BARAKAMON

1

SATSUKI
YOSHINO

Contents

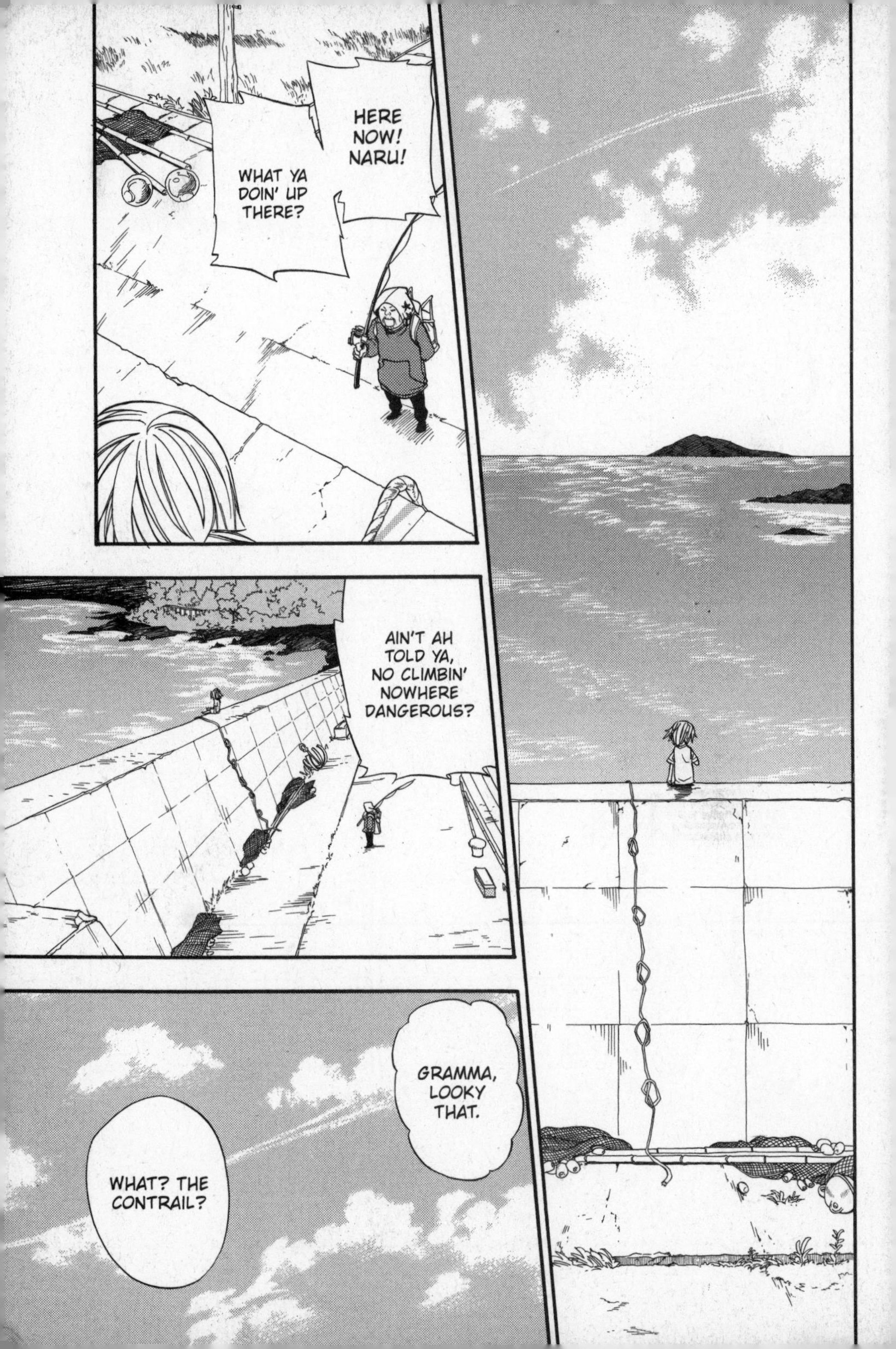
HERE NOW! NARU!
WHAT YA DOIN' UP THERE?
AIN'T AH TOLD YA, NO CLIMBIN' NOWHERE DANGEROUS?
GRAMMA, LOOKY THAT.
WHAT? THE CONTRAIL?

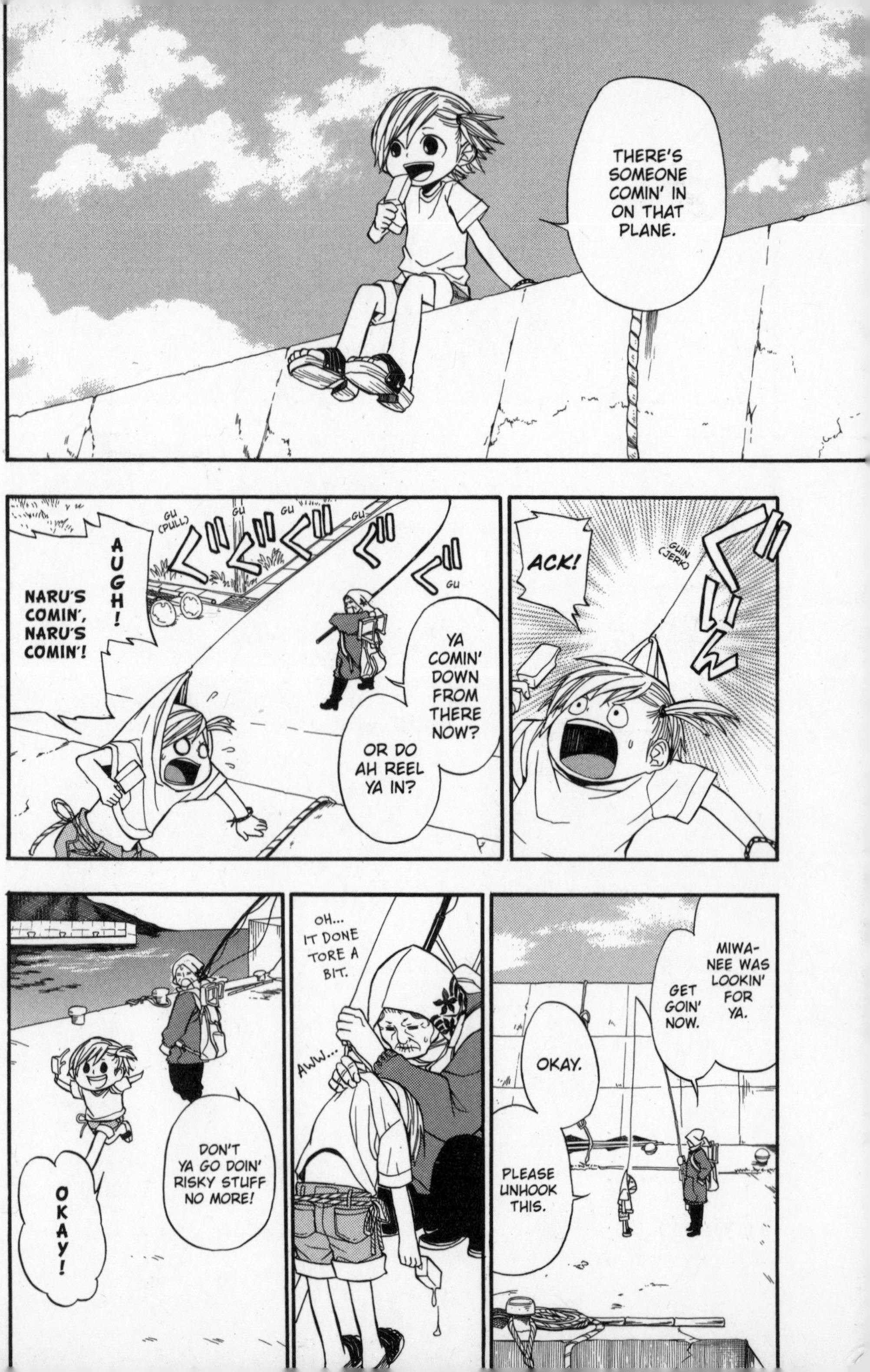
THERE'S SOMEONE COMIN' IN ON THAT PLANE.
GUIN (JERK)
ACK!
GU (PULL)
GU
GU
GU
GU
YA COMIN' DOWN FROM THERE NOW?
OR DO AH REEL YA IN?
AUGH!
NARU'S COMIN', NARU'S COMIN'!
MIWA-NEE WAS LOOKIN' FOR YA.
GET GOIN' NOW.
OKAY.
PLEASE UNHOOK THIS.
OH... IT DONE TORE A BIT.
AWW...
DON'T YA GO DOIN' RISKY STUFF NO MORE!
OKAY!

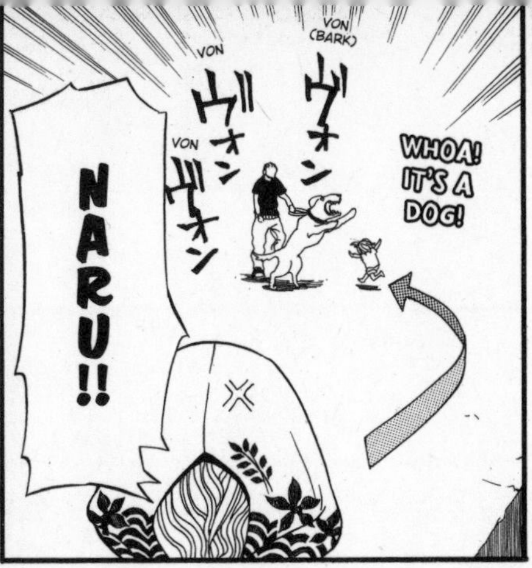
VON (BARK)
ヴォン
WHOA! IT'S A DOG!
VON
ヴォン
VON
ヴォン
NARU!!

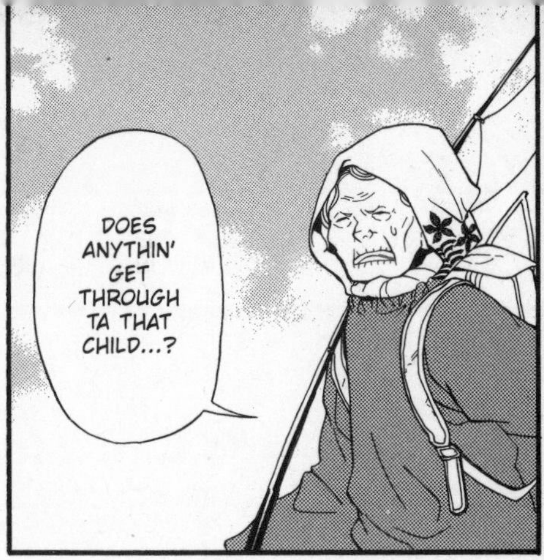
DOES ANYTHIN' GET THROUGH TA THAT CHILD...?

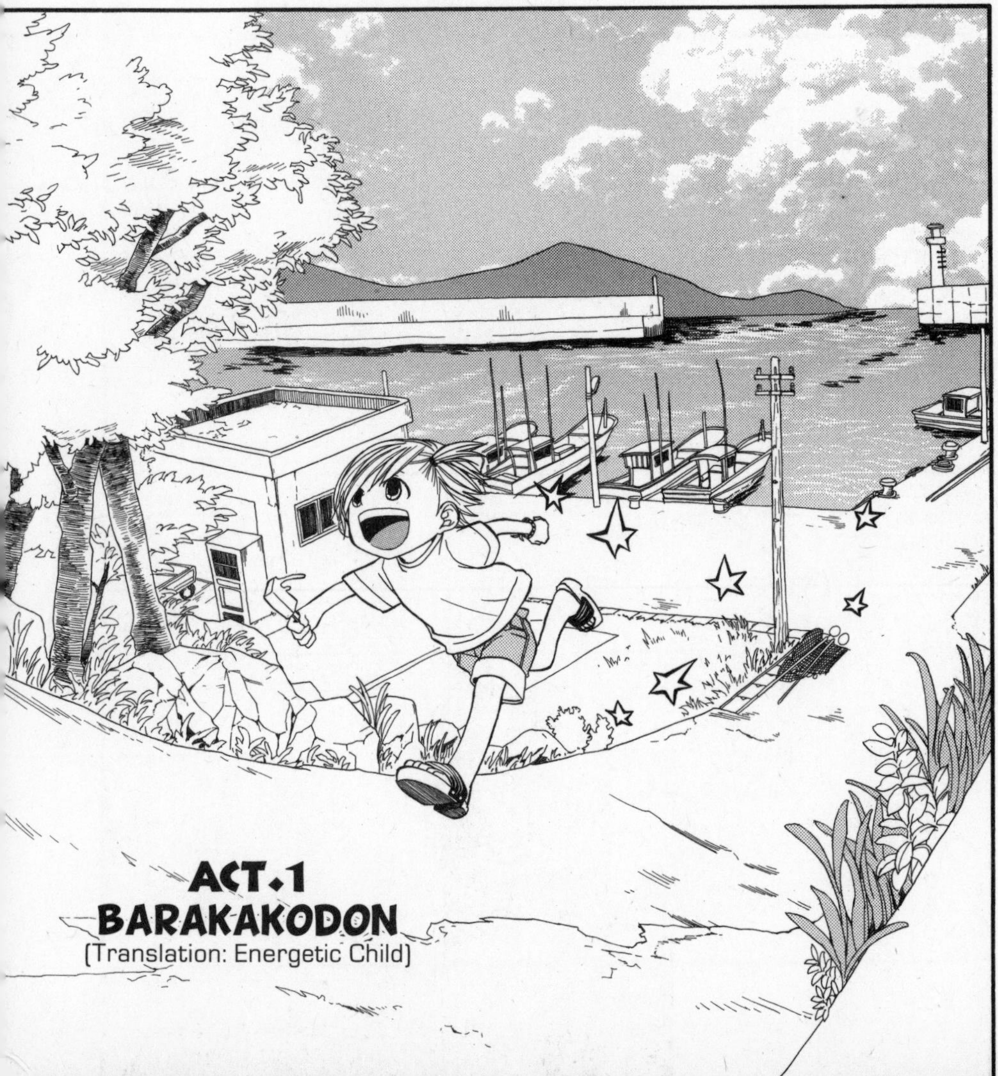
ACT.1
BARAKAKODON
[Translation: Energetic Child]

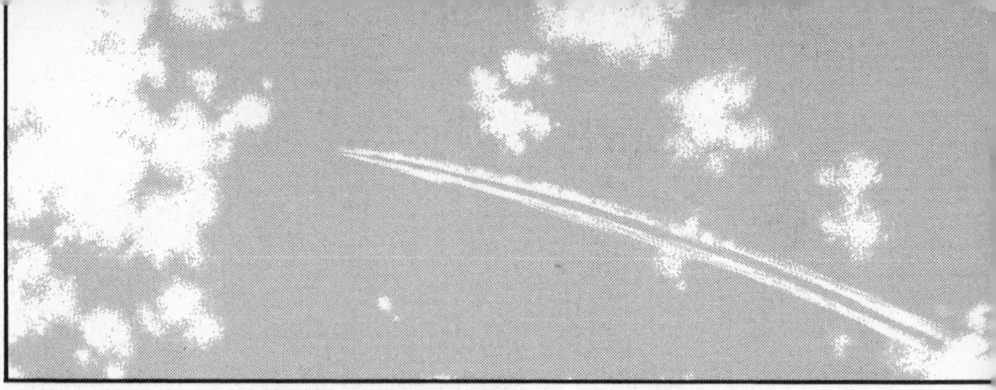

SIGNS: MARINE PRODUCTS, KAMABOKO FISH SAUSAGE / WINDOWS: ARRIVALS

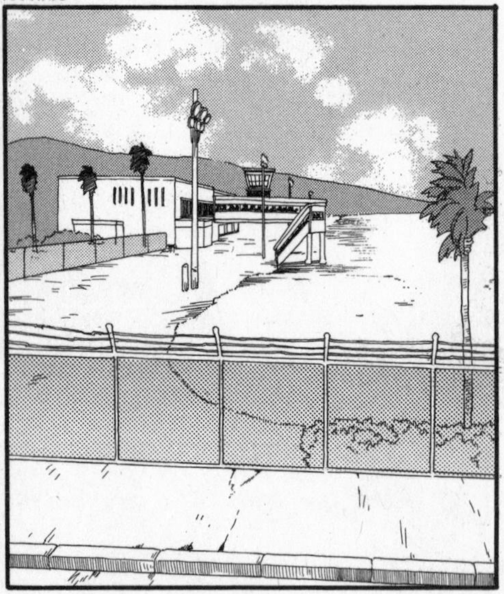

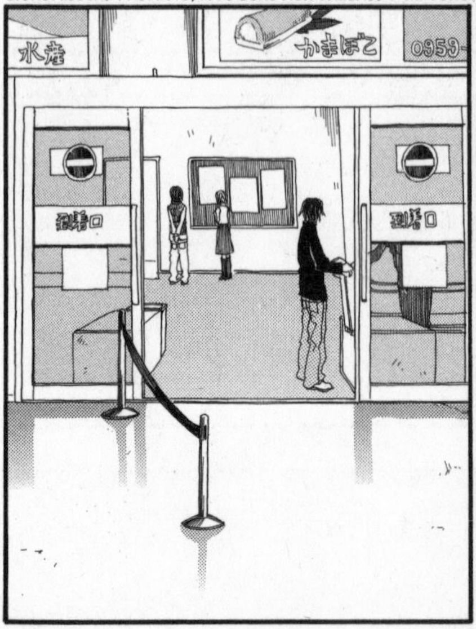
水産
かまぼこ
0959-
到着口
到着口

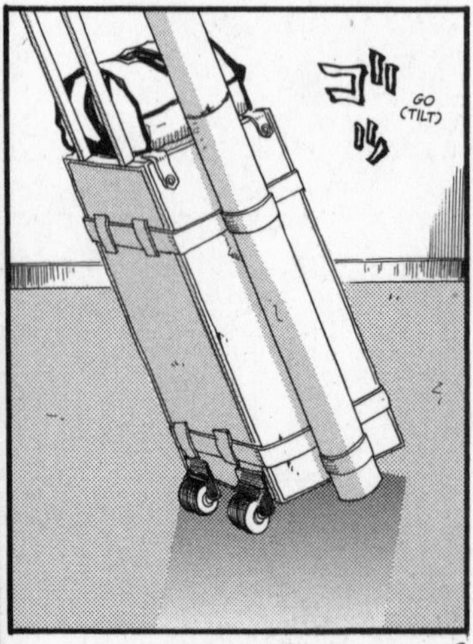
ゴッ
GO (TILT)

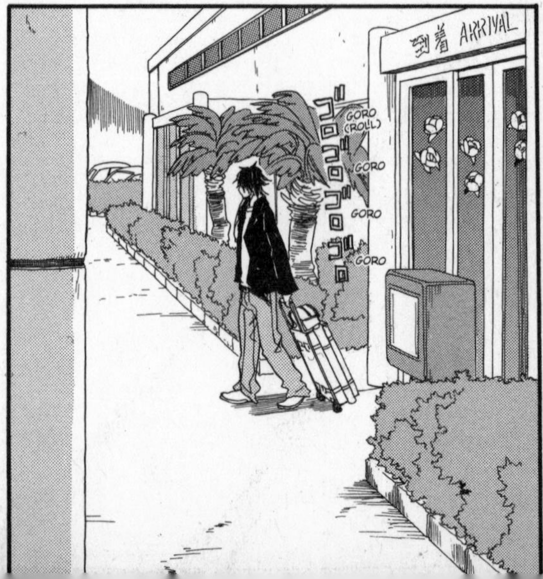
到着 ARRIVAL
ゴロ
GORO (ROLL)
ゴロ
GORO
ゴロ
GORO
ゴロ
GORO

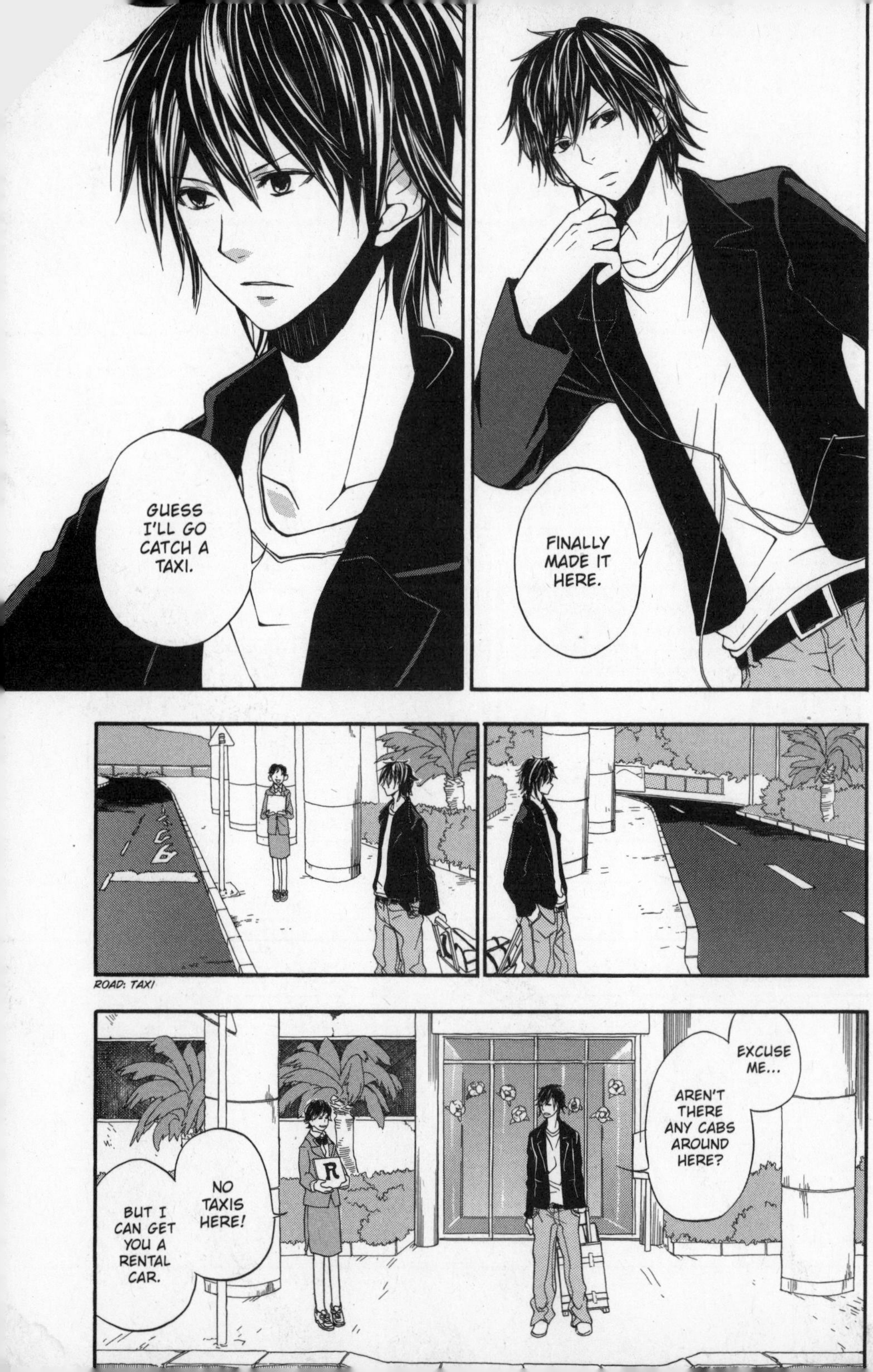
FINALLY MADE IT HERE.
GUESS I'LL GO CATCH A TAXI.
ROAD: TAXI
EXCUSE ME...
AREN'T THERE ANY CABS AROUND HERE?
NO TAXIS HERE!
BUT I CAN GET YOU A RENTAL CAR.

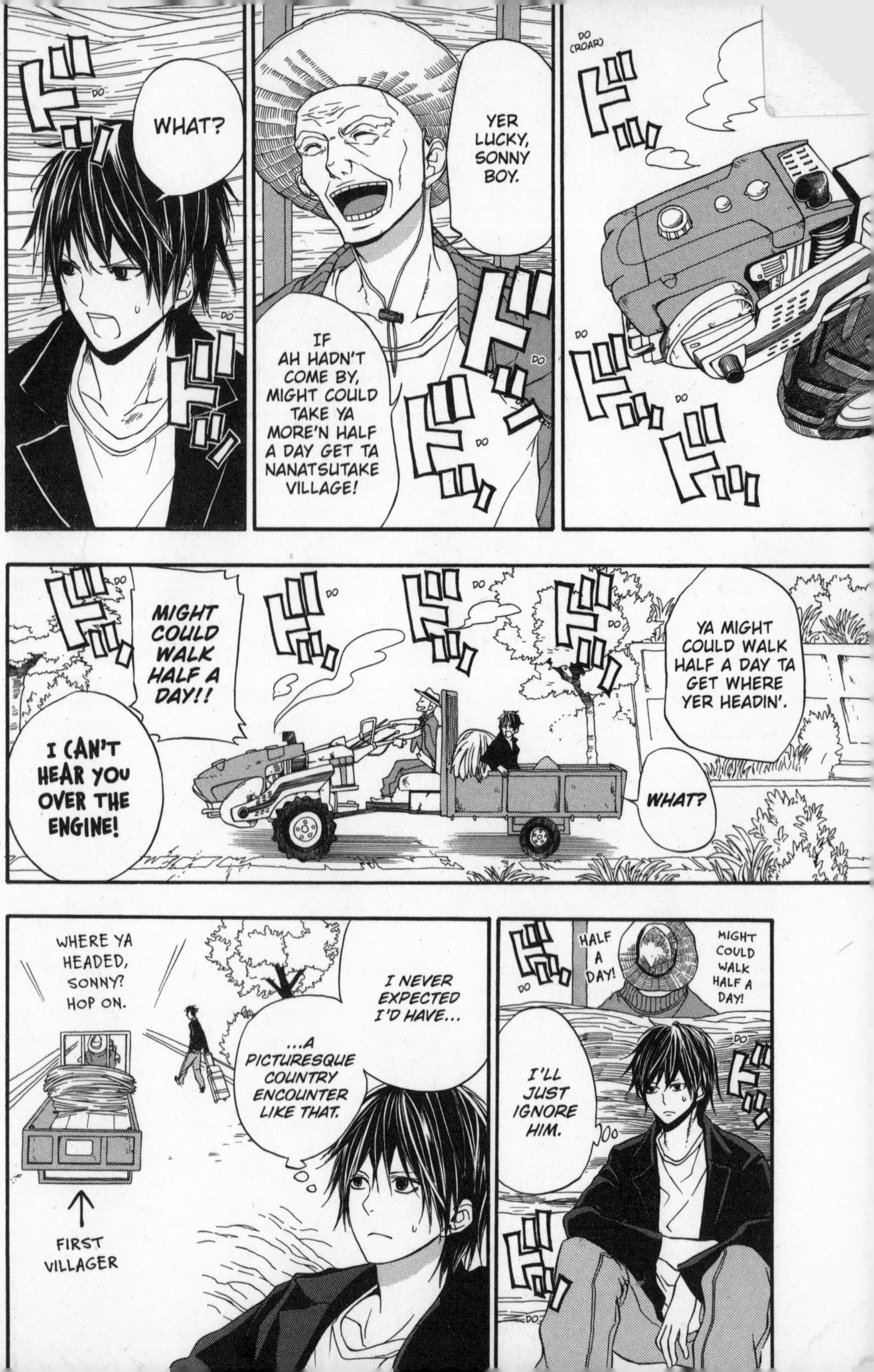
DO (ROAR)
YER LUCKY, SONNY BOY.
IF AH HADN'T COME BY, MIGHT COULD TAKE YA MORE'N HALF A DAY GET TA NANATSUTAKE VILLAGE!
WHAT?
YA MIGHT COULD WALK HALF A DAY TA GET WHERE YER HEADIN'.
WHAT?
MIGHT COULD WALK HALF A DAY!!
I CAN'T HEAR YOU OVER THE ENGINE!
MIGHT COULD WALK HALF A DAY!
HALF A DAY!
I'LL JUST IGNORE HIM.
I NEVER EXPECTED I'D HAVE...
...A PICTURESQUE COUNTRY ENCOUNTER LIKE THAT.
WHERE YA HEADED, SONNY? HOP ON.
FIRST VILLAGER

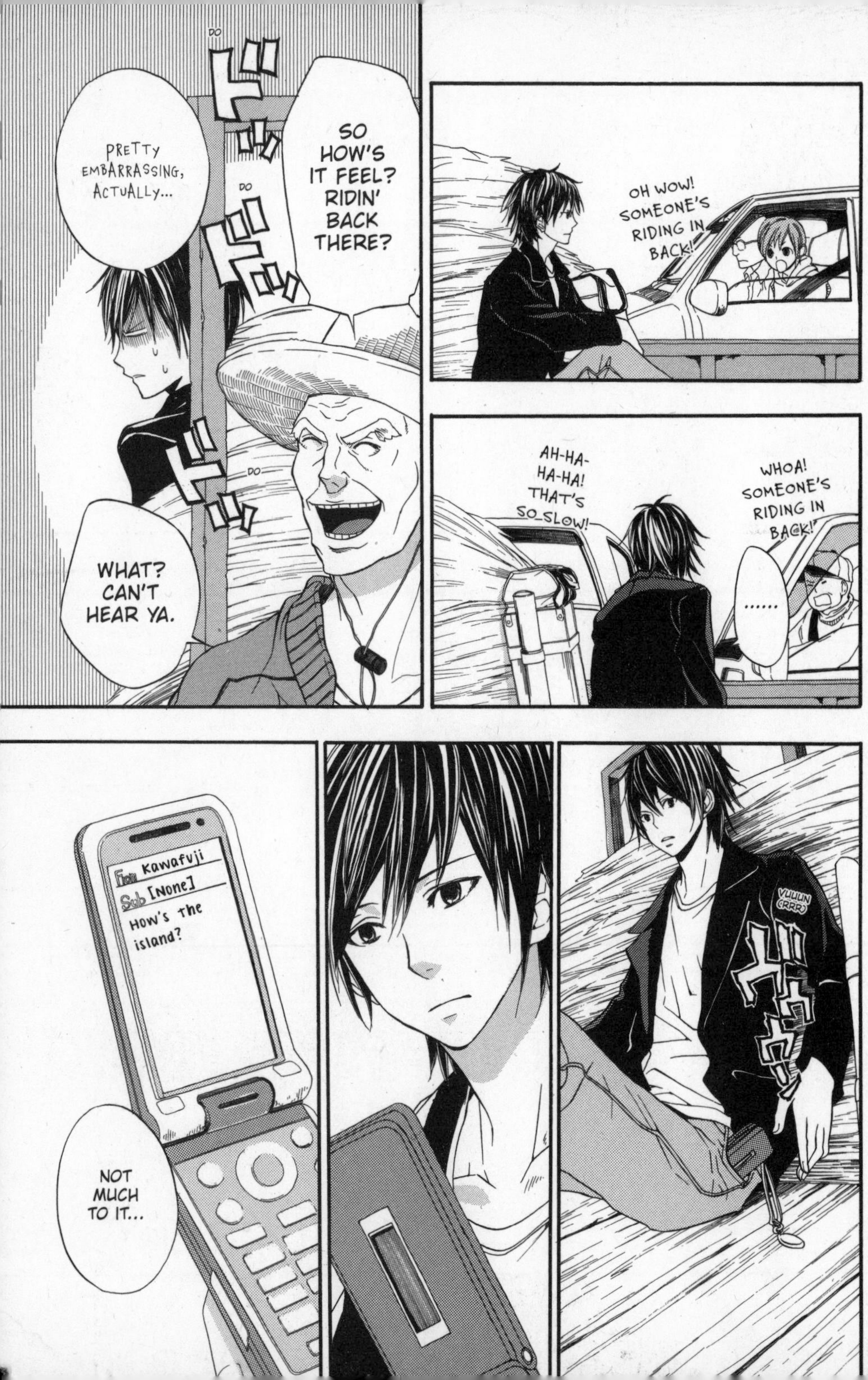
OH WOW! SOMEONE'S RIDING IN BACK!
WHOA! SOMEONE'S RIDING IN BACK!
AH-HA-HA-HA! THAT'S SO SLOW!
......
SO HOW'S IT FEEL? RIDIN' BACK THERE?
DO
DO
PRETTY EMBARRASSING, ACTUALLY...
DO
WHAT? CAN'T HEAR YA.
VUUUN (RRR)
From Kawafuji
Sub [None]
How's the island?
NOT MUCH TO IT...

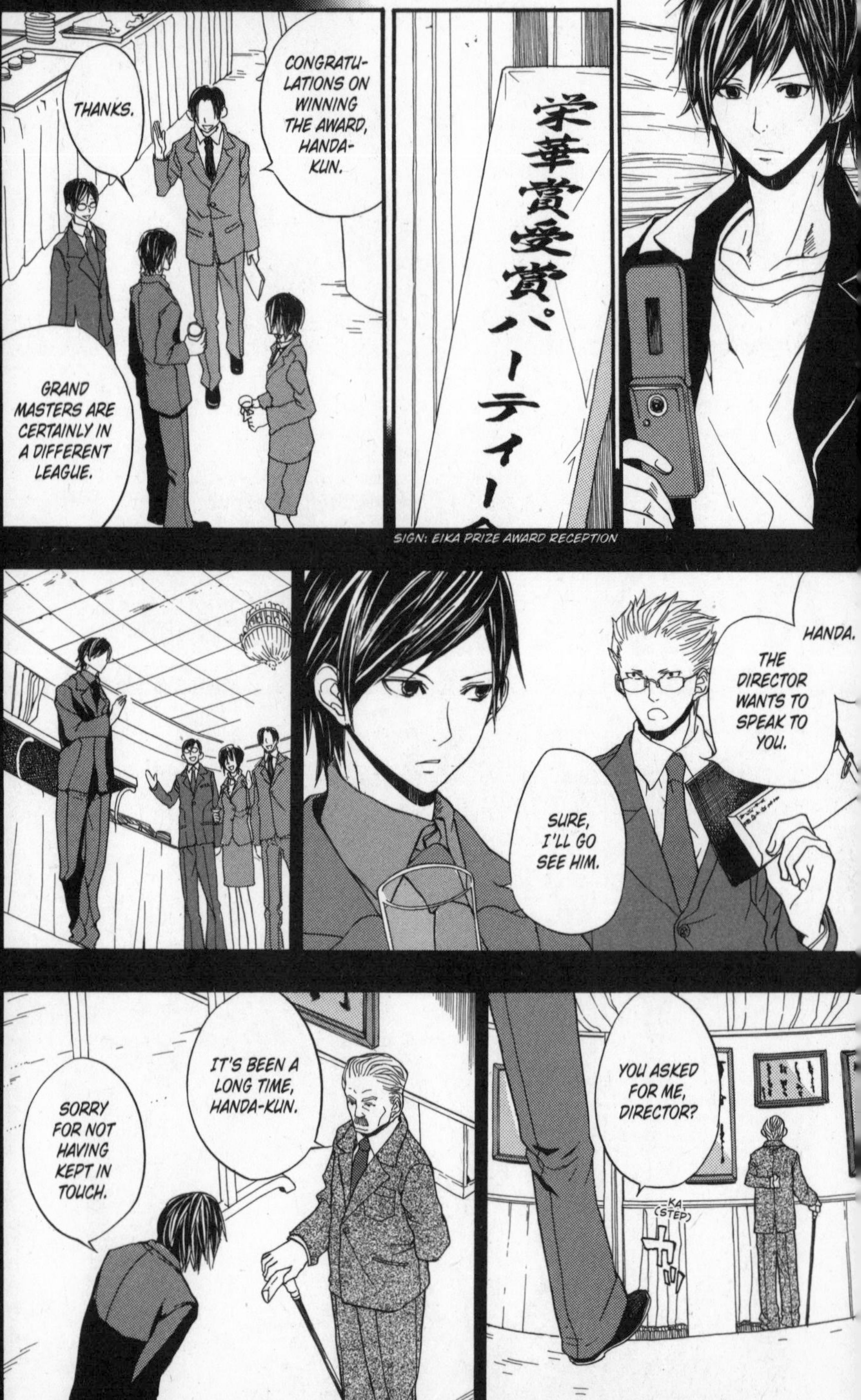

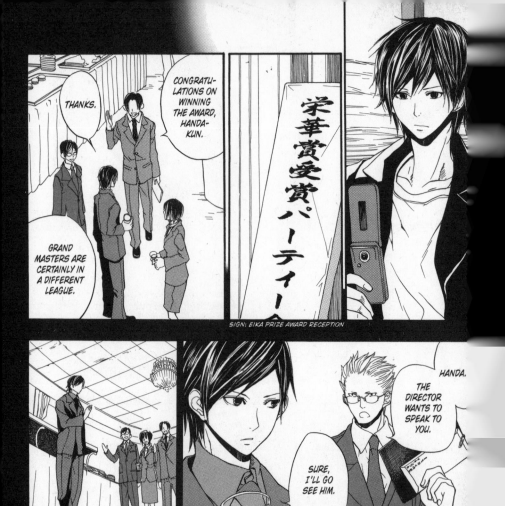

栄華賞受賞パーティー
CONGRATULATIONS ON WINNING THE AWARD, HANDA-KUN.
THANKS.
GRAND MASTERS ARE CERTAINLY IN A DIFFERENT LEAGUE.
SIGN: EIKA PRIZE AWARD RECEPTION
HANDA. THE DIRECTOR WANTS TO SPEAK TO YOU.
SURE, I'LL GO SEE HIM.
YOU ASKED FOR ME, DIRECTOR?
KA (STEP)
IT'S BEEN A LONG TIME, HANDA-KUN.
SORRY FOR NOT HAVING KEPT IN TOUCH.

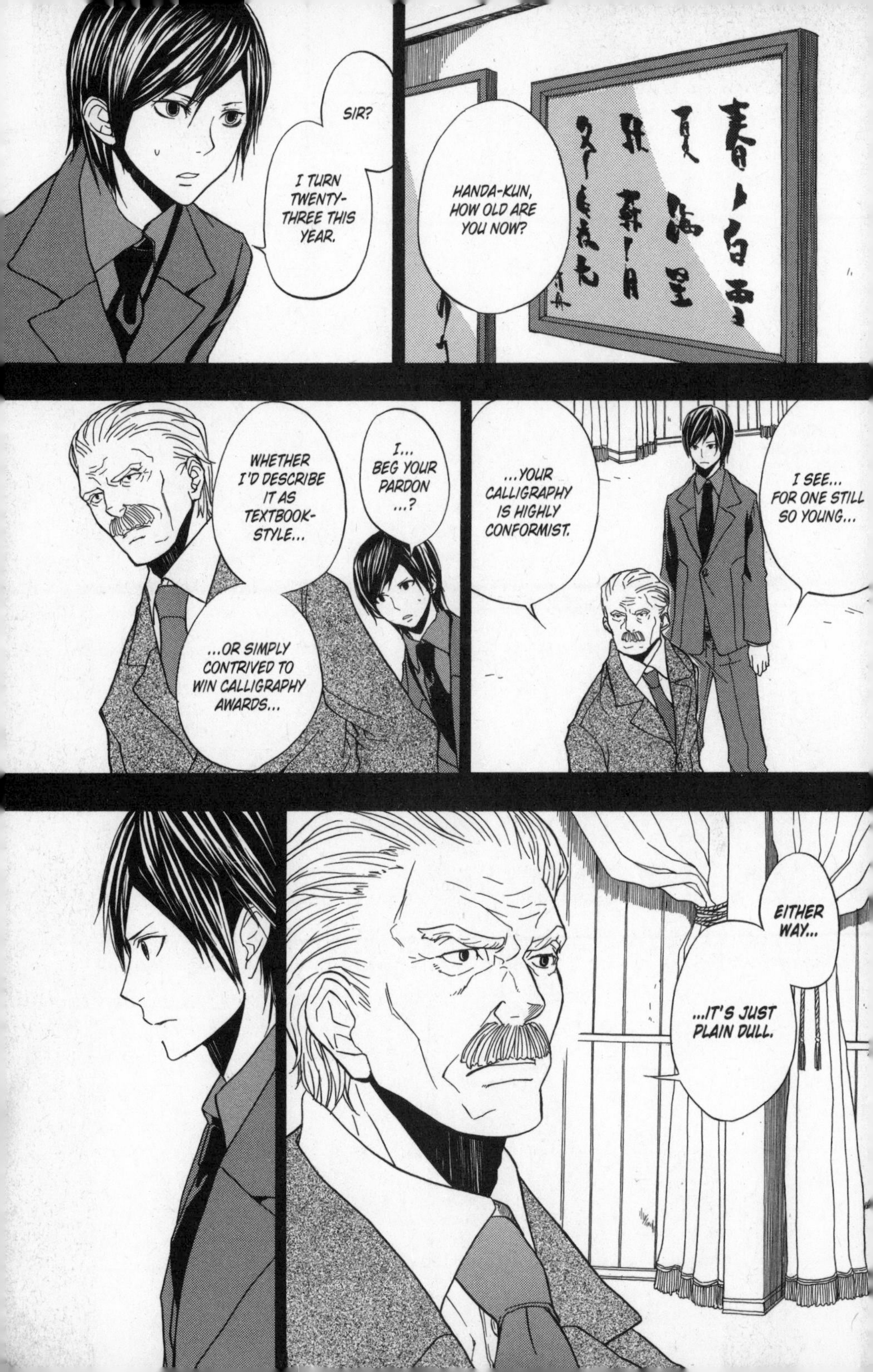
HANDA-KUN, HOW OLD ARE YOU NOW?
SIR?
I TURN TWENTY-THREE THIS YEAR.
I SEE... FOR ONE STILL SO YOUNG...
...YOUR CALLIGRAPHY IS HIGHLY CONFORMIST.
I... BEG YOUR PARDON ...?
WHETHER I'D DESCRIBE IT AS TEXTBOOK-STYLE...
...OR SIMPLY CONTRIVED TO WIN CALLIGRAPHY AWARDS...
EITHER WAY...
...IT'S JUST PLAIN DULL.

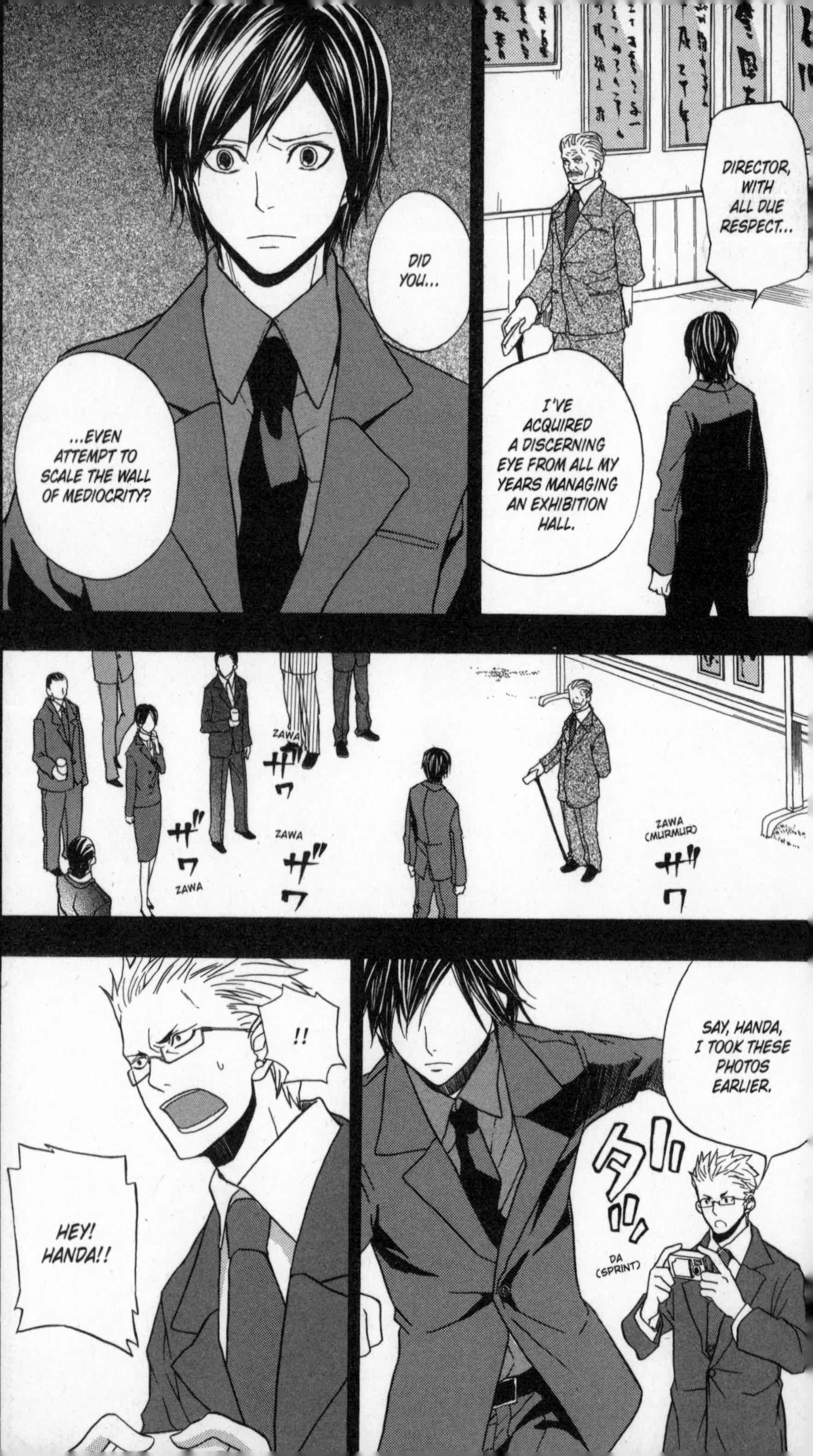
DIRECTOR, WITH ALL DUE RESPECT...
I'VE ACQUIRED A DISCERNING EYE FROM ALL MY YEARS MANAGING AN EXHIBITION HALL.
DID YOU...
...EVEN ATTEMPT TO SCALE THE WALL OF MEDIOCRITY?
ZAWA (MURMUR)
ザワ
ZAWA
ザワ
ZAWA
ザワ
ザワ
ZAWA
SAY, HANDA, I TOOK THESE PHOTOS EARLIER.
ダッ
DA (SPRINT)
!!
HEY! HANDA!!

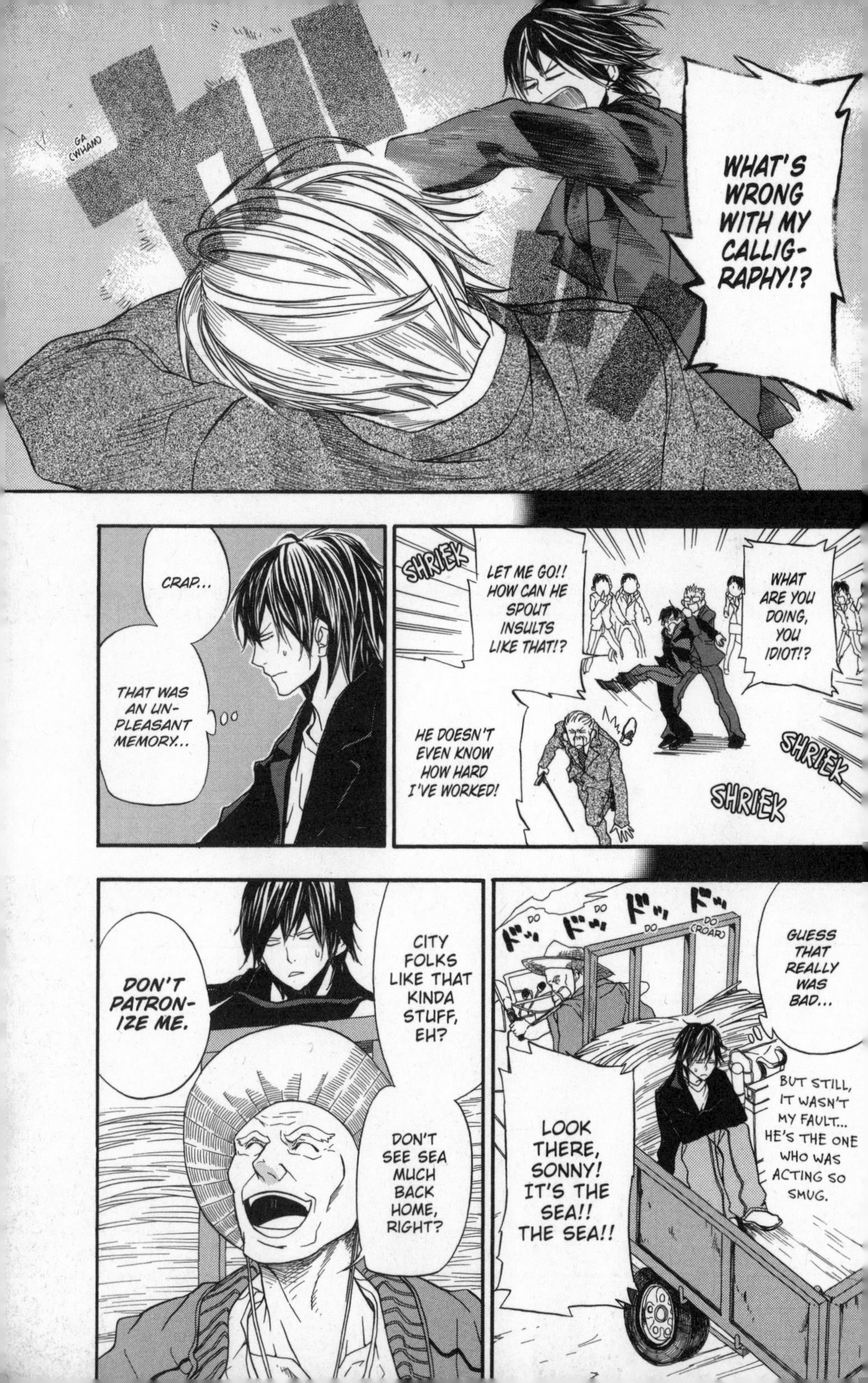
WHAT'S WRONG WITH MY CALLIG-RAPHY!?
GA (WHAM)
WHAT ARE YOU DOING, YOU IDIOT!?
LET ME GO!! HOW CAN HE SPOUT INSULTS LIKE THAT!?
SHRIEK
HE DOESN'T EVEN KNOW HOW HARD I'VE WORKED!
SHRIEK
SHRIEK
CRAP...
THAT WAS AN UN-PLEASANT MEMORY...
DO DO DO DO (ROAR)
GUESS THAT REALLY WAS BAD...
BUT STILL, IT WASN'T MY FAULT... HE'S THE ONE WHO WAS ACTING SO SMUG.
LOOK THERE, SONNY! IT'S THE SEA!! THE SEA!!
CITY FOLKS LIKE THAT KINDA STUFF, EH?
DON'T PATRON-IZE ME.
DON'T SEE SEA MUCH BACK HOME, RIGHT?

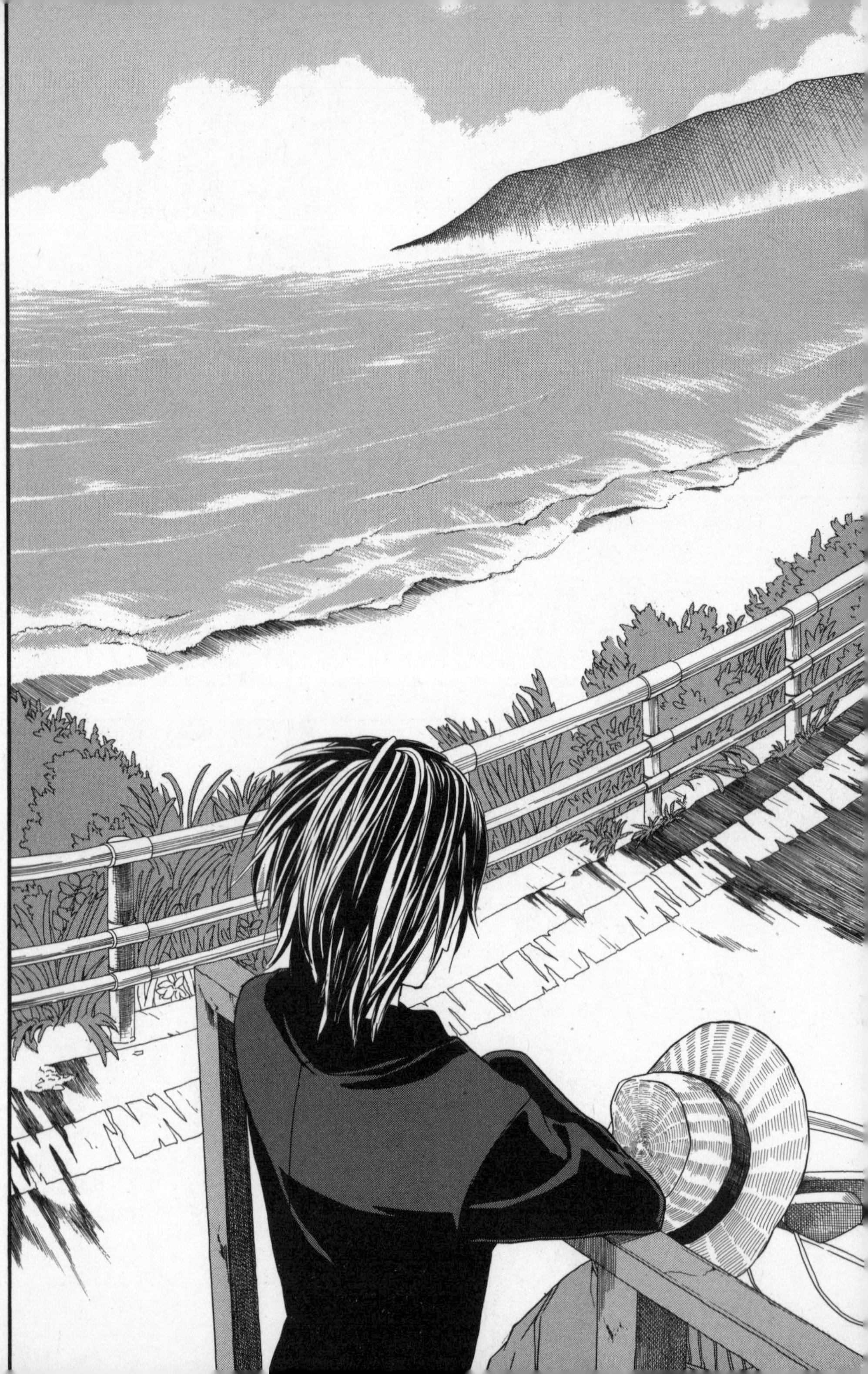

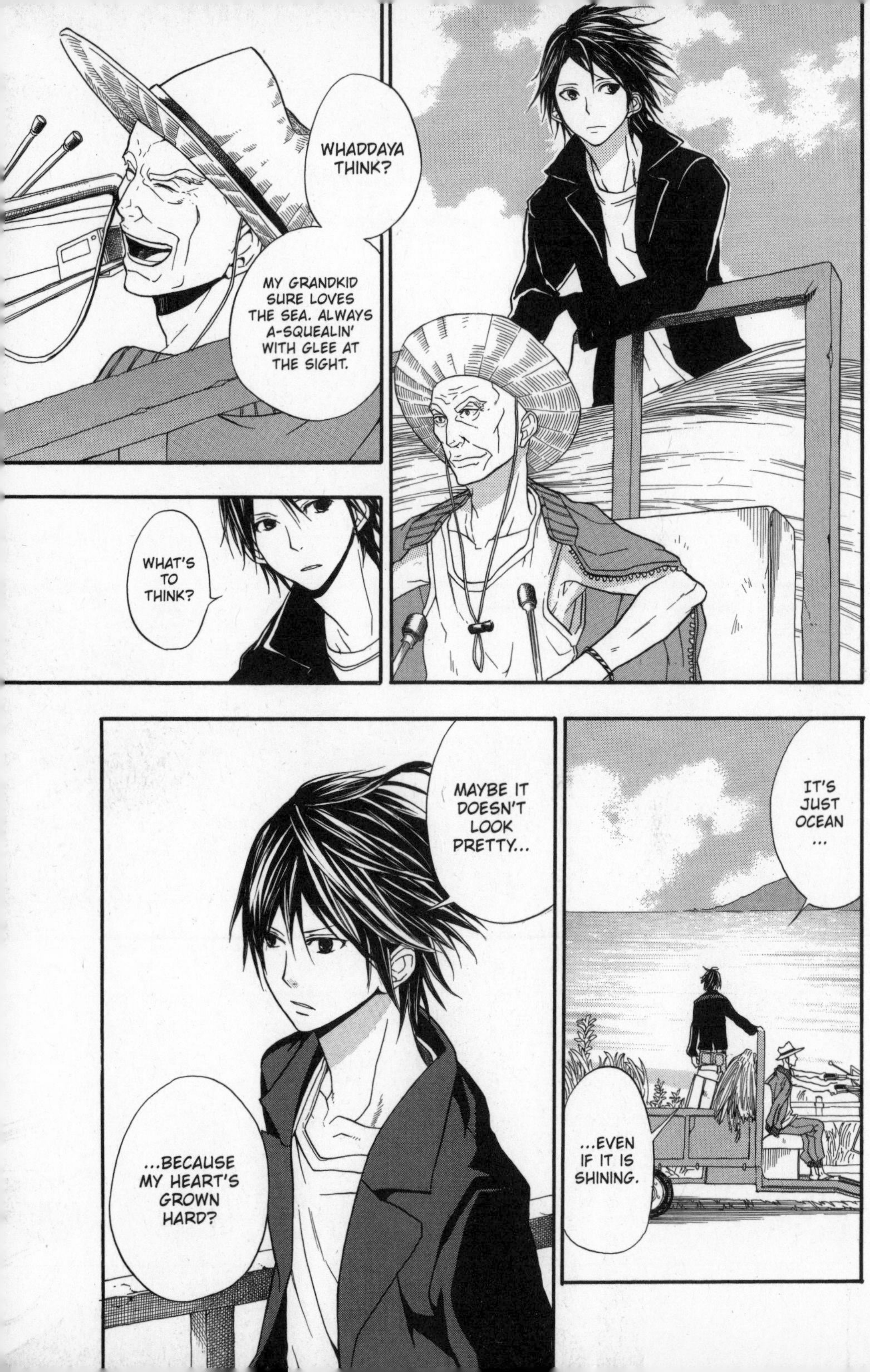
WHADDAYA THINK?
MY GRANDKID SURE LOVES THE SEA. ALWAYS A-SQUEALIN' WITH GLEE AT THE SIGHT.
WHAT'S TO THINK?
IT'S JUST OCEAN ...
...EVEN IF IT IS SHINING.
MAYBE IT DOESN'T LOOK PRETTY...
...BECAUSE MY HEART'S GROWN HARD?

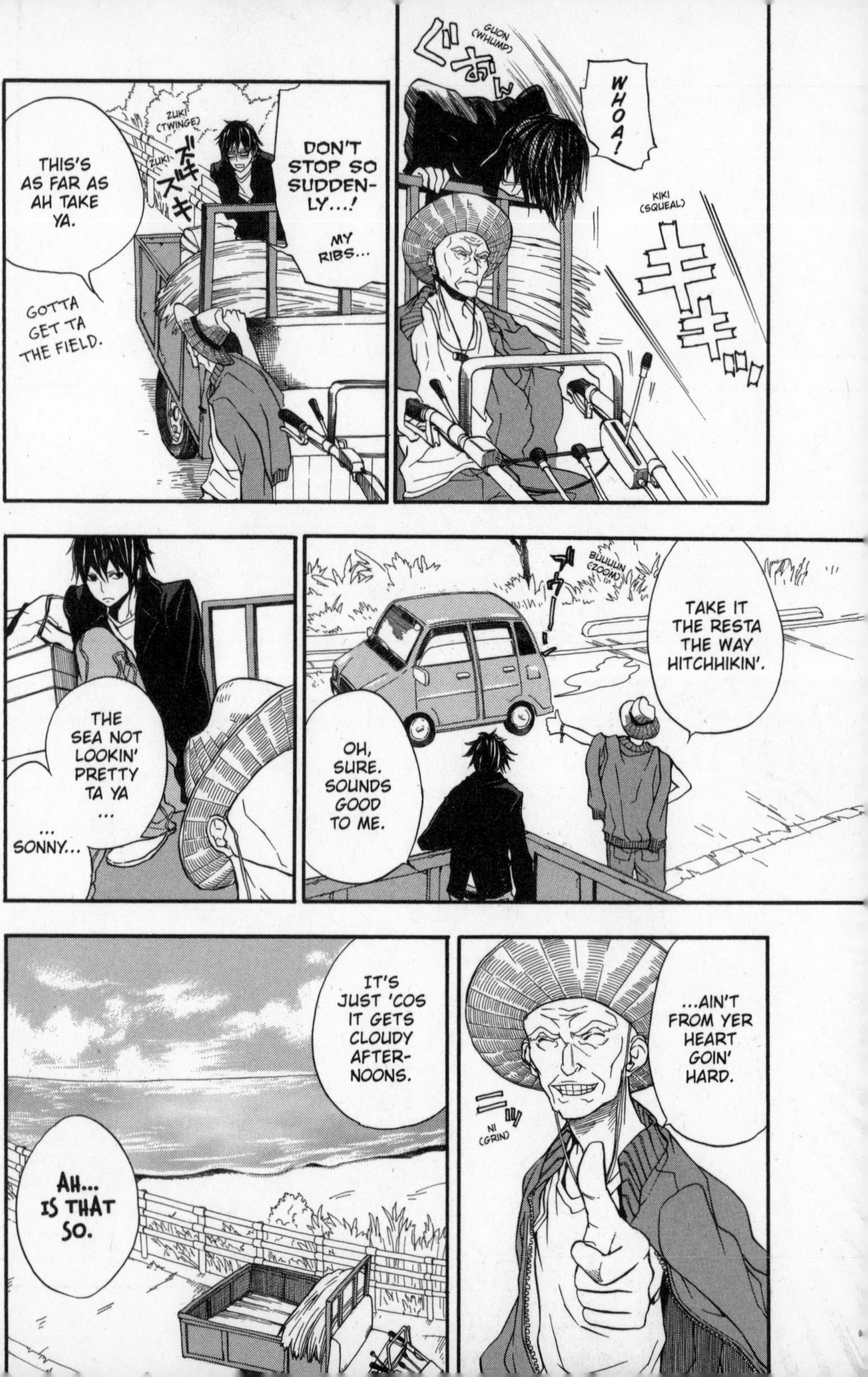
GUON (WHUMP)
WHOA!
KIKI (SQUEAL)
DON'T STOP SO SUDDEN-LY...!
MY RIBS...
ZUKI (TWINGE)
ZUKI
THIS'S AS FAR AS AH TAKE YA.
GOTTA GET TA THE FIELD.
TAKE IT THE RESTA THE WAY HITCHHIKIN'.
BUUUUN (ZOOM)
OH, SURE. SOUNDS GOOD TO ME.
THE SEA NOT LOOKIN' PRETTY TA YA ... SONNY...
...AIN'T FROM YER HEART GOIN' HARD.
NI (GRIN)
IT'S JUST 'COS IT GETS CLOUDY AFTER-NOONS.
AH... IS THAT SO.

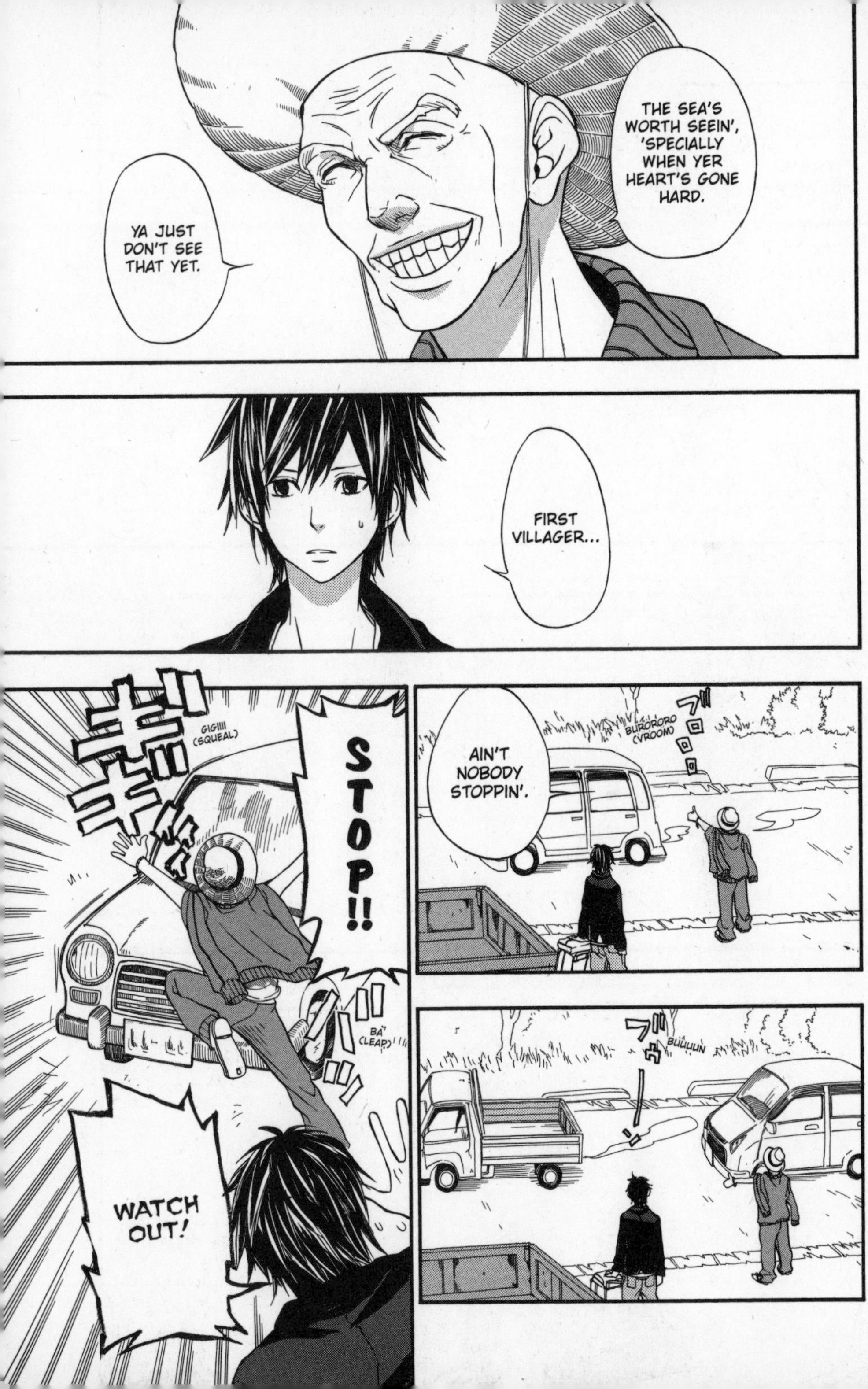
THE SEA'S WORTH SEEIN', 'SPECIALLY WHEN YER HEART'S GONE HARD.
YA JUST DON'T SEE THAT YET.
FIRST VILLAGER...
BURORORO (VROOM)
AIN'T NOBODY STOPPIN'.
BUUUUN
STOP!!
GIGIII (SQUEAL)
BA (LEAP)
WATCH OUT!

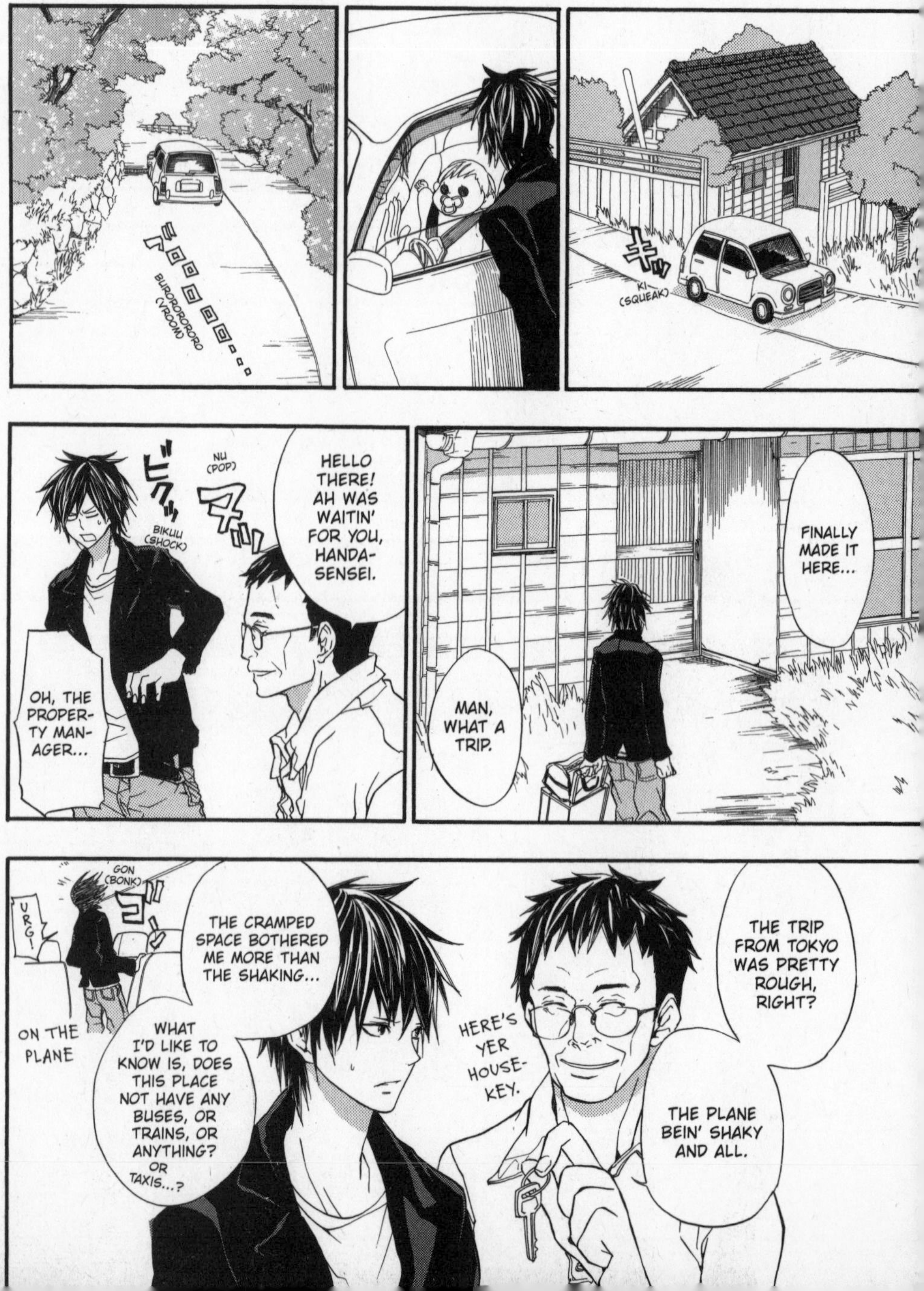
KI (SQUEAK)
BUROROROROR... (VROOM)
FINALLY MADE IT HERE...
MAN, WHAT A TRIP.
HELLO THERE! AH WAS WAITIN' FOR YOU, HANDA-SENSEI.
NU (POP)
BIKUU (SHOCK)
OH, THE PROPERTY MANAGER...
THE TRIP FROM TOKYO WAS PRETTY ROUGH, RIGHT?
THE PLANE BEIN' SHAKY AND ALL.
HERE'S YER HOUSE-KEY.
THE CRAMPED SPACE BOTHERED ME MORE THAN THE SHAKING...
WHAT I'D LIKE TO KNOW IS, DOES THIS PLACE NOT HAVE ANY BUSES, OR TRAINS, OR ANYTHING?
OR TAXIS...?
GON (BONK)
URG!
ON THE PLANE

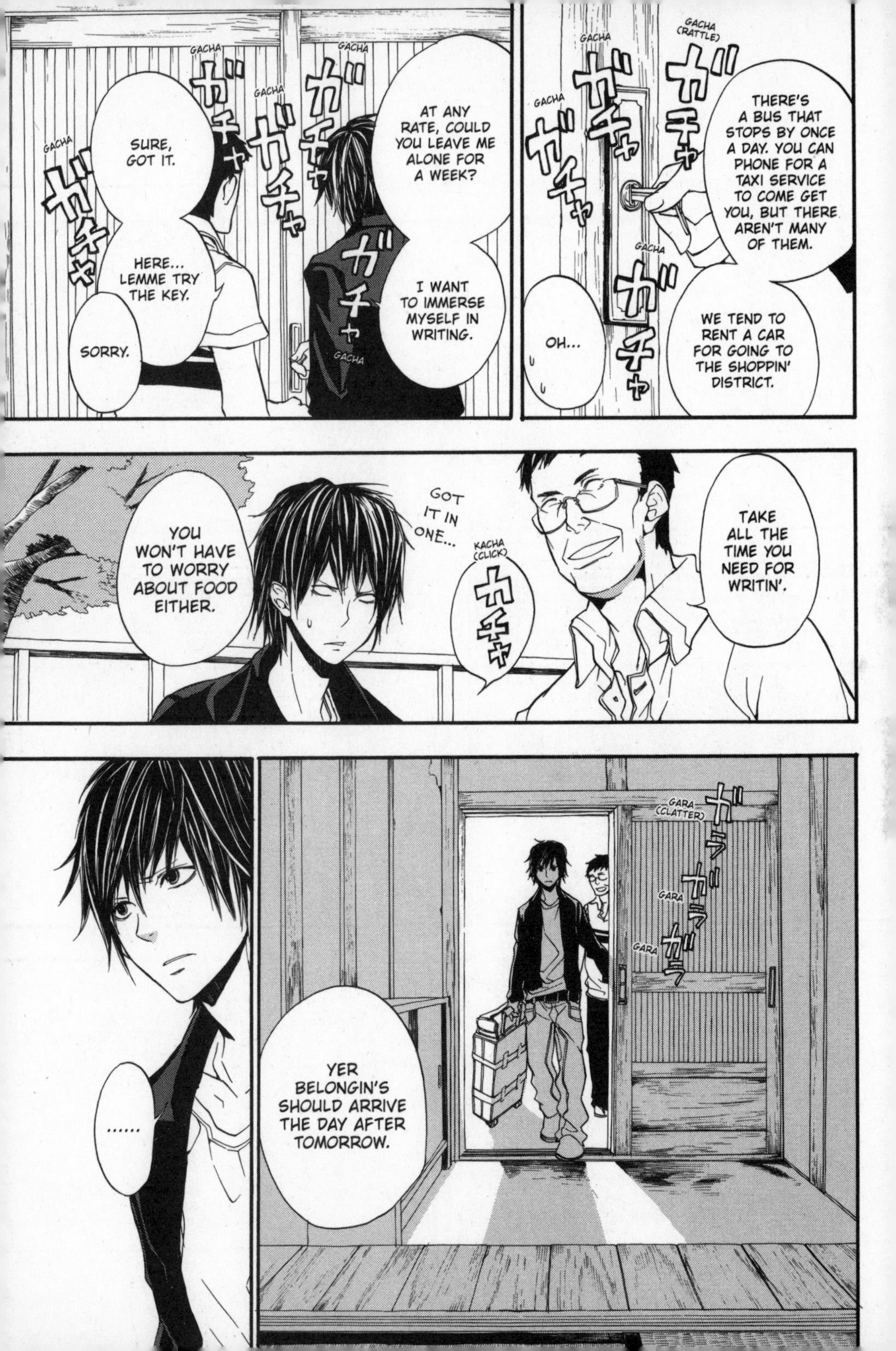
GACHA (RATTLE)
GACHA
GACHA
THERE'S A BUS THAT STOPS BY ONCE A DAY. YOU CAN PHONE FOR A TAXI SERVICE TO COME GET YOU, BUT THERE AREN'T MANY OF THEM.
GACHA
WE TEND TO RENT A CAR FOR GOING TO THE SHOPPIN' DISTRICT.
OH...
GACHA
AT ANY RATE, COULD YOU LEAVE ME ALONE FOR A WEEK?
I WANT TO IMMERSE MYSELF IN WRITING.
GACHA
GACHA
SURE, GOT IT.
HERE... LEMME TRY THE KEY.
GACHA
SORRY.
TAKE ALL THE TIME YOU NEED FOR WRITIN'.
KACHA (CLICK)
GOT IT IN ONE...
YOU WON'T HAVE TO WORRY ABOUT FOOD EITHER.
GARA (CLATTER)
GARA
GARA
YER BELONGIN'S SHOULD ARRIVE THE DAY AFTER TOMORROW.
......

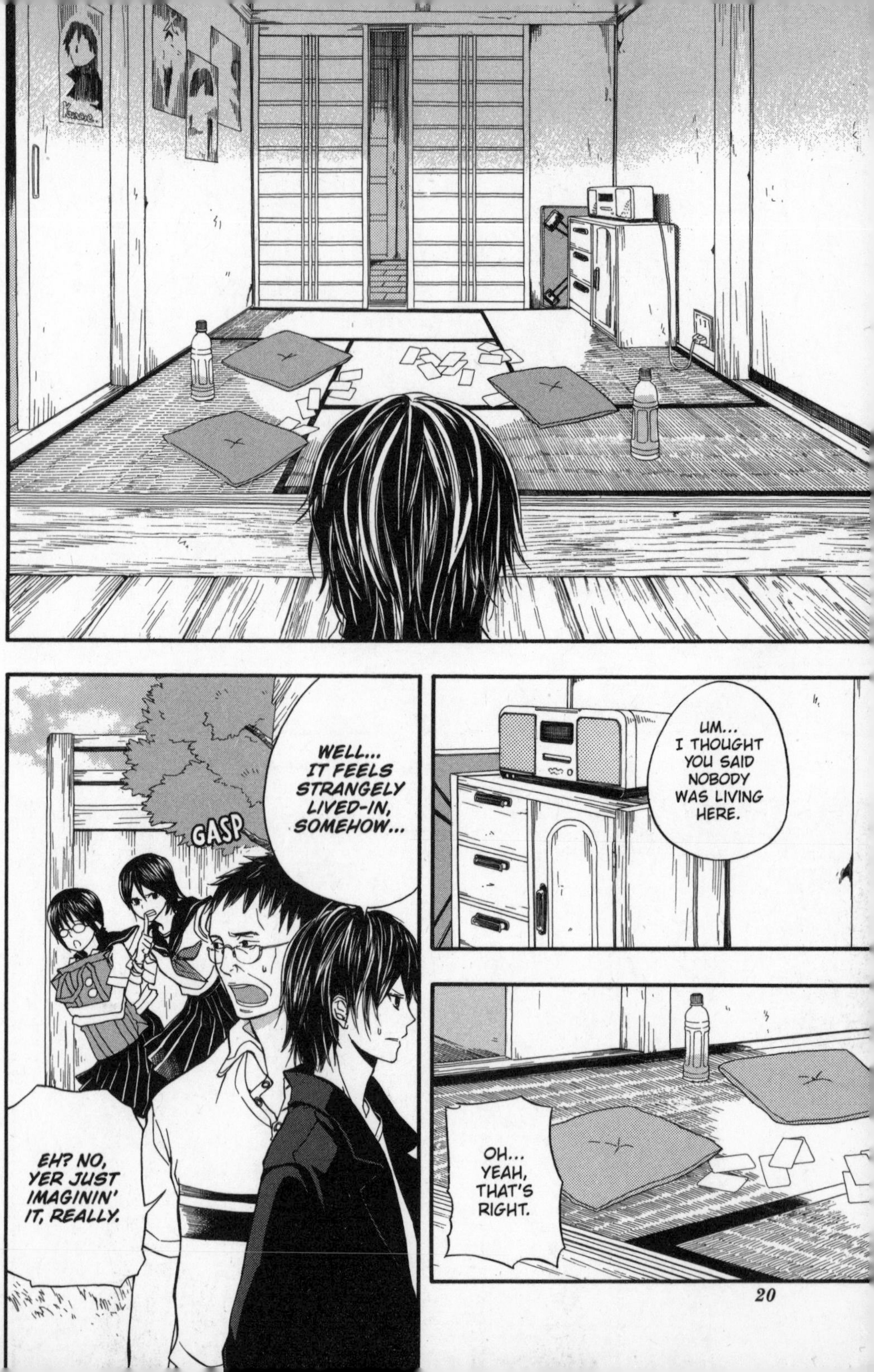
UM... I THOUGHT YOU SAID NOBODY WAS LIVING HERE.
OH... YEAH, THAT'S RIGHT.
WELL... IT FEELS STRANGELY LIVED-IN, SOMEHOW...
GASP
EH? NO, YER JUST IMAGININ' IT, REALLY.

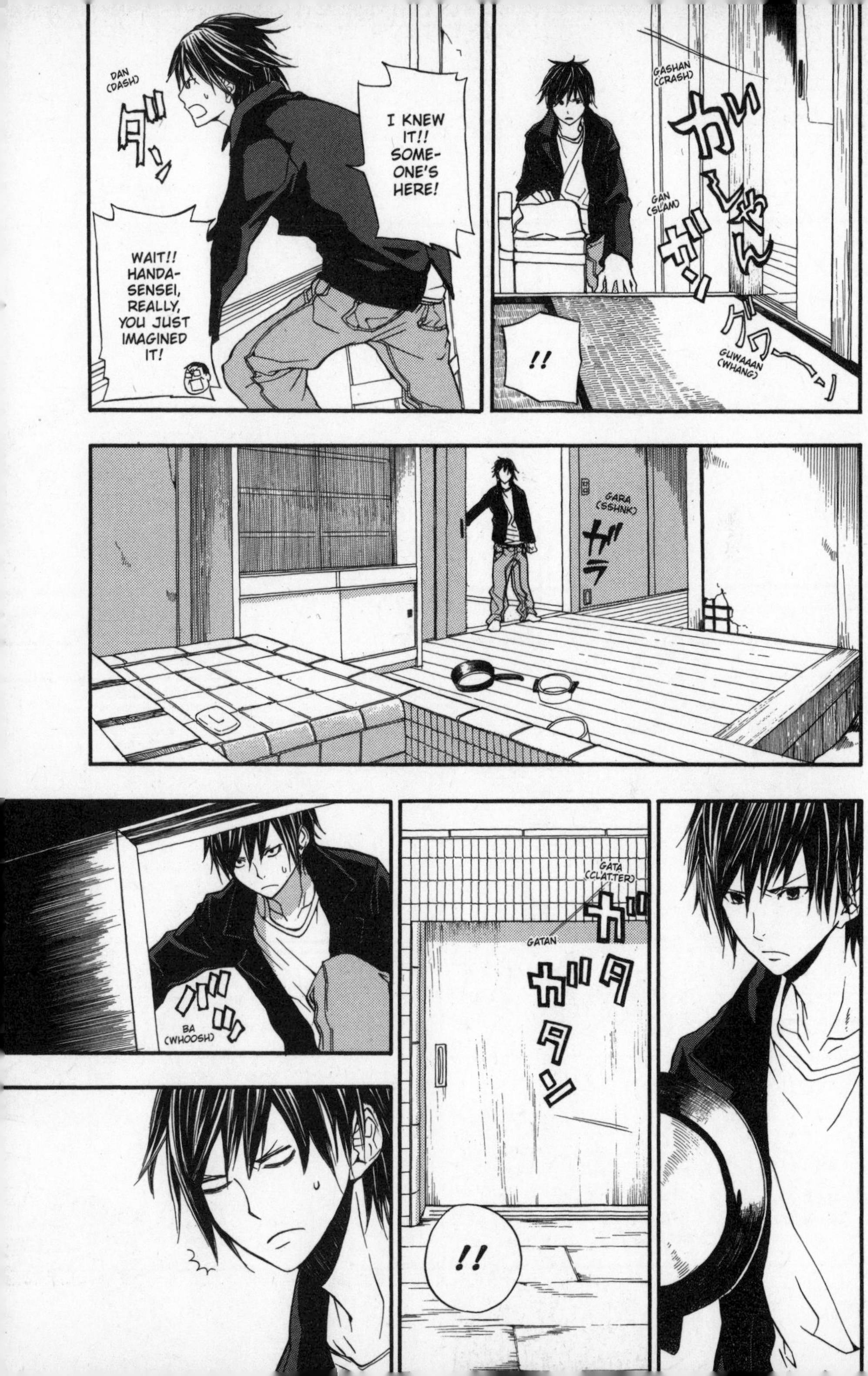
GASHAN (CRASH)
GAN (SLAM)
!!
GUWAAAN (WHANG)
I KNEW IT!! SOME-ONE'S HERE!
DAN (DASH)
WAIT!! HANDA-SENSEI, REALLY, YOU JUST IMAGINED IT!
GARA (SSHNK)
GATA (CLATTER)
GATAN
!!
BA (WHOOSH)

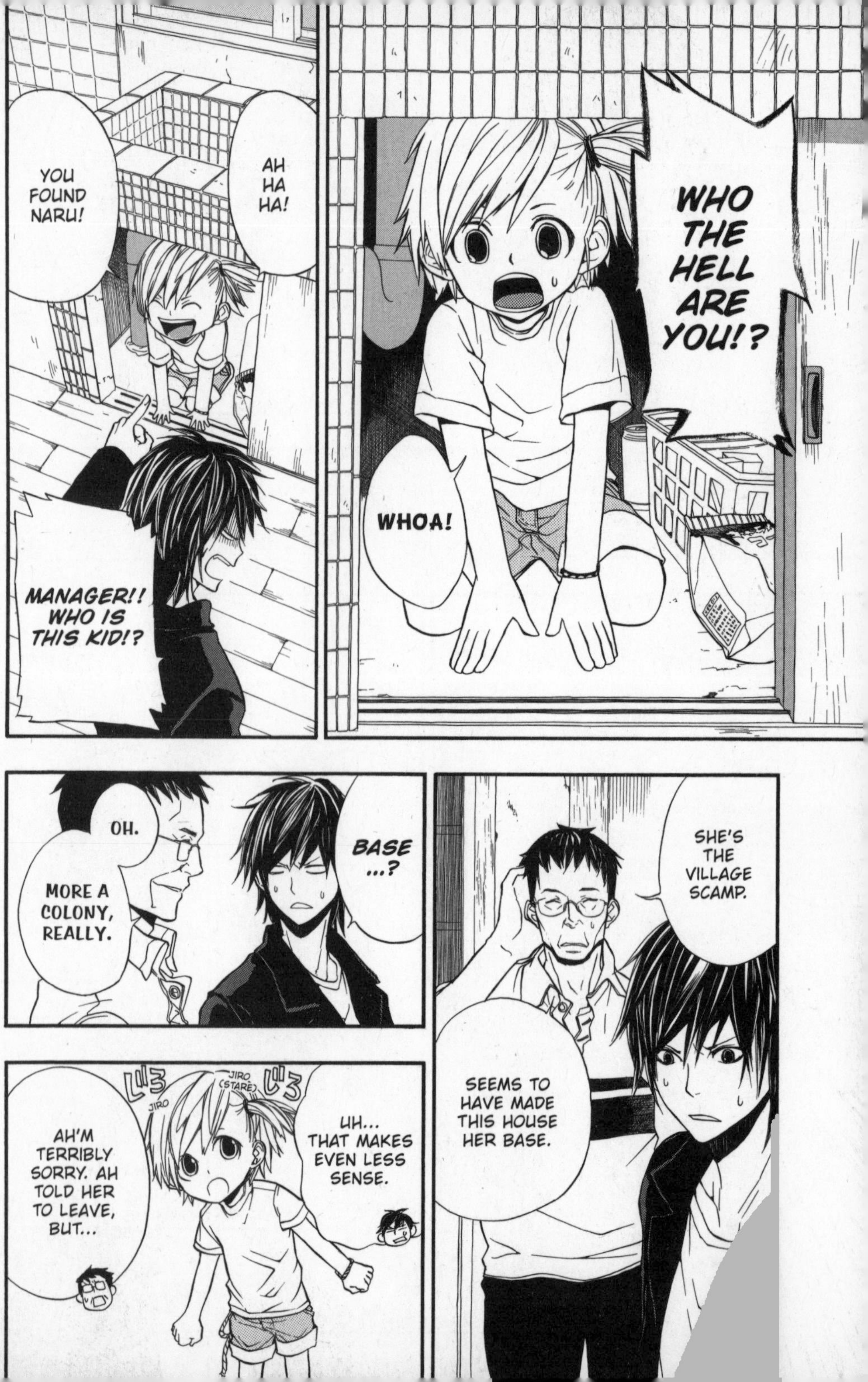
WHO THE HELL ARE YOU!?
WHOA!
AH HA HA!
YOU FOUND NARU!
MANAGER!! WHO IS THIS KID!?
SHE'S THE VILLAGE SCAMP.
SEEMS TO HAVE MADE THIS HOUSE HER BASE.
BASE ...?
OH.
MORE A COLONY, REALLY.
じろ
JIRO (STARE)
じろ
JIRO
UH... THAT MAKES EVEN LESS SENSE.
AH'M TERRIBLY SORRY. AH TOLD HER TO LEAVE, BUT...

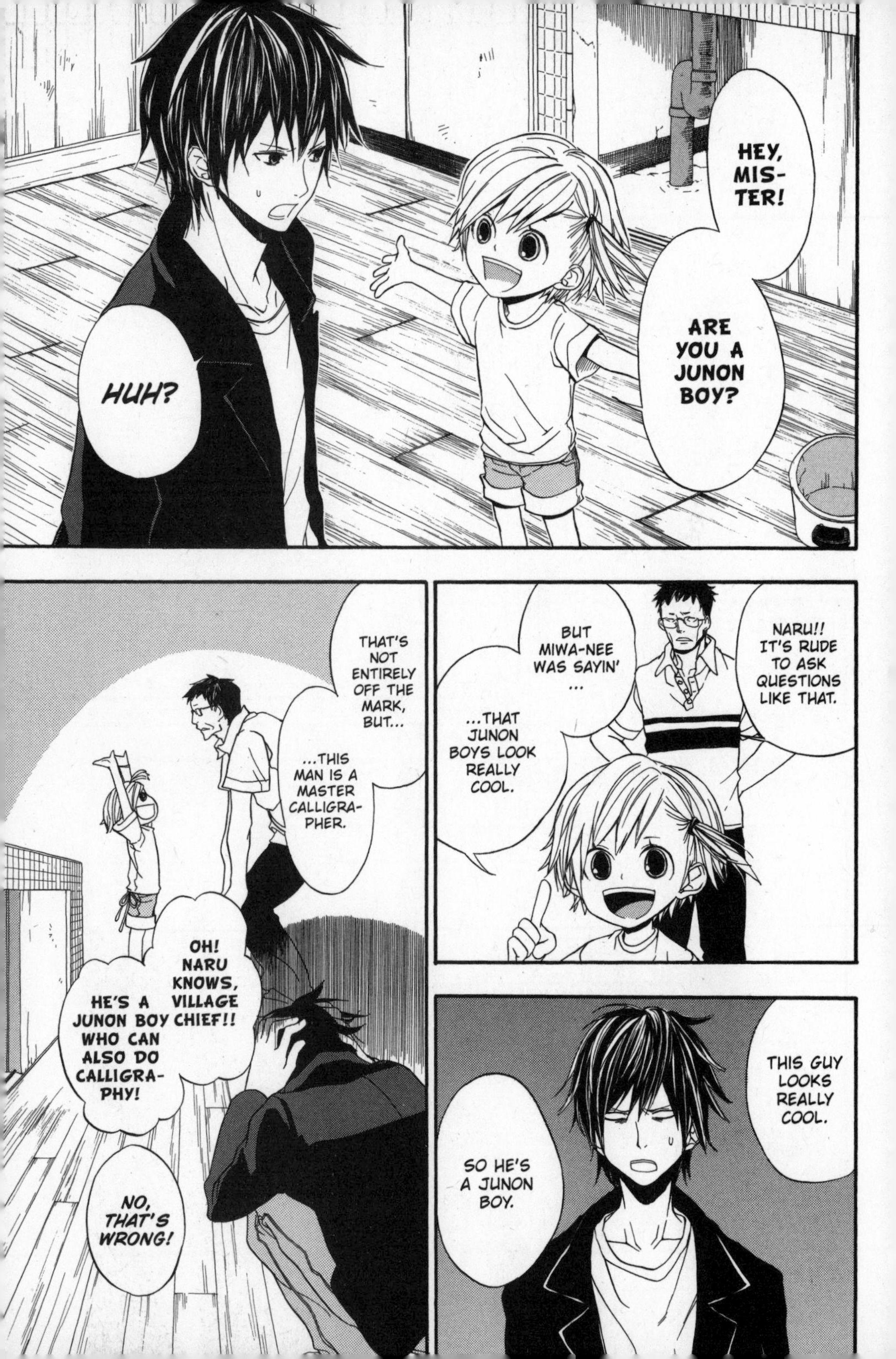

HEY, MISTER!
ARE YOU A JUNON BOY?
HUH?
NARU!! IT'S RUDE TO ASK QUESTIONS LIKE THAT.
BUT MIWA-NEE WAS SAYIN'...
...THAT JUNON BOYS LOOK REALLY COOL.
THIS GUY LOOKS REALLY COOL.
SO HE'S A JUNON BOY.
THAT'S NOT ENTIRELY OFF THE MARK, BUT...
...THIS MAN IS A MASTER CALLIGRAPHER.
OH! NARU KNOWS, VILLAGE CHIEF!!
HE'S A JUNON BOY WHO CAN ALSO DO CALLIGRAPHY!
NO, THAT'S WRONG!

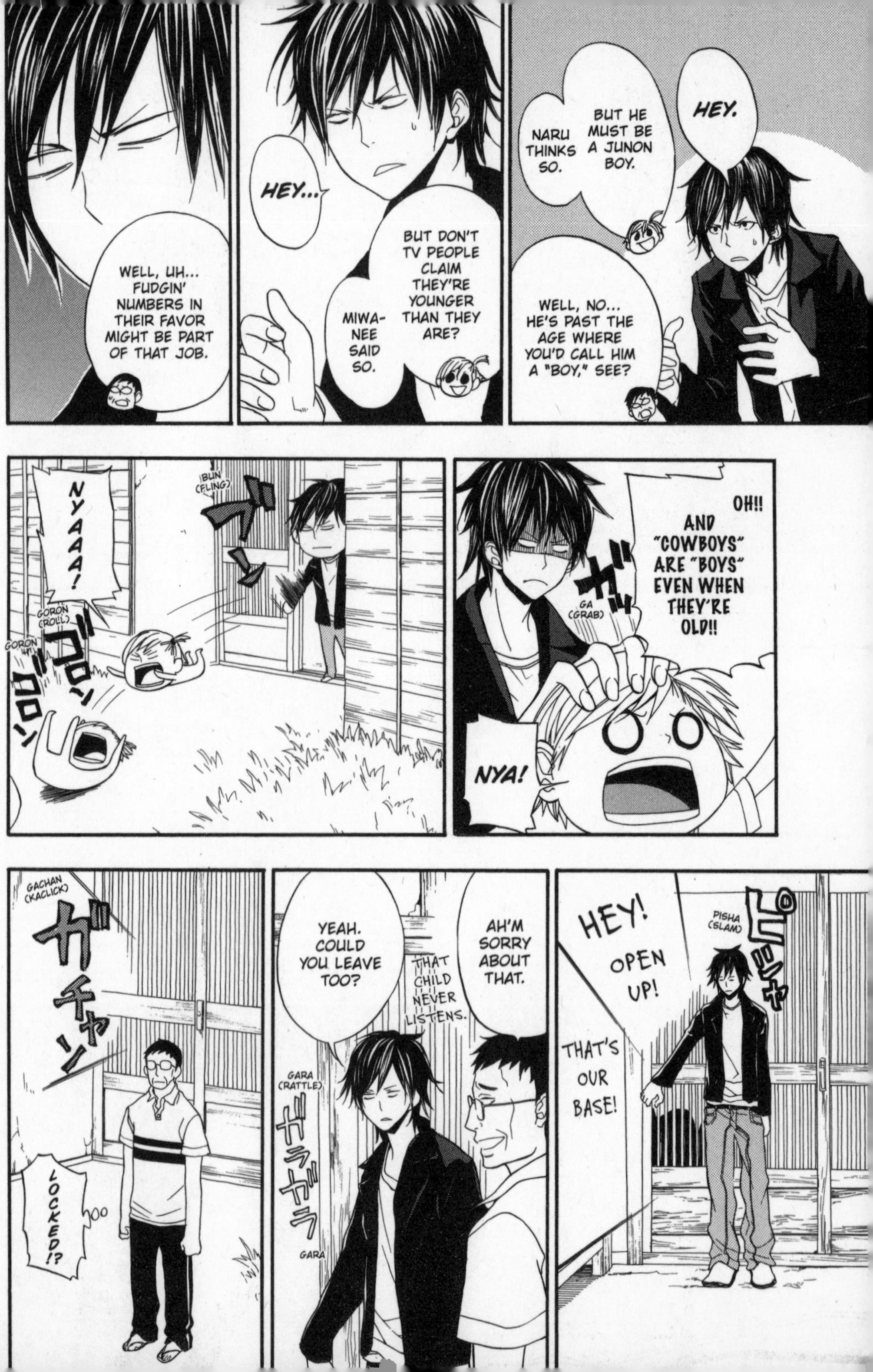
HEY.
BUT HE MUST BE A JUNON BOY.
NARU THINKS SO.
WELL, NO... HE'S PAST THE AGE WHERE YOU'D CALL HIM A "BOY," SEE?
HEY...
BUT DON'T TV PEOPLE CLAIM THEY'RE YOUNGER THAN THEY ARE?
MIWA-NEE SAID SO.
WELL, UH... FUDGIN' NUMBERS IN THEIR FAVOR MIGHT BE PART OF THAT JOB.
OH!!
AND "COWBOYS" ARE "BOYS" EVEN WHEN THEY'RE OLD!!
GA (GRAB)
NYA!
BUN (FLING)
NYAAA!
GORON (ROLL)
GORON
HEY!
OPEN UP!
PISHA (SLAM)
THAT'S OUR BASE!
AH'M SORRY ABOUT THAT.
THAT CHILD NEVER LISTENS.
YEAH. COULD YOU LEAVE TOO?
GARA (RATTLE)
GARA
GACHAN (KACLICK)
LOCKED!?

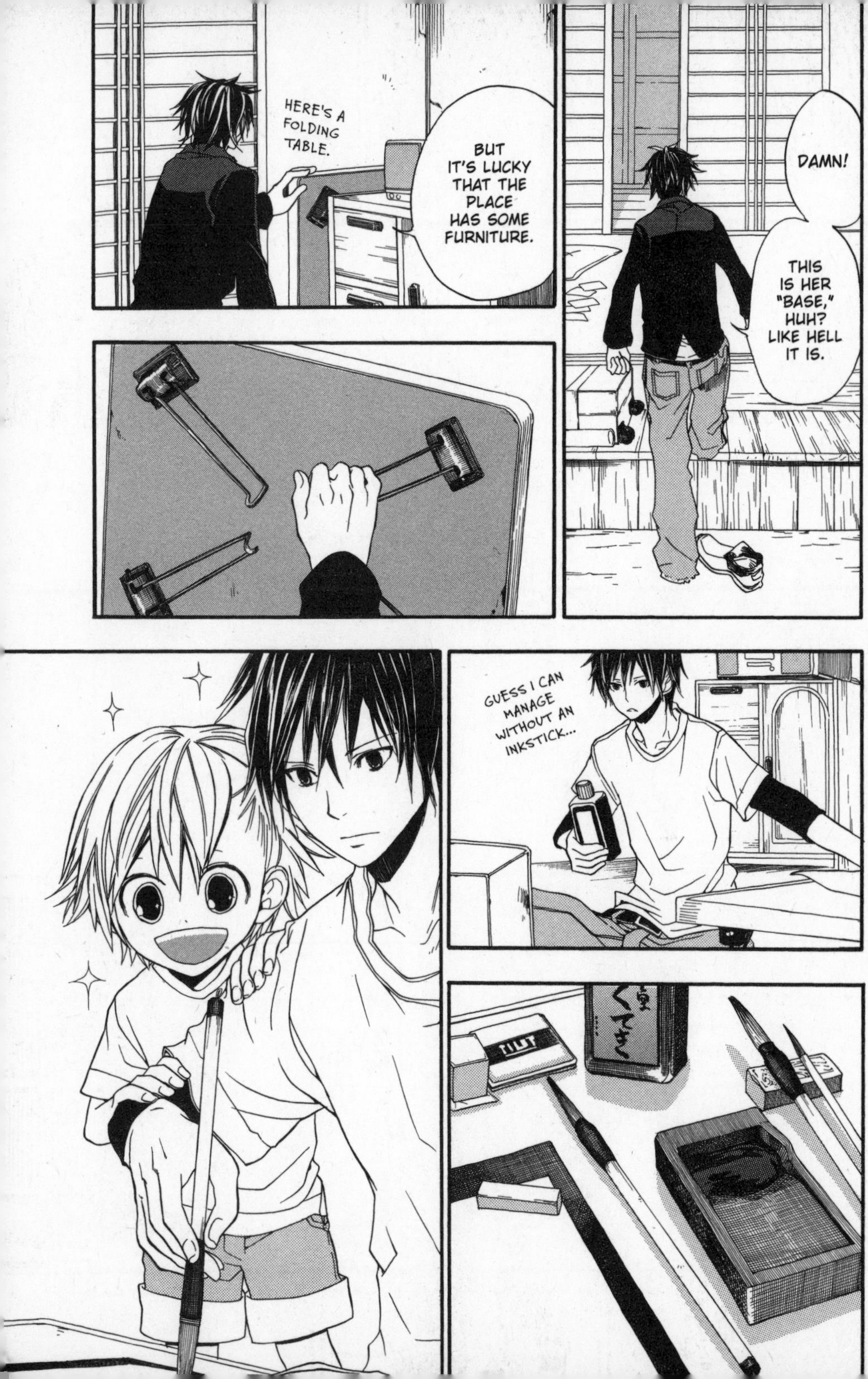
DAMN!
THIS IS HER "BASE," HUH? LIKE HELL IT IS.
BUT IT'S LUCKY THAT THE PLACE HAS SOME FURNITURE.
HERE'S A FOLDING TABLE.
GUESS I CAN MANAGE WITHOUT AN INKSTICK...

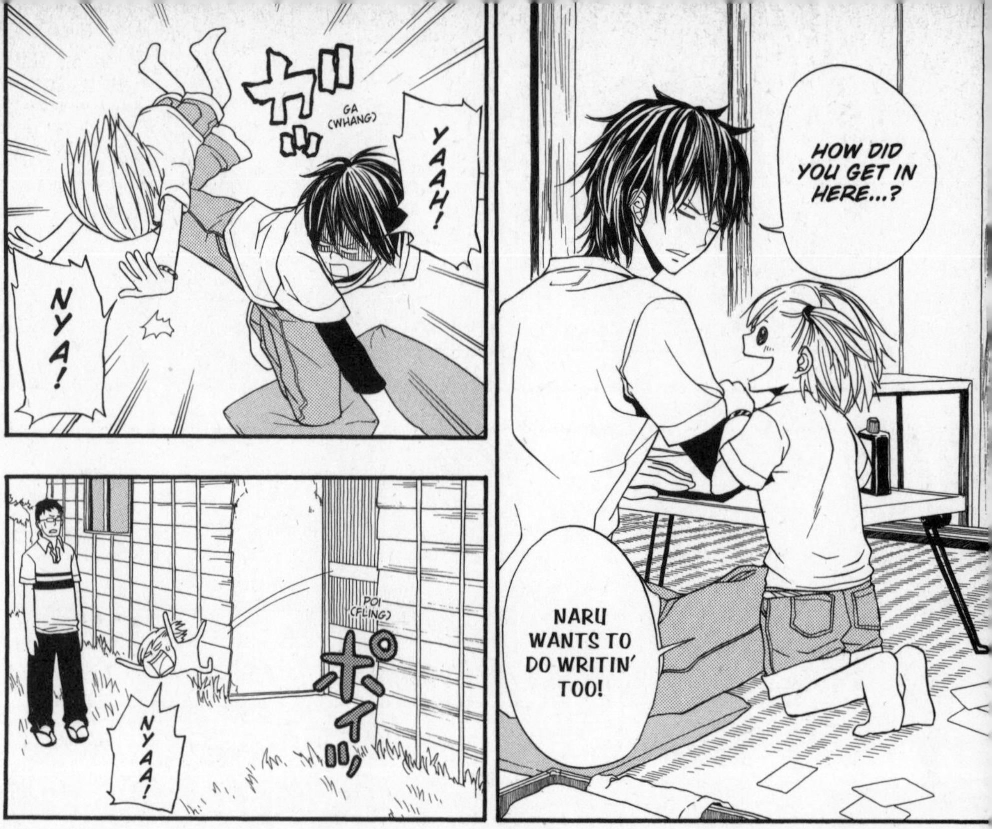
HOW DID YOU GET IN HERE...?
NARU WANTS TO DO WRITIN' TOO!
GA (WHANG)
YAAH!
NYA!
POI (FLING)
NYAA!

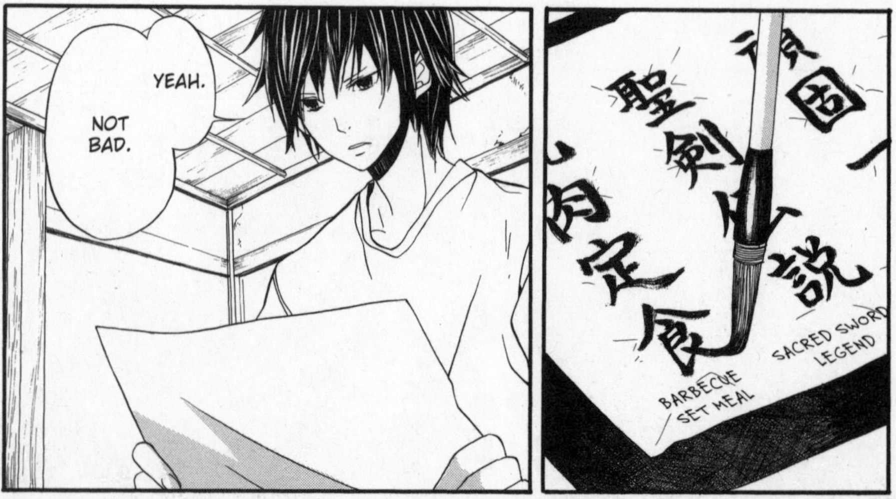
SACRED SWORD LEGEND
BARBECUE SET MEAL
YEAH.
NOT BAD.

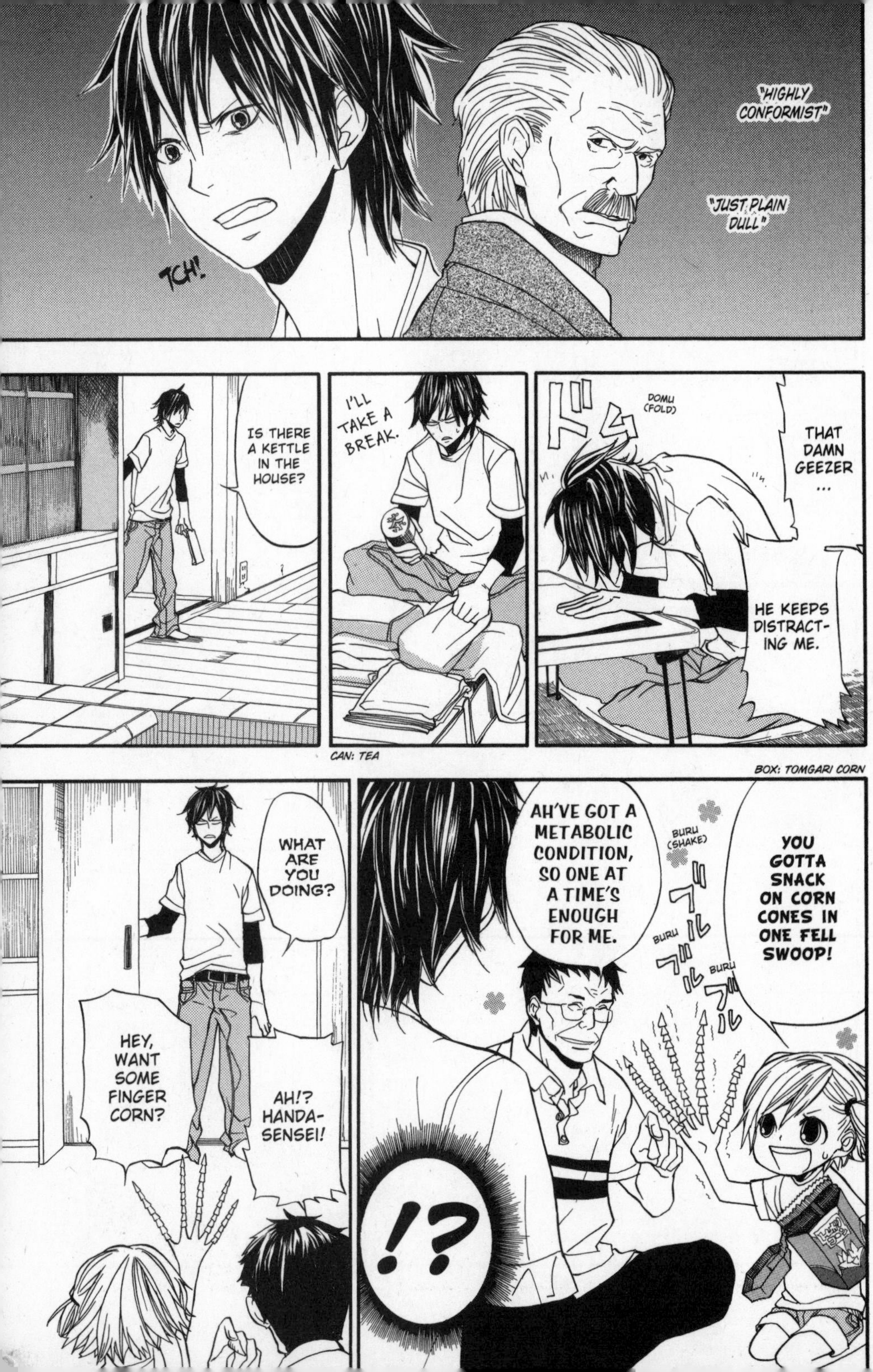
"HIGHLY CONFORMIST"
"JUST PLAIN DULL"
TCH!
DOMU (FOLD)
THAT DAMN GEEZER...
HE KEEPS DISTRACTING ME.
I'LL TAKE A BREAK.
CAN: TEA
IS THERE A KETTLE IN THE HOUSE?
BOX: TOMGARI CORN
YOU GOTTA SNACK ON CORN CONES IN ONE FELL SWOOP!
BURU (SHAKE)
BURU
BURU
AH'VE GOT A METABOLIC CONDITION, SO ONE AT A TIME'S ENOUGH FOR ME.
!?
WHAT ARE YOU DOING?
HEY, WANT SOME FINGER CORN?
AH!? HANDA-SENSEI!

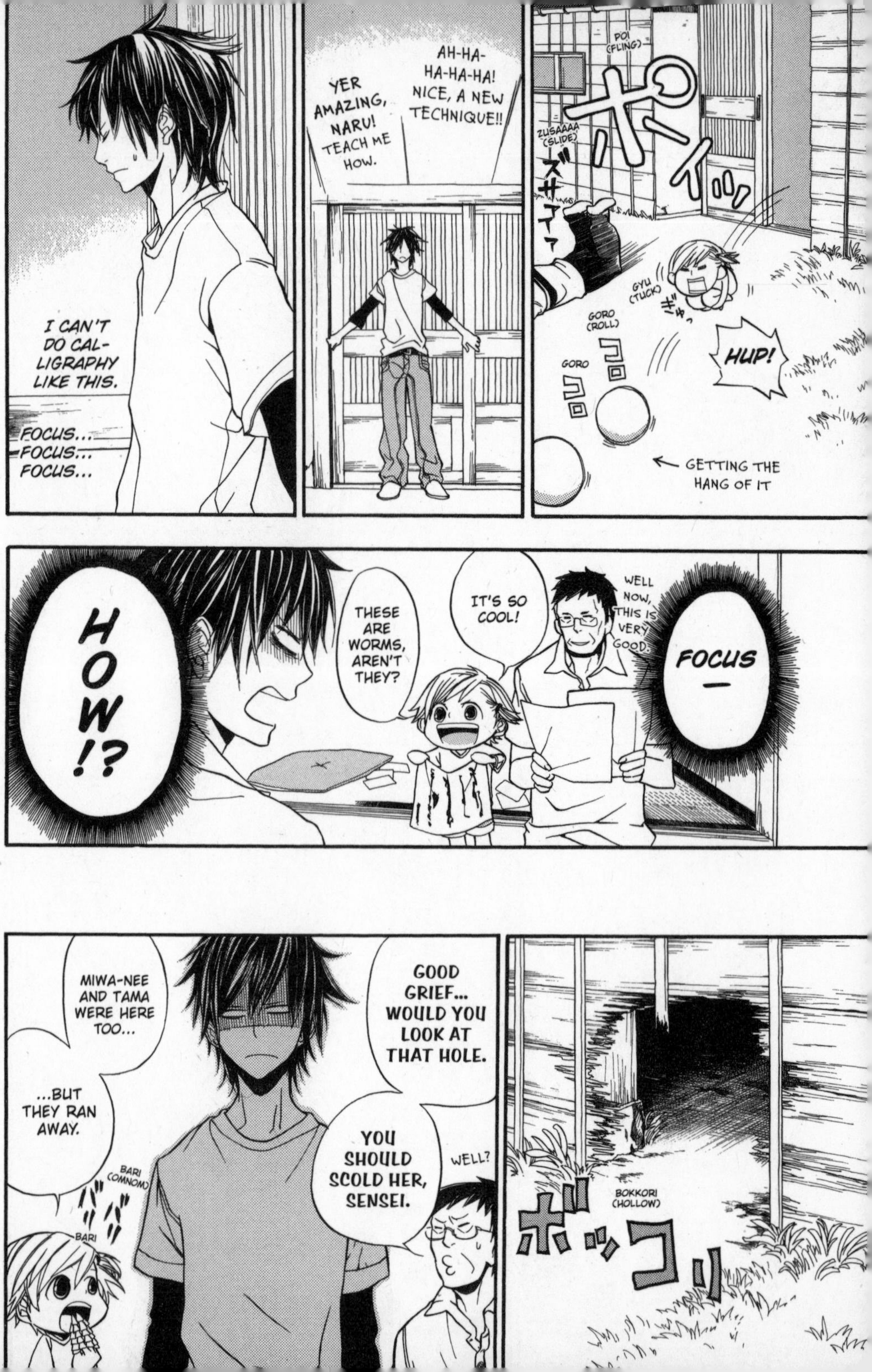
PO! (FLING)
ポイッ
ZUSAAAA (SLIDE)
ズサァァ
GYU (TUCK)
ぎゅっ
HUP!
GORO (ROLL)
コロ
GORO
コロ
GETTING THE HANG OF IT
AH-HA-HA-HA-HA! NICE, A NEW TECHNIQUE!!
YER AMAZING, NARU! TEACH ME HOW.
I CAN'T DO CAL-LIGRAPHY LIKE THIS.
FOCUS... FOCUS... FOCUS...
FOCUS —
WELL NOW, THIS IS VERY GOOD.
IT'S SO COOL!
THESE ARE WORMS, AREN'T THEY?
HOW!?
BOKKORI (HOLLOW)
ボッコリ
GOOD GRIEF... WOULD YOU LOOK AT THAT HOLE.
WELL?
YOU SHOULD SCOLD HER, SENSEI.
MIWA-NEE AND TAMA WERE HERE TOO...
...BUT THEY RAN AWAY.
BARI (OMNOM)
バリ
BARI

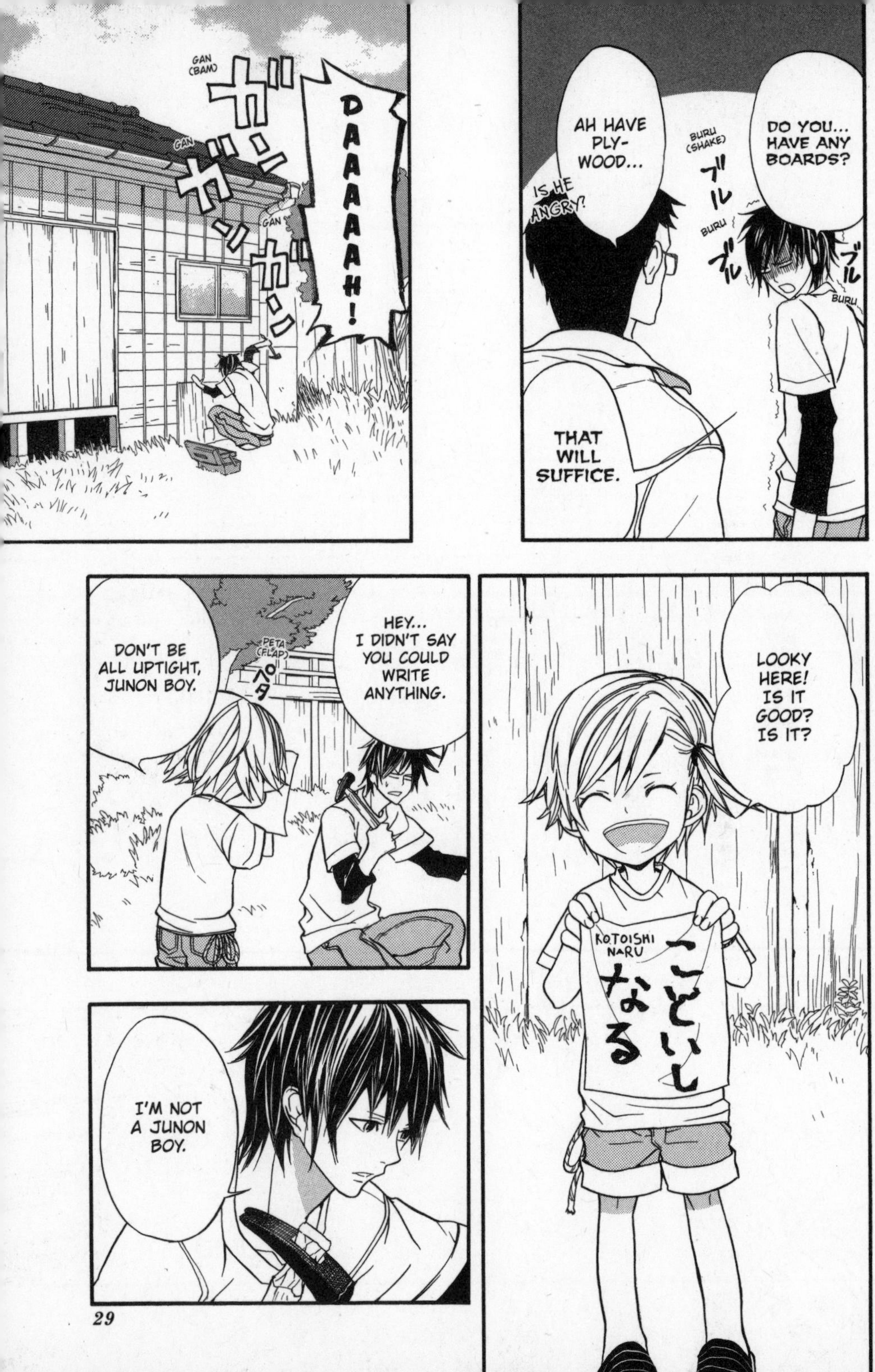
DO YOU... HAVE ANY BOARDS?
BURU (SHAKE) ブル
BURU ブル
BURU ブル
AH HAVE PLY-WOOD...
IS HE ANGRY?
THAT WILL SUFFICE.
GAN (BAM) ガン
GAN ガッ
GAN ガン
DAAAAAAH!
LOOKY HERE! IS IT GOOD? IS IT?
KOTOISHI NARU
こといし なる
HEY... I DIDN'T SAY YOU COULD WRITE ANYTHING.
PETA (FLAP) ペタ
DON'T BE ALL UPTIGHT, JUNON BOY.
I'M NOT A JUNON BOY.

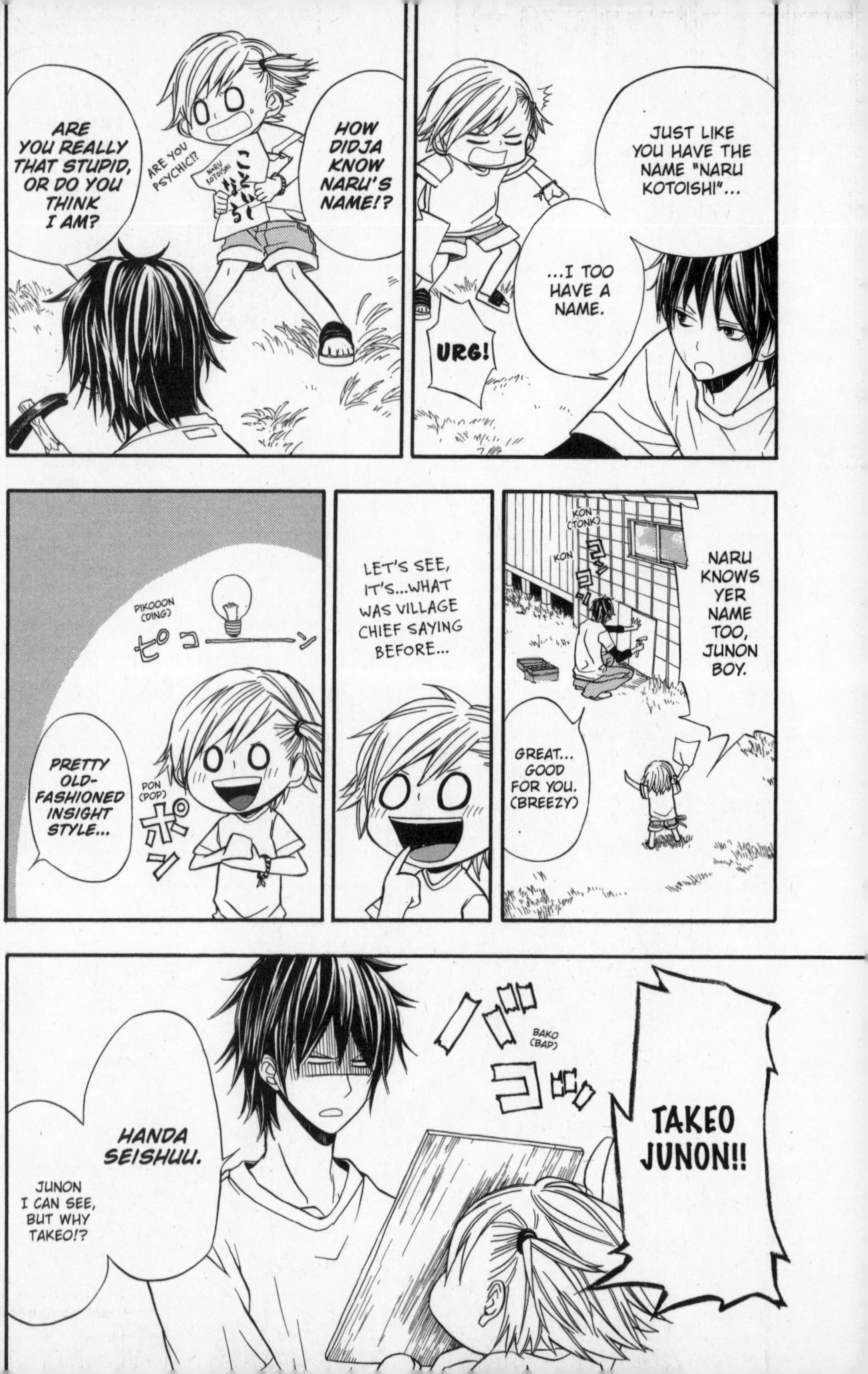
JUST LIKE YOU HAVE THE NAME "NARU KOTOISHI"...
...I TOO HAVE A NAME.
URG!
HOW DIDJA KNOW NARU'S NAME!?
ARE YOU PSYCHIC!?
NARU KOTOISHI
ARE YOU REALLY THAT STUPID, OR DO YOU THINK I AM?
KON (TONK)
KON
NARU KNOWS YER NAME TOO, JUNON BOY.
GREAT... GOOD FOR YOU. (BREEZY)
LET'S SEE, IT'S...WHAT WAS VILLAGE CHIEF SAYING BEFORE...
PIKOOON (DING)
ピコーーン
PON (POP)
ポン
PRETTY OLD-FASHIONED INSIGHT STYLE...
BAKO (BAP)
TAKEO JUNON!!
HANDA SEISHUU.
JUNON I CAN SEE, BUT WHY TAKEO!?

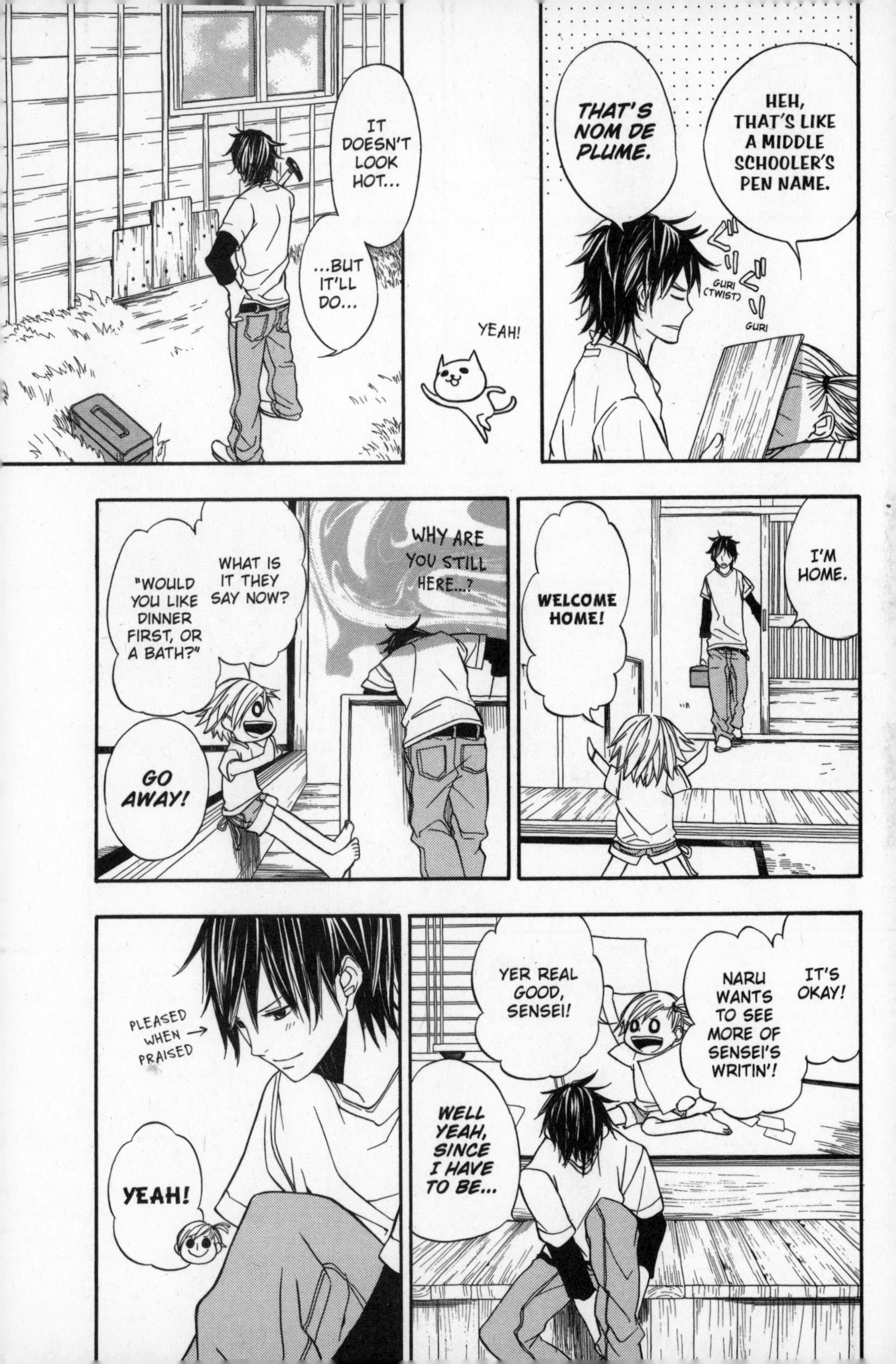
HEH, THAT'S LIKE A MIDDLE SCHOOLER'S PEN NAME.
THAT'S NOM DE PLUME.
GURI (TWIST)
GURI
IT DOESN'T LOOK HOT...
...BUT IT'LL DO...
YEAH!
I'M HOME.
WELCOME HOME!
WHY ARE YOU STILL HERE...?
WHAT IS IT THEY SAY NOW?
"WOULD YOU LIKE DINNER FIRST, OR A BATH?"
GO AWAY!
IT'S OKAY!
NARU WANTS TO SEE MORE OF SENSEI'S WRITIN'!
YER REAL GOOD, SENSEI!
WELL YEAH, SINCE I HAVE TO BE...
PLEASED WHEN PRAISED
YEAH!

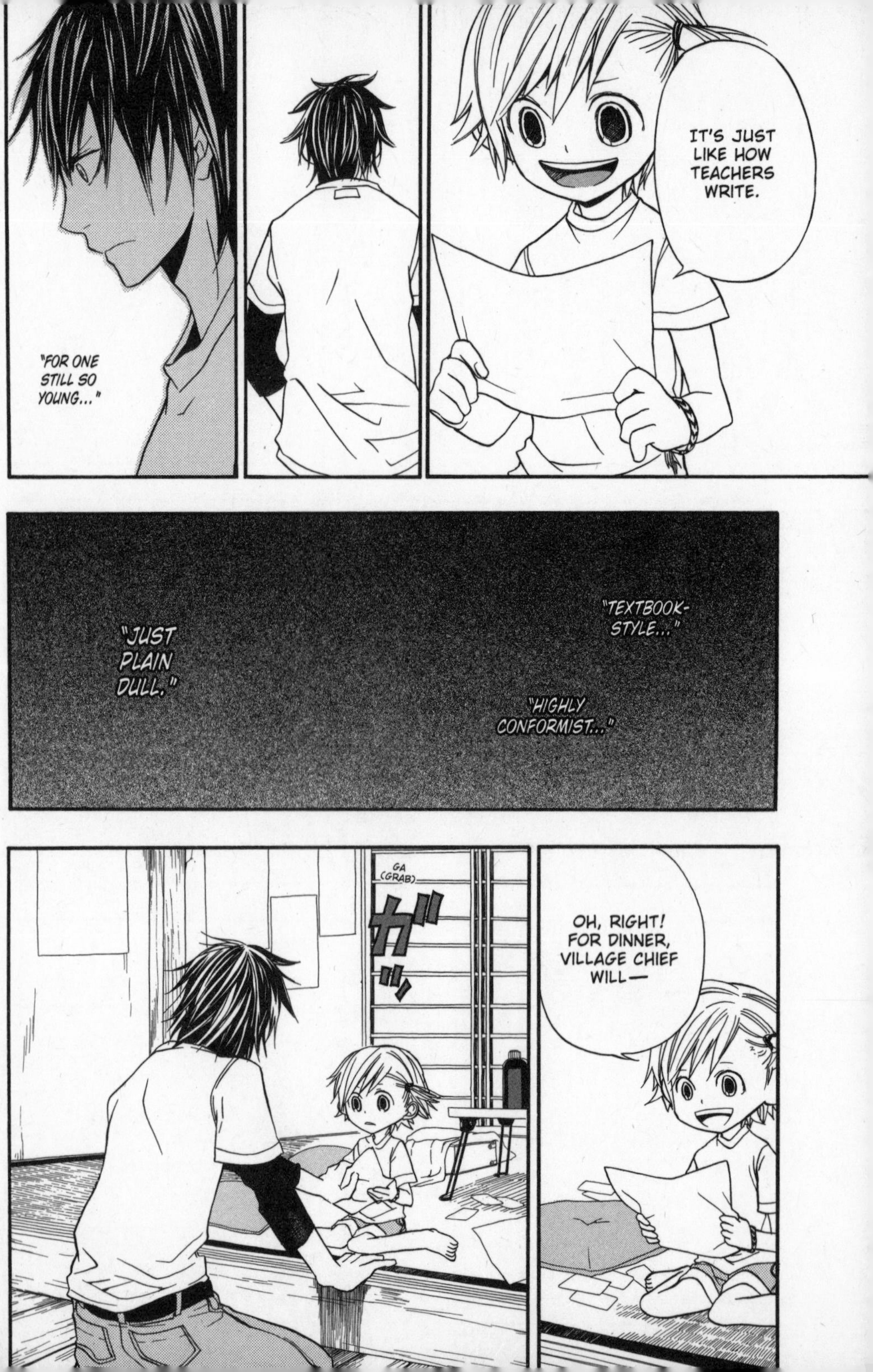
IT'S JUST LIKE HOW TEACHERS WRITE.
"FOR ONE STILL SO YOUNG..."
"TEXTBOOK-STYLE..."
"HIGHLY CONFORMIST..."
"JUST PLAIN DULL."
OH, RIGHT! FOR DINNER, VILLAGE CHIEF WILL—
ガッ
GA (GRAB)

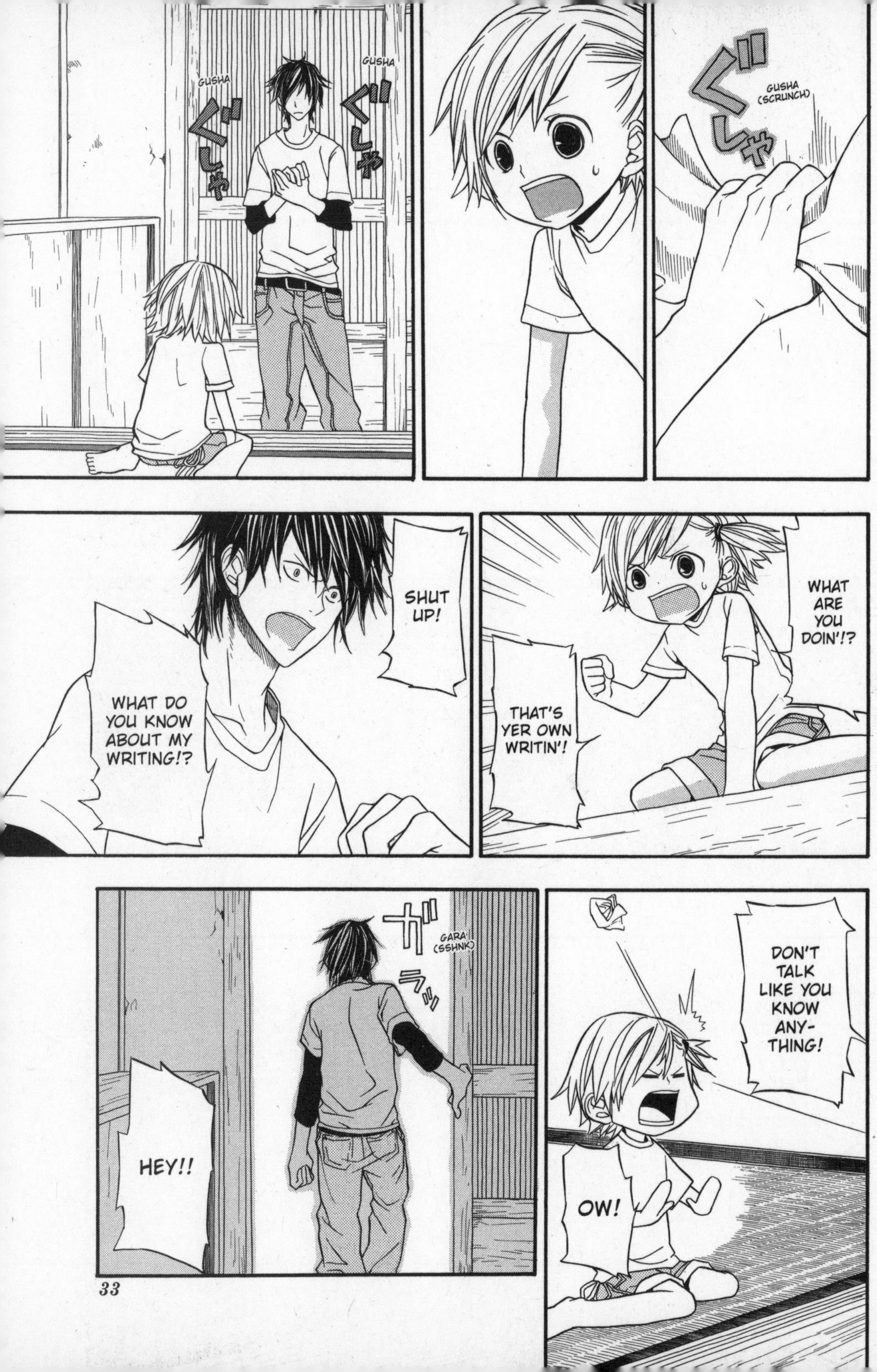
ぐしゃ
GUSHA (SCRUNCH)
ぐしゃ
GUSHA
ぐしゃ
GUSHA
WHAT ARE YOU DOIN'!?
THAT'S YER OWN WRITIN'!
SHUT UP!
WHAT DO YOU KNOW ABOUT MY WRITING!?
DON'T TALK LIKE YOU KNOW ANY-THING!
OW!
ガラッ
GARA (SSHNK)
HEY!!

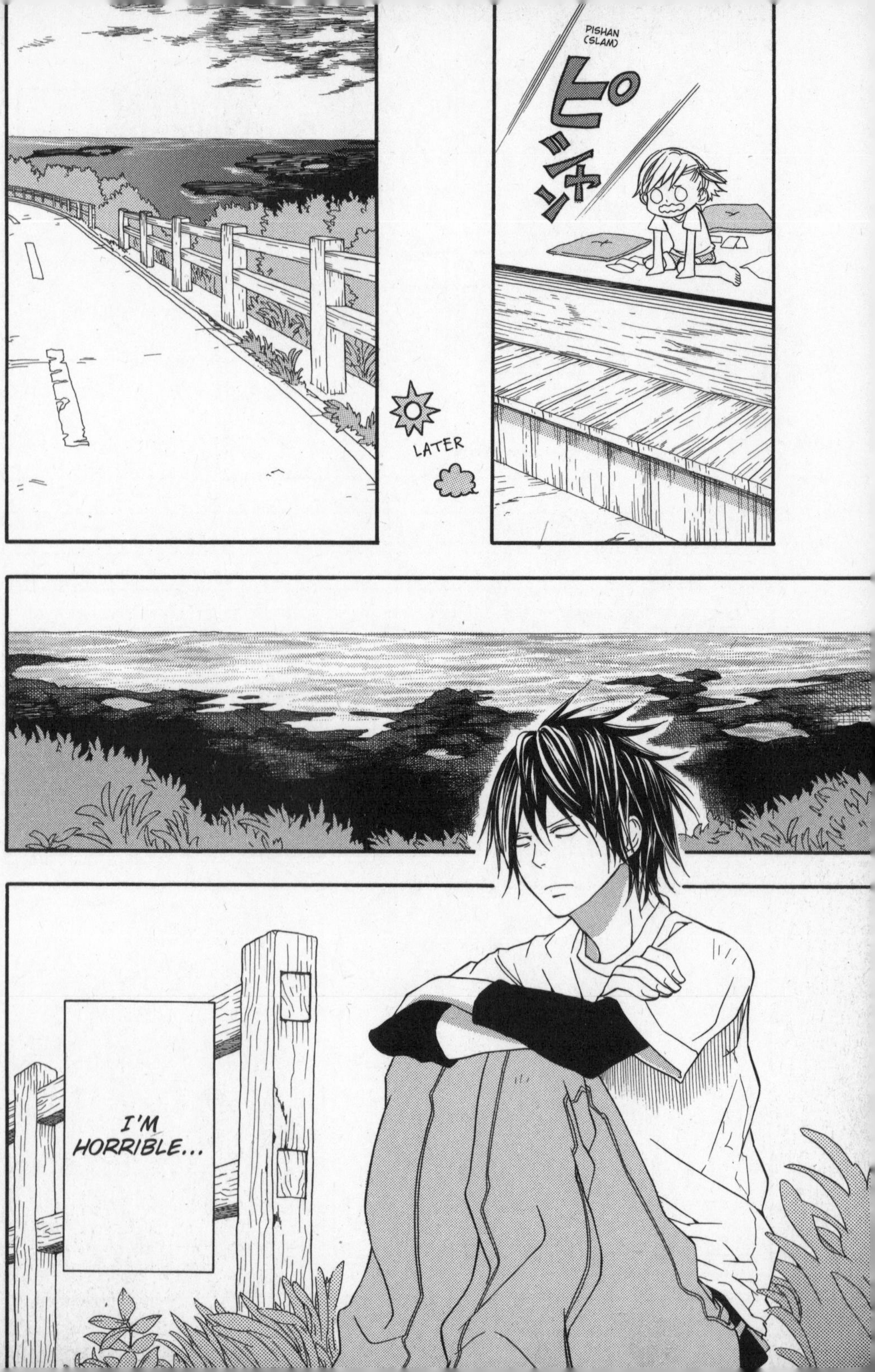
PISHAN (SLAM)
ピシャン
LATER
I'M HORRIBLE...

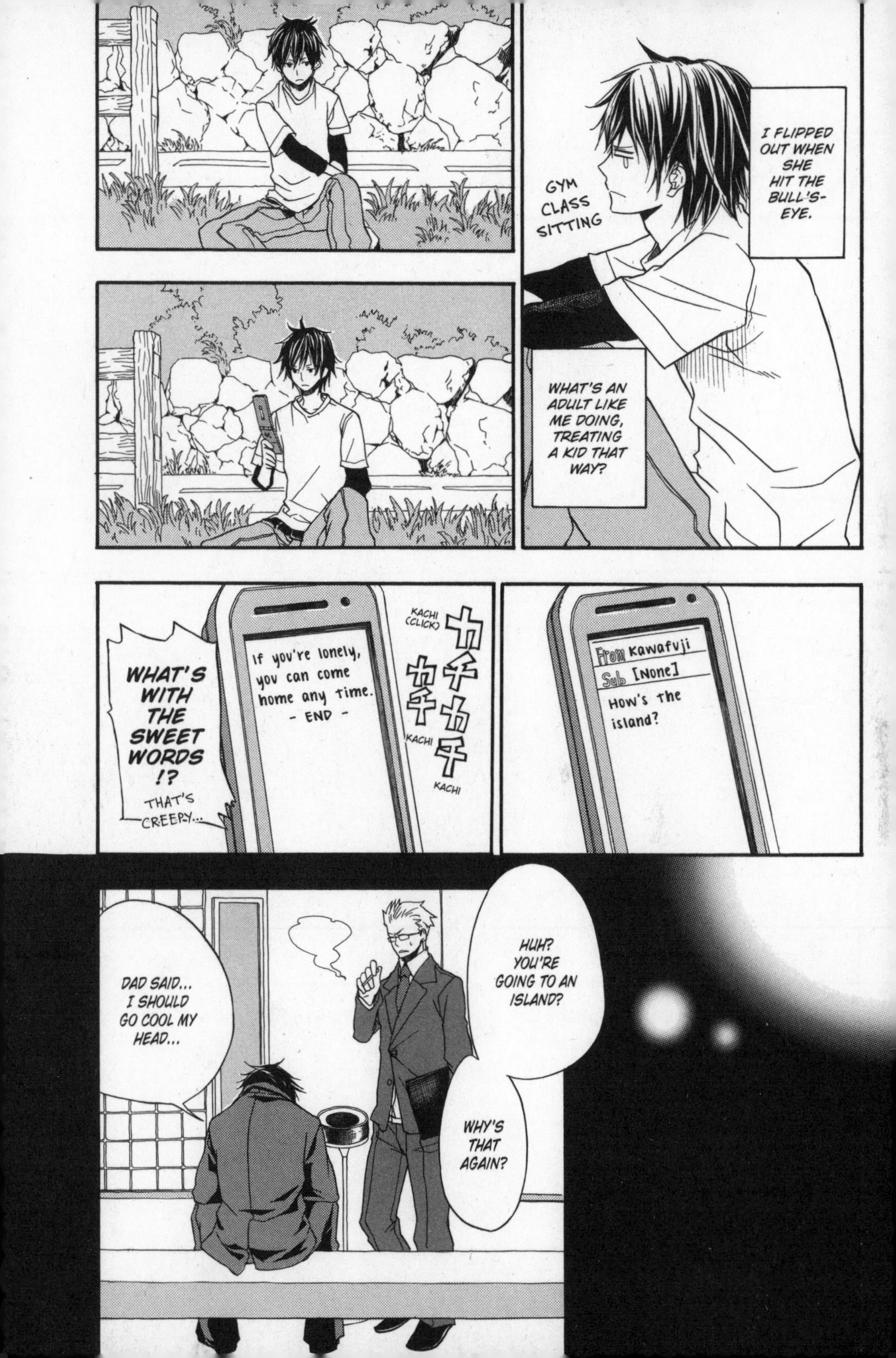
I FLIPPED OUT WHEN SHE HIT THE BULL'S-EYE.
GYM CLASS SITTING
WHAT'S AN ADULT LIKE ME DOING, TREATING A KID THAT WAY?
From Kawafuji
Sub [None]
How's the island?
KACHI (CLICK)
KACHI
KACHI
If you're lonely, you can come home any time.
- END -
WHAT'S WITH THE SWEET WORDS!?
THAT'S CREEPY...
HUH? YOU'RE GOING TO AN ISLAND?
WHY'S THAT AGAIN?
DAD SAID... I SHOULD GO COOL MY HEAD...

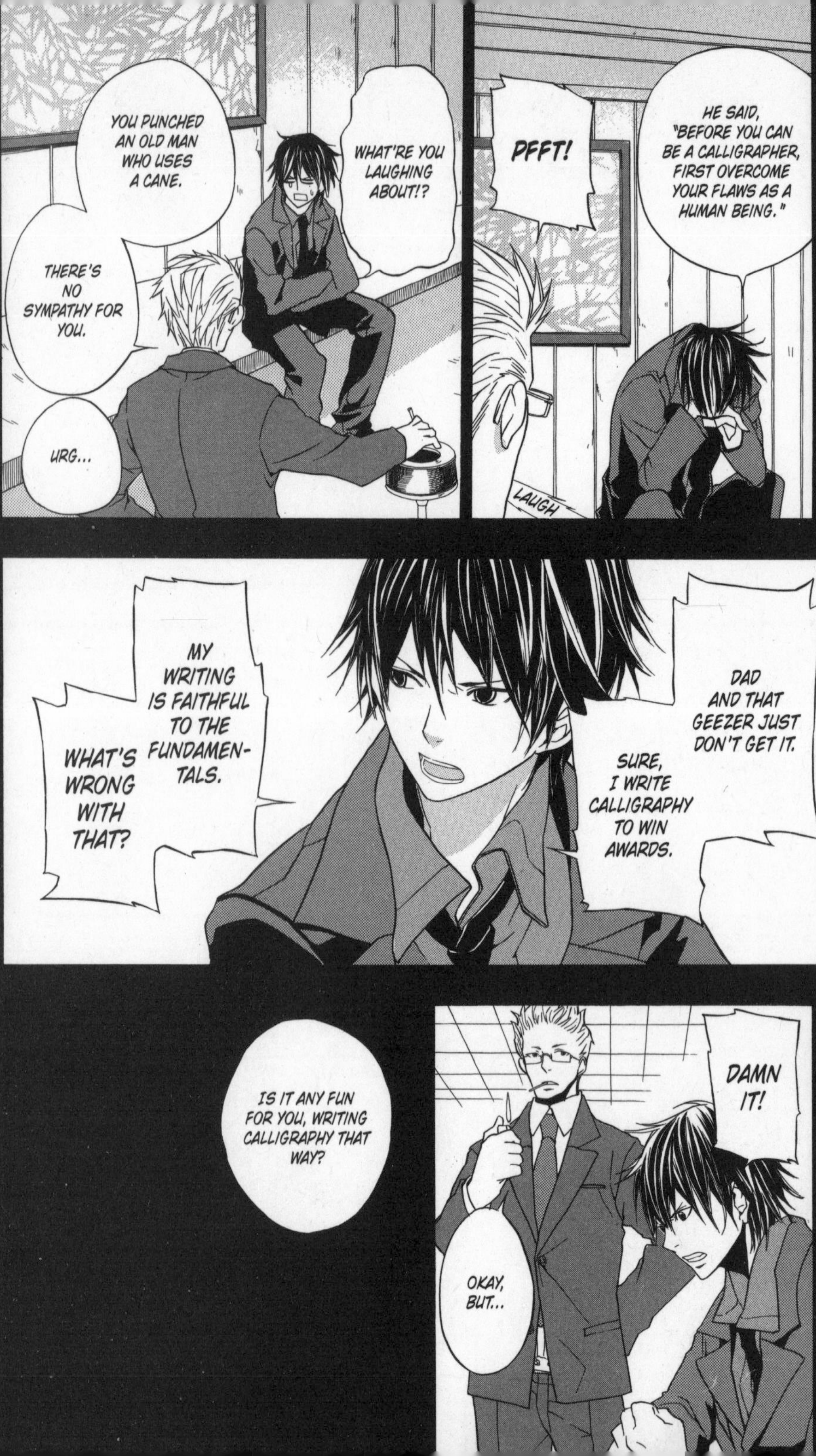
HE SAID, "BEFORE YOU CAN BE A CALLIGRAPHER, FIRST OVERCOME YOUR FLAWS AS A HUMAN BEING."
PFFT!
LAUGH
WHAT'RE YOU LAUGHING ABOUT!?
YOU PUNCHED AN OLD MAN WHO USES A CANE.
THERE'S NO SYMPATHY FOR YOU.
URG...
DAD AND THAT GEEZER JUST DON'T GET IT.
SURE, I WRITE CALLIGRAPHY TO WIN AWARDS.
MY WRITING IS FAITHFUL TO THE FUNDAMEN-TALS.
WHAT'S WRONG WITH THAT?
DAMN IT!
OKAY, BUT...
IS IT ANY FUN FOR YOU, WRITING CALLIGRAPHY THAT WAY?

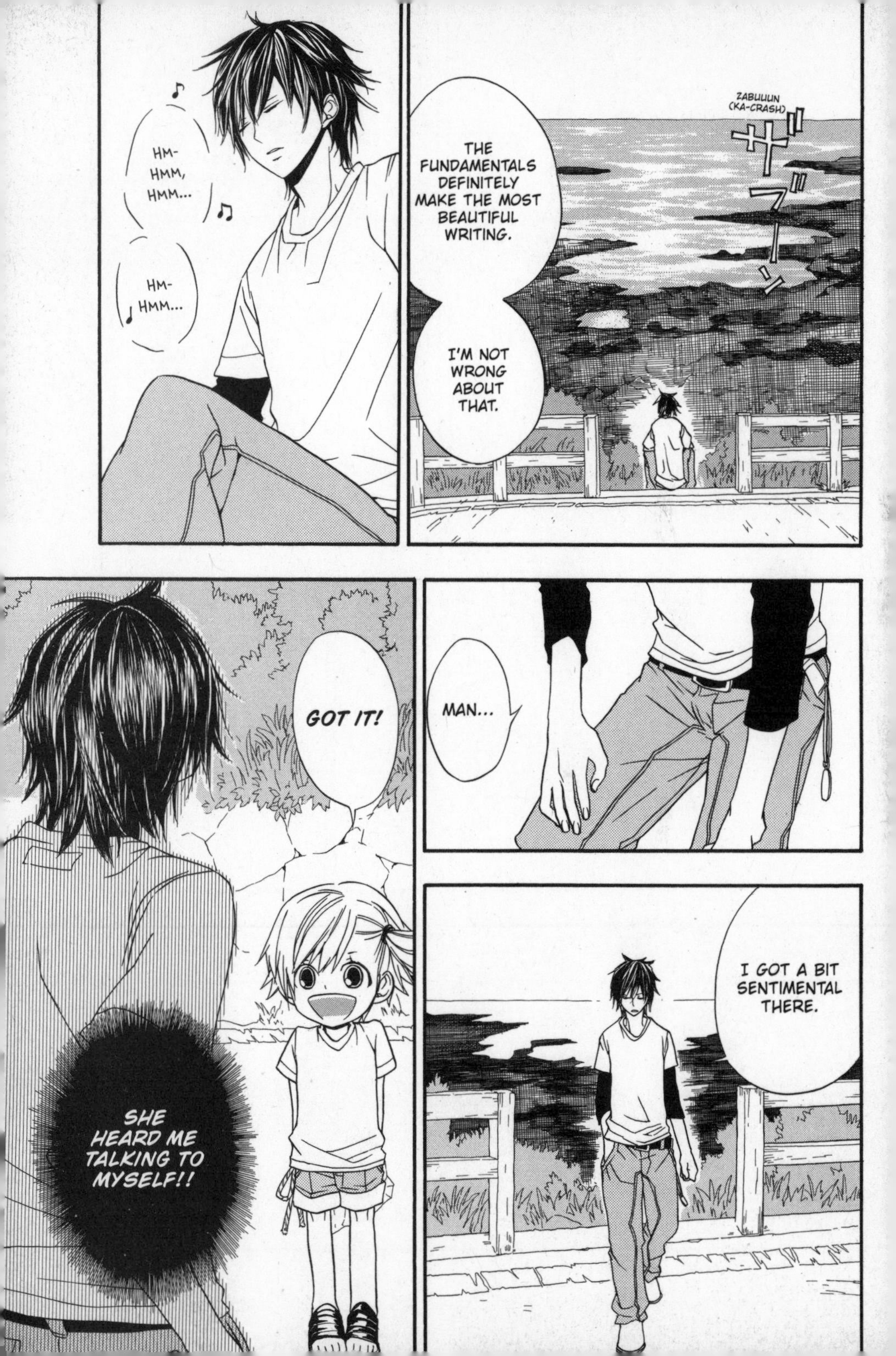
ZABUUUN (KA-CRASH)
ザブーン
THE FUNDAMENTALS DEFINITELY MAKE THE MOST BEAUTIFUL WRITING.
I'M NOT WRONG ABOUT THAT.
HM-HMM, HMM...
HM-HMM...
MAN...
I GOT A BIT SENTIMENTAL THERE.
GOT IT!
SHE HEARD ME TALKING TO MYSELF!!

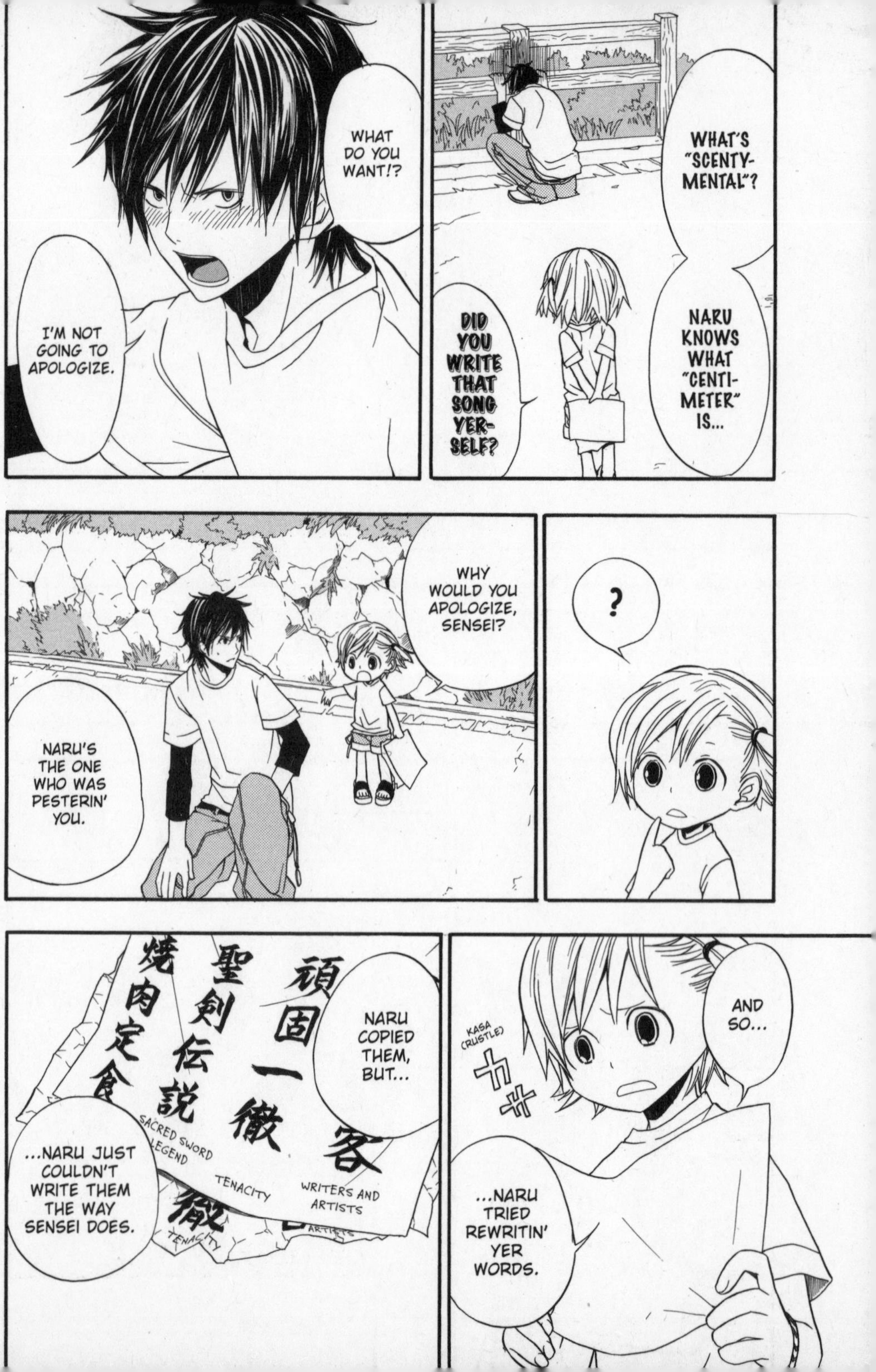
WHAT'S "SCENTY-MENTAL"?
NARU KNOWS WHAT "CENTI-METER" IS...
DID YOU WRITE THAT SONG YER-SELF?
WHAT DO YOU WANT!?
I'M NOT GOING TO APOLOGIZE.
?
WHY WOULD YOU APOLOGIZE, SENSEI?
NARU'S THE ONE WHO WAS PESTERIN' YOU.
AND SO...
KASA (RUSTLE)
...NARU TRIED REWRITIN' YER WORDS.
NARU COPIED THEM, BUT...
頑固一徹
客
聖剣伝説
焼肉定食
SACRED SWORD LEGEND
TENACITY
WRITERS AND ARTISTS
...NARU JUST COULDN'T WRITE THEM THE WAY SENSEI DOES.
TENACITY
ARTISTS

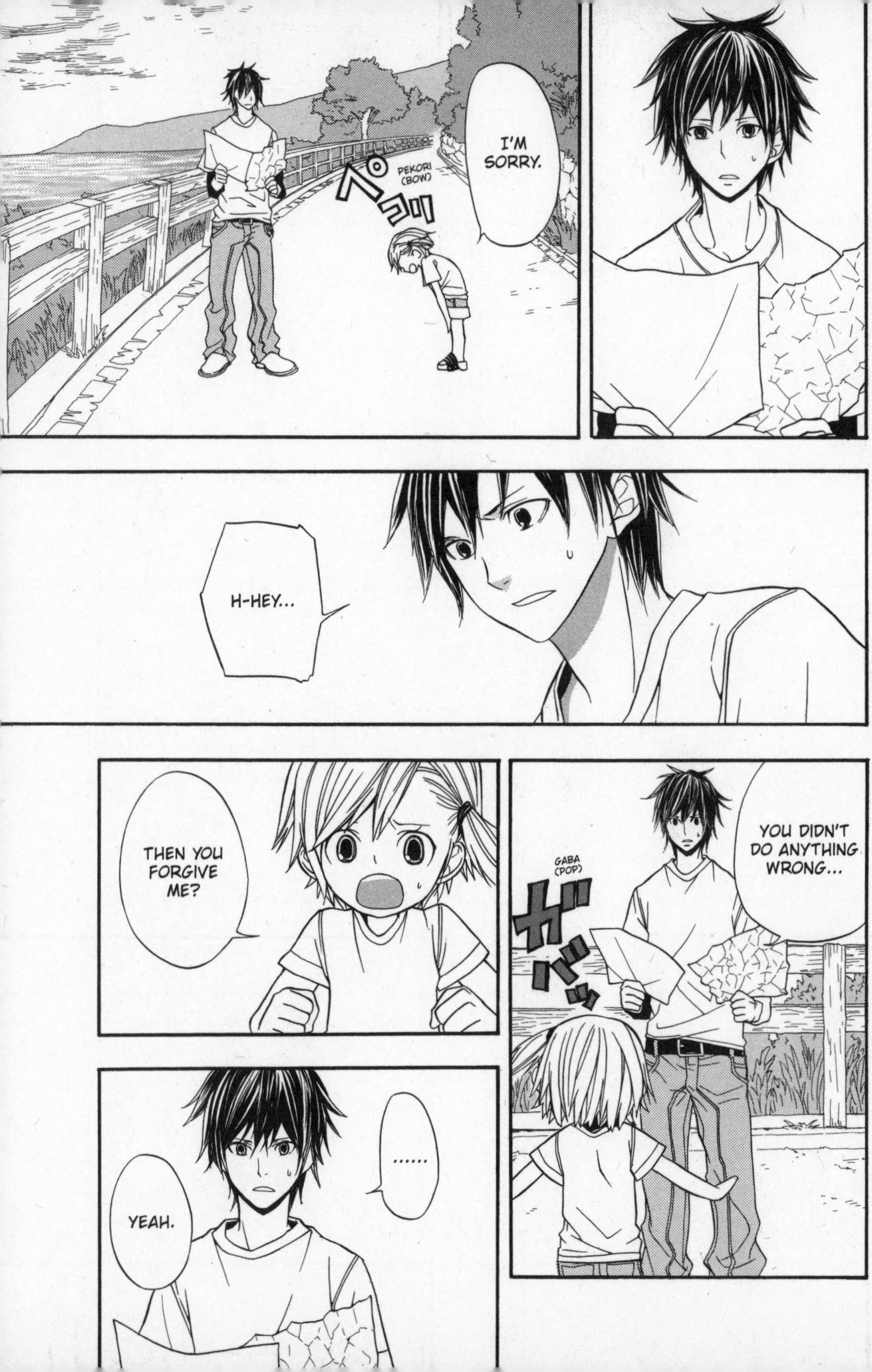
PEKORI (BOW)
I'M SORRY.
H-HEY...
GABA (POP)
YOU DIDN'T DO ANYTHING WRONG...
THEN YOU FORGIVE ME?
......
YEAH.

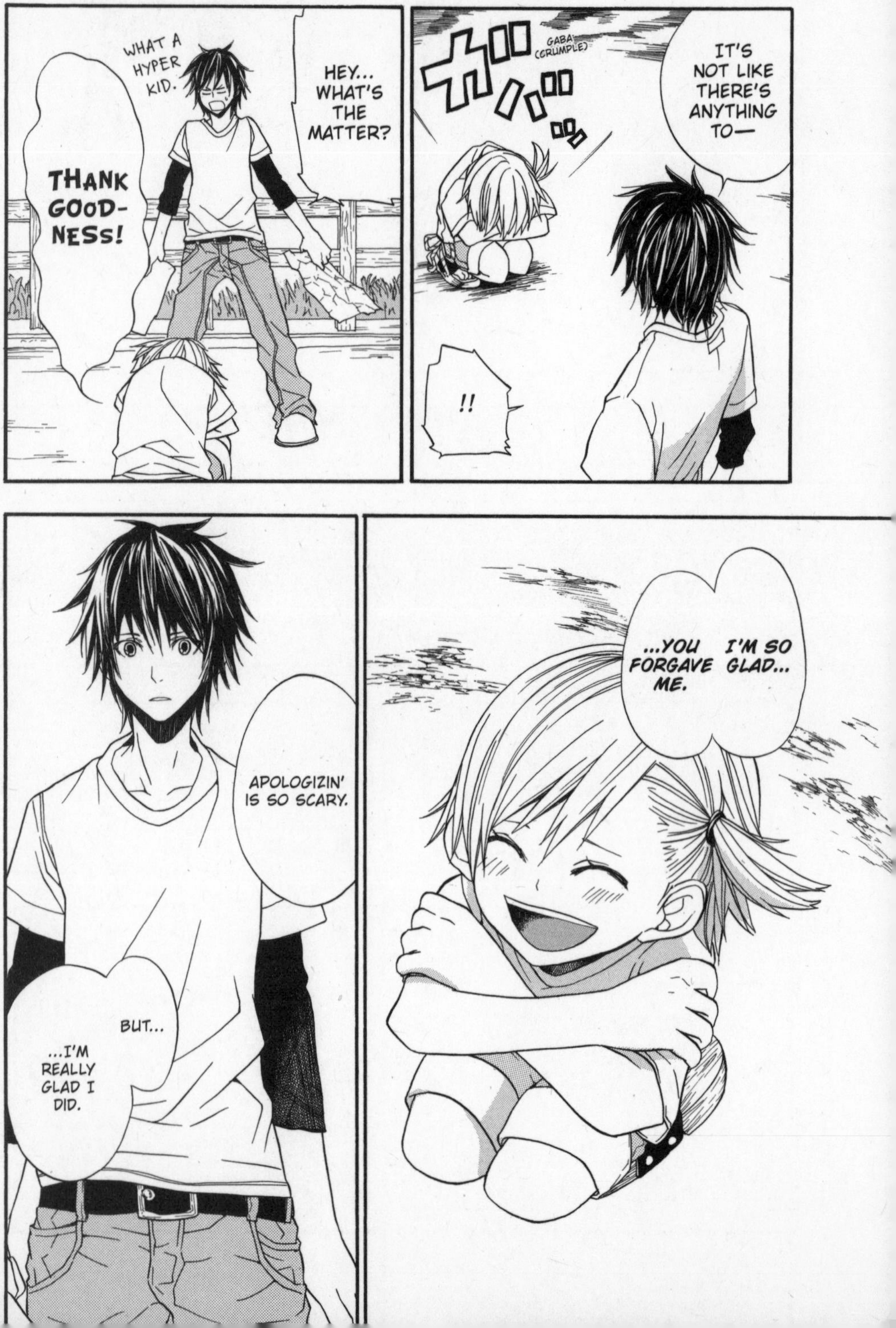
IT'S NOT LIKE THERE'S ANYTHING TO—
GABA (CRUMPLE)
!!
HEY... WHAT'S THE MATTER?
WHAT A HYPER KID.
THANK GOOD-NESS!
I'M SO GLAD...
...YOU FORGAVE ME.
APOLOGIZIN' IS SO SCARY.
BUT...
...I'M REALLY GLAD I DID.

HM?

....

I'M SORRY ...

...I YELLED AT YOU.

OKAY!

IT'S NOTHING.

COME ON, GET UP.

....

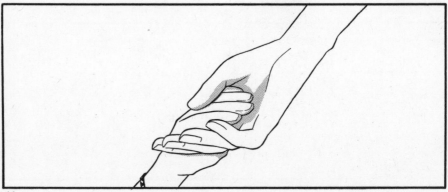

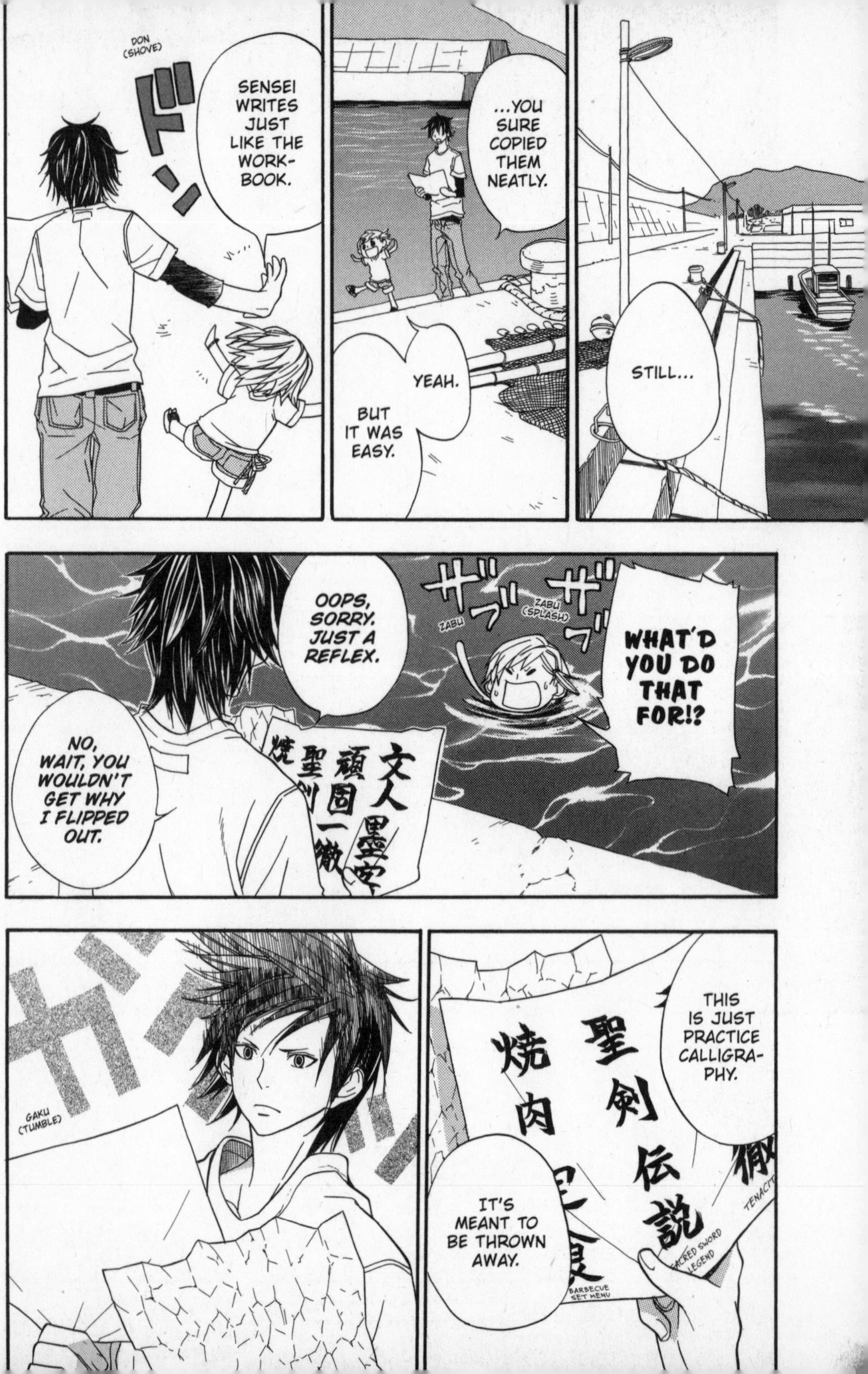
STILL...
...YOU SURE COPIED THEM NEATLY.
YEAH.
BUT IT WAS EASY.
SENSEI WRITES JUST LIKE THE WORK-BOOK.
DON (SHOVE)
WHAT'D YOU DO THAT FOR!?
ZABU (SPLASH)
ZABU
OOPS, SORRY. JUST A REFLEX.
NO, WAIT, YOU WOULDN'T GET WHY I FLIPPED OUT.
THIS IS JUST PRACTICE CALLIGRA-PHY.
TENACITY
SACRED SWORD LEGEND
IT'S MEANT TO BE THROWN AWAY.
BARBECUE SET MENU
GAKU (TUMBLE)

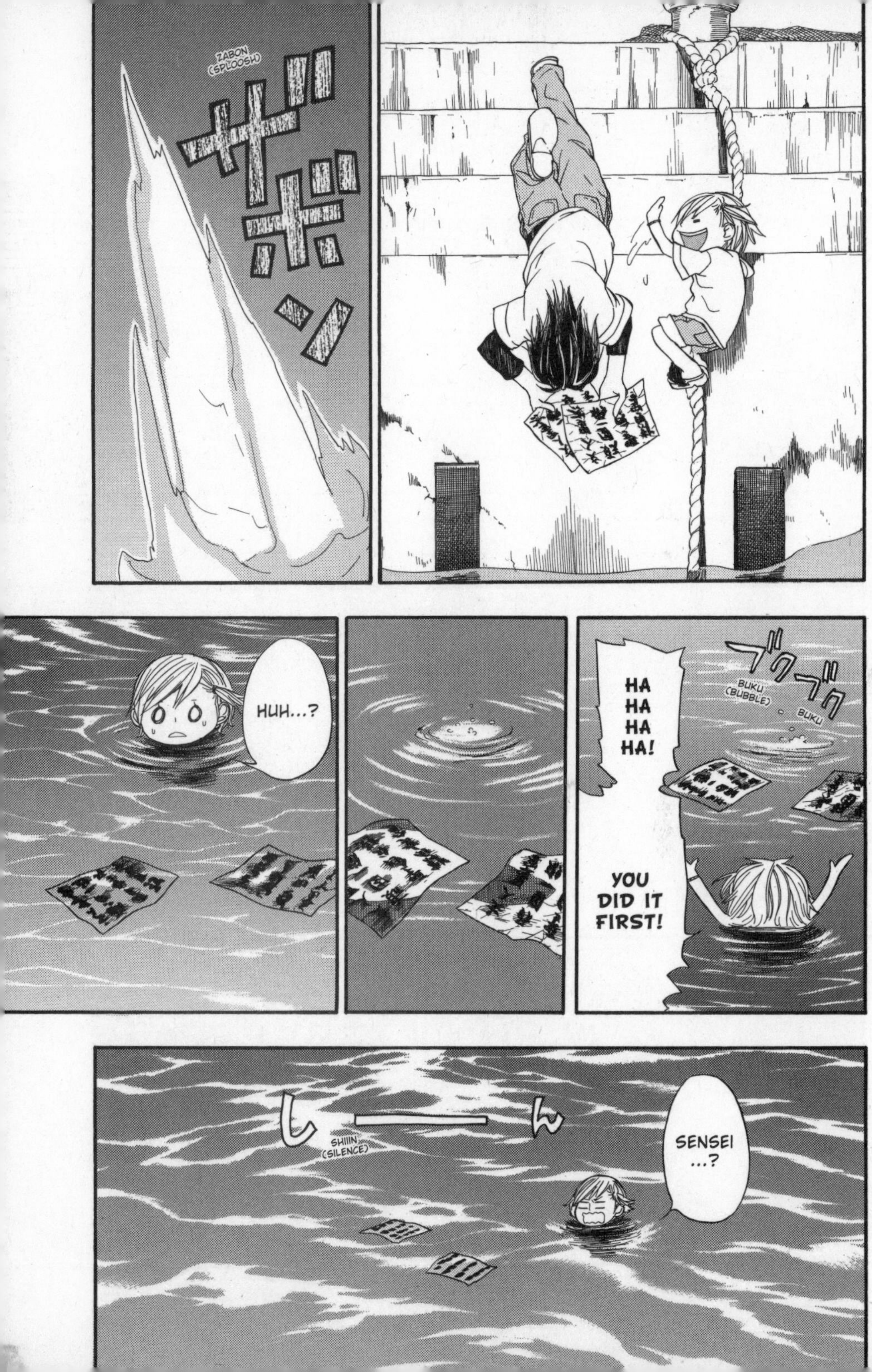
ZABON (SPLOOSH)
ブクブク
BUKU (BUBBLE)
BUKU
HA HA HA HA!
YOU DID IT FIRST!
HUH...?
しーん
SHIIIN (SILENCE)
SENSEI ...?

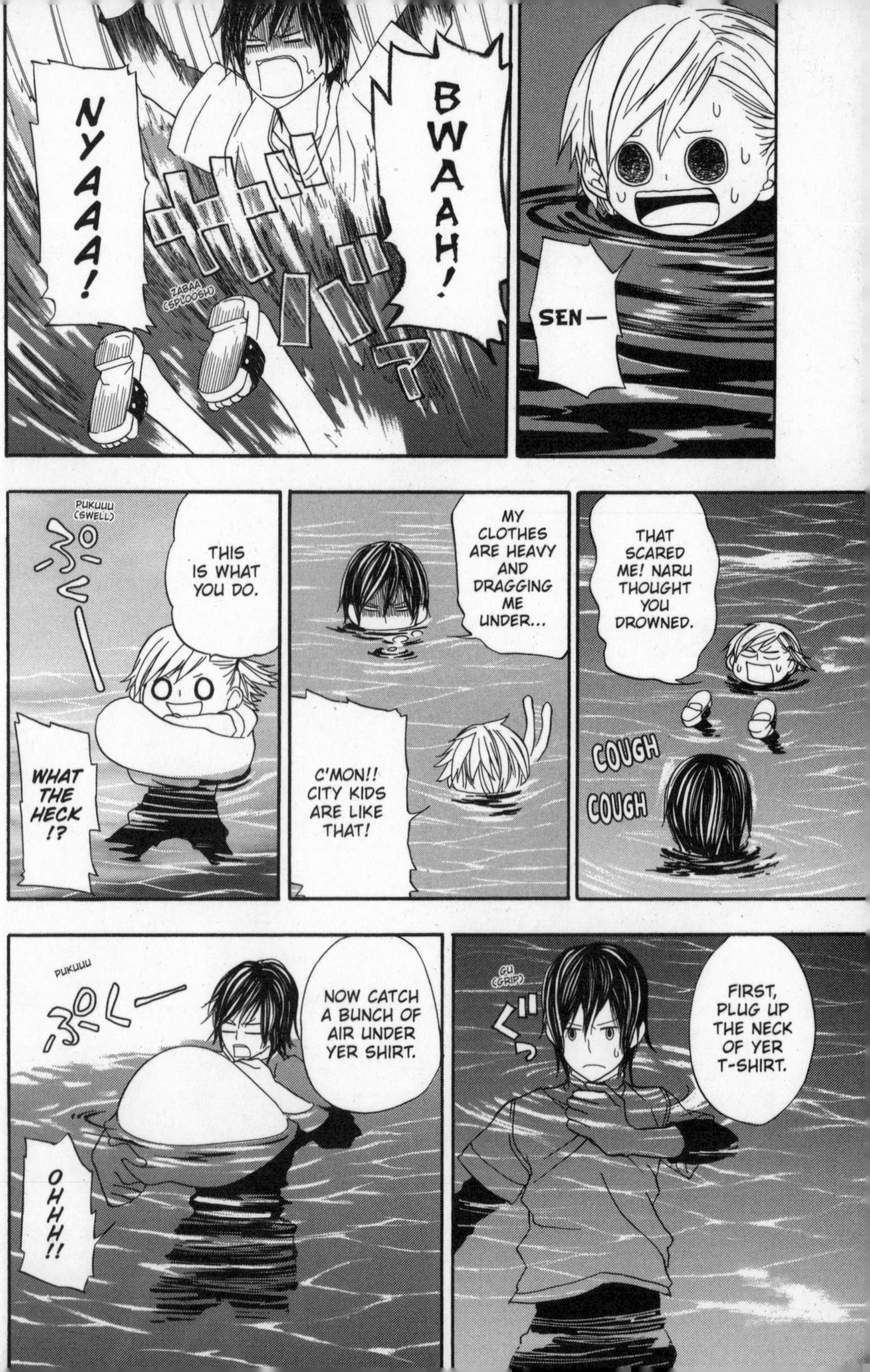
SEN—
BWAAH!
NYAAAA!
ZABAA (SPLOOSH)
THAT SCARED ME! NARU THOUGHT YOU DROWNED.
COUGH
COUGH
MY CLOTHES ARE HEAVY AND DRAGGING ME UNDER...
C'MON!! CITY KIDS ARE LIKE THAT!
THIS IS WHAT YOU DO.
PUKUUU (SWELL)
WHAT THE HECK!?
FIRST, PLUG UP THE NECK OF YER T-SHIRT.
GU (GRIP)
NOW CATCH A BUNCH OF AIR UNDER YER SHIRT.
PUKUUU
OHHH!!

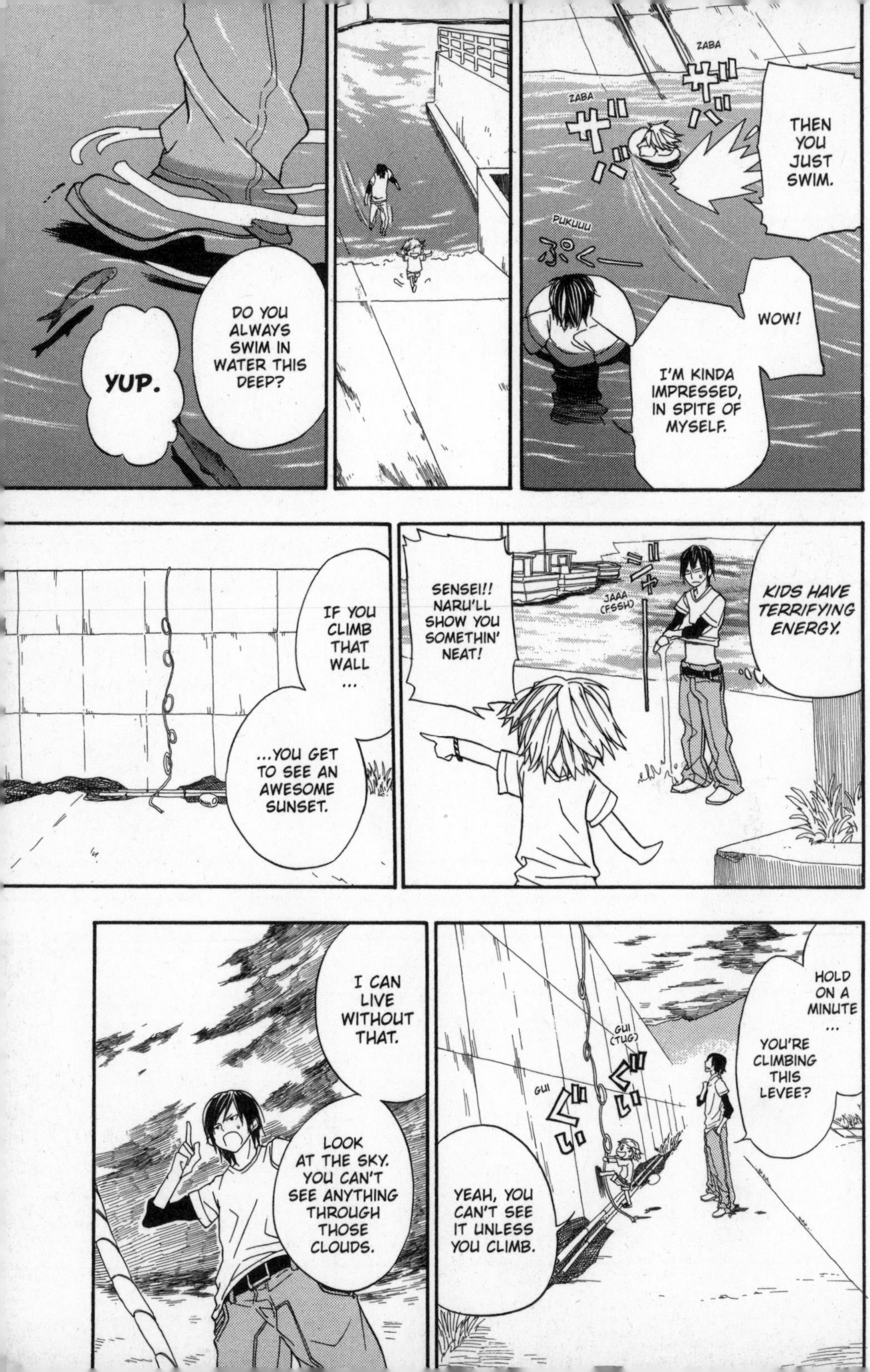
ZABA
ZABA
THEN YOU JUST SWIM.
PUKUUU
WOW!
I'M KINDA IMPRESSED, IN SPITE OF MYSELF.
DO YOU ALWAYS SWIM IN WATER THIS DEEP?
YUP.
KIDS HAVE TERRIFYING ENERGY.
JAAA (FSSH)
SENSEI!! NARU'LL SHOW YOU SOMETHIN' NEAT!
IF YOU CLIMB THAT WALL ...
...YOU GET TO SEE AN AWESOME SUNSET.
HOLD ON A MINUTE ...
YOU'RE CLIMBING THIS LEVEE?
GUI (TUG)
GUI
YEAH, YOU CAN'T SEE IT UNLESS YOU CLIMB.
I CAN LIVE WITHOUT THAT.
LOOK AT THE SKY. YOU CAN'T SEE ANYTHING THROUGH THOSE CLOUDS.

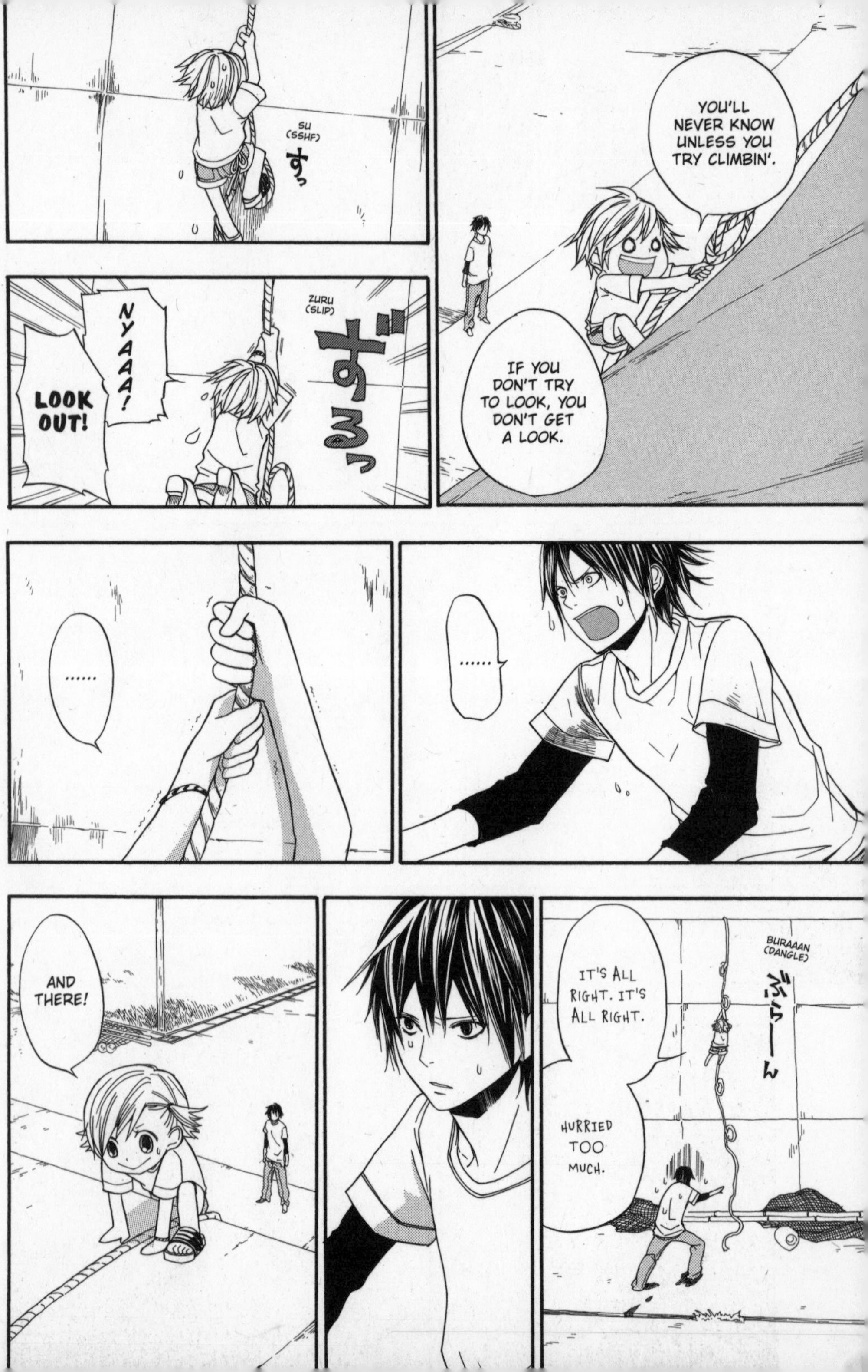
YOU'LL NEVER KNOW UNLESS YOU TRY CLIMBIN'.
IF YOU DON'T TRY TO LOOK, YOU DON'T GET A LOOK.
SU (SSHF)
すっ
ZURU (SLIP)
ずるっ
NYAAA!
LOOK OUT!
......
......
BURAAAN (DANGLE)
ぶらーん
IT'S ALL RIGHT. IT'S ALL RIGHT.
HURRIED TOO MUCH.
AND THERE!

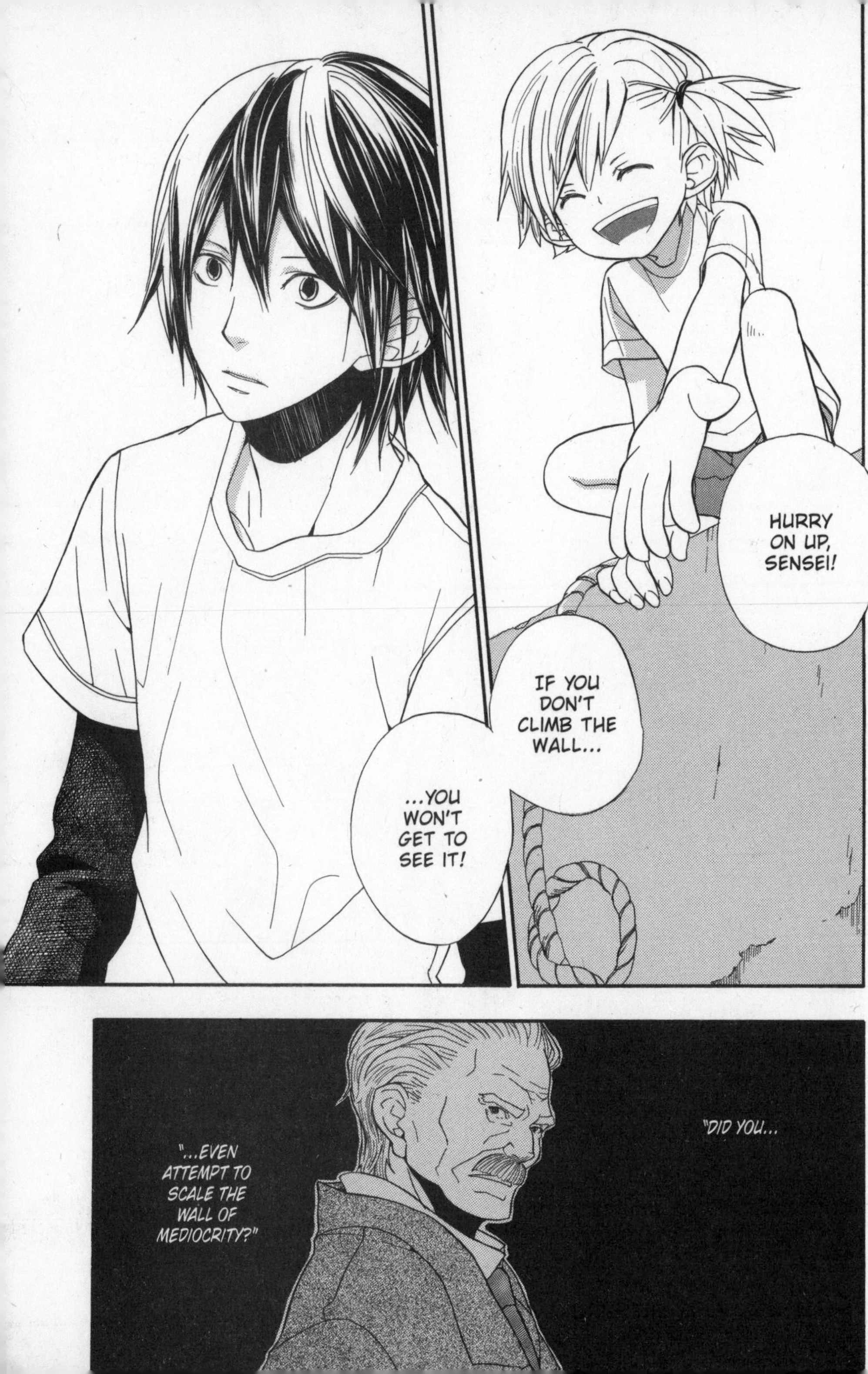
HURRY ON UP, SENSEI!
IF YOU DON'T CLIMB THE WALL...
...YOU WON'T GET TO SEE IT!
"DID YOU...
"...EVEN ATTEMPT TO SCALE THE WALL OF MEDIOCRITY?"

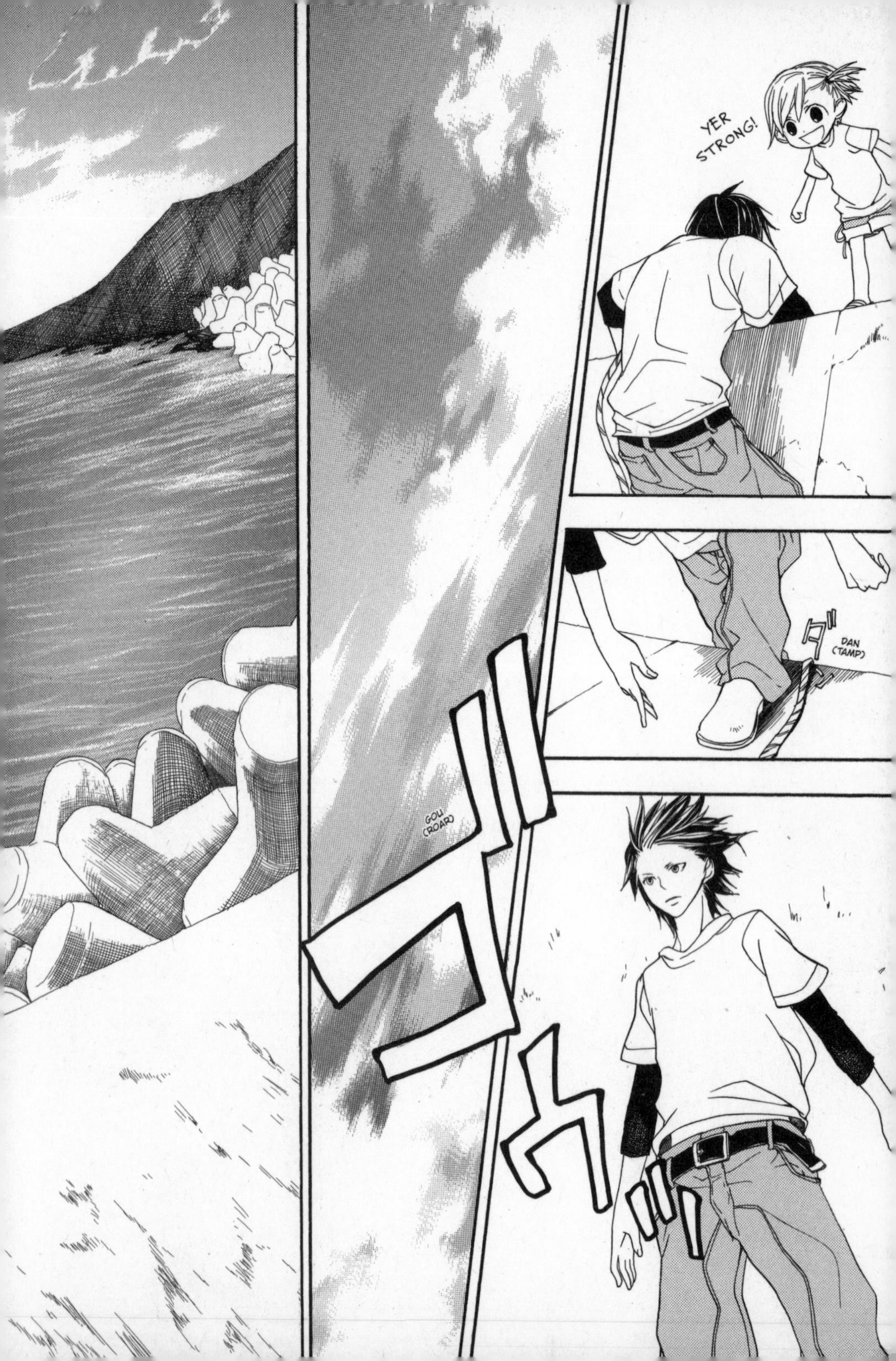
YER STRONG!
DAN (TAMP)
GOU (ROAR)

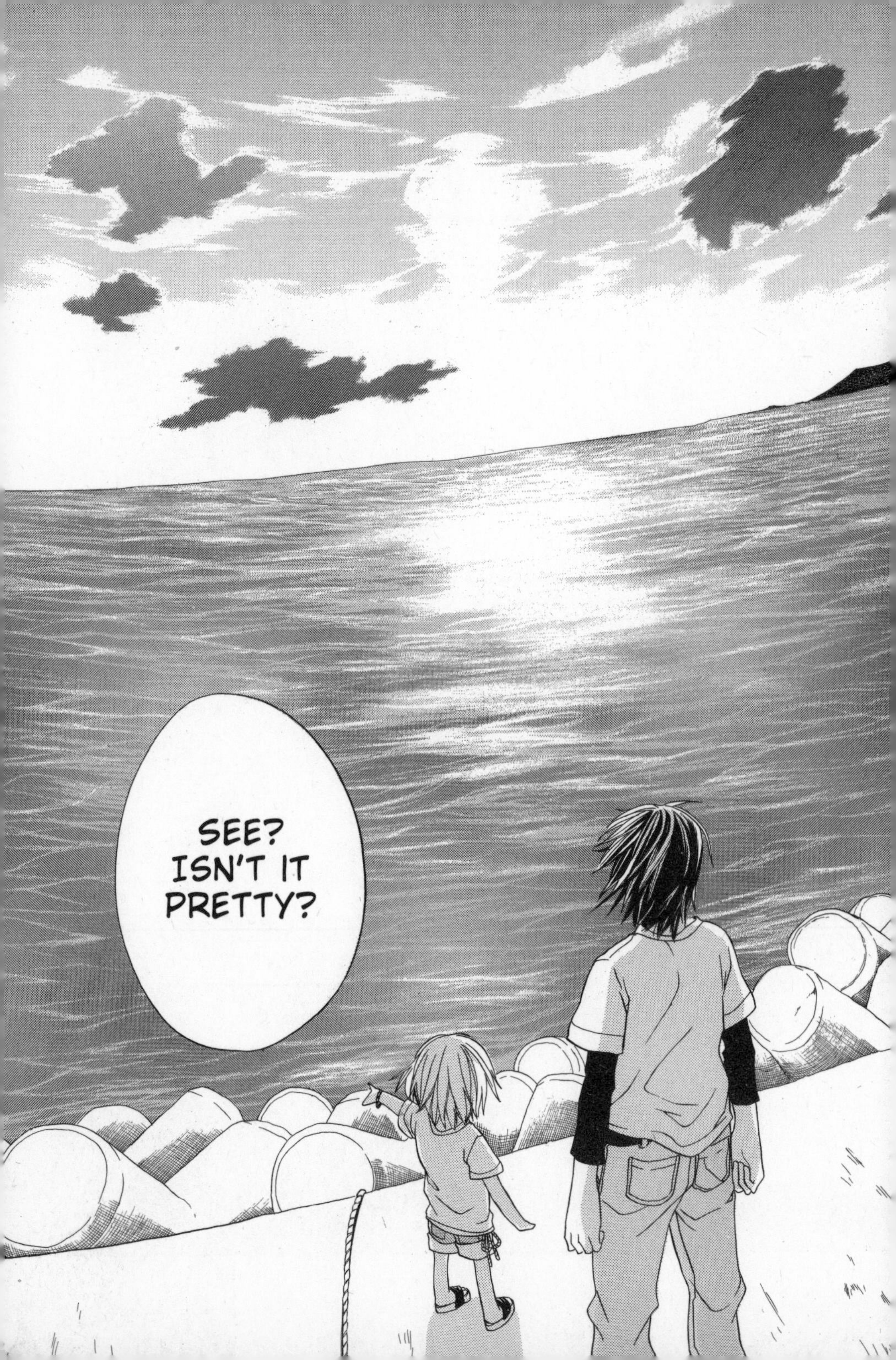
SEE? ISN'T IT PRETTY?

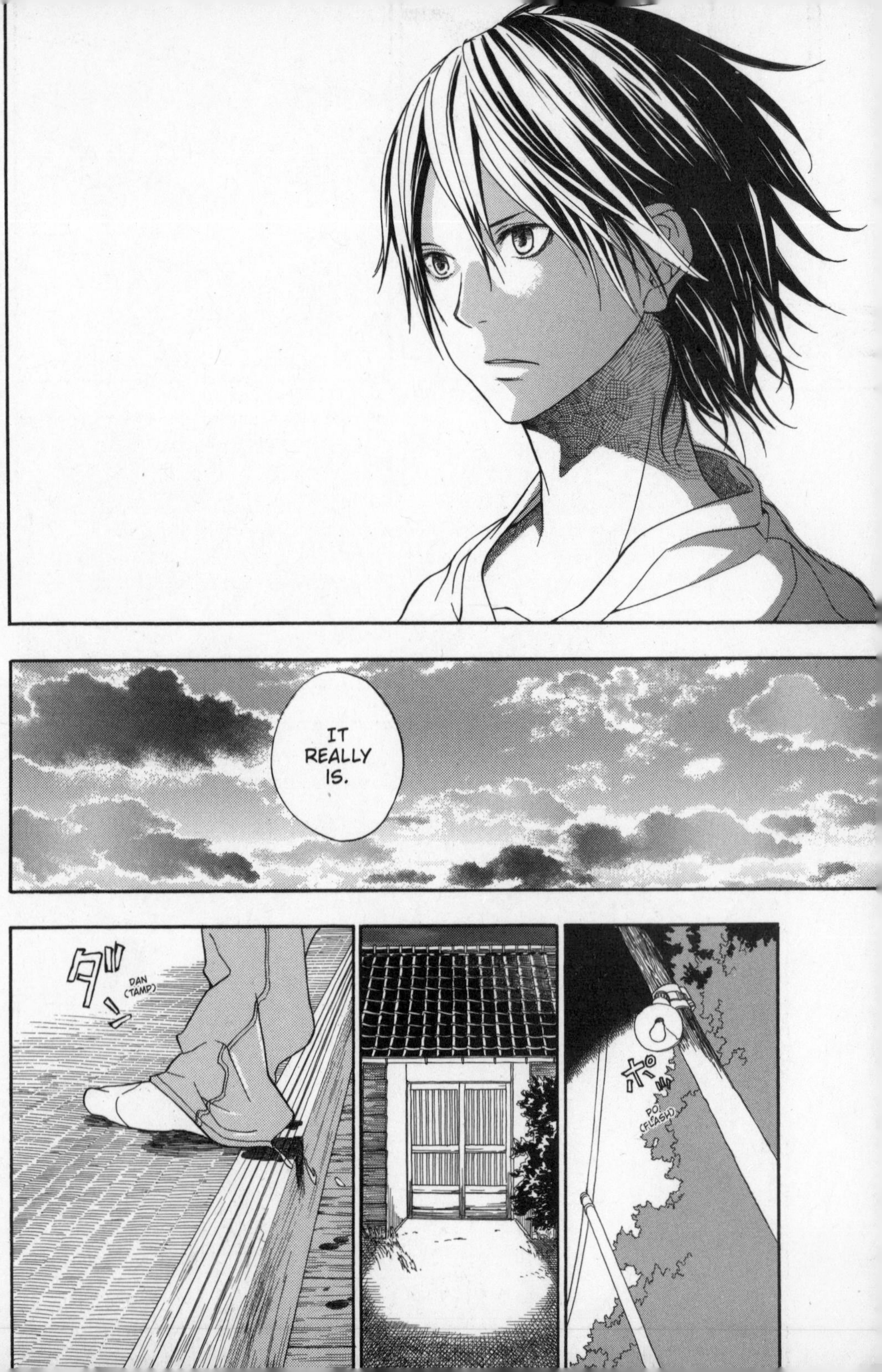
IT REALLY IS.
ポッ
PO (FLASH)
ダッ!
DAN (TAMP)

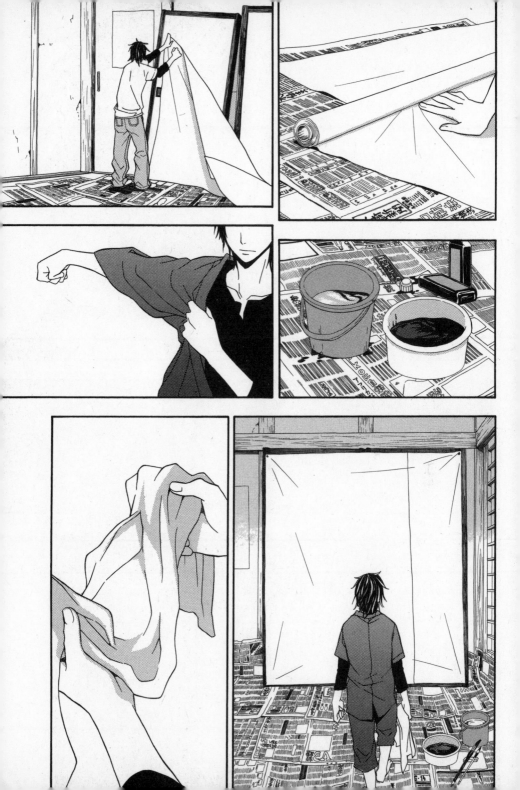

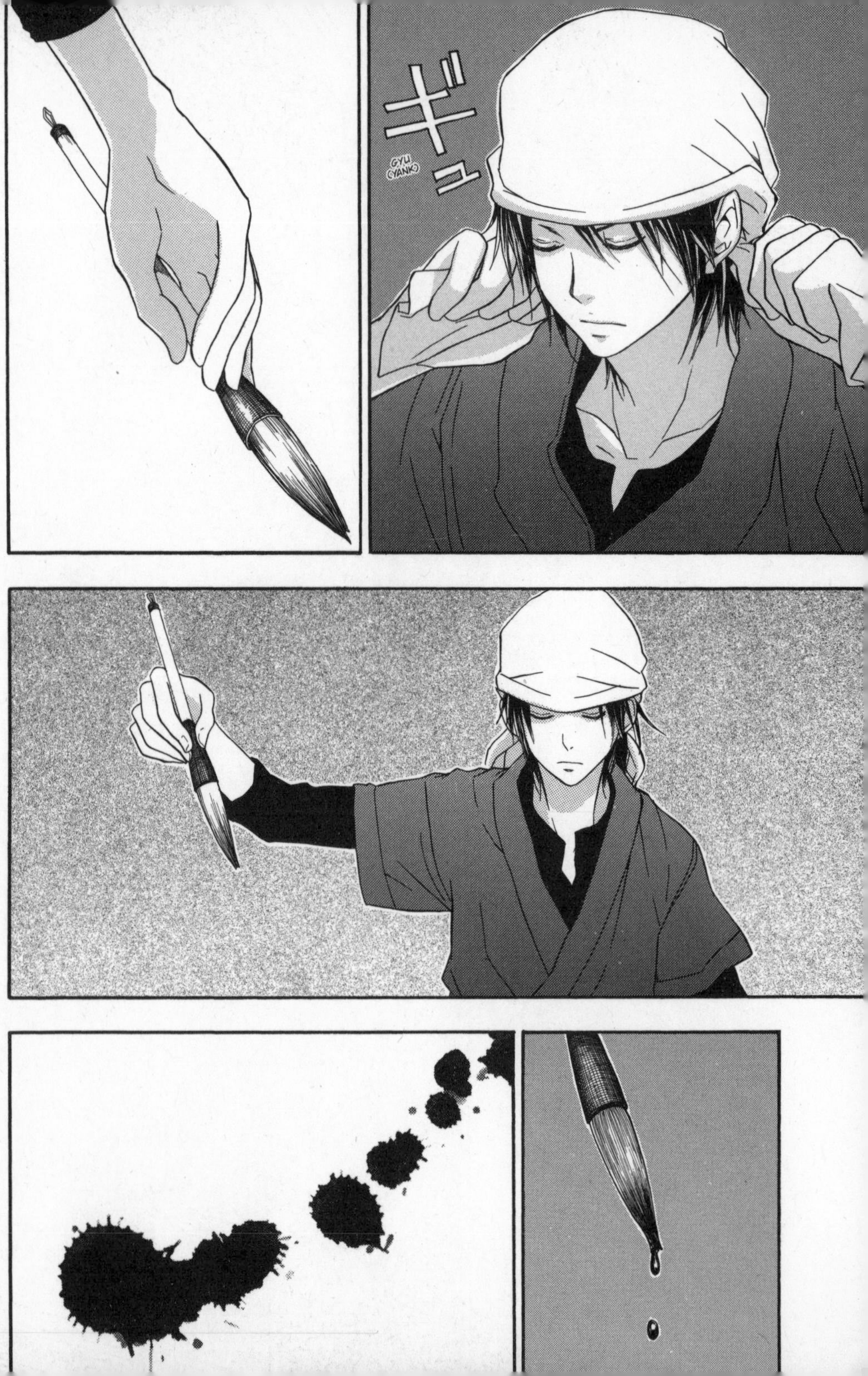
ギュ
GYU (YANK)

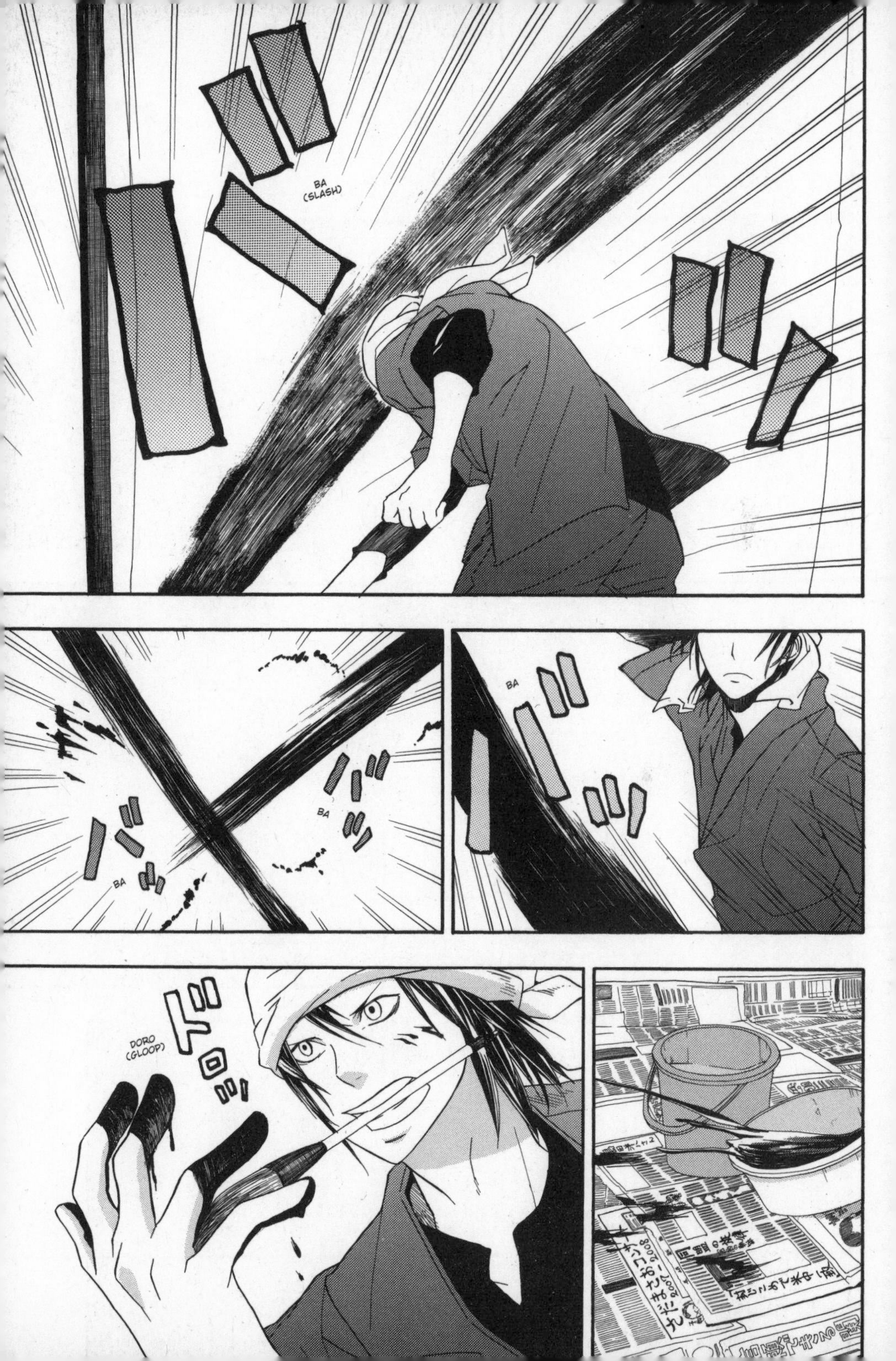
BA
(SLASH)
BA
BA
BA
DORO
(GLOOP)

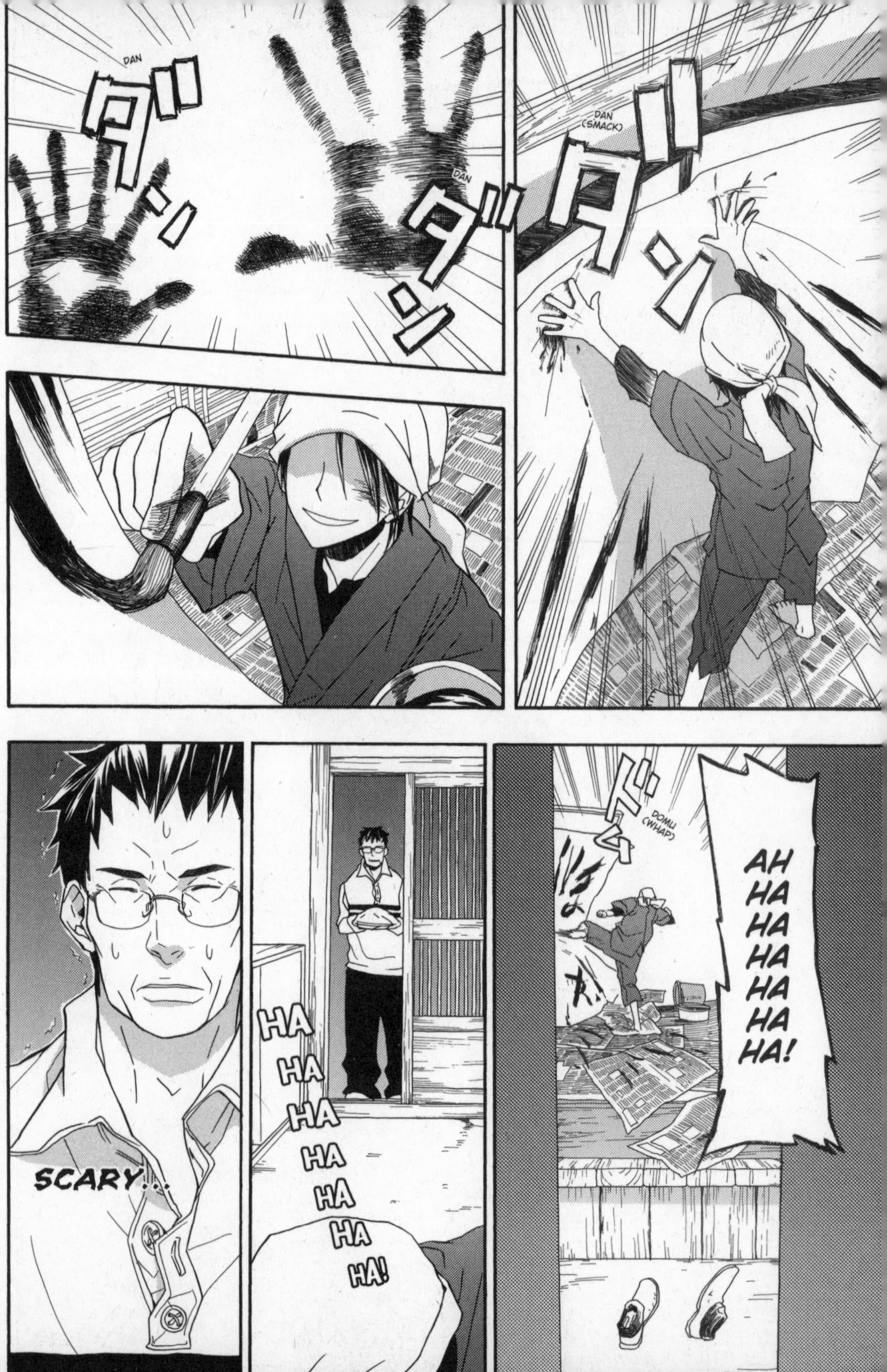
DAN (SMACK)
DAN
DAN
DOMU (WHAP)
AH HA HA HA HA HA HA HA HA!
HA HA HA HA HA HA HA!
SCARY...

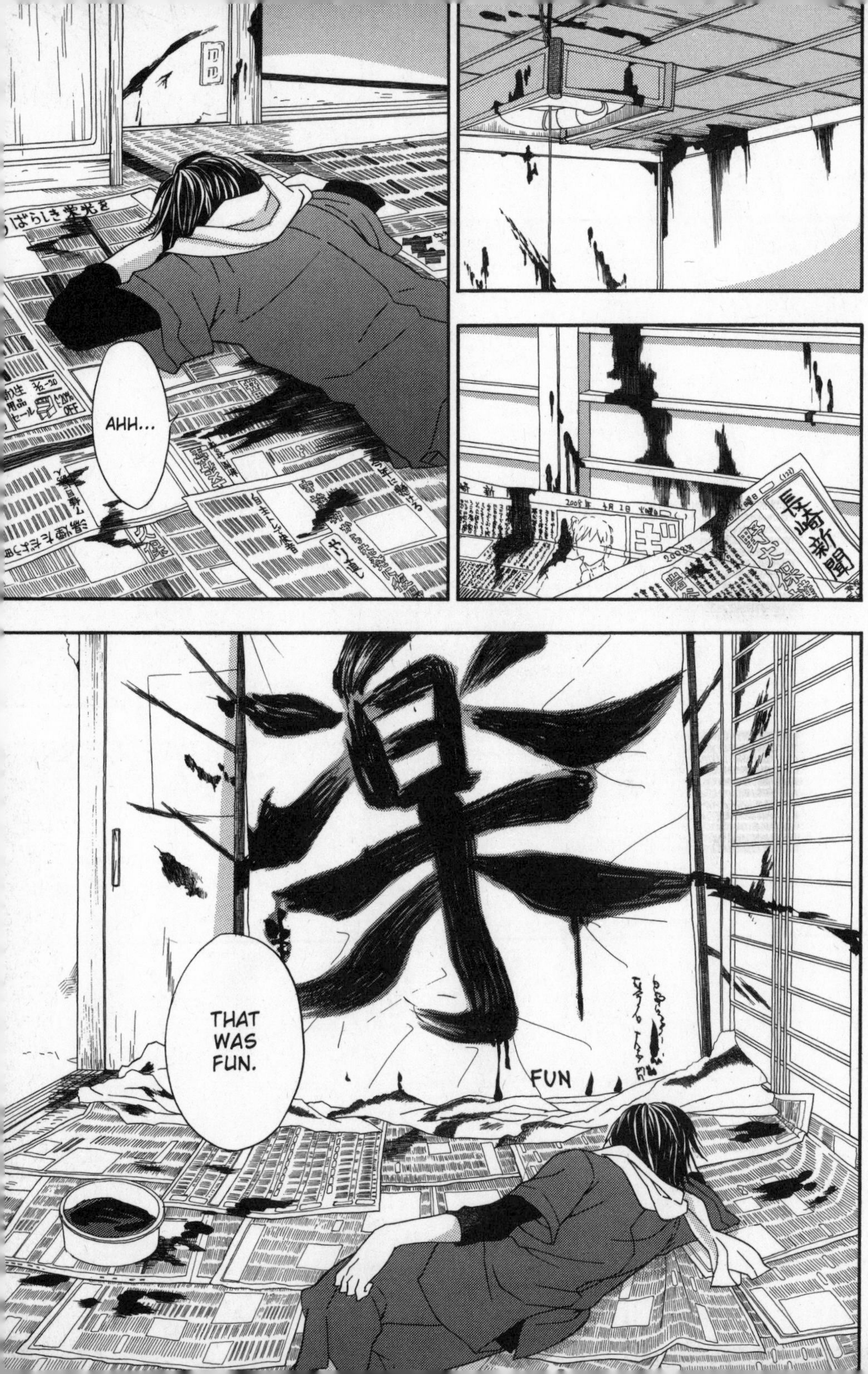
AHH...
THAT WAS FUN.
FUN

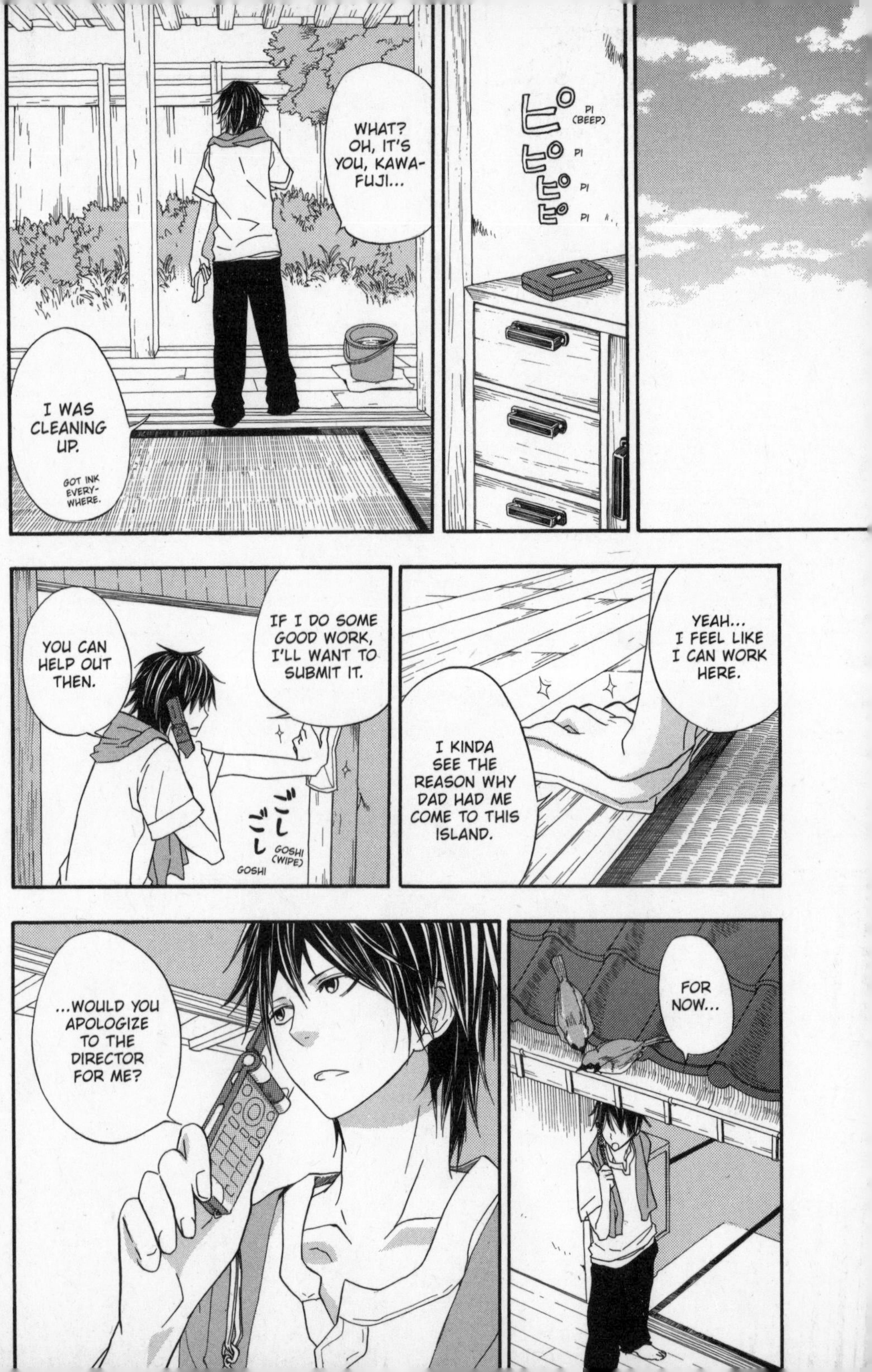
ピピピピ
PI (BEEP) PI PI PI
WHAT? OH, IT'S YOU, KAWA-FUJI...
I WAS CLEANING UP.
GOT INK EVERY-WHERE.
YEAH... I FEEL LIKE I CAN WORK HERE.
I KINDA SEE THE REASON WHY DAD HAD ME COME TO THIS ISLAND.
IF I DO SOME GOOD WORK, I'LL WANT TO SUBMIT IT.
YOU CAN HELP OUT THEN.
ごしごし
GOSHI (WIPE) GOSHI
FOR NOW...
...WOULD YOU APOLOGIZE TO THE DIRECTOR FOR ME?

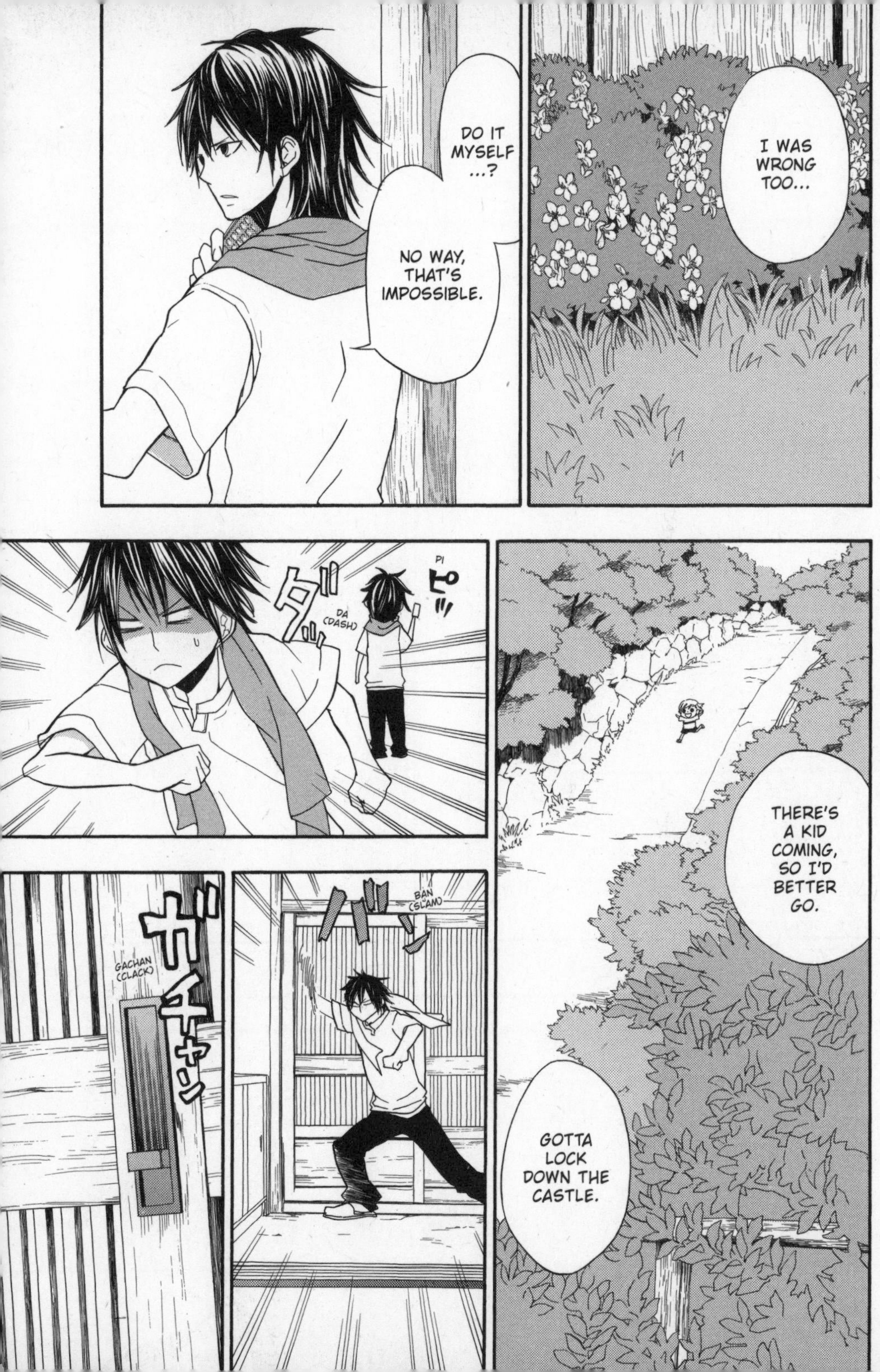
I WAS WRONG TOO...
DO IT MYSELF ...?
NO WAY, THAT'S IMPOSSIBLE.
THERE'S A KID COMING, SO I'D BETTER GO.
GOTTA LOCK DOWN THE CASTLE.
PI
DA (DASH)
BAN (SLAM)
GACHAN (CLACK)

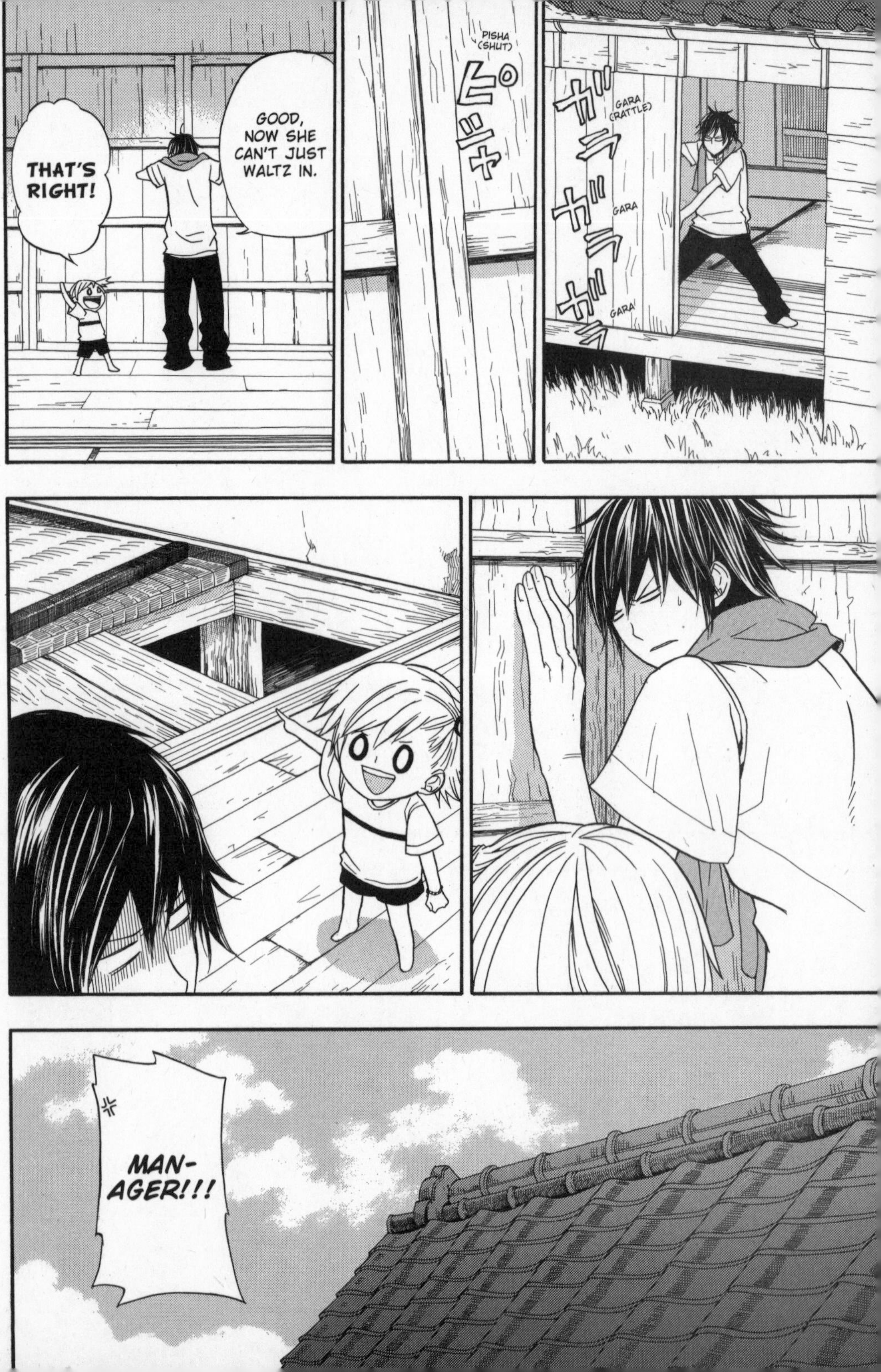
GARA (RATTLE)
GARA
GARA
PISHA (SHUT)
GOOD, NOW SHE CAN'T JUST WALTZ IN.
THAT'S RIGHT!
MAN-AGER!!!

ACT. 2
YANAWA
(Translation: Moving)

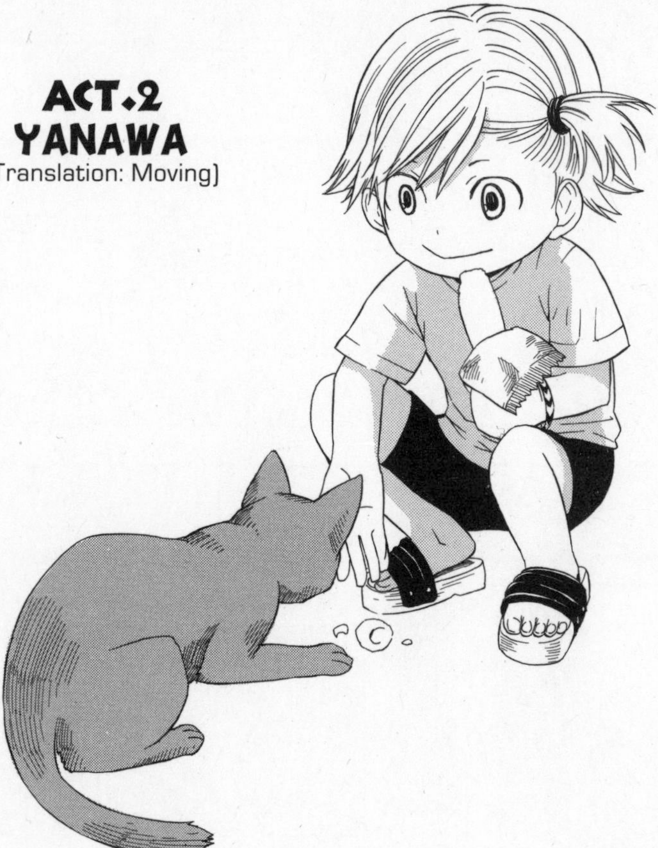

TRUCK: KIJIMA SHIPPING

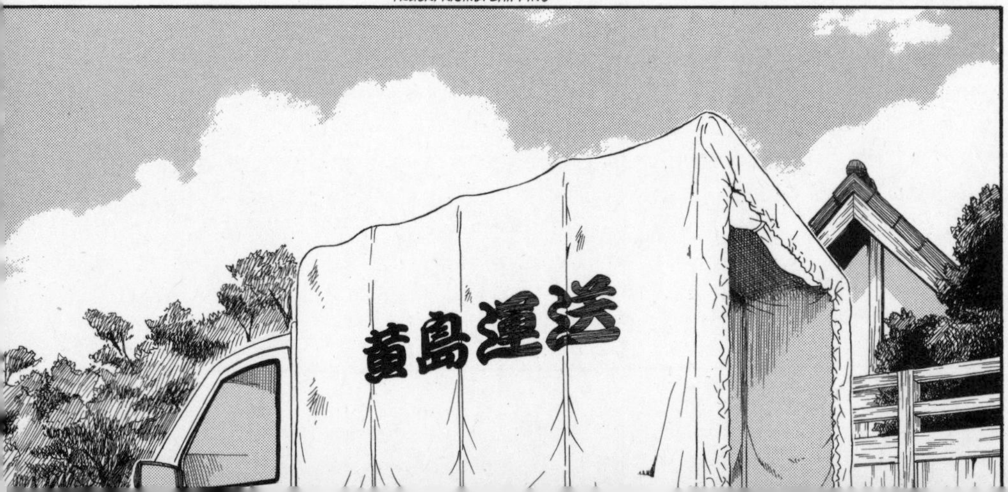
黄島運送

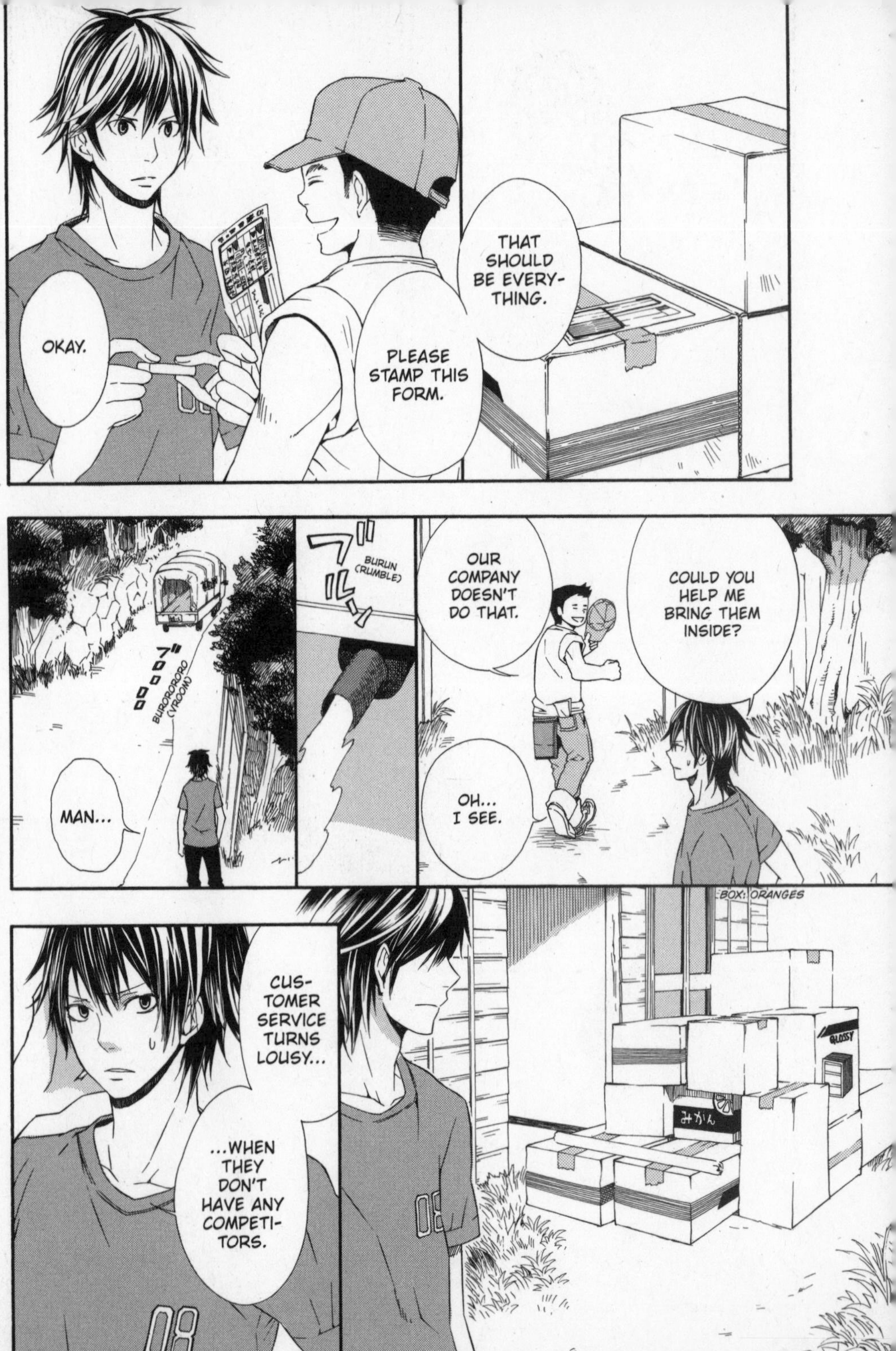
THAT SHOULD BE EVERY-THING.
PLEASE STAMP THIS FORM.
OKAY.
COULD YOU HELP ME BRING THEM INSIDE?
OUR COMPANY DOESN'T DO THAT.
OH... I SEE.
BURUN (RUMBLE)
BURORORORO (VROOM)
MAN...
BOX: ORANGES
みかん
GLOSSY
CUS-TOMER SERVICE TURNS LOUSY...
...WHEN THEY DON'T HAVE ANY COMPETI-TORS.

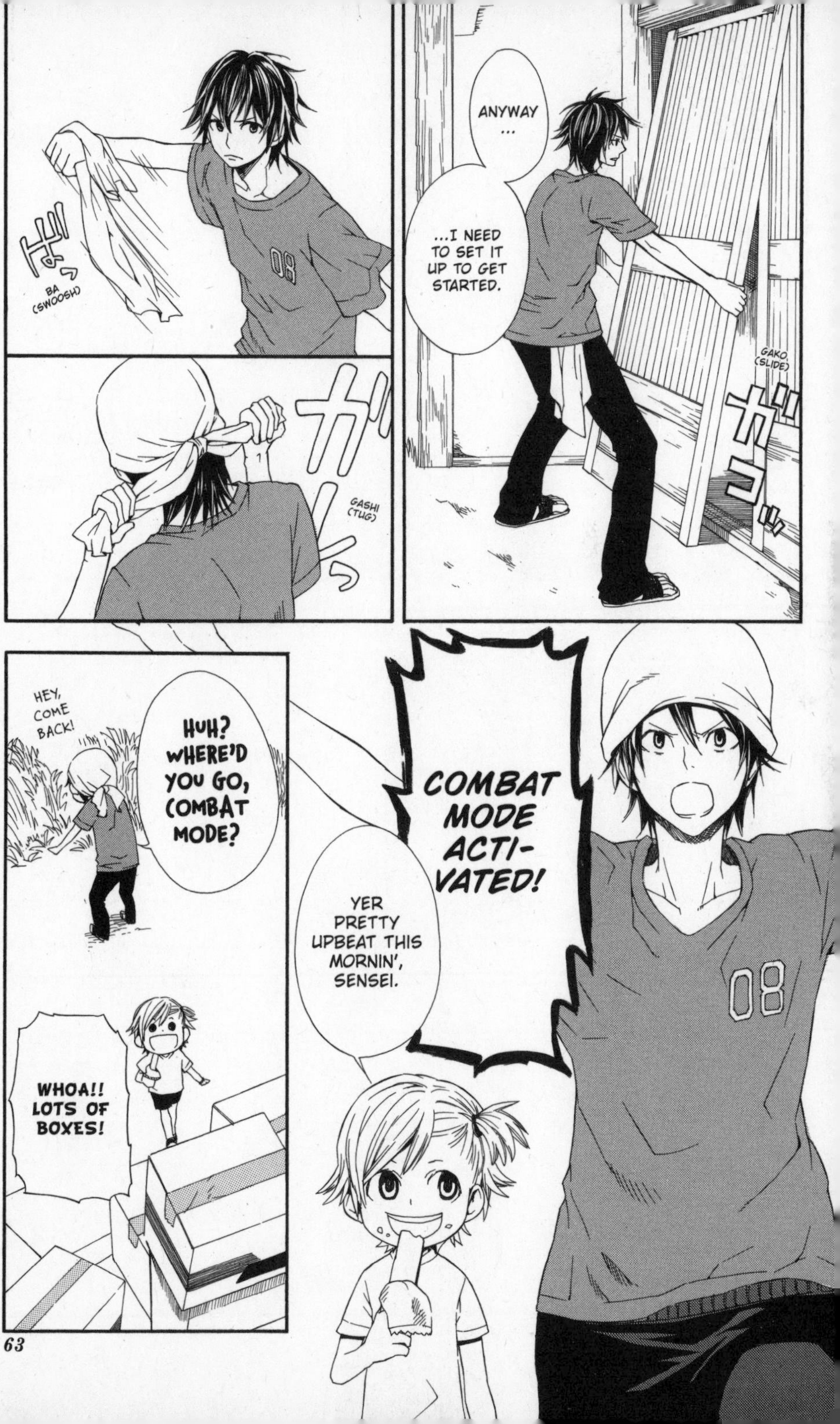
ANYWAY ...
...I NEED TO SET IT UP TO GET STARTED.
GAKO (SLIDE)
BA (SWOOSH)
GASHI (TUG)
COMBAT MODE ACTI-VATED!
YER PRETTY UPBEAT THIS MORNIN', SENSEI.
HEY, COME BACK!
HUH? WHERE'D YOU GO, COMBAT MODE?
WHOA!! LOTS OF BOXES!

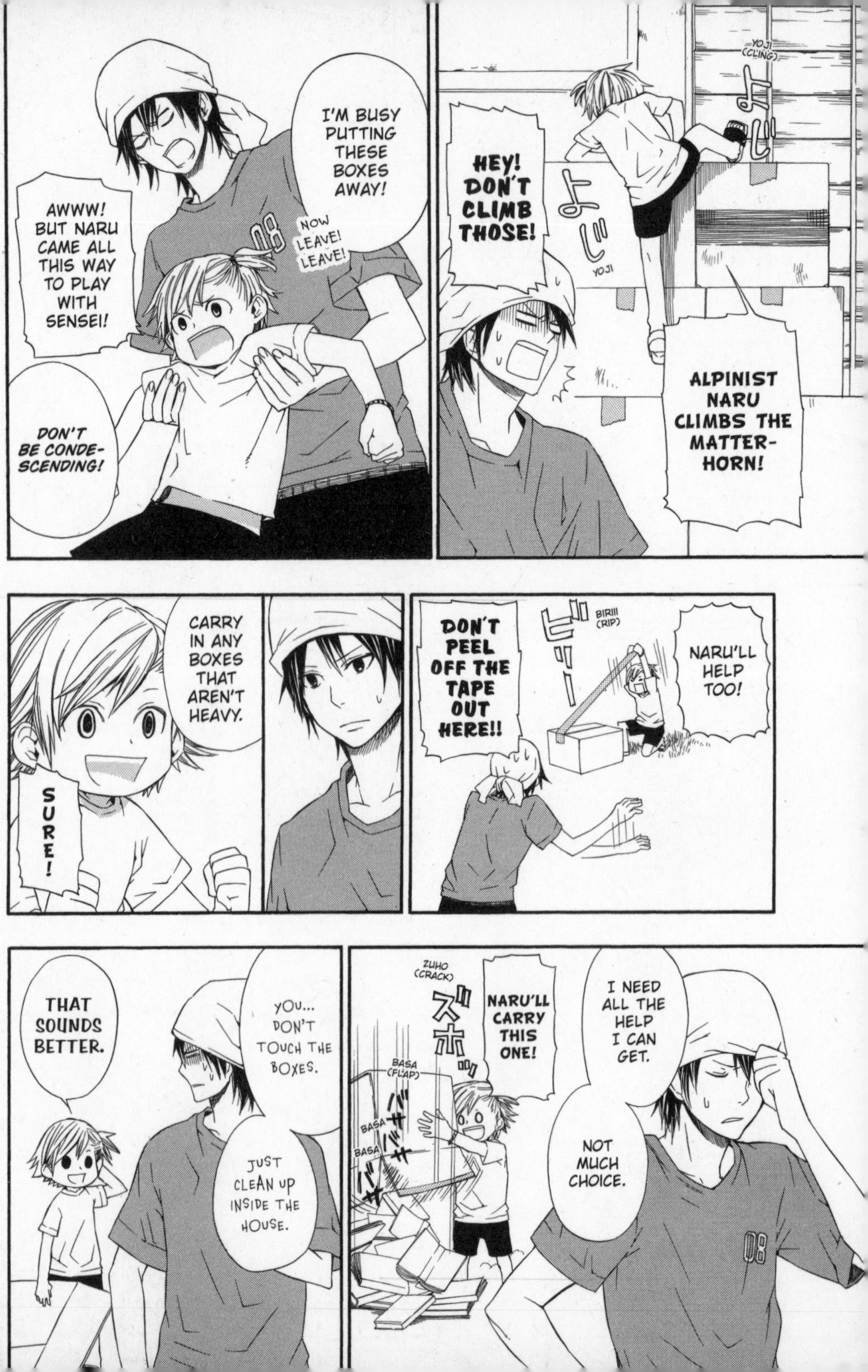
YOJI (CLING)
HEY! DON'T CLIMB THOSE!
YOJI
ALPINIST NARU CLIMBS THE MATTER-HORN!
I'M BUSY PUTTING THESE BOXES AWAY!
NOW LEAVE! LEAVE!
AWWW! BUT NARU CAME ALL THIS WAY TO PLAY WITH SENSEI!
DON'T BE CONDE-SCENDING!
NARU'LL HELP TOO!
BIRIII (RIP)
DON'T PEEL OFF THE TAPE OUT HERE!!
CARRY IN ANY BOXES THAT AREN'T HEAVY.
SURE!
I NEED ALL THE HELP I CAN GET.
NARU'LL CARRY THIS ONE!
ZUHO (CRACK)
BASA (FLAP)
BASA
BASA
NOT MUCH CHOICE.
YOU... DON'T TOUCH THE BOXES.
JUST CLEAN UP INSIDE THE HOUSE.
THAT SOUNDS BETTER.

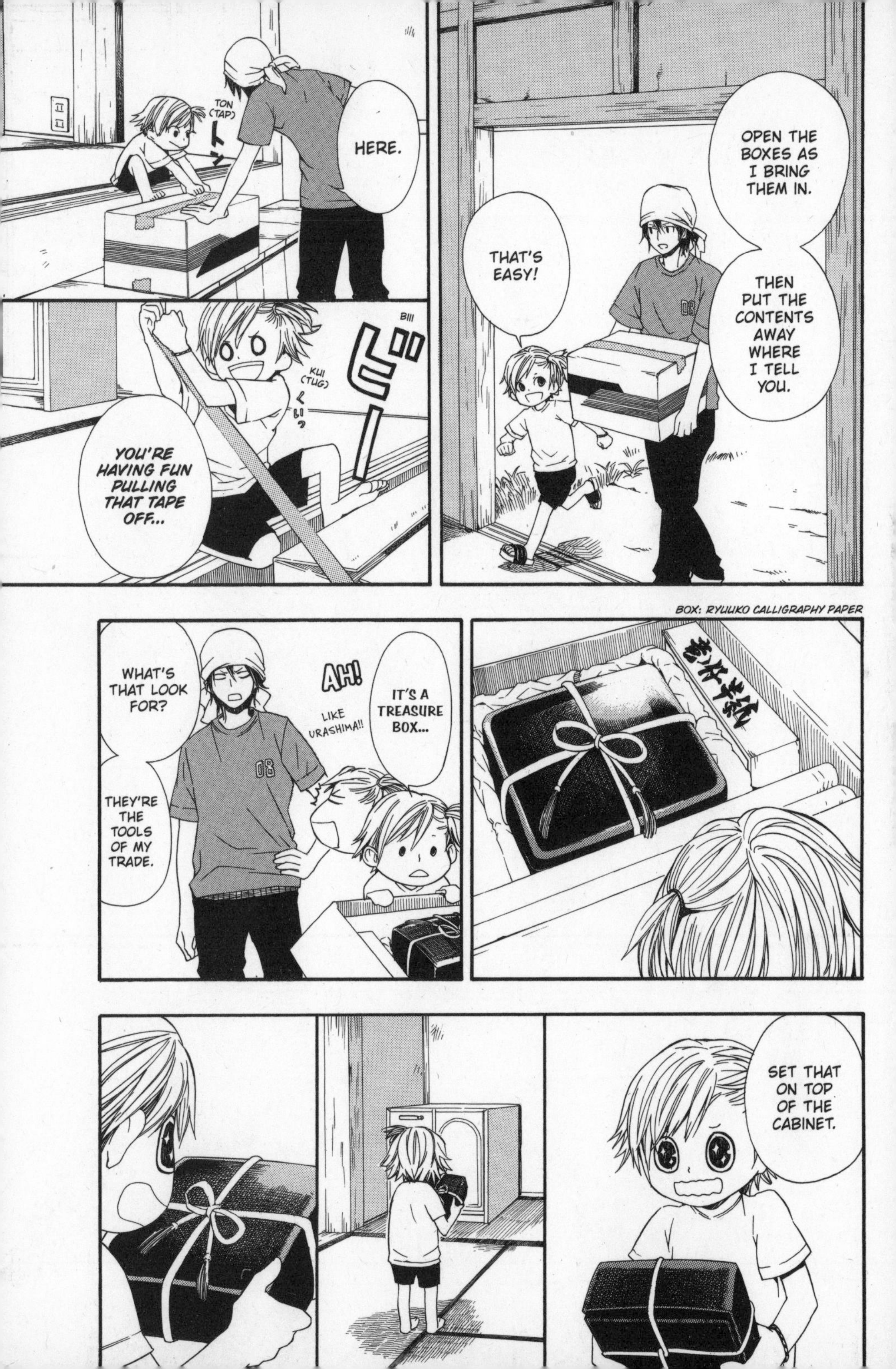
OPEN THE BOXES AS I BRING THEM IN.
THAT'S EASY!
THEN PUT THE CONTENTS AWAY WHERE I TELL YOU.
TON (TAP)
HERE.
BIII
KUI (TUG)
YOU'RE HAVING FUN PULLING THAT TAPE OFF...
BOX: RYUUKO CALLIGRAPHY PAPER
IT'S A TREASURE BOX...
AH!
LIKE URASHIMA!!
WHAT'S THAT LOOK FOR?
THEY'RE THE TOOLS OF MY TRADE.
SET THAT ON TOP OF THE CABINET.

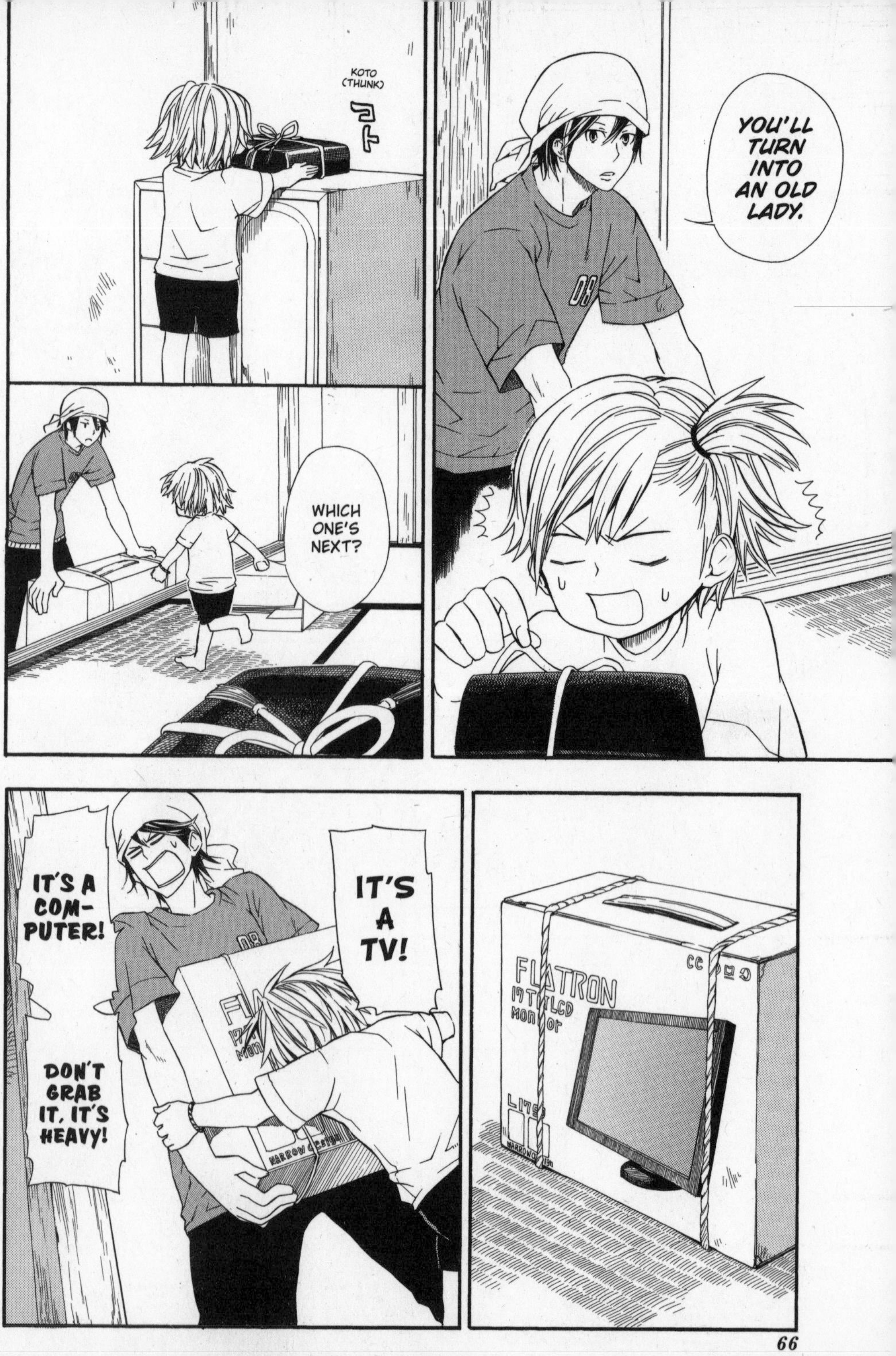
YOU'LL TURN INTO AN OLD LADY.
KOTO (THUNK)
コト
WHICH ONE'S NEXT?
IT'S A TV!
IT'S A COM-PUTER!
DON'T GRAB IT, IT'S HEAVY!
FLATRON
17" TFT LCD Monitor

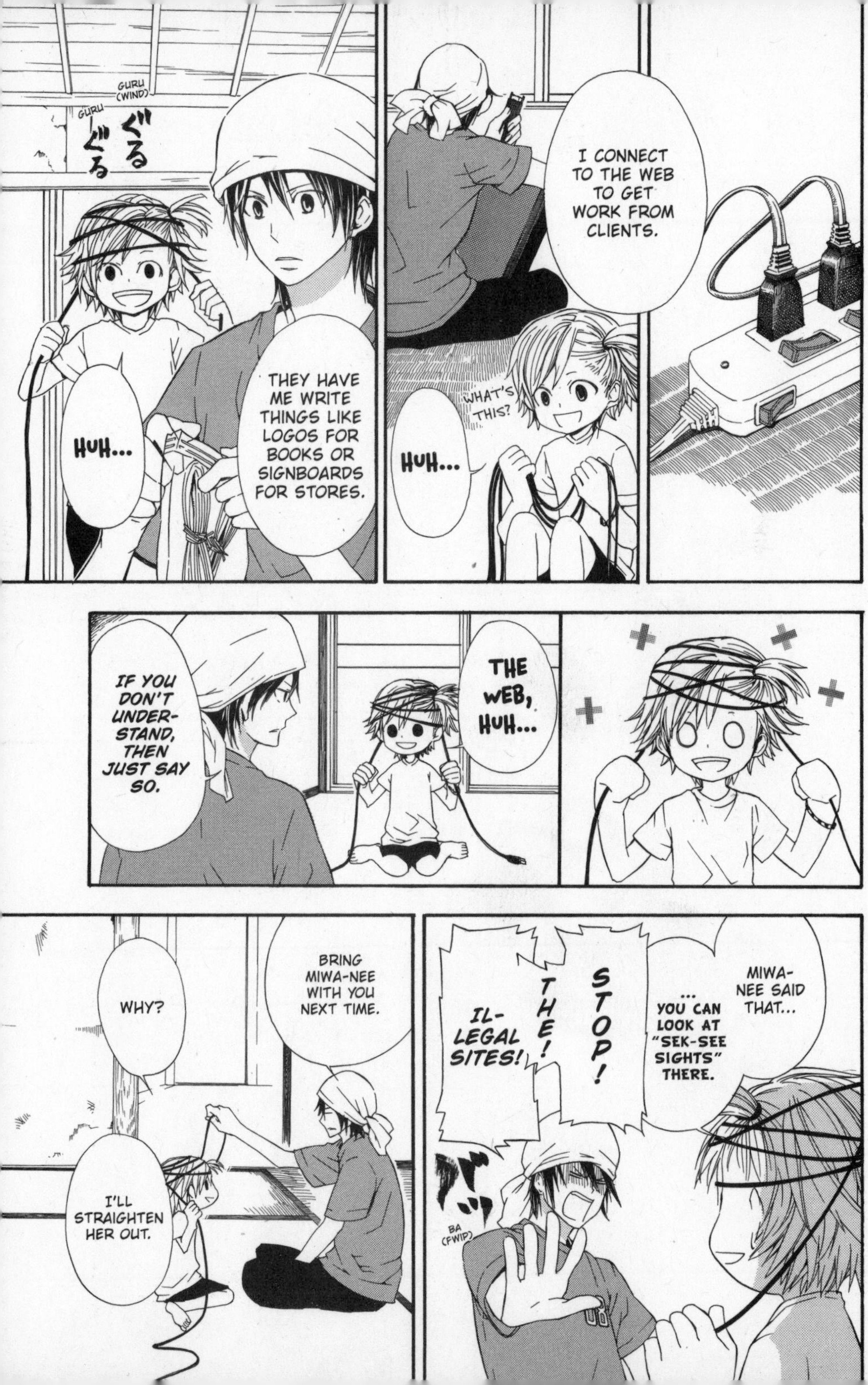
I CONNECT TO THE WEB TO GET WORK FROM CLIENTS.
WHAT'S THIS?
HUH...
ぐるぐる
GURU (WIND) GURU
THEY HAVE ME WRITE THINGS LIKE LOGOS FOR BOOKS OR SIGNBOARDS FOR STORES.
HUH...
THE WEB, HUH...
IF YOU DON'T UNDER-STAND, THEN JUST SAY SO.
MIWA-NEE SAID THAT...
... YOU CAN LOOK AT "SEK-SEE SIGHTS" THERE.
STOP!
THE!
IL-LEGAL SITES!
BA (FWIP)
BRING MIWA-NEE WITH YOU NEXT TIME.
WHY?
I'LL STRAIGHTEN HER OUT.

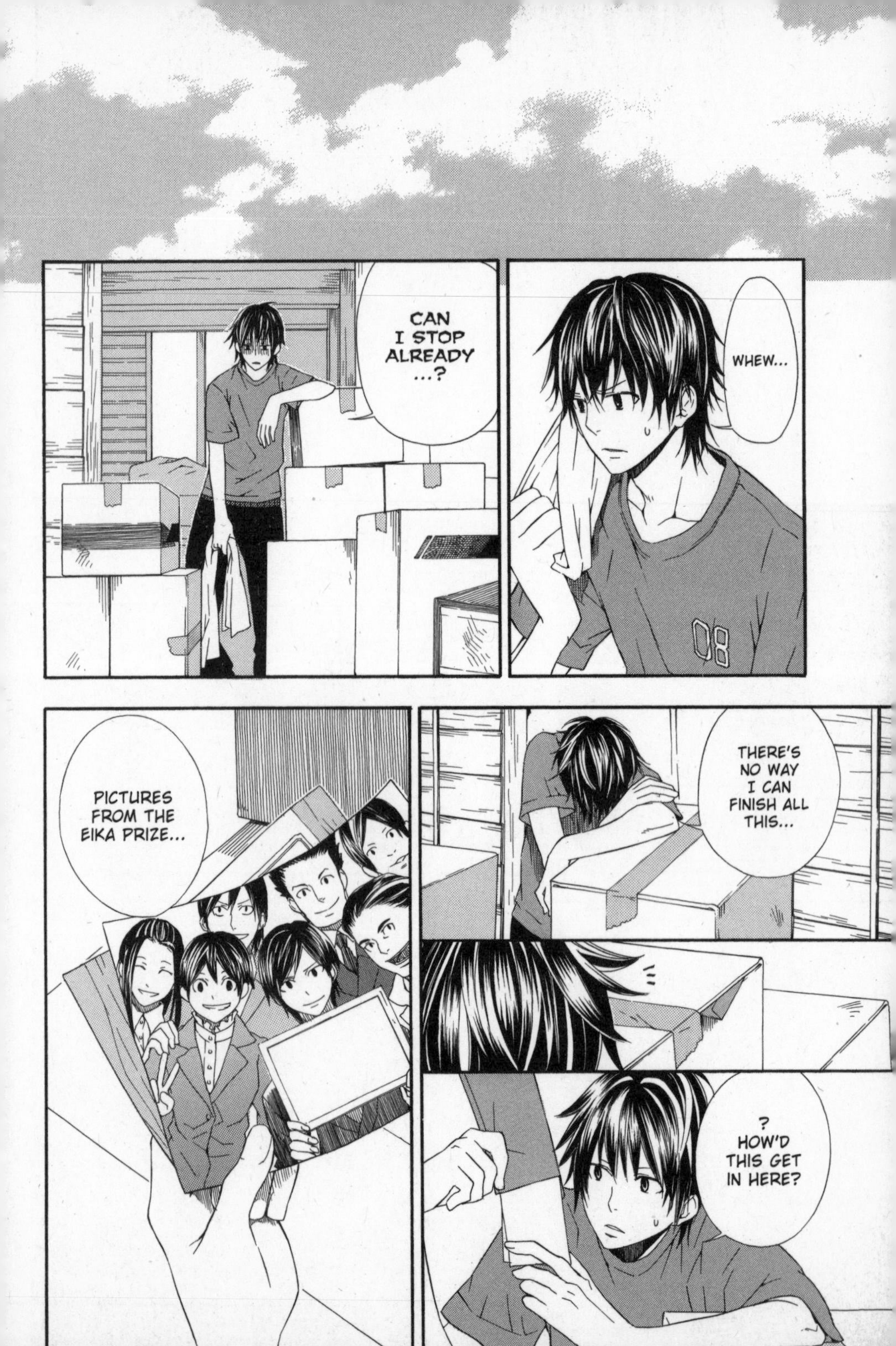
WHEW...
CAN I STOP ALREADY ...?
THERE'S NO WAY I CAN FINISH ALL THIS...
? HOW'D THIS GET IN HERE?
PICTURES FROM THE EIKA PRIZE...

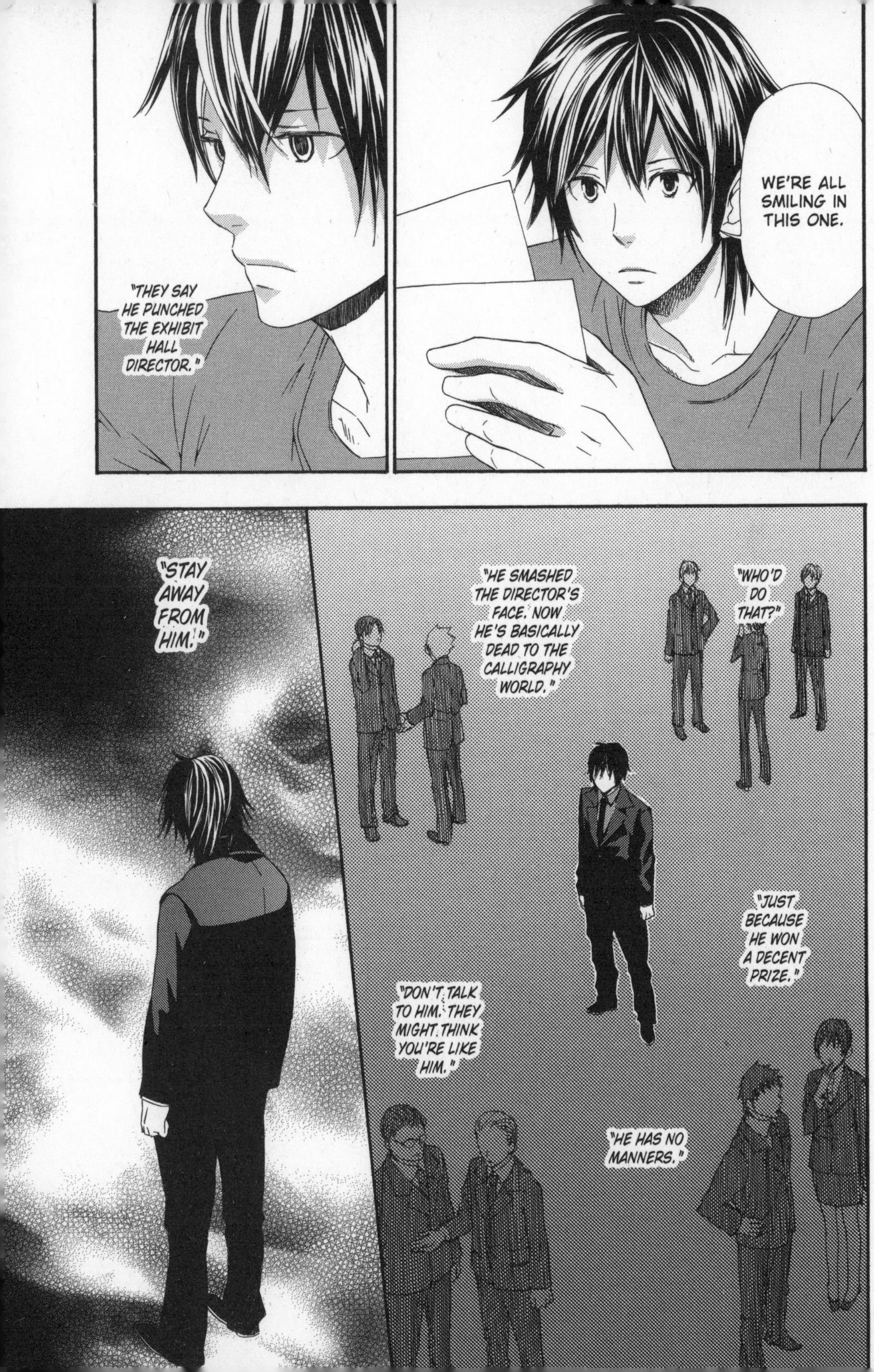
WE'RE ALL SMILING IN THIS ONE.
"THEY SAY HE PUNCHED THE EXHIBIT HALL DIRECTOR."
"WHO'D DO THAT?"
"HE SMASHED THE DIRECTOR'S FACE. NOW HE'S BASICALLY DEAD TO THE CALLIGRAPHY WORLD."
"JUST BECAUSE HE WON A DECENT PRIZE."
"DON'T TALK TO HIM. THEY MIGHT THINK YOU'RE LIKE HIM."
"HE HAS NO MANNERS."
"STAY AWAY FROM HIM."

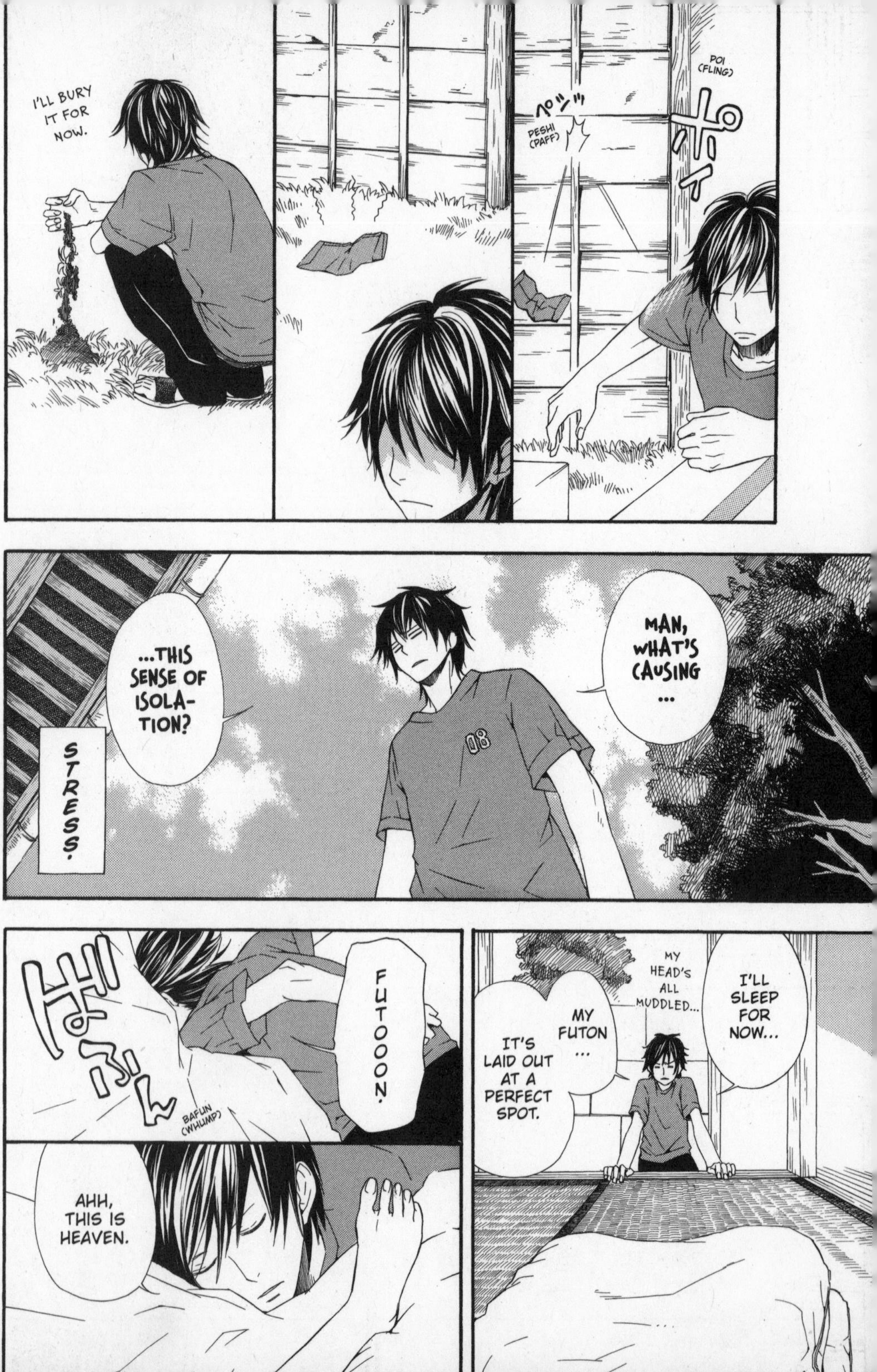
POI (FLING)
PESHI (PAFF)
I'LL BURY IT FOR NOW.
MAN, WHAT'S CAUSING ...
...THIS SENSE OF ISOLATION?
STRESS.
I'LL SLEEP FOR NOW...
MY HEAD'S ALL MUDDLED...
MY FUTON ...
IT'S LAID OUT AT A PERFECT SPOT.
. . .
FUTOOON.
BAFUN (WHUMP)
AHH, THIS IS HEAVEN.

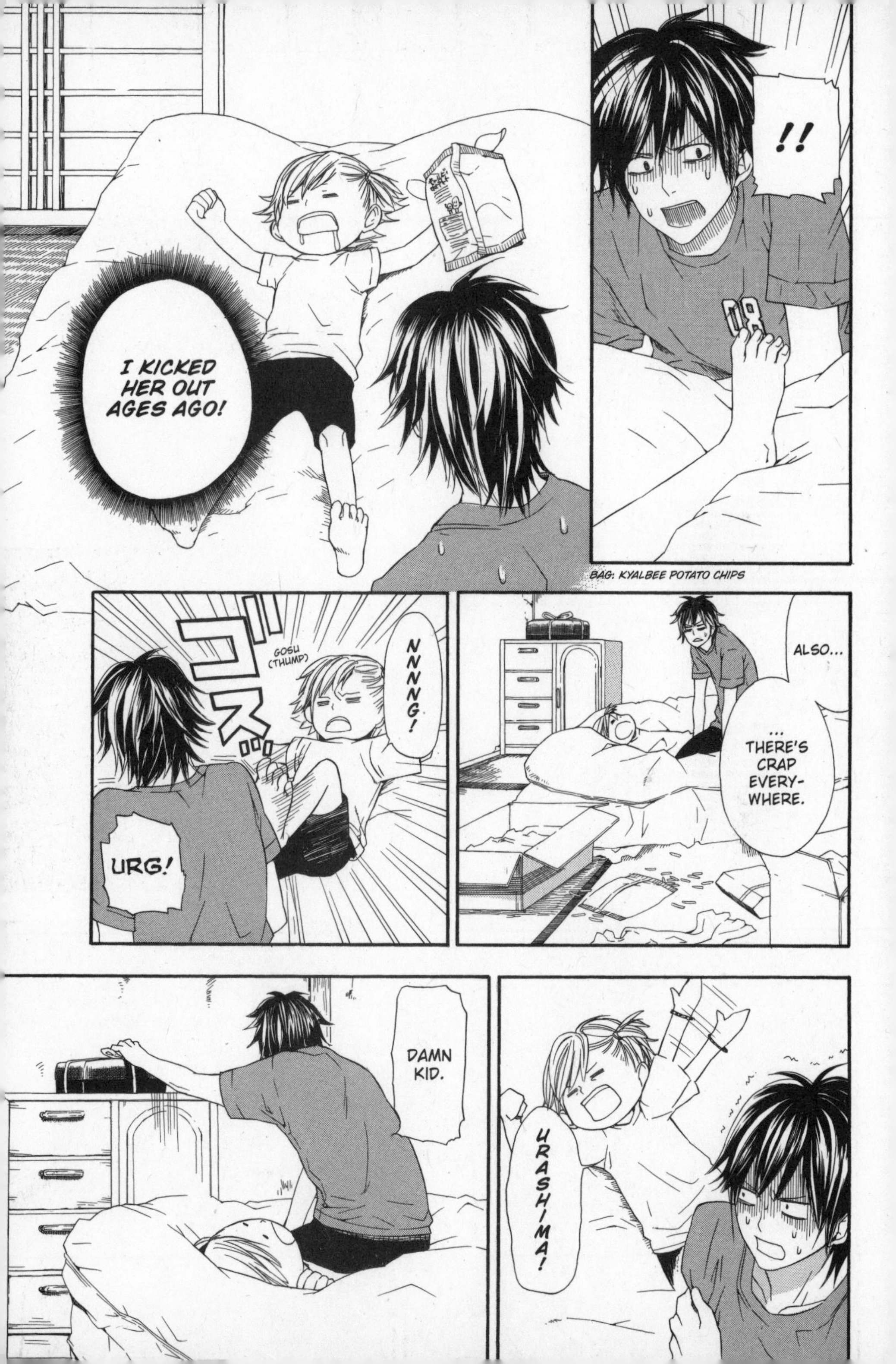
!!
I KICKED HER OUT AGES AGO!
BAG: KYALBEE POTATO CHIPS
ALSO...
...THERE'S CRAP EVERY-WHERE.
NNNNG!
GOSU (THUMP)
URG!
URASHIMA!
DAMN KID.

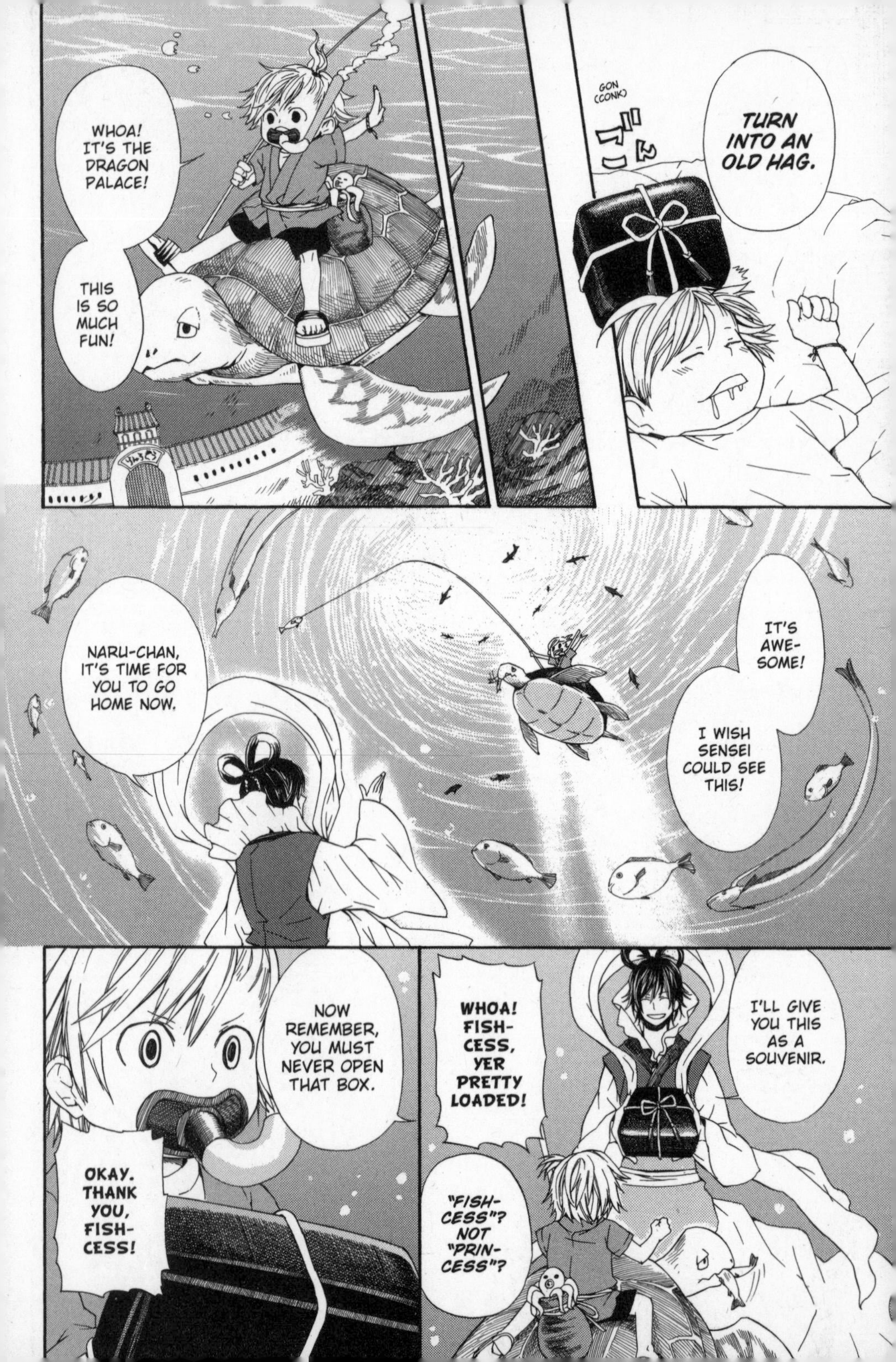
GON (CONK)
TURN INTO AN OLD HAG.
WHOA! IT'S THE DRAGON PALACE!
THIS IS SO MUCH FUN!
IT'S AWE-SOME!
I WISH SENSEI COULD SEE THIS!
NARU-CHAN, IT'S TIME FOR YOU TO GO HOME NOW.
I'LL GIVE YOU THIS AS A SOUVENIR.
WHOA! FISH-CESS, YER PRETTY LOADED!
"FISH-CESS"? NOT "PRIN-CESS"?
NOW REMEMBER, YOU MUST NEVER OPEN THAT BOX.
OKAY. THANK YOU, FISH-CESS!

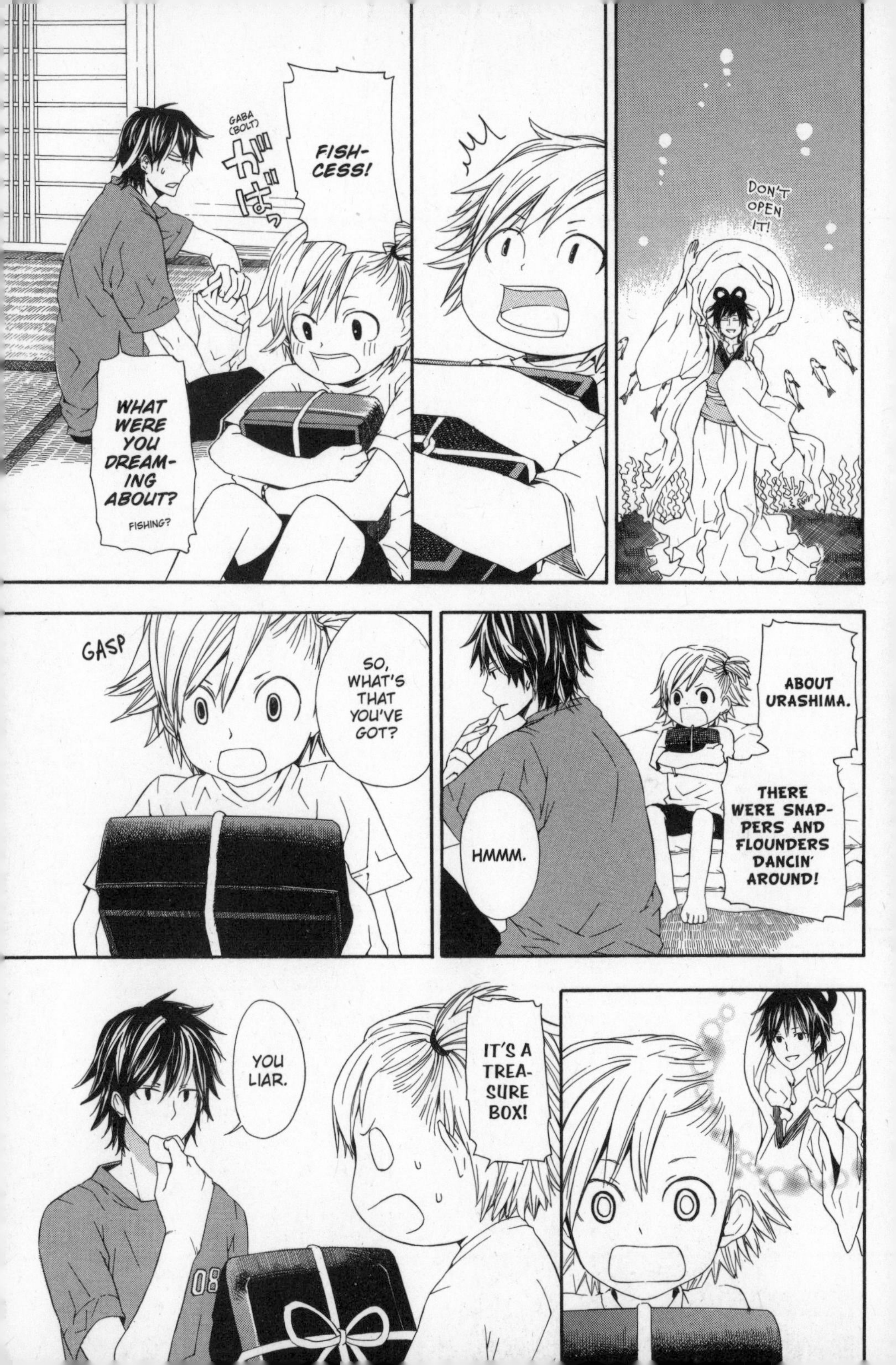
DON'T OPEN IT!
FISH-CESS!
GABA (BOLT)
がばっ
WHAT WERE YOU DREAMING ABOUT?
FISHING?
ABOUT URASHIMA.
THERE WERE SNAPPERS AND FLOUNDERS DANCIN' AROUND!
HMMM.
SO, WHAT'S THAT YOU'VE GOT?
GASP
IT'S A TREASURE BOX!
YOU LIAR.

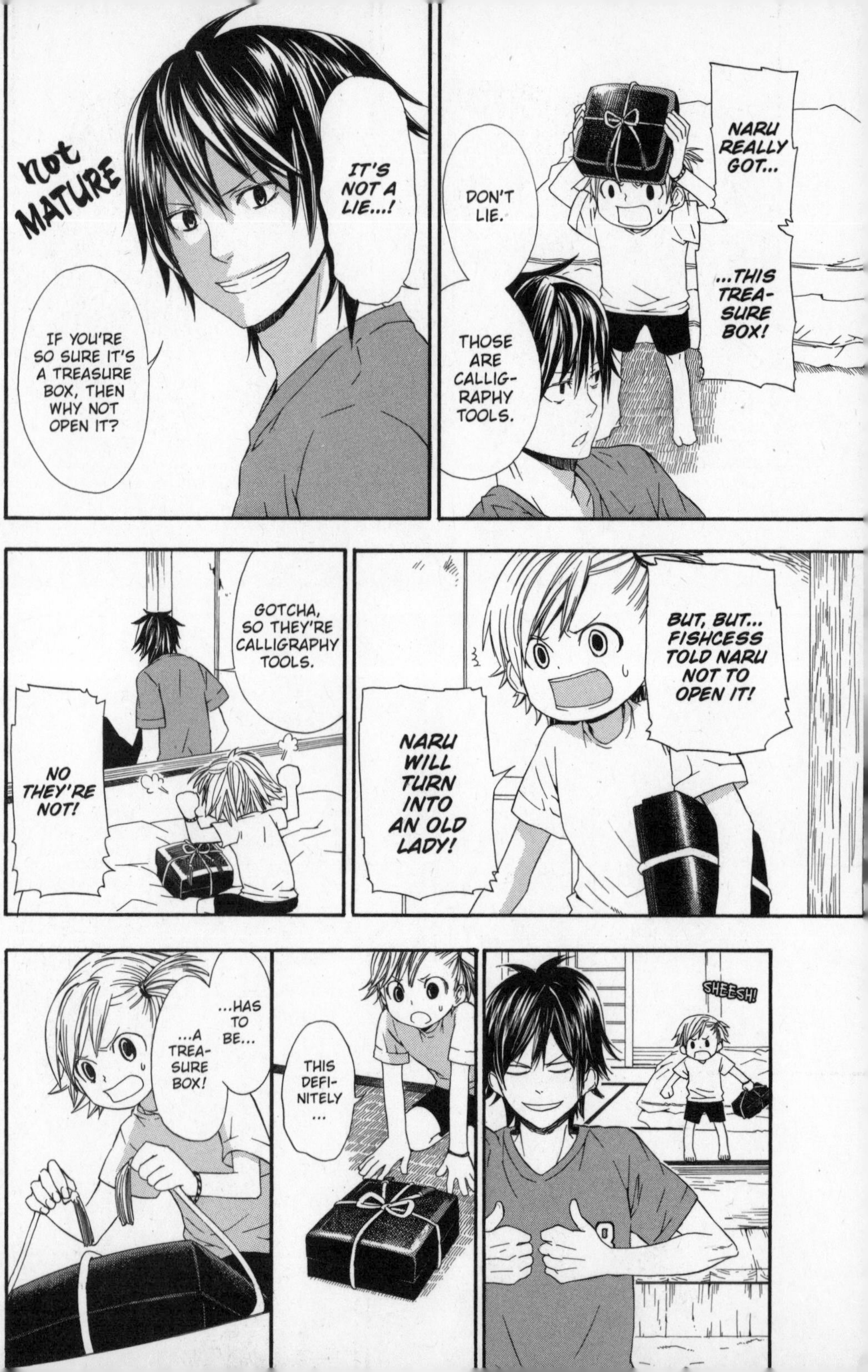
NARU REALLY GOT...
...THIS TREASURE BOX!
DON'T LIE.
THOSE ARE CALLIGRAPHY TOOLS.
IT'S NOT A LIE...!
not MATURE
IF YOU'RE SO SURE IT'S A TREASURE BOX, THEN WHY NOT OPEN IT?
BUT, BUT... FISHCESS TOLD NARU NOT TO OPEN IT!
NARU WILL TURN INTO AN OLD LADY!
GOTCHA, SO THEY'RE CALLIGRAPHY TOOLS.
NO THEY'RE NOT!
SHEESH!
THIS DEFINITELY...
...HAS TO BE...
...A TREASURE BOX!

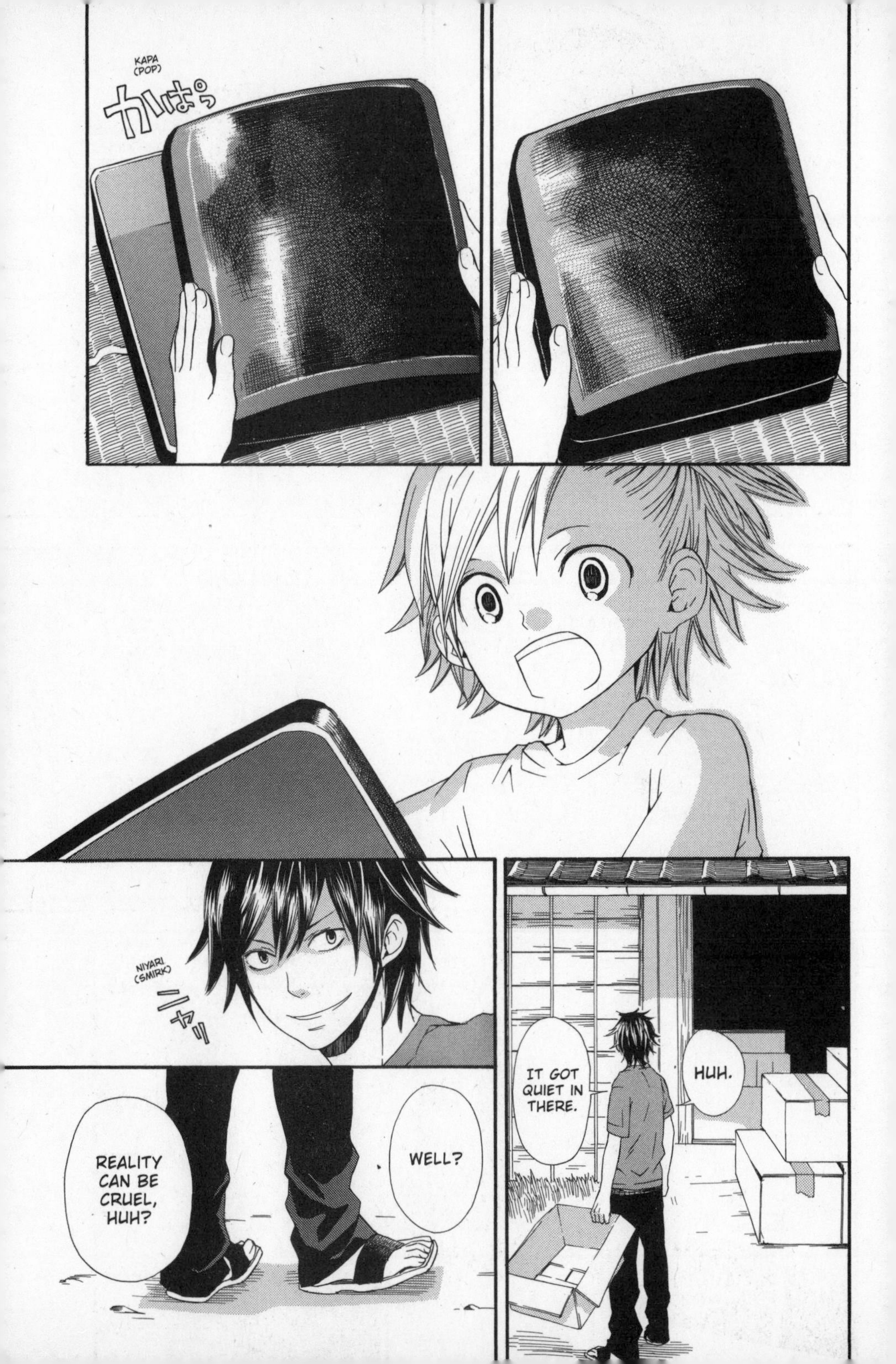
KAPA (POP)
かぱっ
HUH.
IT GOT QUIET IN THERE.
NIYARI (SMIRK)
ニヤリ
WELL?
REALITY CAN BE CRUEL, HUH?

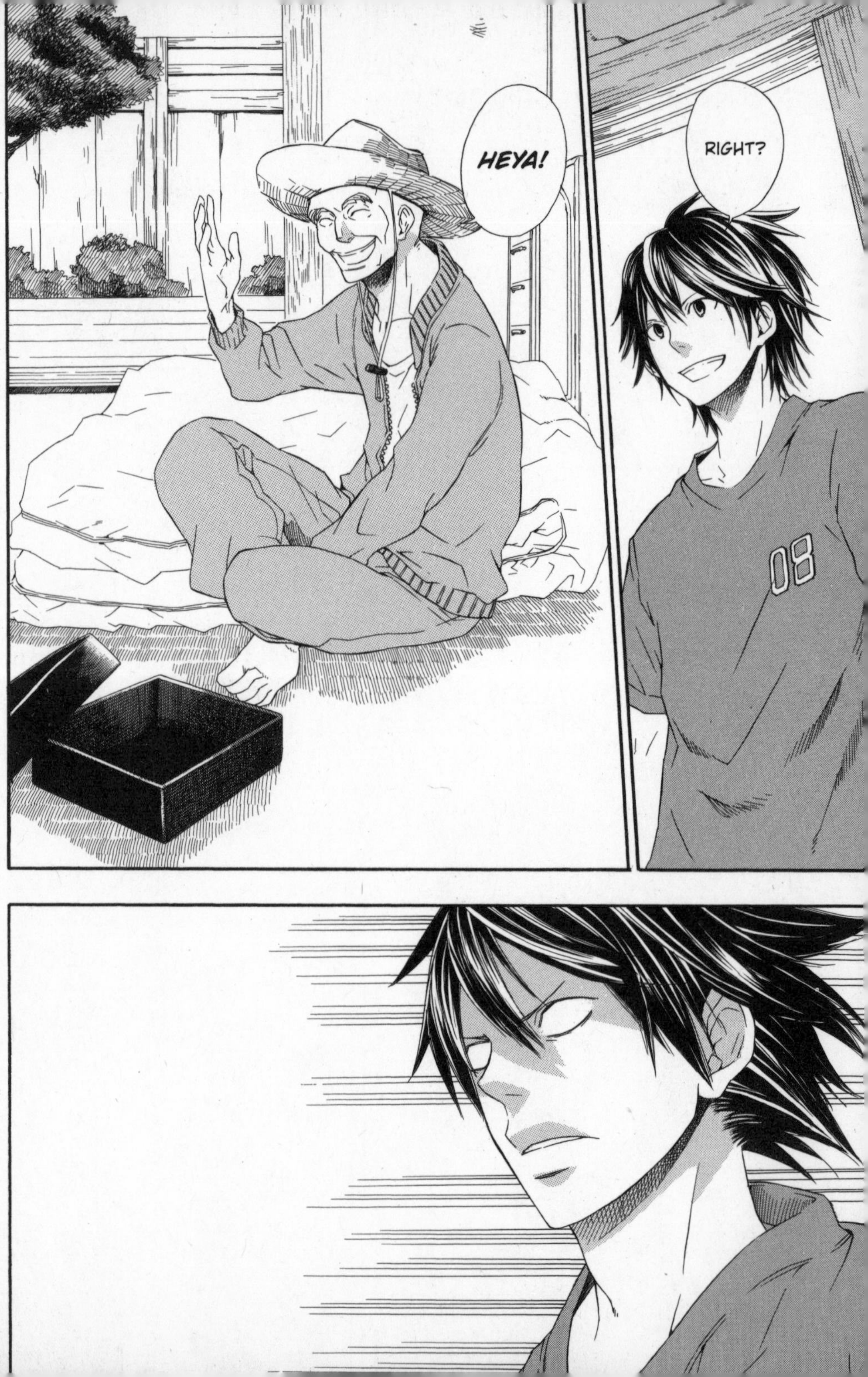
RIGHT?
HEYA!

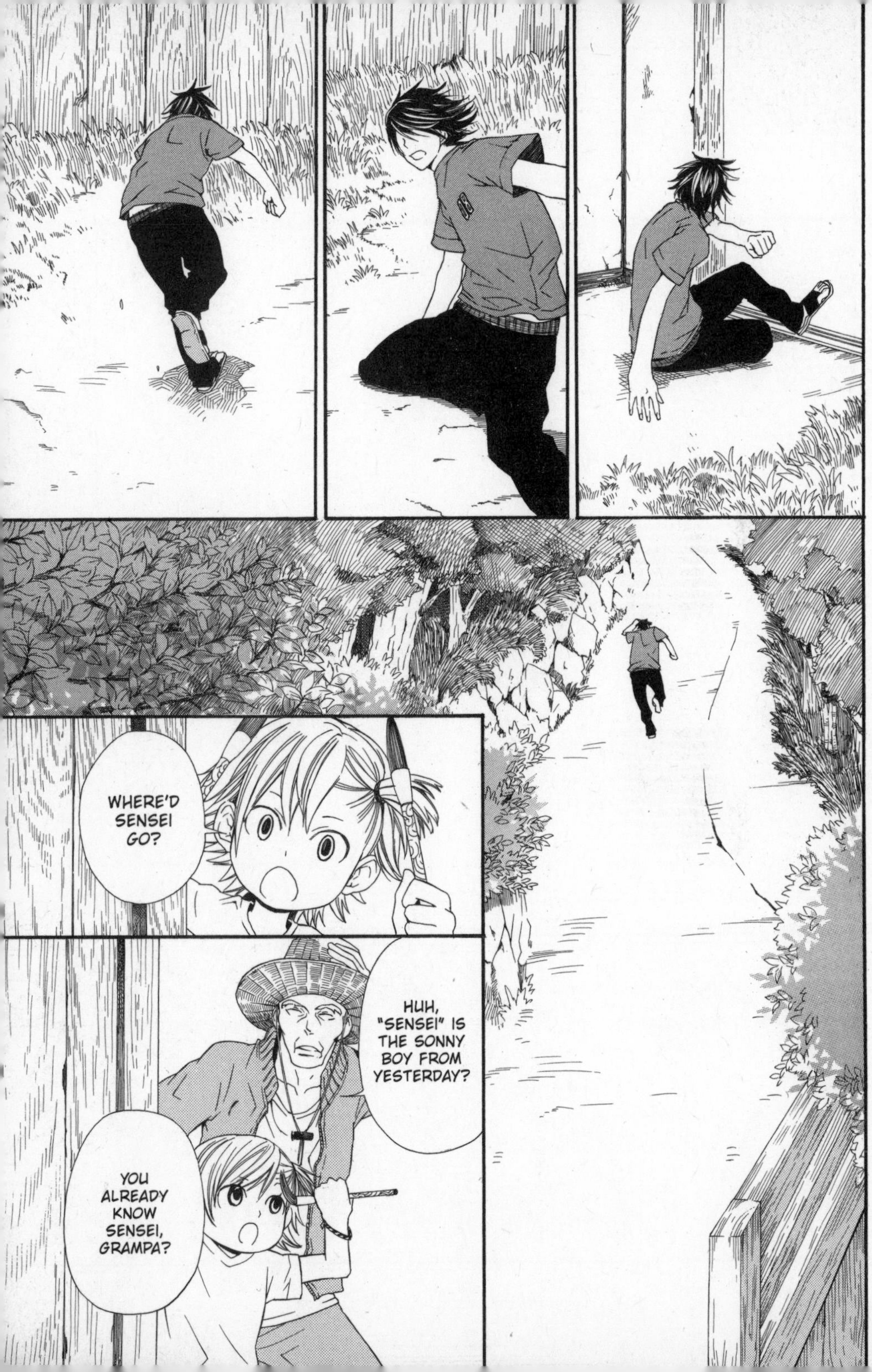
WHERE'D SENSEI GO?
HUH, "SENSEI" IS THE SONNY BOY FROM YESTERDAY?
YOU ALREADY KNOW SENSEI, GRAMPA?

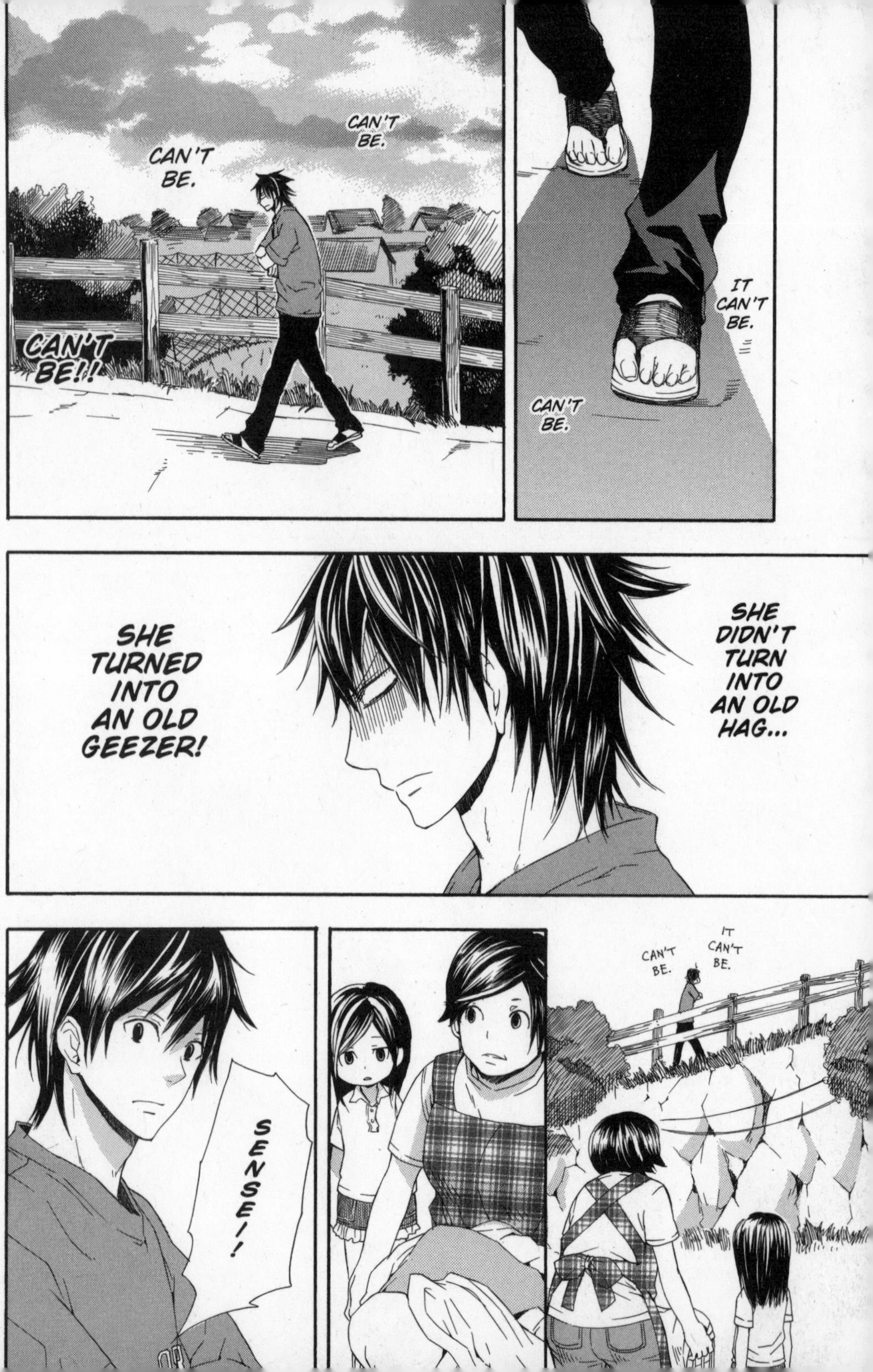
IT CAN'T BE.
CAN'T BE.
CAN'T BE.
CAN'T BE.
CAN'T BE!!
SHE DIDN'T TURN INTO AN OLD HAG...
SHE TURNED INTO AN OLD GEEZER!
IT CAN'T BE.
CAN'T BE.
SENSEI!!

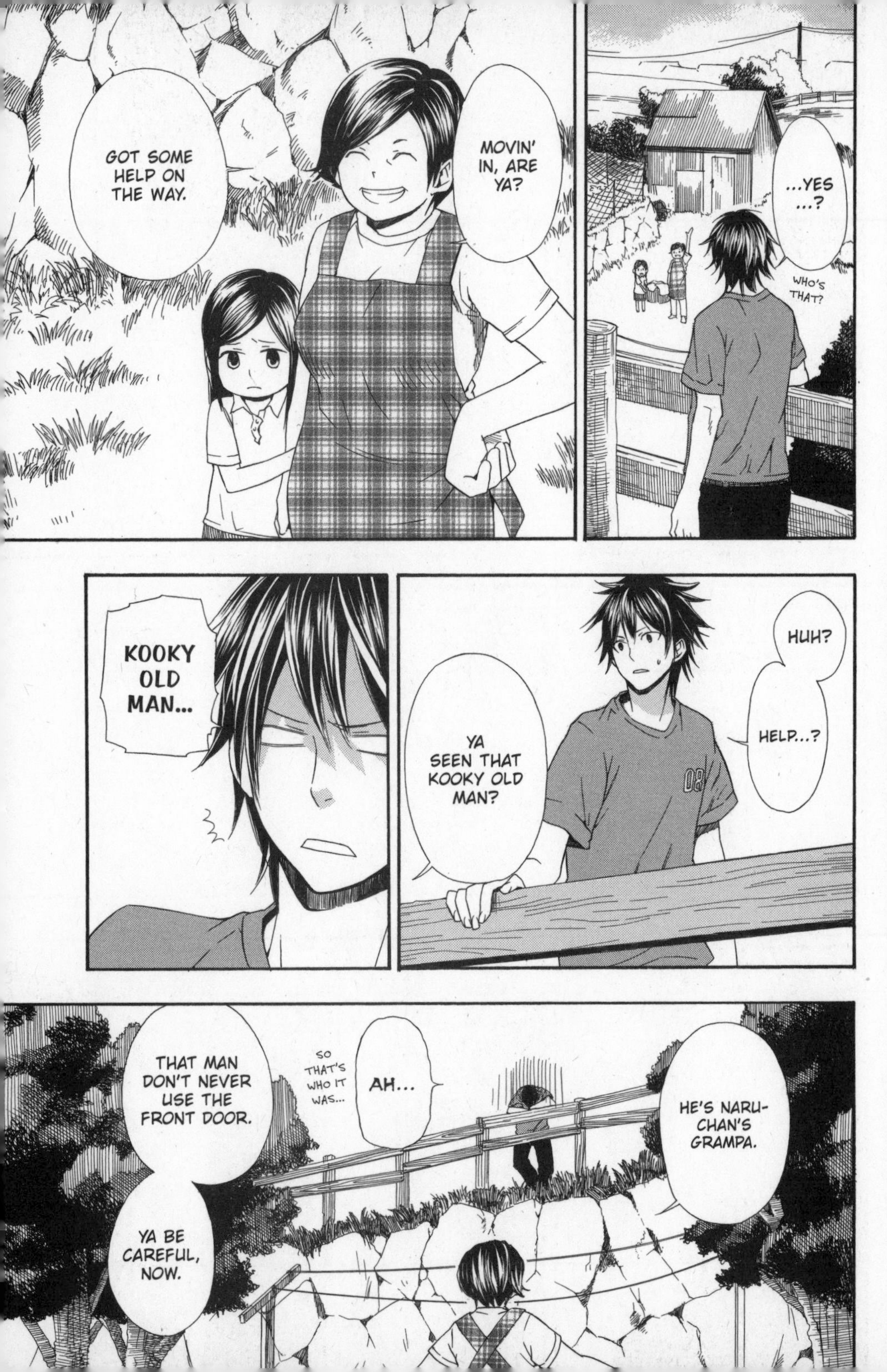
...YES ...?
WHO'S THAT?
MOVIN' IN, ARE YA?
GOT SOME HELP ON THE WAY.
HUH?
HELP...?
YA SEEN THAT KOOKY OLD MAN?
KOOKY OLD MAN...
HE'S NARU-CHAN'S GRAMPA.
AH...
SO THAT'S WHO IT WAS...
THAT MAN DON'T NEVER USE THE FRONT DOOR.
YA BE CAREFUL, NOW.

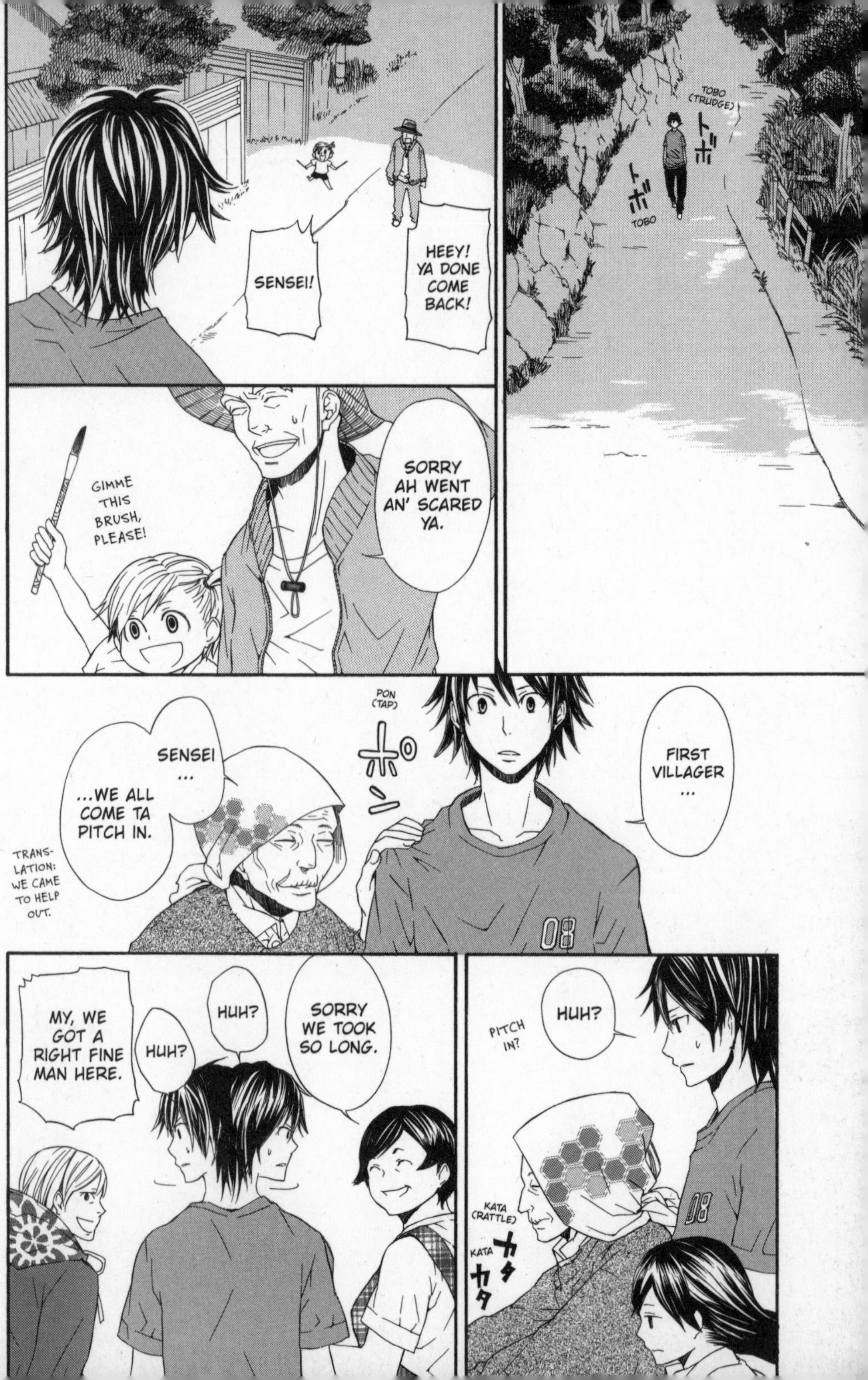
TOBO (TRUDGE)
トボ
トボ
TOBO
HEEY! YA DONE COME BACK!
SENSEI!
SORRY AH WENT AN' SCARED YA.
GIMME THIS BRUSH, PLEASE!
FIRST VILLAGER ...
PON (TAP)
ポン
SENSEI ...
...WE ALL COME TA PITCH IN.
TRANS-LATION: WE CAME TO HELP OUT.
HUH?
PITCH IN?
KATA (RATTLE)
カタ
カタ
KATA
SORRY WE TOOK SO LONG.
HUH?
HUH?
MY, WE GOT A RIGHT FINE MAN HERE.

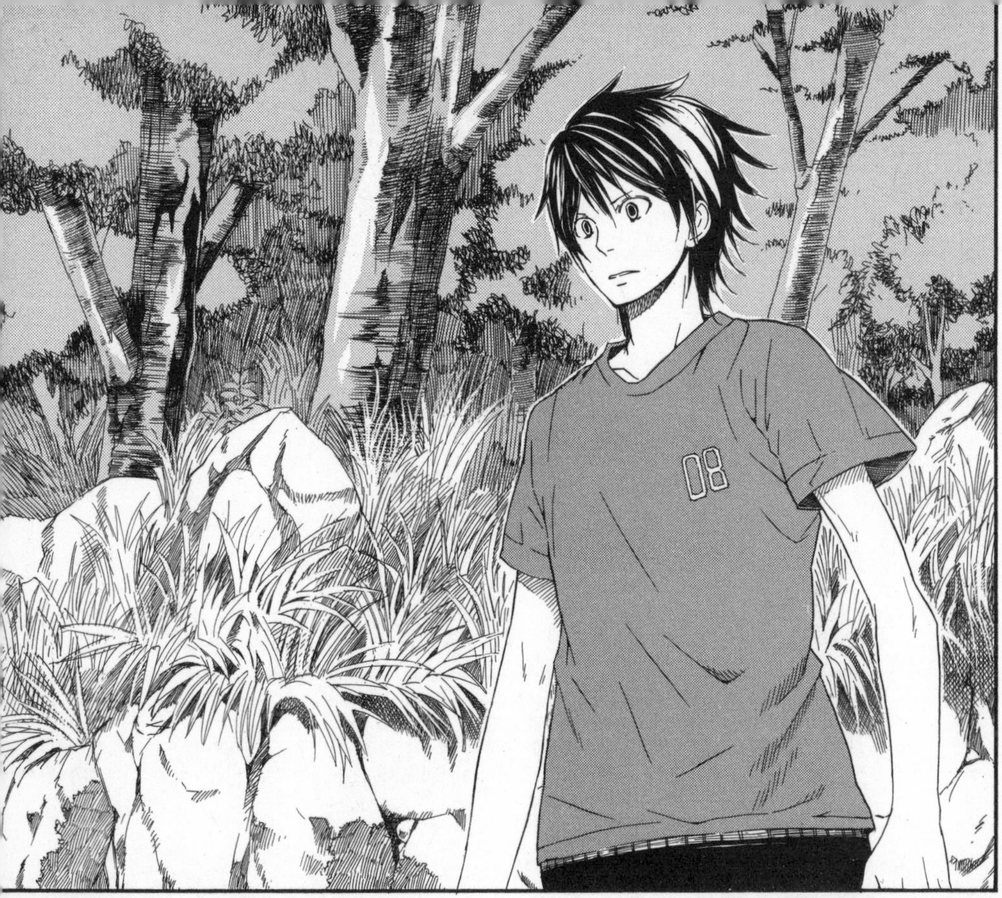

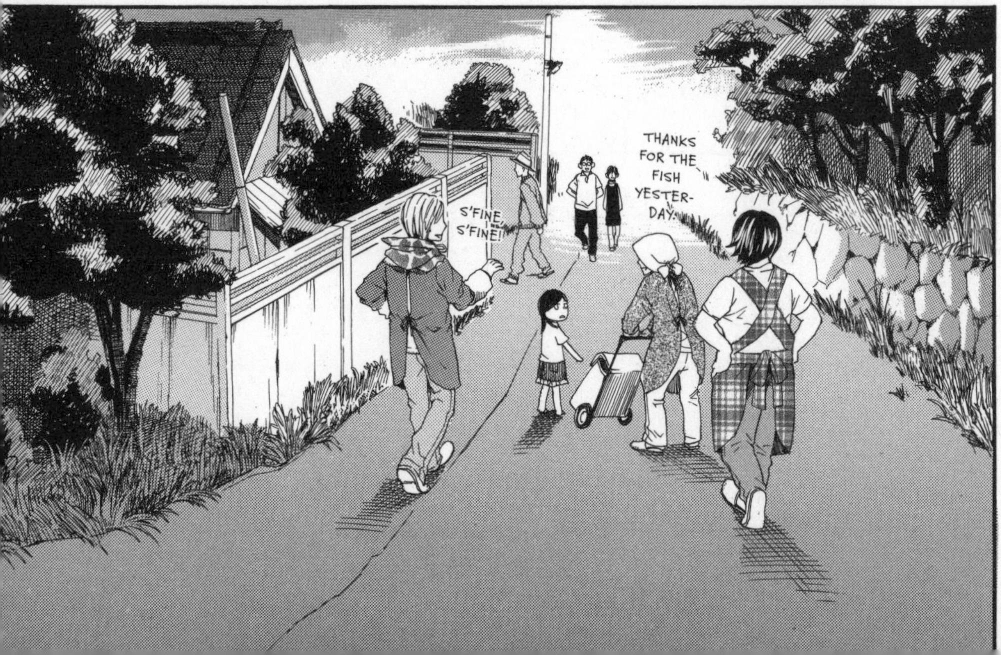
THANKS FOR THE FISH YESTER-DAY.
S'FINE, S'FINE!!

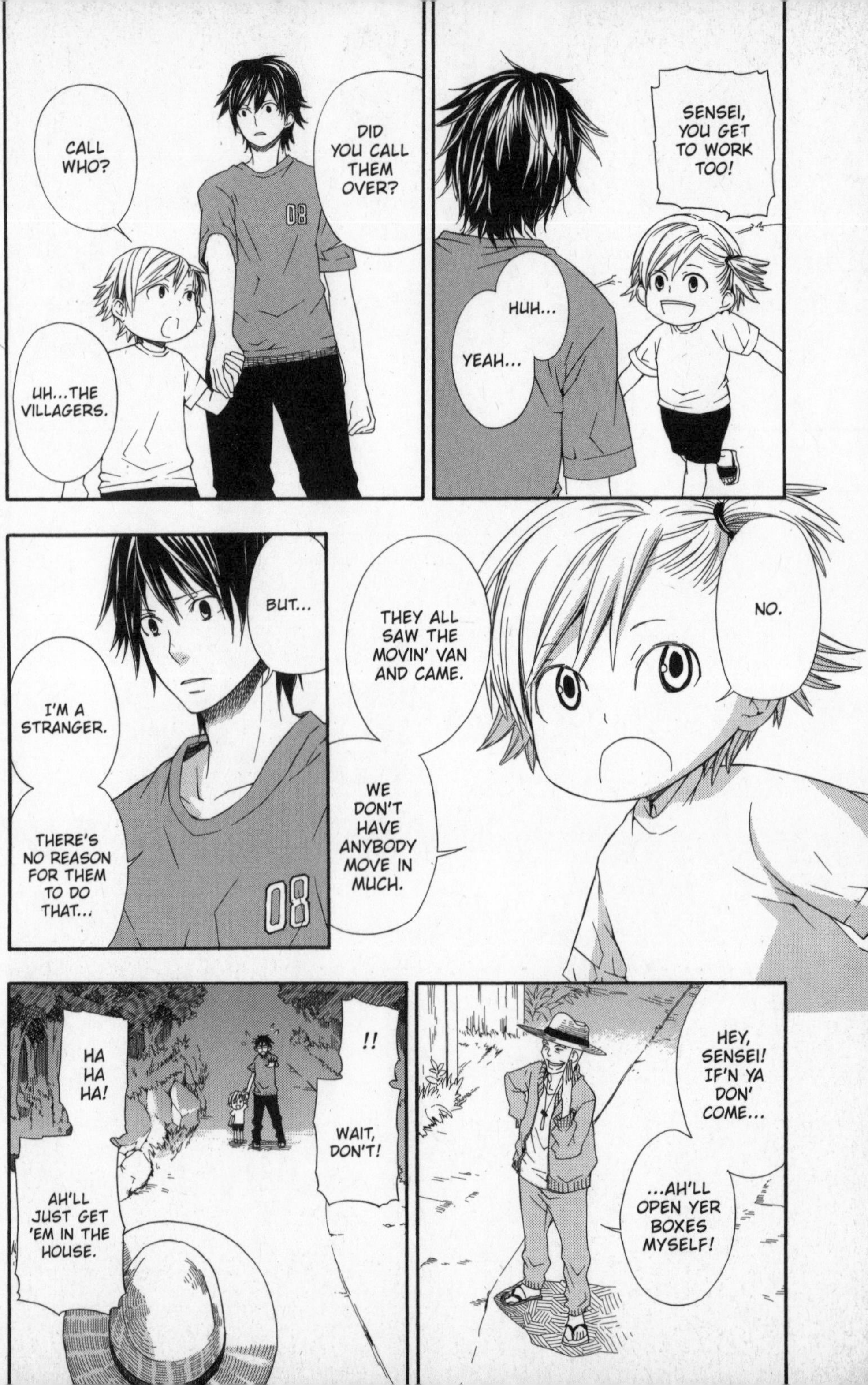
SENSEI, YOU GET TO WORK TOO!
HUH...
YEAH...
DID YOU CALL THEM OVER?
CALL WHO?
UH...THE VILLAGERS.
NO.
THEY ALL SAW THE MOVIN' VAN AND CAME.
WE DON'T HAVE ANYBODY MOVE IN MUCH.
BUT...
I'M A STRANGER.
THERE'S NO REASON FOR THEM TO DO THAT...
HEY, SENSEI! IF'N YA DON' COME...
...AH'LL OPEN YER BOXES MYSELF!
!!
WAIT, DON'T!
HA HA HA!
AH'LL JUST GET 'EM IN THE HOUSE.

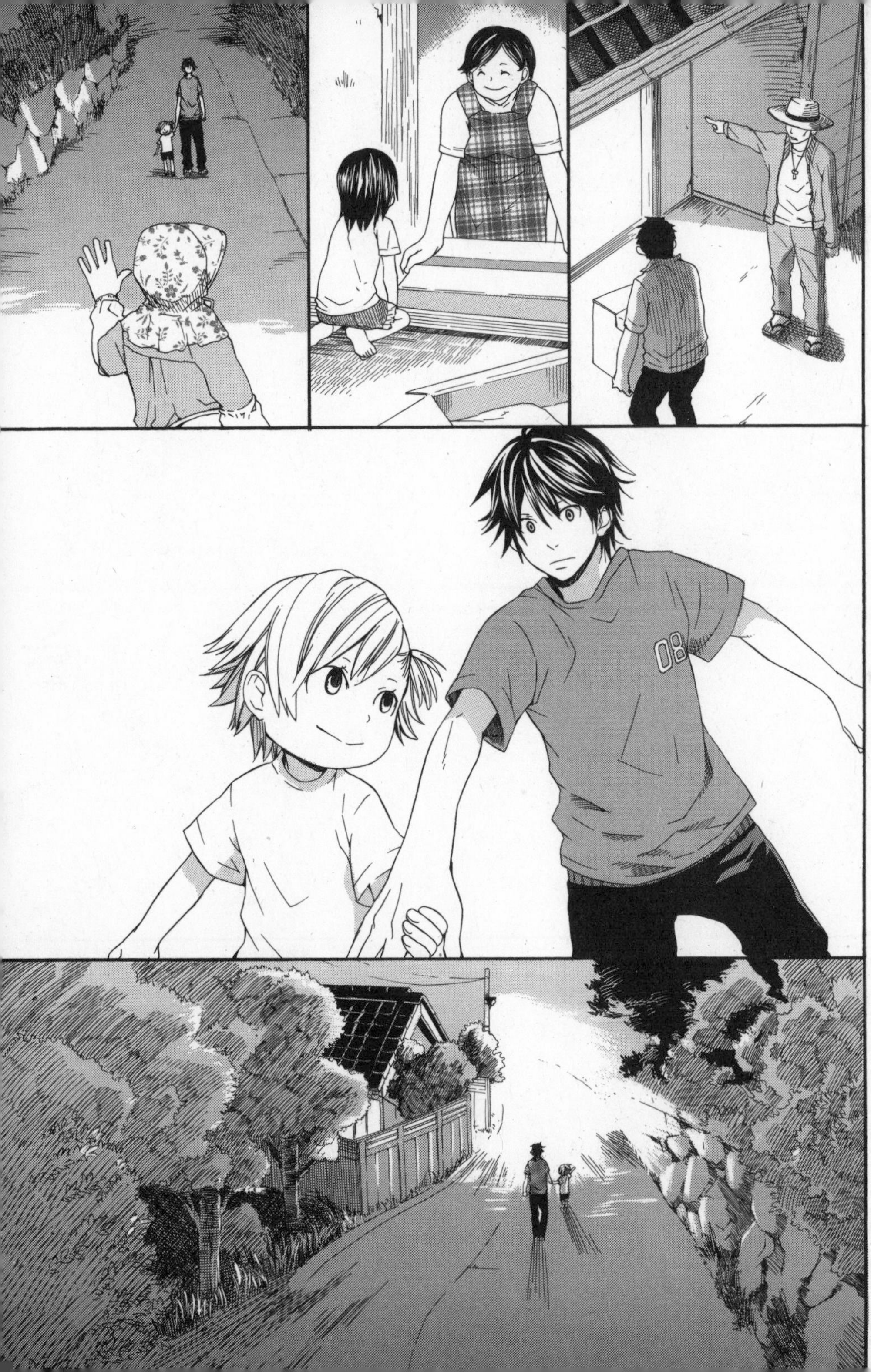
08

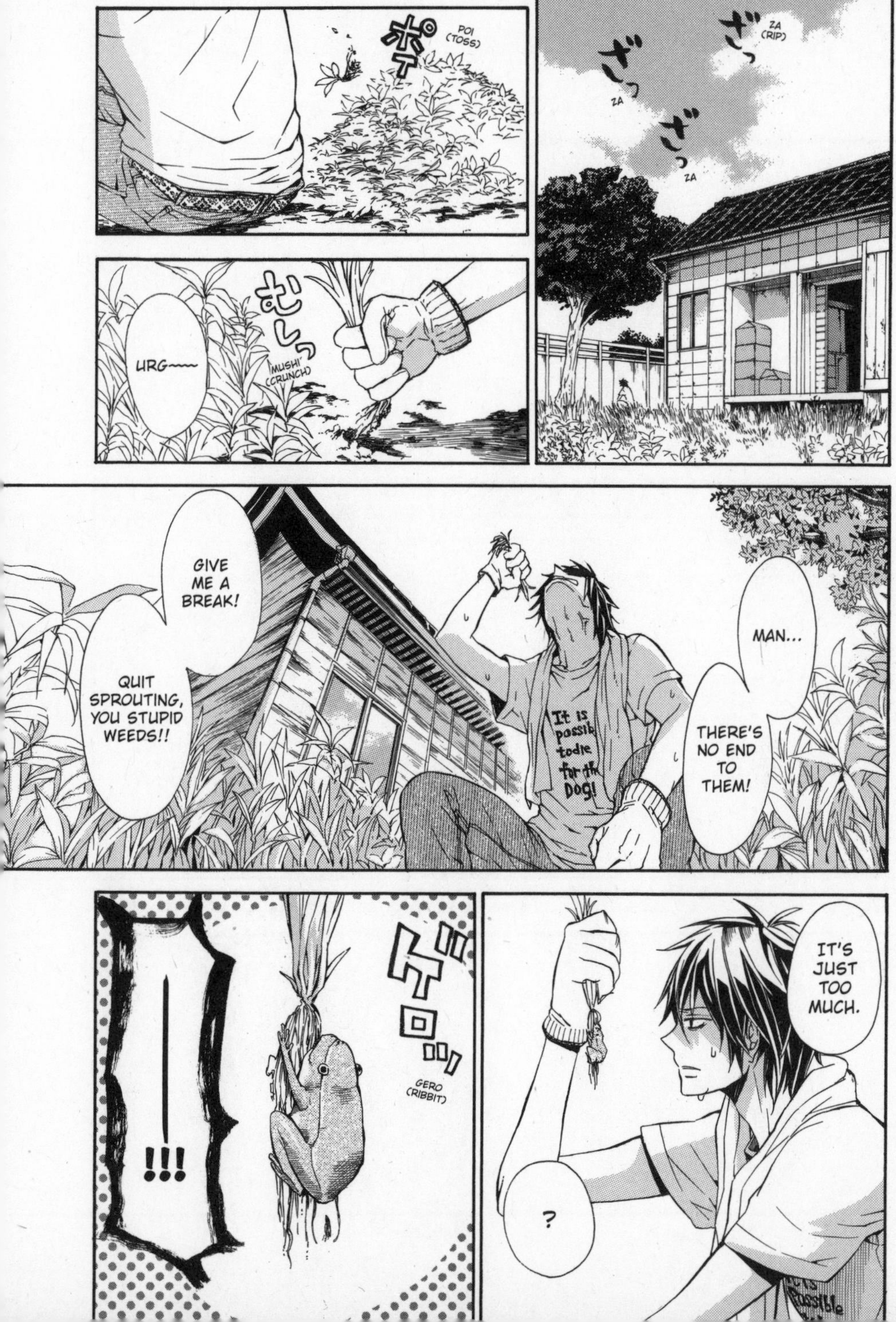
ZA (RIP)
ZA
ZA
POI (TOSS)
URG~~~
MUSHI (CRUNCH)
MAN...
THERE'S NO END TO THEM!
GIVE ME A BREAK!
QUIT SPROUTING, YOU STUPID WEEDS!!
IT'S JUST TOO MUCH.
?
GERO (RIBBIT)
—!!!

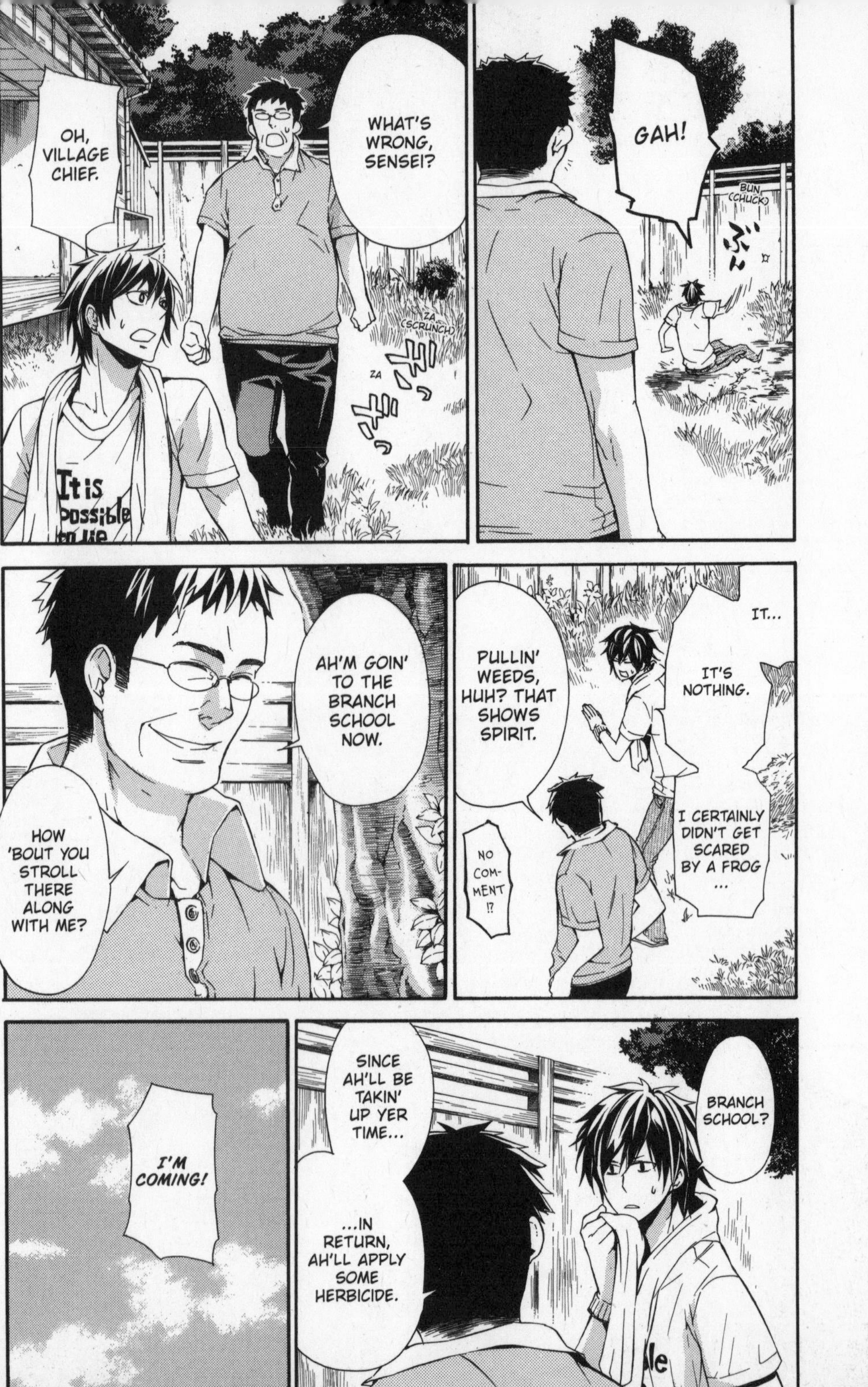
GAH!
BUN (CHUCK)
ぶん
WHAT'S WRONG, SENSEI?
OH, VILLAGE CHIEF.
ZA (SCRUNCH)
ZA
IT...
IT'S NOTHING.
I CERTAINLY DIDN'T GET SCARED BY A FROG...
PULLIN' WEEDS, HUH? THAT SHOWS SPIRIT.
NO COM-MENT!?
AH'M GOIN' TO THE BRANCH SCHOOL NOW.
HOW 'BOUT YOU STROLL THERE ALONG WITH ME?
BRANCH SCHOOL?
SINCE AH'LL BE TAKIN' UP YER TIME...
...IN RETURN, AH'LL APPLY SOME HERBICIDE.
I'M COMING!

ACT.3
DONKUDON
(Translation: Frog)
SO THAT'S THE SCHOOL BUILDING, RIGHT?
IS IT OKAY FOR IT TO BE SO SMALL?
THERE'S ONLY NINE STUDENTS TOTAL.
HA HA HA!
NINE!?
THERE'S FIVE FIRST-GRADERS AND FOUR SECOND-GRADERS.
SIGN: TOMIE MUNICIPAL SCHOOL - NANATSUTAKE BRANCH
富江町立七ツ岳分校
STARTIN' IN THIRD GRADE, THEY COMMUTE BY BIKE...
...TO THE MAIN SCHOOL THREE KILOMETERS AWAY.

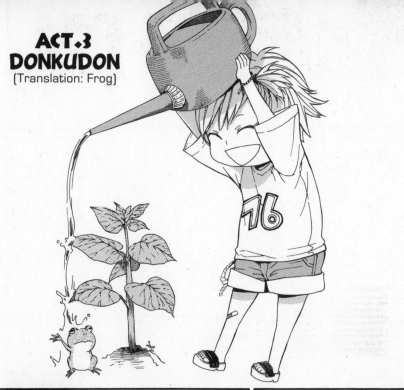

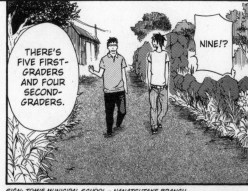

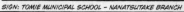

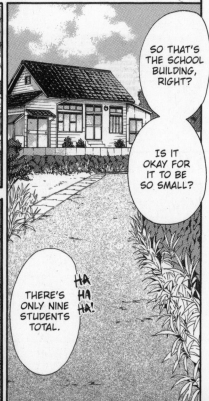

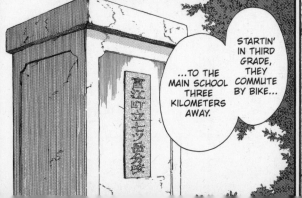

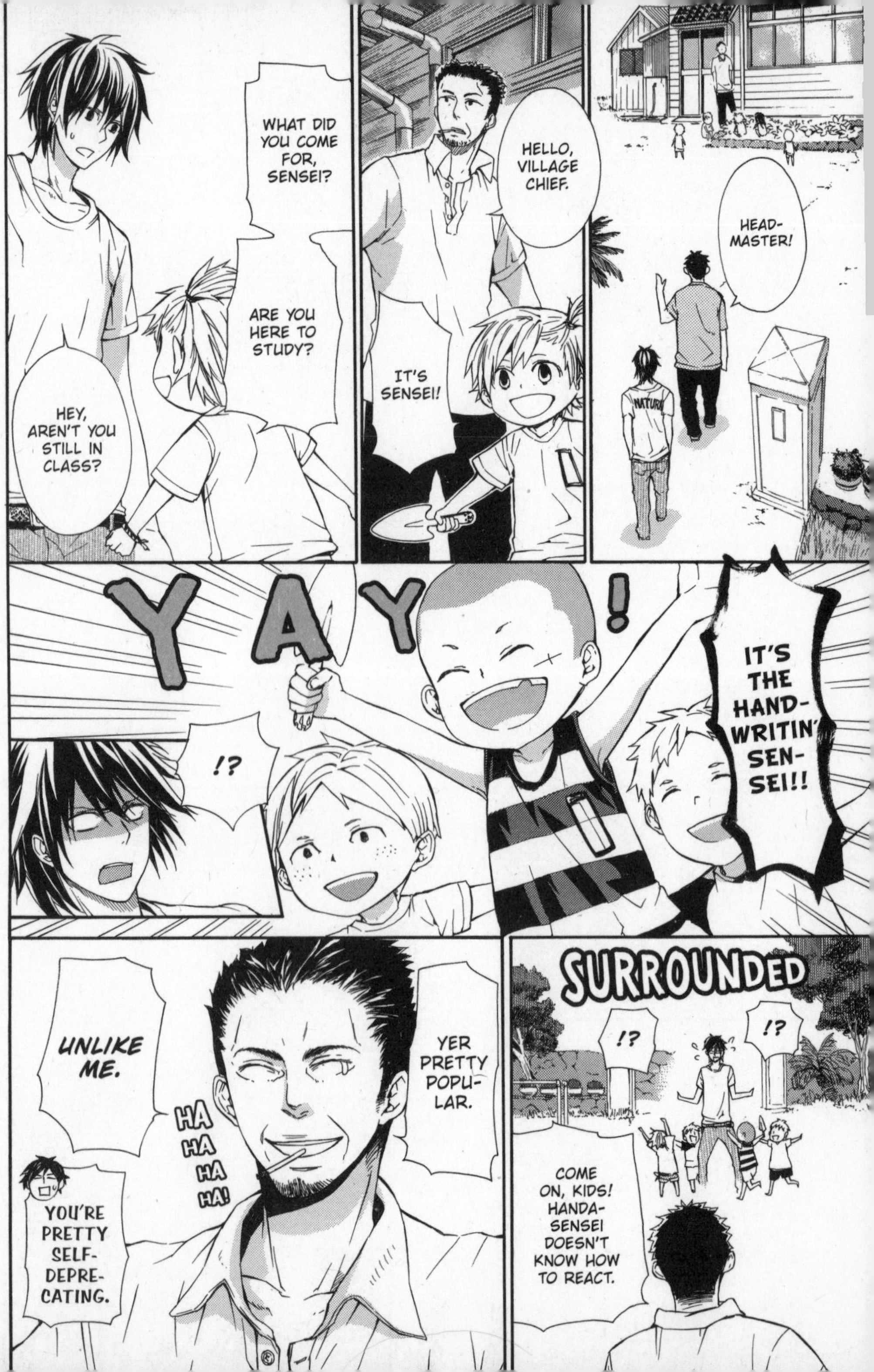
HEAD-MASTER!
HELLO, VILLAGE CHIEF.
IT'S SENSEI!
WHAT DID YOU COME FOR, SENSEI?
ARE YOU HERE TO STUDY?
HEY, AREN'T YOU STILL IN CLASS?
YAY!
IT'S THE HAND-WRITIN' SEN-SEI!!
!?
SURROUNDED
!?
!?
COME ON, KIDS! HANDA-SENSEI DOESN'T KNOW HOW TO REACT.
YER PRETTY POPU-LAR.
HA HA HA HA!
UNLIKE ME.
YOU'RE PRETTY SELF-DEPRE-CATING.

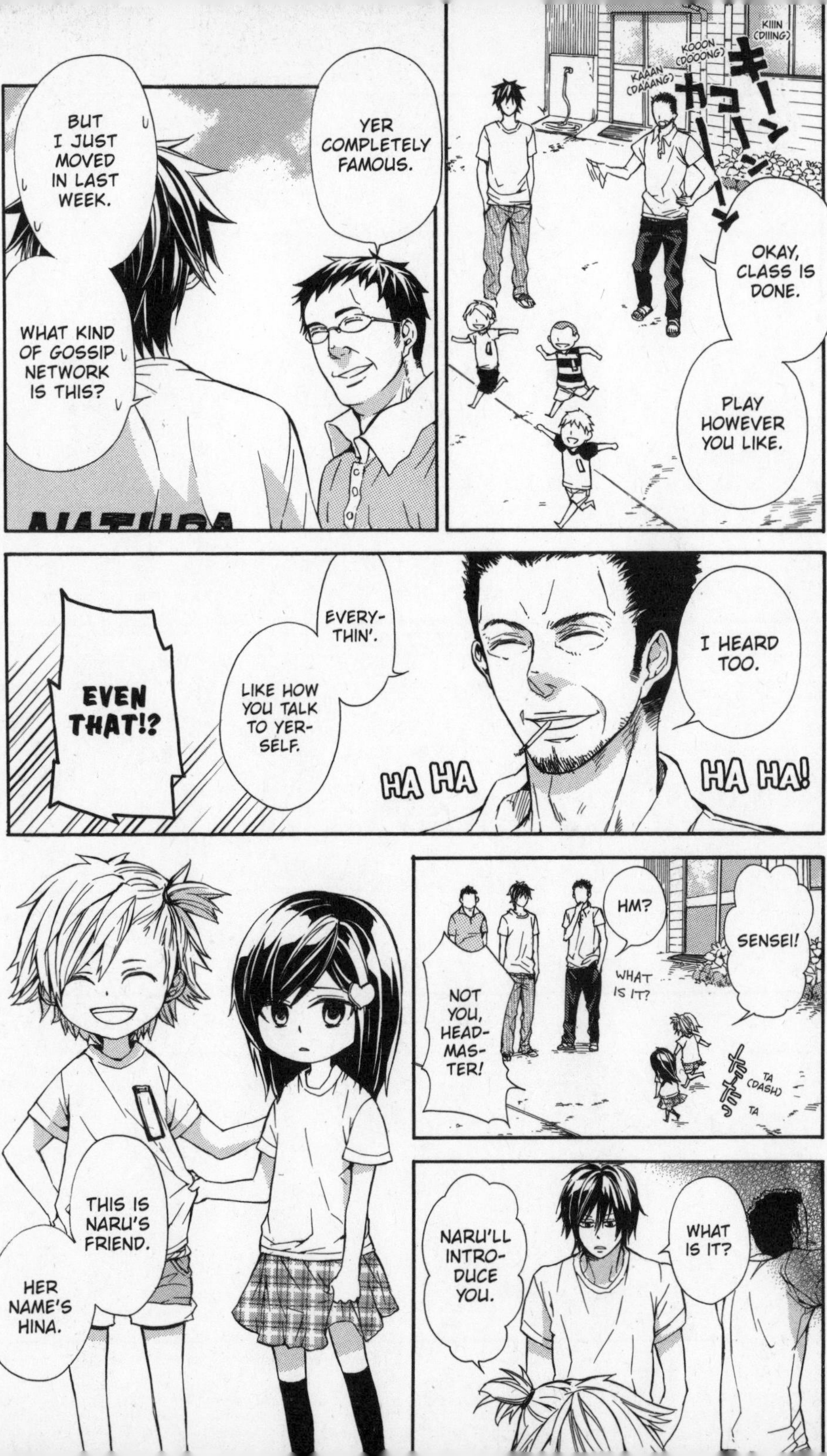
KIIN (DIIING)
KOOON (DOOONG)
KAAAN (DAAANG)
OKAY, CLASS IS DONE.
PLAY HOWEVER YOU LIKE.
YER COMPLETELY FAMOUS.
BUT I JUST MOVED IN LAST WEEK.
WHAT KIND OF GOSSIP NETWORK IS THIS?
I HEARD TOO.
HA HA!
HA HA
EVERY-THIN'.
LIKE HOW YOU TALK TO YER-SELF.
EVEN THAT!?
SENSEI!
HM?
WHAT IS IT?
NOT YOU, HEAD-MAS-TER!
TA (DASH) TA
WHAT IS IT?
NARU'LL INTRO-DUCE YOU.
THIS IS NARU'S FRIEND.
HER NAME'S HINA.

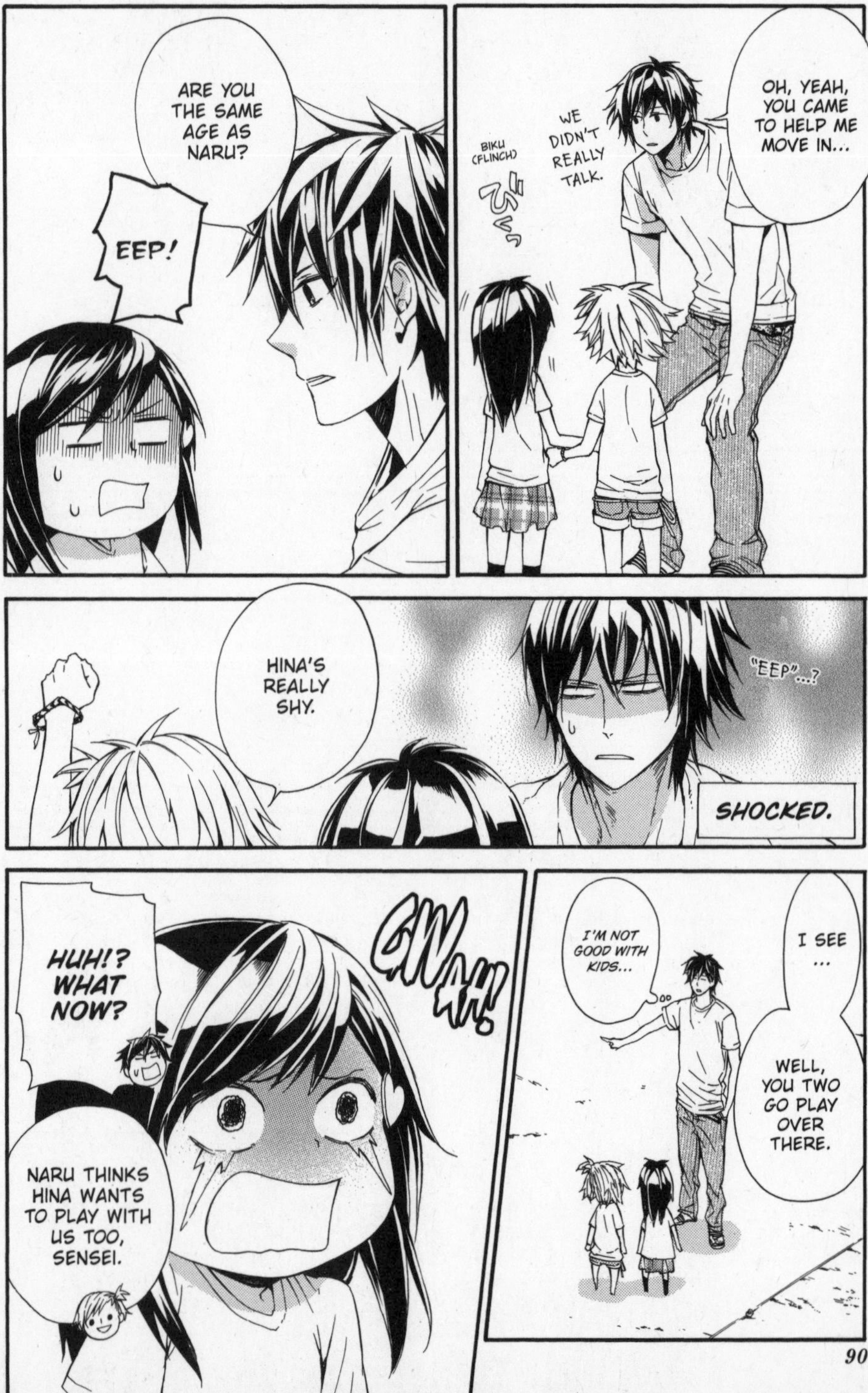
OH, YEAH, YOU CAME TO HELP ME MOVE IN...
WE DIDN'T REALLY TALK.
BIKU (FLINCH)
ARE YOU THE SAME AGE AS NARU?
EEP!
"EEP"...?
SHOCKED.
HINA'S REALLY SHY.
I SEE ...
I'M NOT GOOD WITH KIDS...
WELL, YOU TWO GO PLAY OVER THERE.
GWAH!
HUH!? WHAT NOW?
NARU THINKS HINA WANTS TO PLAY WITH US TOO, SENSEI.

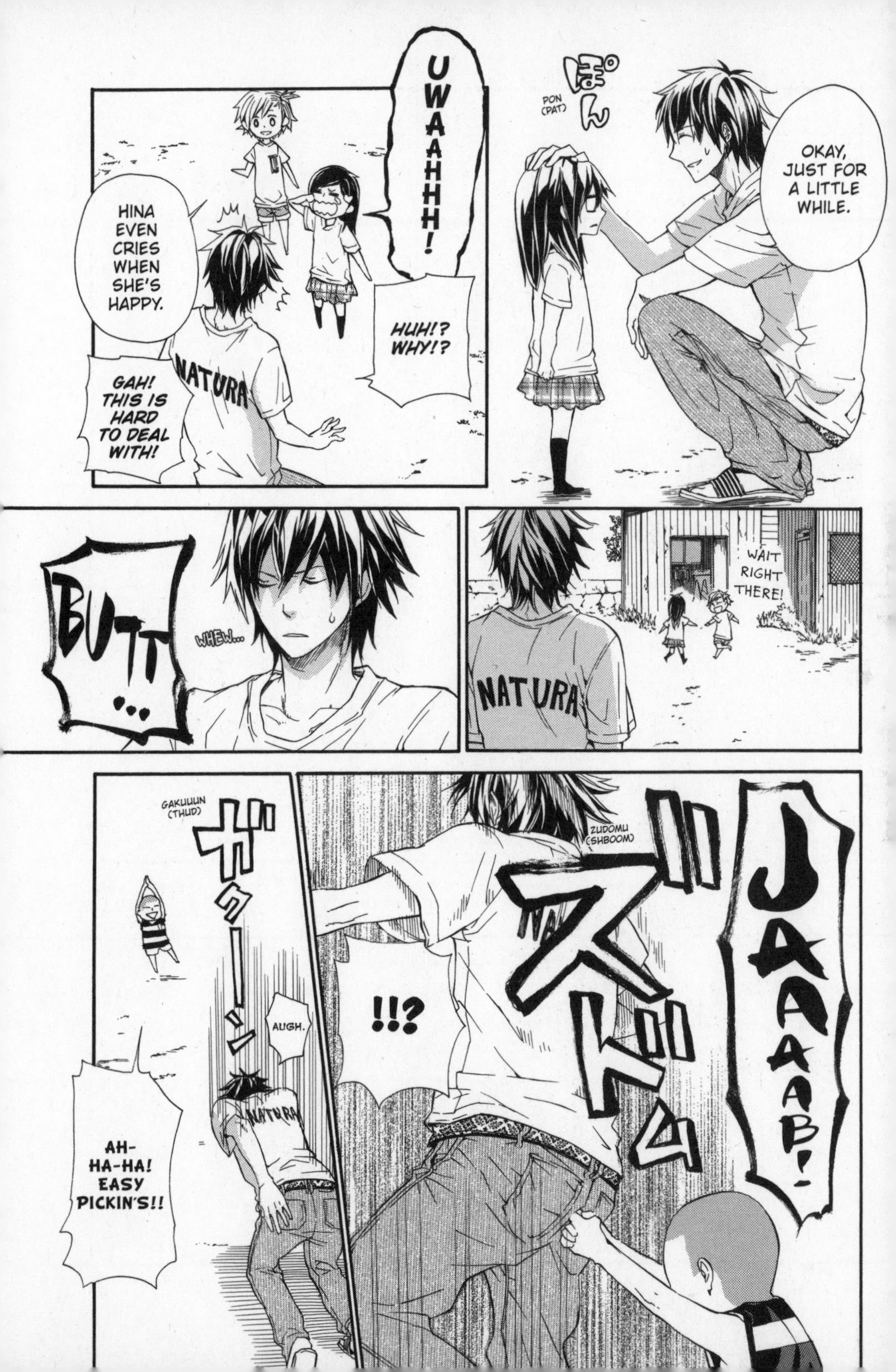
ぽん
PON (PAT)
OKAY, JUST FOR A LITTLE WHILE.
UWAAHHH!
HINA EVEN CRIES WHEN SHE'S HAPPY.
HUH!? WHY!?
GAH! THIS IS HARD TO DEAL WITH!
WAIT RIGHT THERE!
BUTT...
WHEW...
JAAAAB!
ズドム
ZUDOMU (SHBOOM)
!!?
ガクーン
GAKUUUN (THUD)
AUGH.
AH-HA-HA! EASY PICKIN'S!!

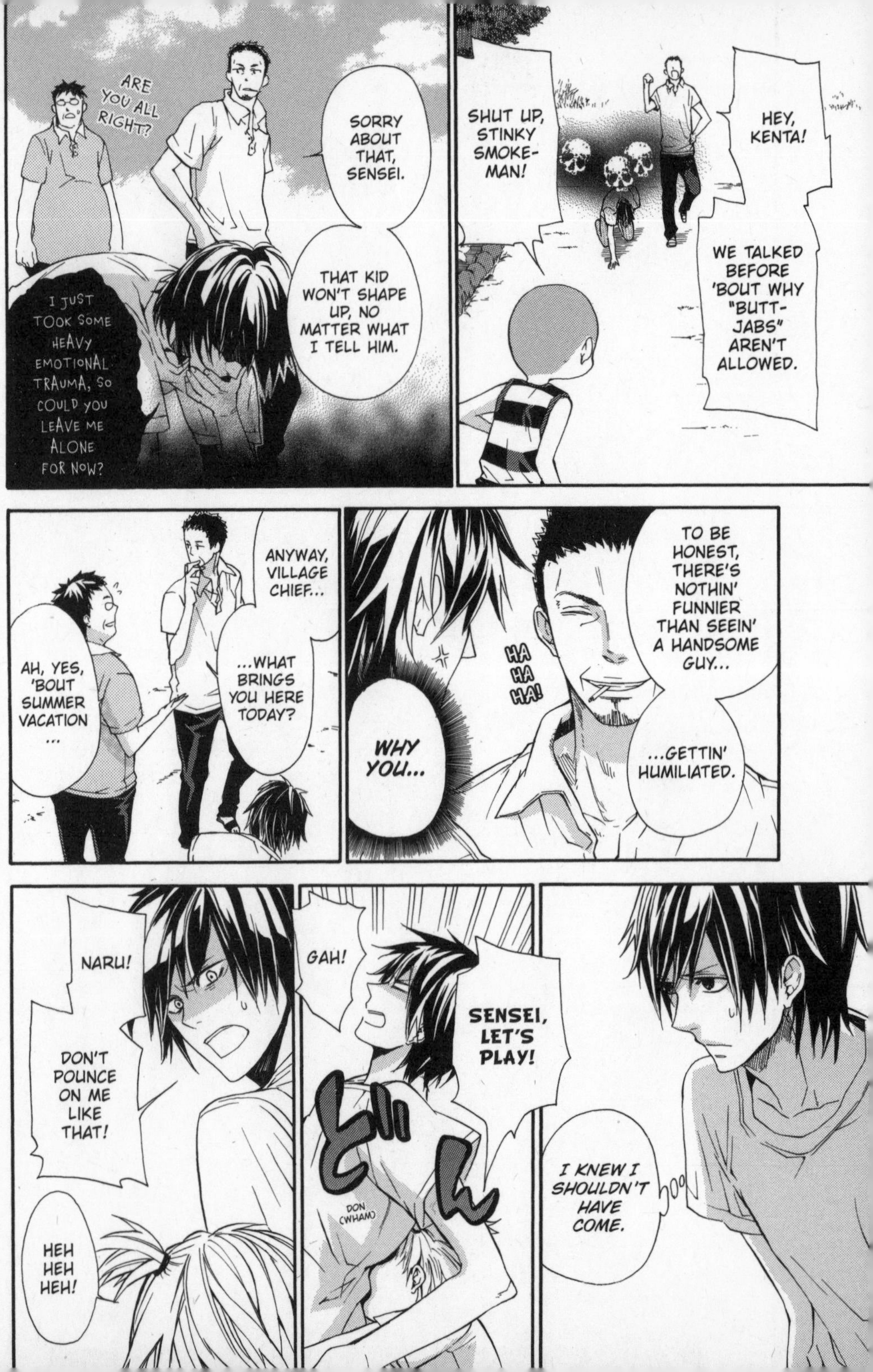
HEY, KENTA!
WE TALKED BEFORE 'BOUT WHY "BUTT-JABS" AREN'T ALLOWED.
SHUT UP, STINKY SMOKE-MAN!
SORRY ABOUT THAT, SENSEI.
THAT KID WON'T SHAPE UP, NO MATTER WHAT I TELL HIM.
ARE YOU ALL RIGHT?
I JUST TOOK SOME HEAVY EMOTIONAL TRAUMA, SO COULD YOU LEAVE ME ALONE FOR NOW?
TO BE HONEST, THERE'S NOTHIN' FUNNIER THAN SEEIN' A HANDSOME GUY...
...GETTIN' HUMILIATED.
HA HA HA!
WHY YOU...
ANYWAY, VILLAGE CHIEF...
...WHAT BRINGS YOU HERE TODAY?
AH, YES, 'BOUT SUMMER VACATION ...
I KNEW I SHOULDN'T HAVE COME.
SENSEI, LET'S PLAY!
GAH!
DON (WHAM)
NARU!
DON'T POUNCE ON ME LIKE THAT!
HEH HEH HEH!

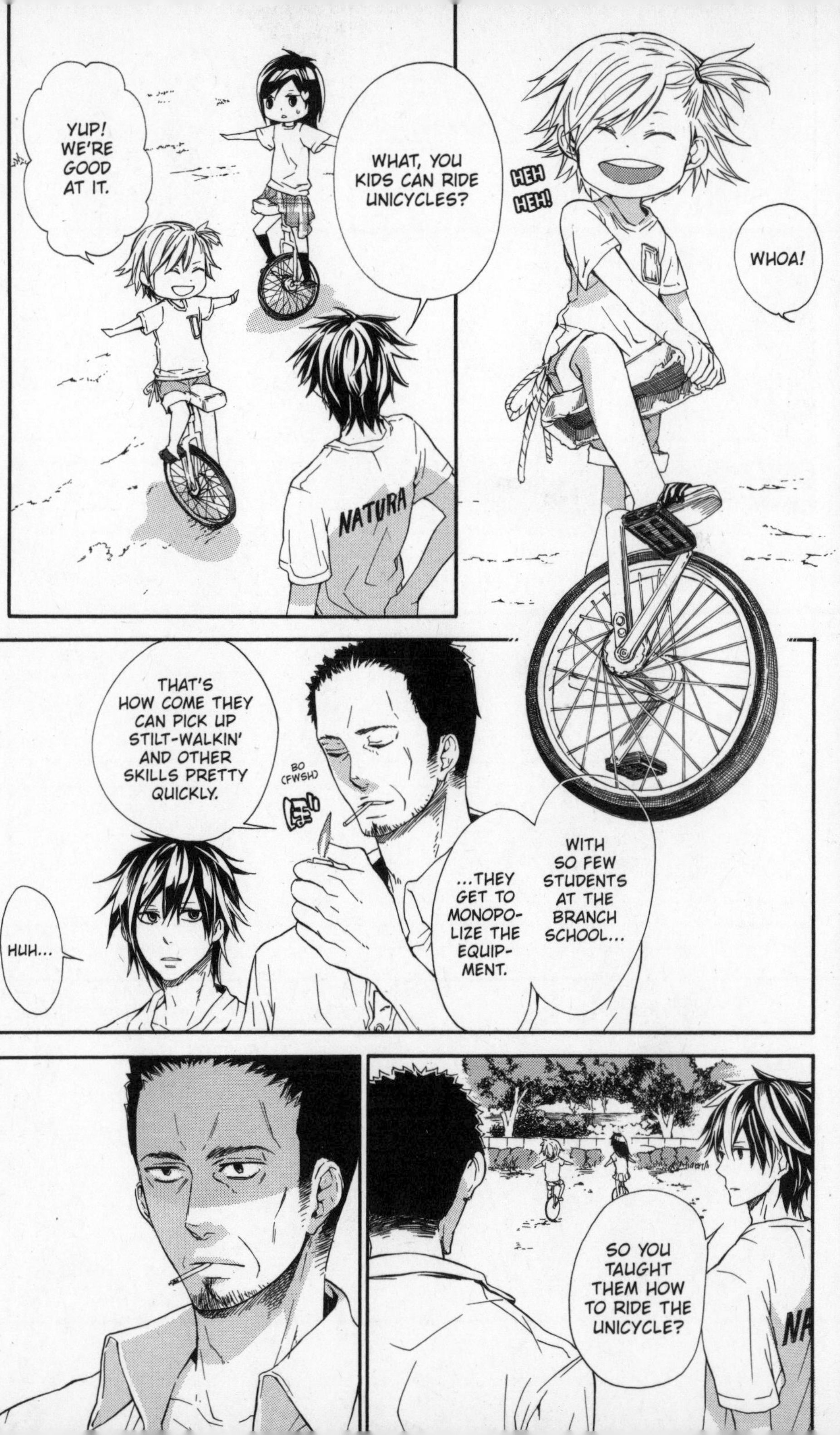

HEH HEH!
WHOA!
WHAT, YOU KIDS CAN RIDE UNICYCLES?
YUP! WE'RE GOOD AT IT.
NATURA
WITH SO FEW STUDENTS AT THE BRANCH SCHOOL...
...THEY GET TO MONOPOLIZE THE EQUIPMENT.
ぼ
BO (FWSH)
THAT'S HOW COME THEY CAN PICK UP STILT-WALKIN' AND OTHER SKILLS PRETTY QUICKLY.
HUH...
SO YOU TAUGHT THEM HOW TO RIDE THE UNICYCLE?

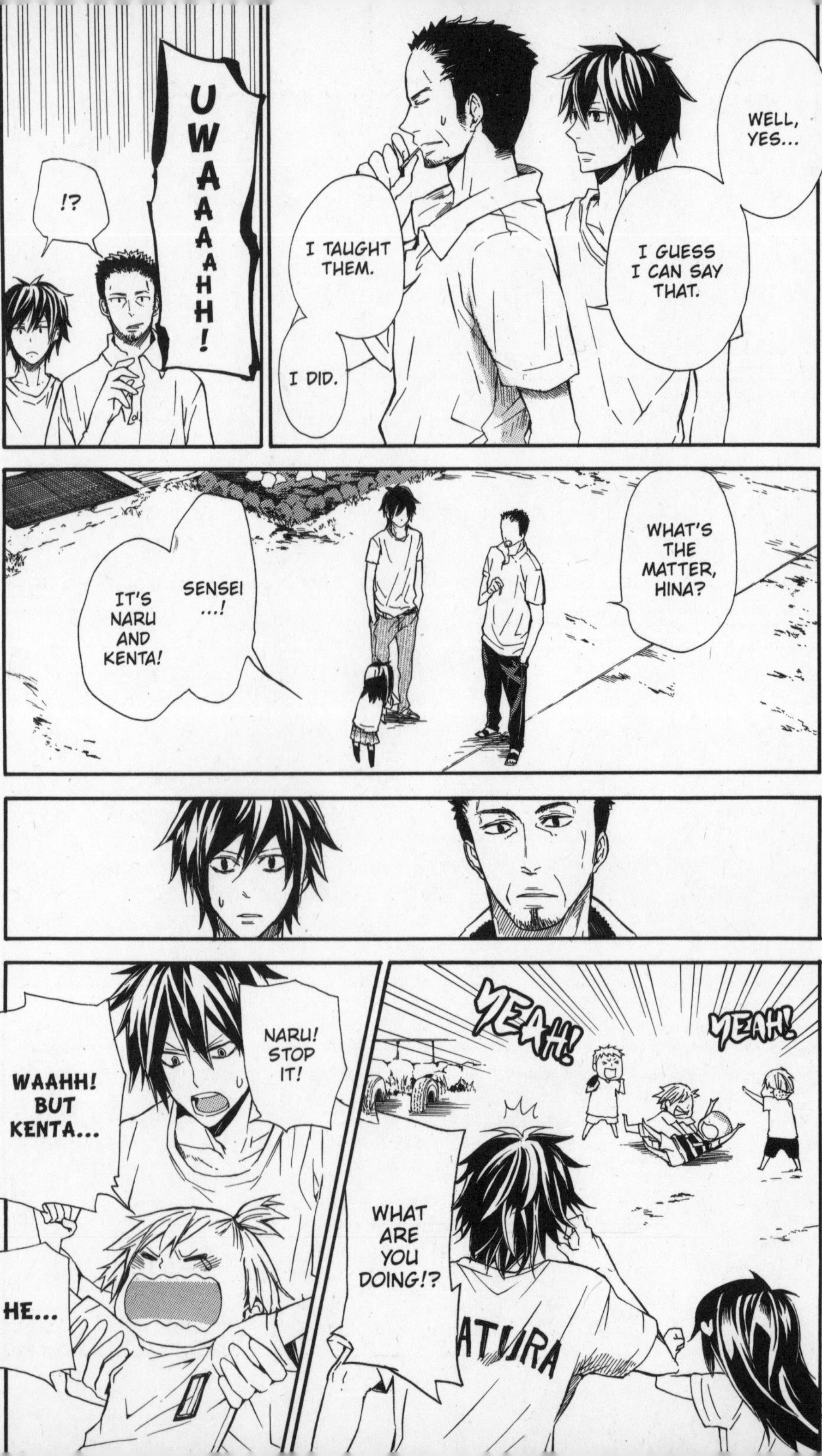
WELL, YES...
I GUESS I CAN SAY THAT.
I TAUGHT THEM.
I DID.
UWAAAAAHH!
!?
WHAT'S THE MATTER, HINA?
SENSEI...!
IT'S NARU AND KENTA!
YEAH!
YEAH!
WHAT ARE YOU DOING!?
NARU! STOP IT!
WAAHH! BUT KENTA...
HE...

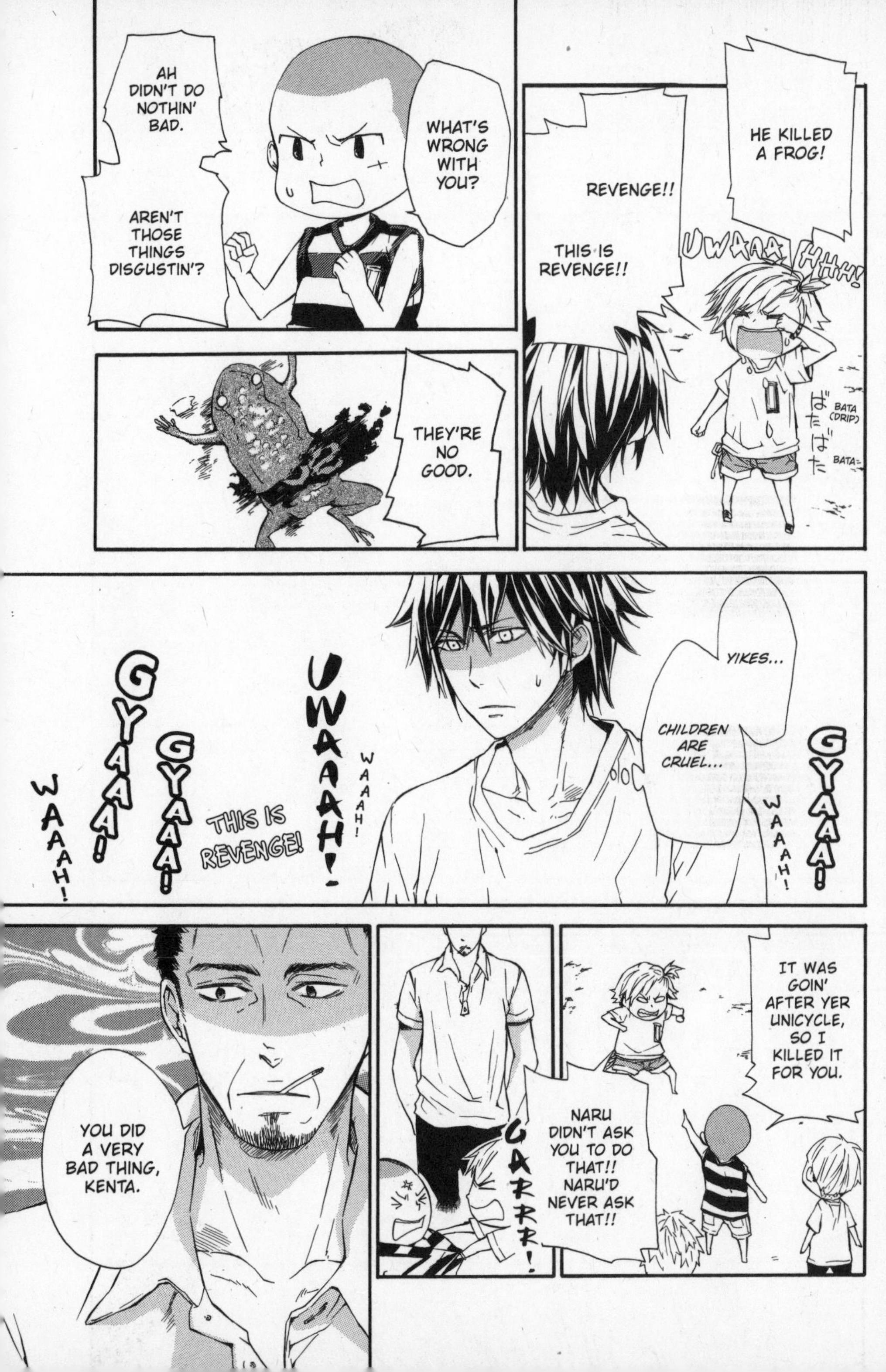
HE KILLED A FROG!
REVENGE!!
THIS IS REVENGE!!
UWAAAHHH!
ばたばた
BATA (DRIP)
BATA=
WHAT'S WRONG WITH YOU?
AH DIDN'T DO NOTHIN' BAD.
AREN'T THOSE THINGS DISGUSTIN'?
THEY'RE NO GOOD.
GYAAA!
WAAAH!
YIKES...
CHILDREN ARE CRUEL...
UWAAAH!
WAAAH!
THIS IS REVENGE!
GYAAA!
GYAAA!
WAAAH!
IT WAS GOIN' AFTER YER UNICYCLE, SO I KILLED IT FOR YOU.
NARU DIDN'T ASK YOU TO DO THAT!! NARU'D NEVER ASK THAT!!
GARRR!
YOU DID A VERY BAD THING, KENTA.

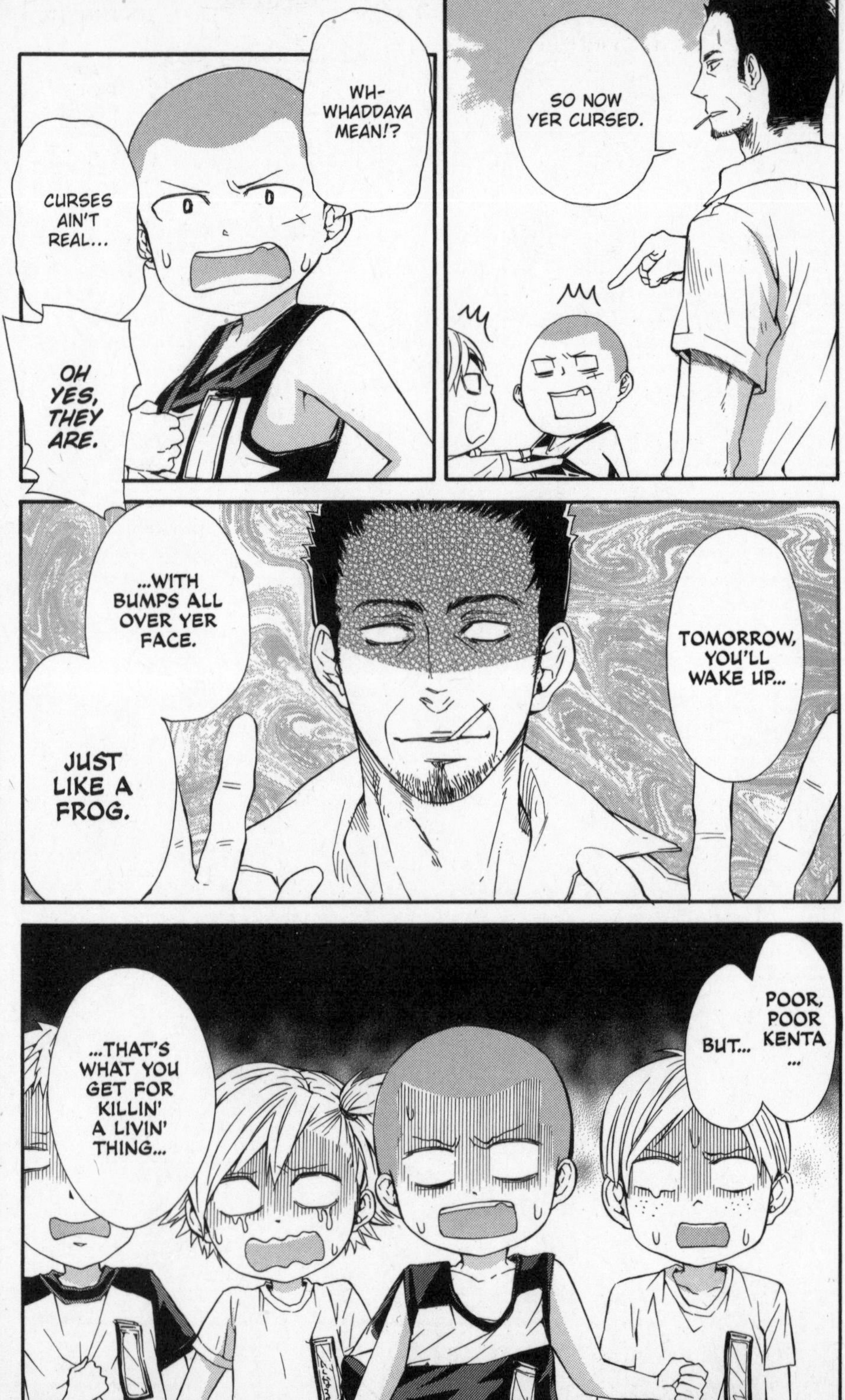
SO NOW YER CURSED.
WH- WHADDAYA MEAN!?
CURSES AIN'T REAL...
OH YES, THEY ARE.
TOMORROW, YOU'LL WAKE UP...
...WITH BUMPS ALL OVER YER FACE.
JUST LIKE A FROG.
POOR, POOR KENTA ...
BUT...
...THAT'S WHAT YOU GET FOR KILLIN' A LIVIN' THING...

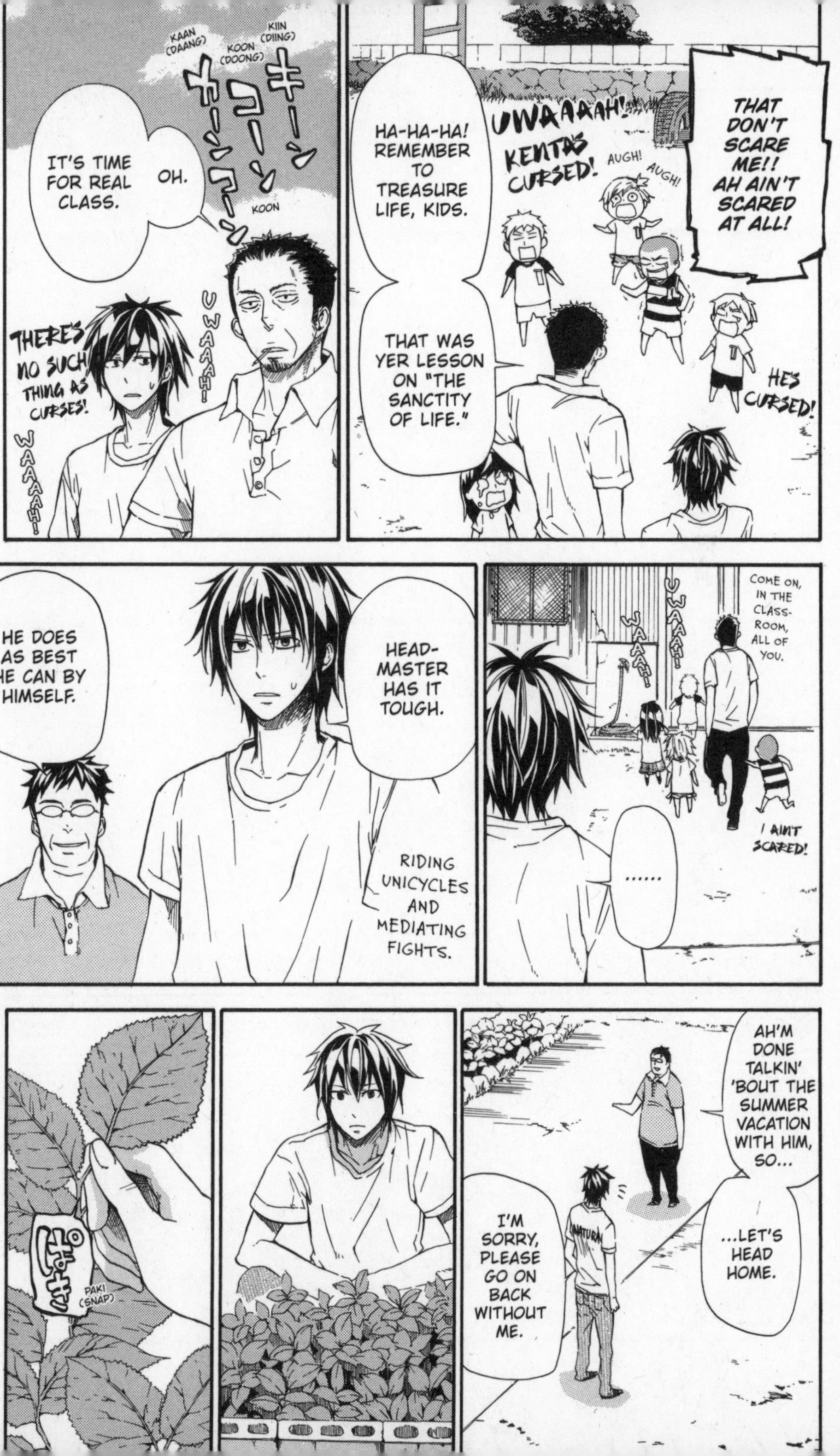
THAT DON'T SCARE ME!! AH AIN'T SCARED AT ALL!
UWAAAAH! KENTA'S CURSED!
AUGH!
AUGH!
HA-HA-HA! REMEMBER TO TREASURE LIFE, KIDS.
THAT WAS YER LESSON ON "THE SANCTITY OF LIFE."
HE'S CURSED!
KIIN (DIING)
KOON (DOONG)
KAAN (DAANG)
KOON
OH.
IT'S TIME FOR REAL CLASS.
UWAAAAH!
THERE'S NO SUCH THING AS CURSES!
WAAAAAH!
COME ON, IN THE CLASS-ROOM, ALL OF YOU.
UWAAAH!
WAAAH!
I AIN'T SCARED!
......
HEAD-MASTER HAS IT TOUGH.
HE DOES AS BEST HE CAN BY HIMSELF.
RIDING UNICYCLES AND MEDIATING FIGHTS.
AH'M DONE TALKIN' 'BOUT THE SUMMER VACATION WITH HIM, SO...
...LET'S HEAD HOME.
I'M SORRY, PLEASE GO ON BACK WITHOUT ME.
PAKI (SNAP)

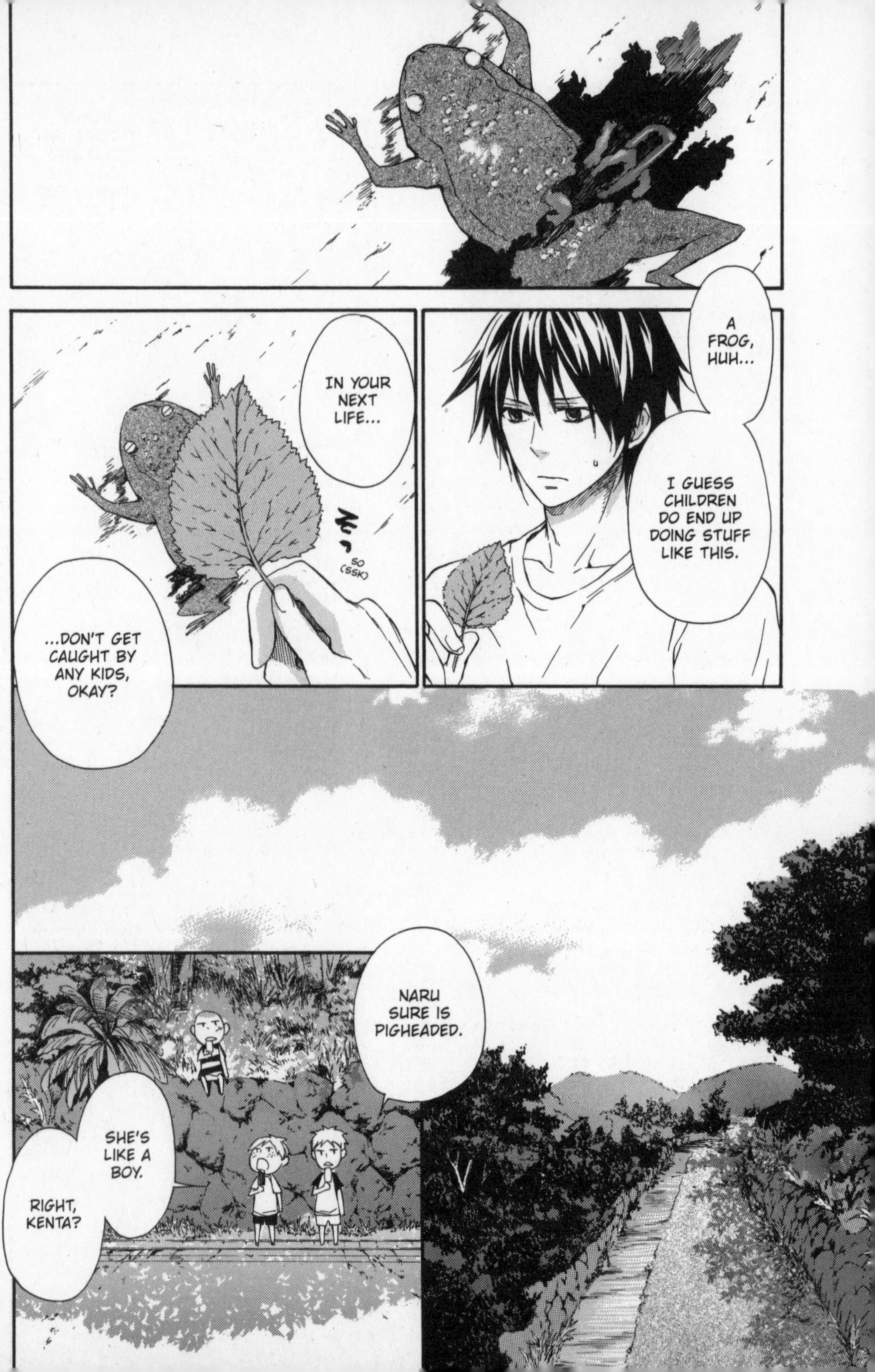
A FROG, HUH...
I GUESS CHILDREN DO END UP DOING STUFF LIKE THIS.
IN YOUR NEXT LIFE...
SO (SSK)
...DON'T GET CAUGHT BY ANY KIDS, OKAY?
NARU SURE IS PIGHEADED.
SHE'S LIKE A BOY.
RIGHT, KENTA?

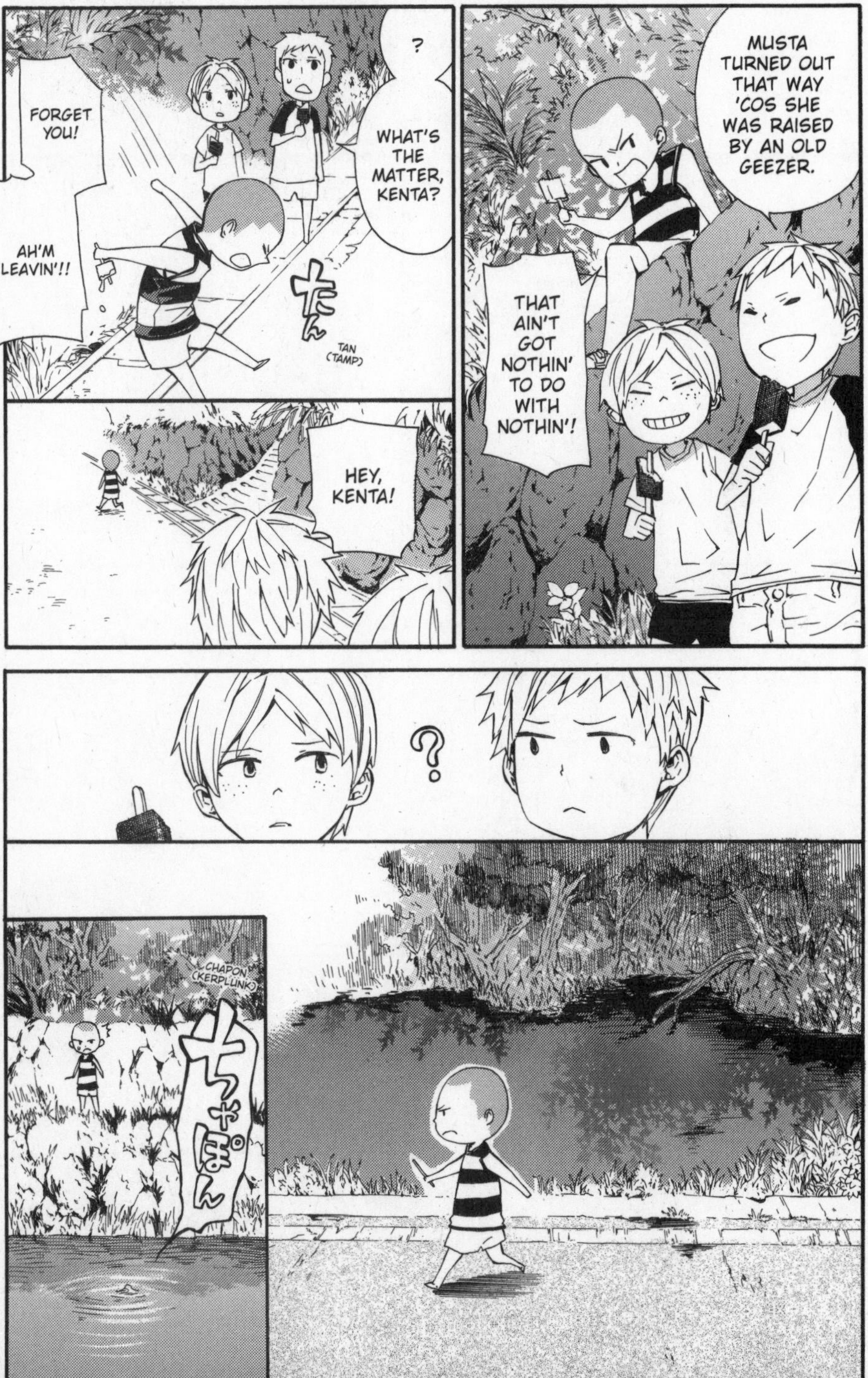
MUSTA TURNED OUT THAT WAY 'COS SHE WAS RAISED BY AN OLD GEEZER.
THAT AIN'T GOT NOTHIN' TO DO WITH NOTHIN'!
?
WHAT'S THE MATTER, KENTA?
たん
TAN (TAMP)
FORGET YOU!
AH'M LEAVIN'!!
HEY, KENTA!
?
ちゃぽん
CHAPON (KERPLUNK)

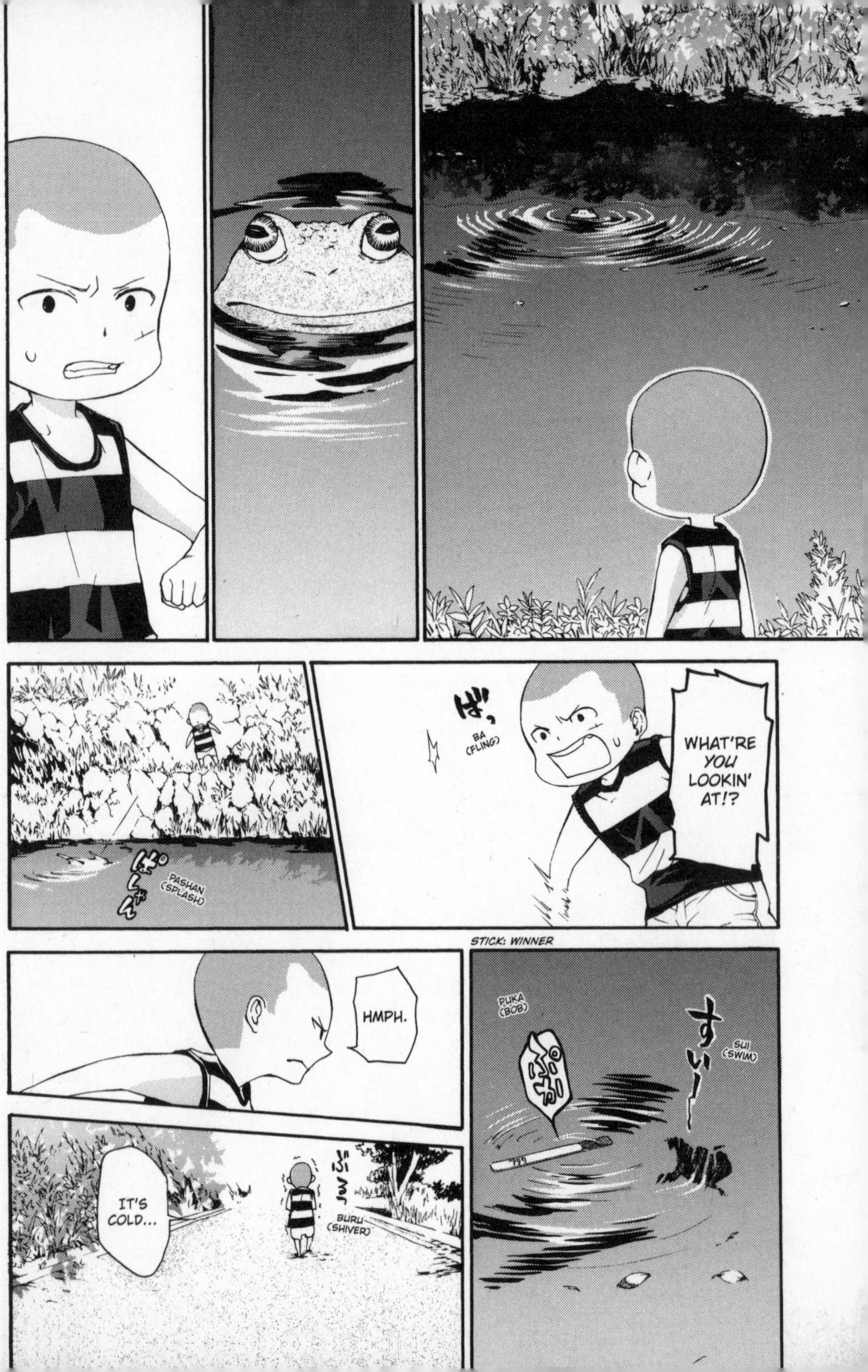
BA
(FLING)
WHAT'RE YOU LOOKIN' AT!?
PASHAN
(SPLASH)
STICK: WINNER
PUKA
(BOB)
SUI
(SWIM)
HMPH.
BURU
(SHIVER)
IT'S COLD...

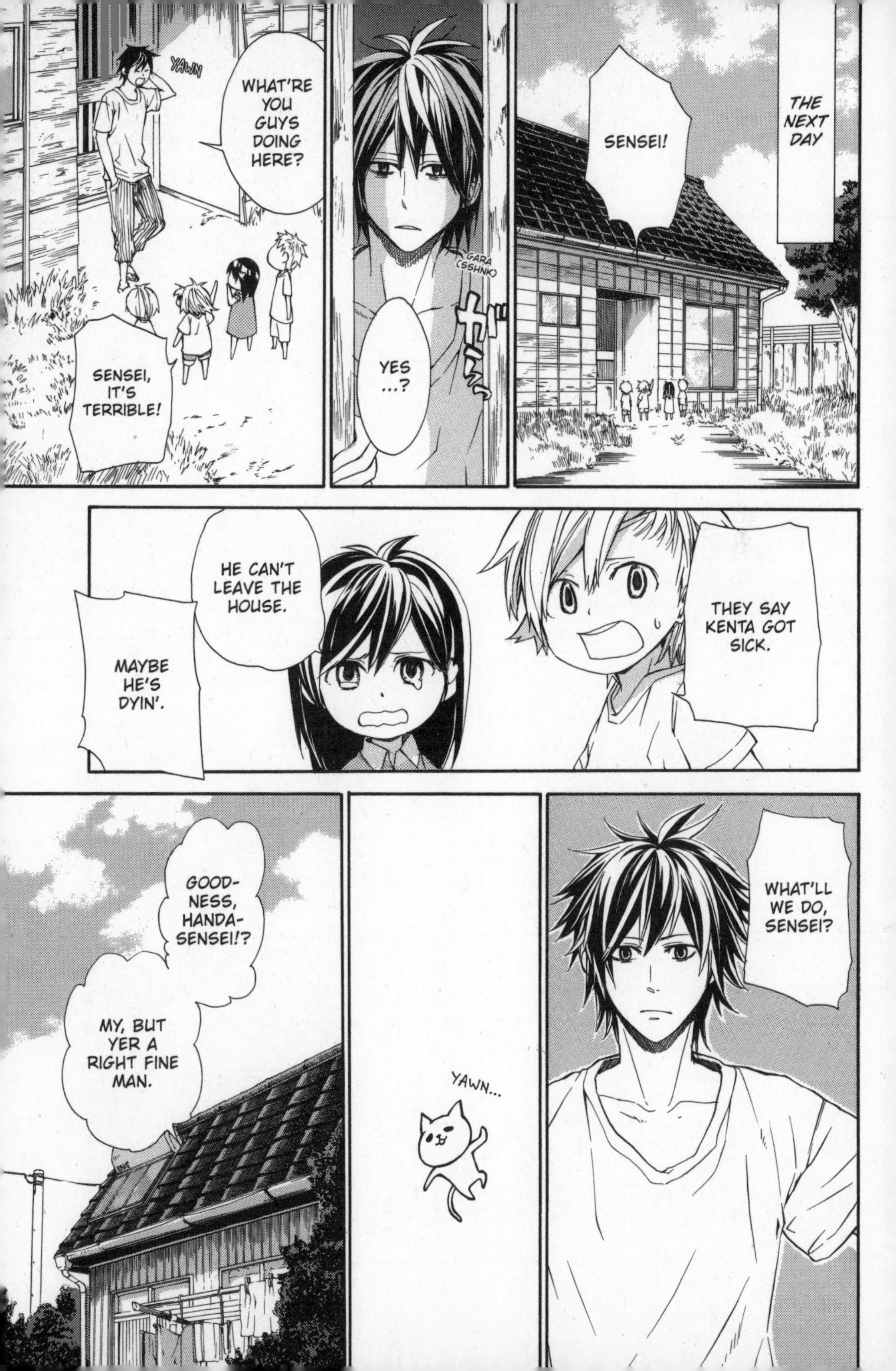
THE NEXT DAY
SENSEI!
GARA (SSHNK)
YES ...?
WHAT'RE YOU GUYS DOING HERE?
YAWN
SENSEI, IT'S TERRIBLE!
THEY SAY KENTA GOT SICK.
HE CAN'T LEAVE THE HOUSE.
MAYBE HE'S DYIN'.
WHAT'LL WE DO, SENSEI?
YAWN...
GOOD-NESS, HANDA-SENSEI!?
MY, BUT YER A RIGHT FINE MAN.

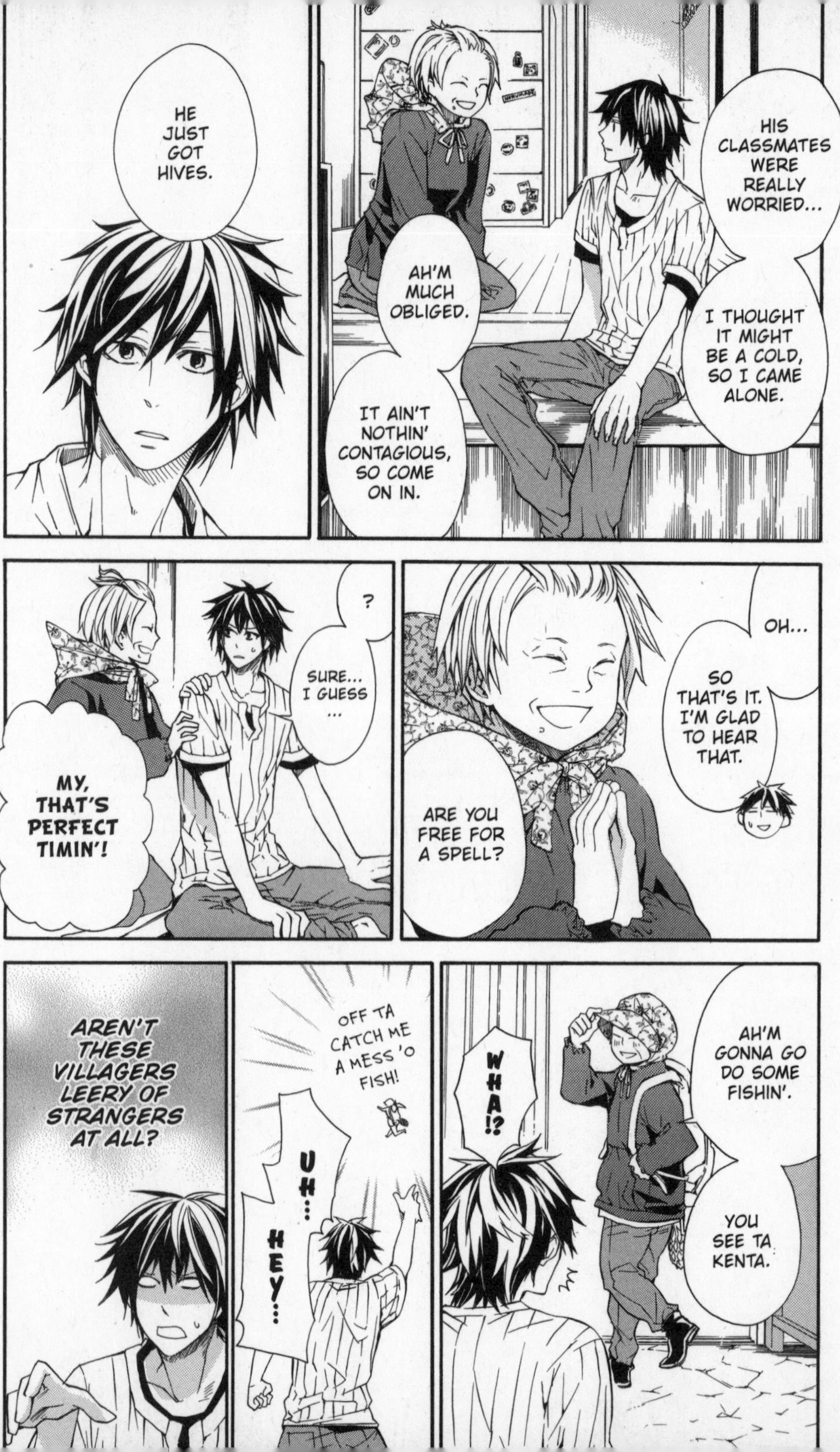
HIS CLASSMATES WERE REALLY WORRIED...
I THOUGHT IT MIGHT BE A COLD, SO I CAME ALONE.
AH'M MUCH OBLIGED.
IT AIN'T NOTHIN' CONTAGIOUS, SO COME ON IN.
HE JUST GOT HIVES.
OH...
SO THAT'S IT. I'M GLAD TO HEAR THAT.
ARE YOU FREE FOR A SPELL?
?
SURE... I GUESS ...
MY, THAT'S PERFECT TIMIN'!
AH'M GONNA GO DO SOME FISHIN'.
YOU SEE TA KENTA.
WHA!?
OFF TA CATCH ME A MESS 'O FISH!
UH... HEY...
AREN'T THESE VILLAGERS LEERY OF STRANGERS AT ALL?

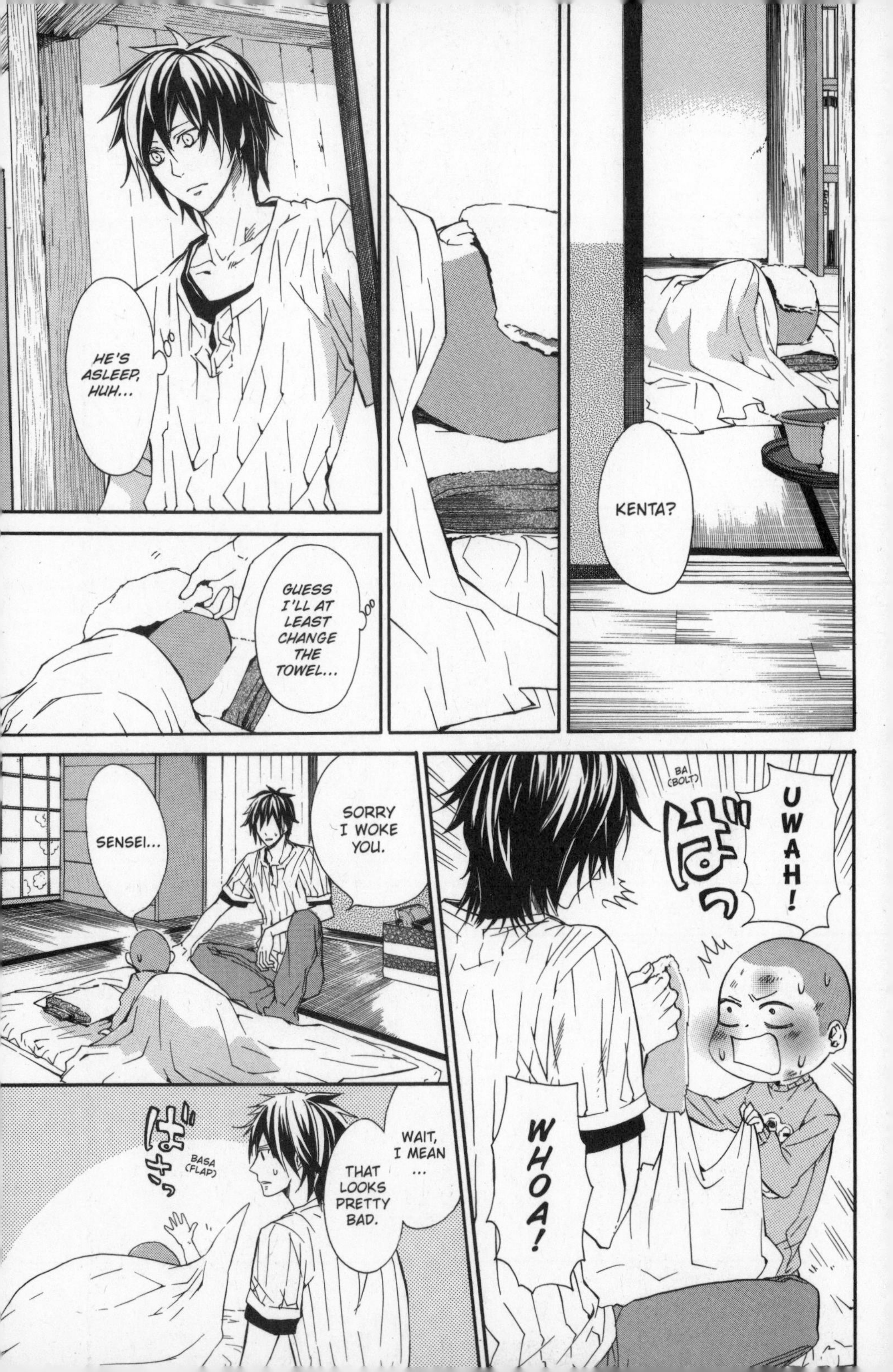
KENTA?
HE'S ASLEEP, HUH...
GUESS I'LL AT LEAST CHANGE THE TOWEL...
ばっ
BA (BOLT)
UWAH!
WHOA!
SORRY I WOKE YOU.
SENSEI...
WAIT, I MEAN ...
THAT LOOKS PRETTY BAD.
ばさっ
BASA (FLAP)

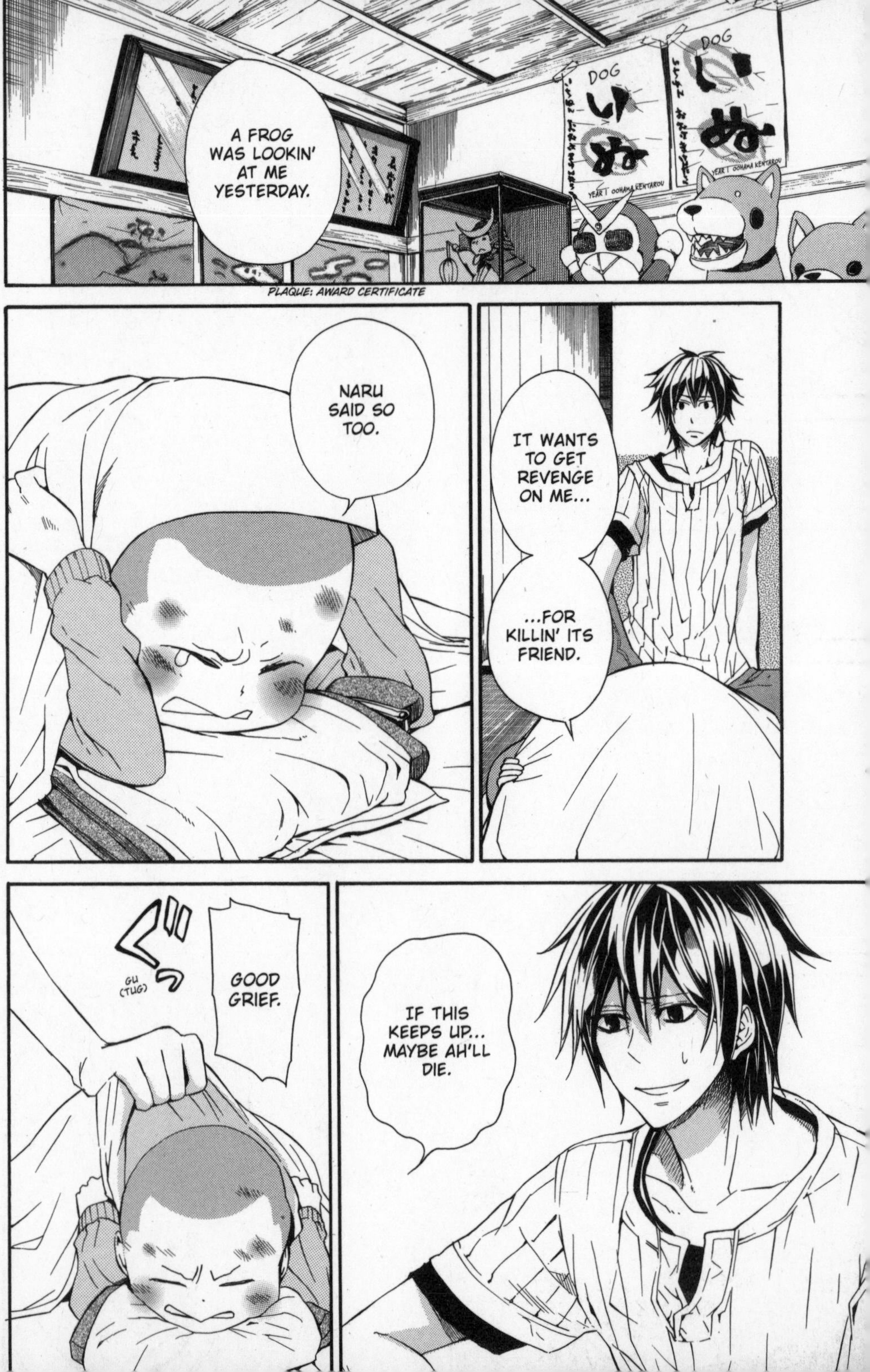
A FROG WAS LOOKIN' AT ME YESTERDAY.
DOG
YEAR 1 OOHAMA KENTAROU
DOG
YEAR 1 OOHAMA KENTAROU
PLAQUE: AWARD CERTIFICATE
IT WANTS TO GET REVENGE ON ME...
...FOR KILLIN' ITS FRIEND.
NARU SAID SO TOO.
IF THIS KEEPS UP... MAYBE AH'LL DIE.
GOOD GRIEF.
GU (TUG)

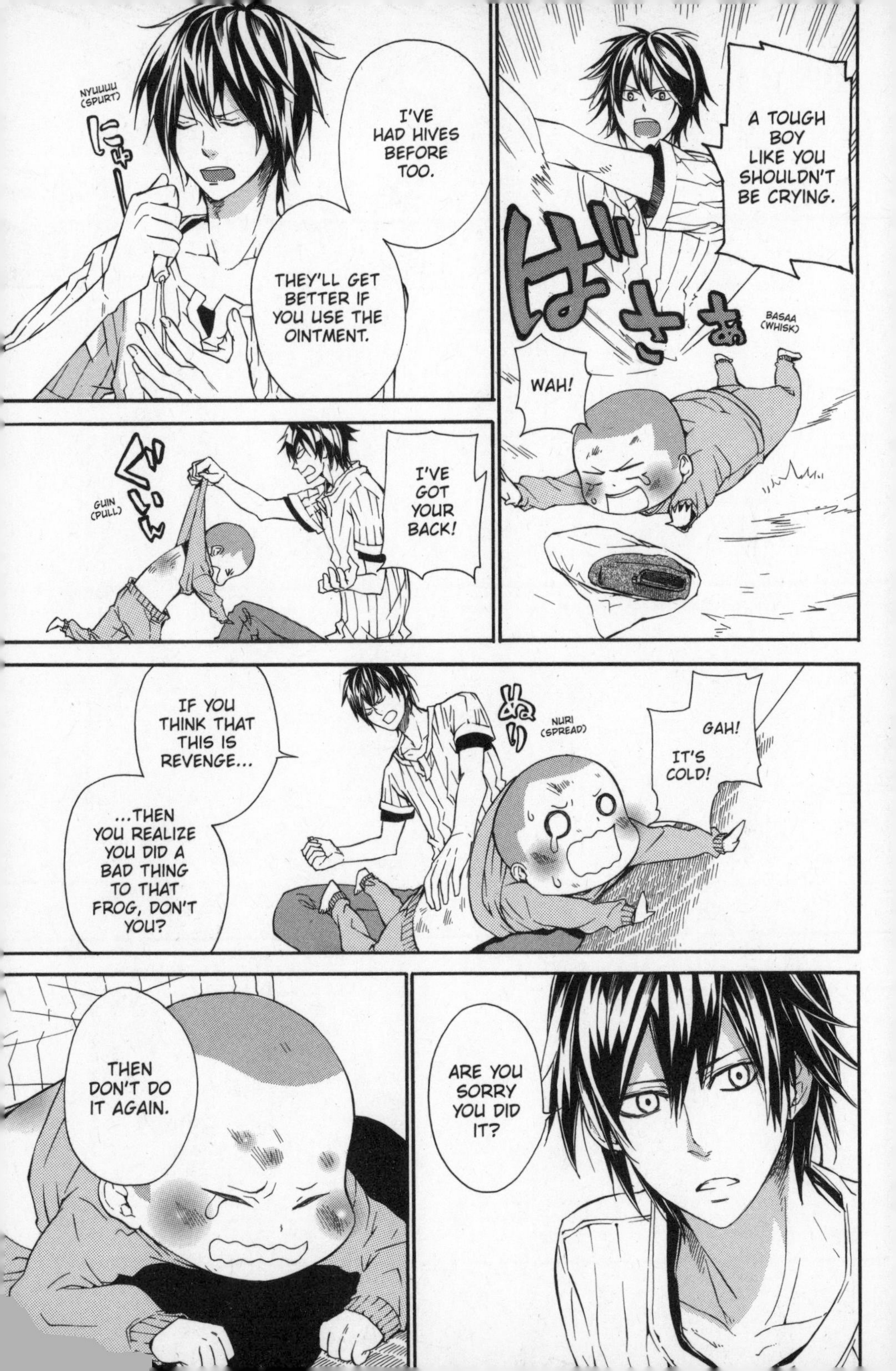

A TOUGH BOY LIKE YOU SHOULDN'T BE CRYING.
ばさぁ
BASAA (WHISK)
WAH!
I'VE HAD HIVES BEFORE TOO.
THEY'LL GET BETTER IF YOU USE THE OINTMENT.
にゅ
NYUUUU (SPURT)
I'VE GOT YOUR BACK!
ぐいん
GUIN (PULL)
GAH!
IT'S COLD!
ぬり
NURI (SPREAD)
IF YOU THINK THAT THIS IS REVENGE...
...THEN YOU REALIZE YOU DID A BAD THING TO THAT FROG, DON'T YOU?
ARE YOU SORRY YOU DID IT?
THEN DON'T DO IT AGAIN.

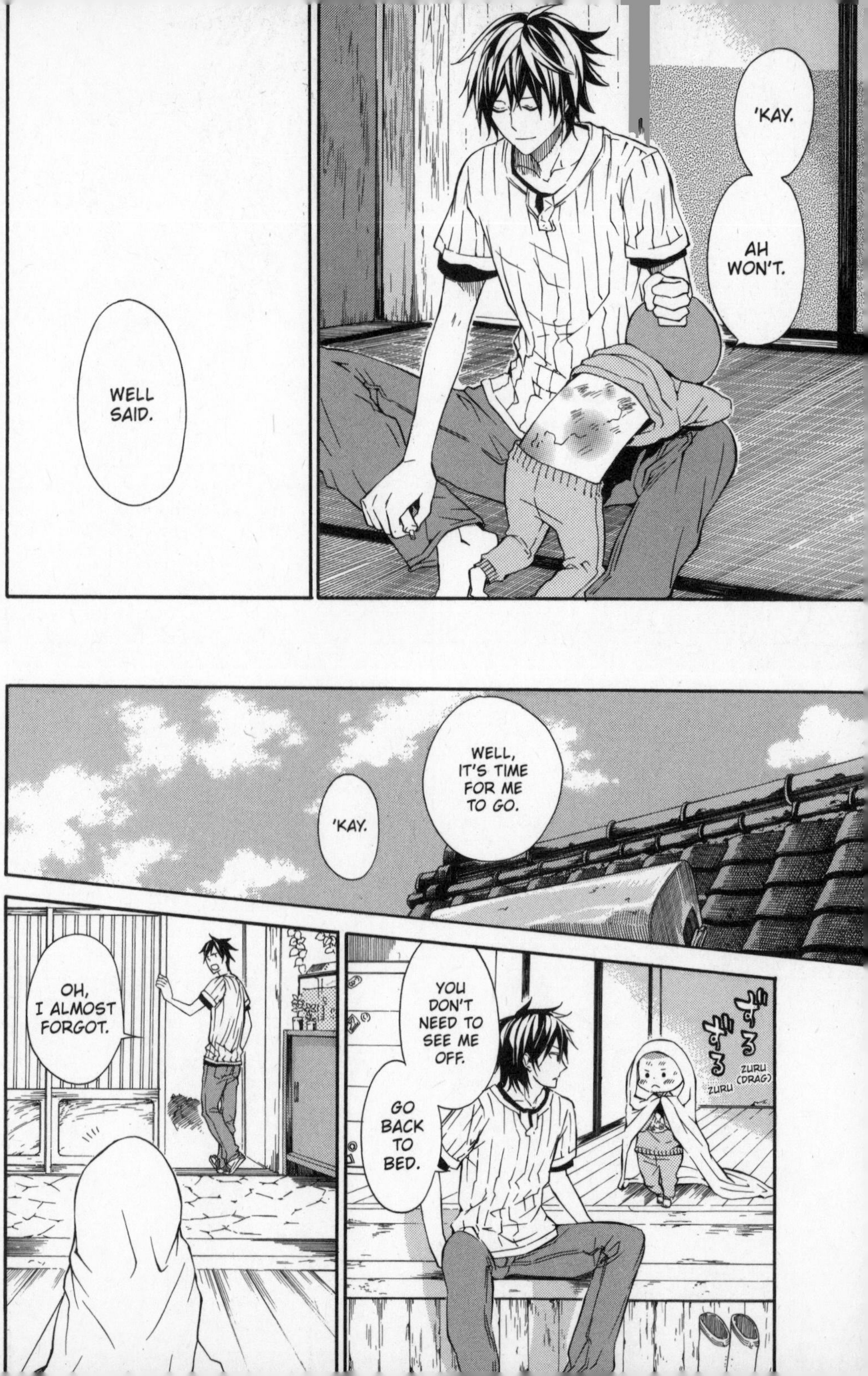
'KAY.
AH WON'T.
WELL SAID.
WELL, IT'S TIME FOR ME TO GO.
'KAY.
YOU DON'T NEED TO SEE ME OFF.
GO BACK TO BED.
ずるずる
ZURU ZURU (DRAG)
OH, I ALMOST FORGOT.

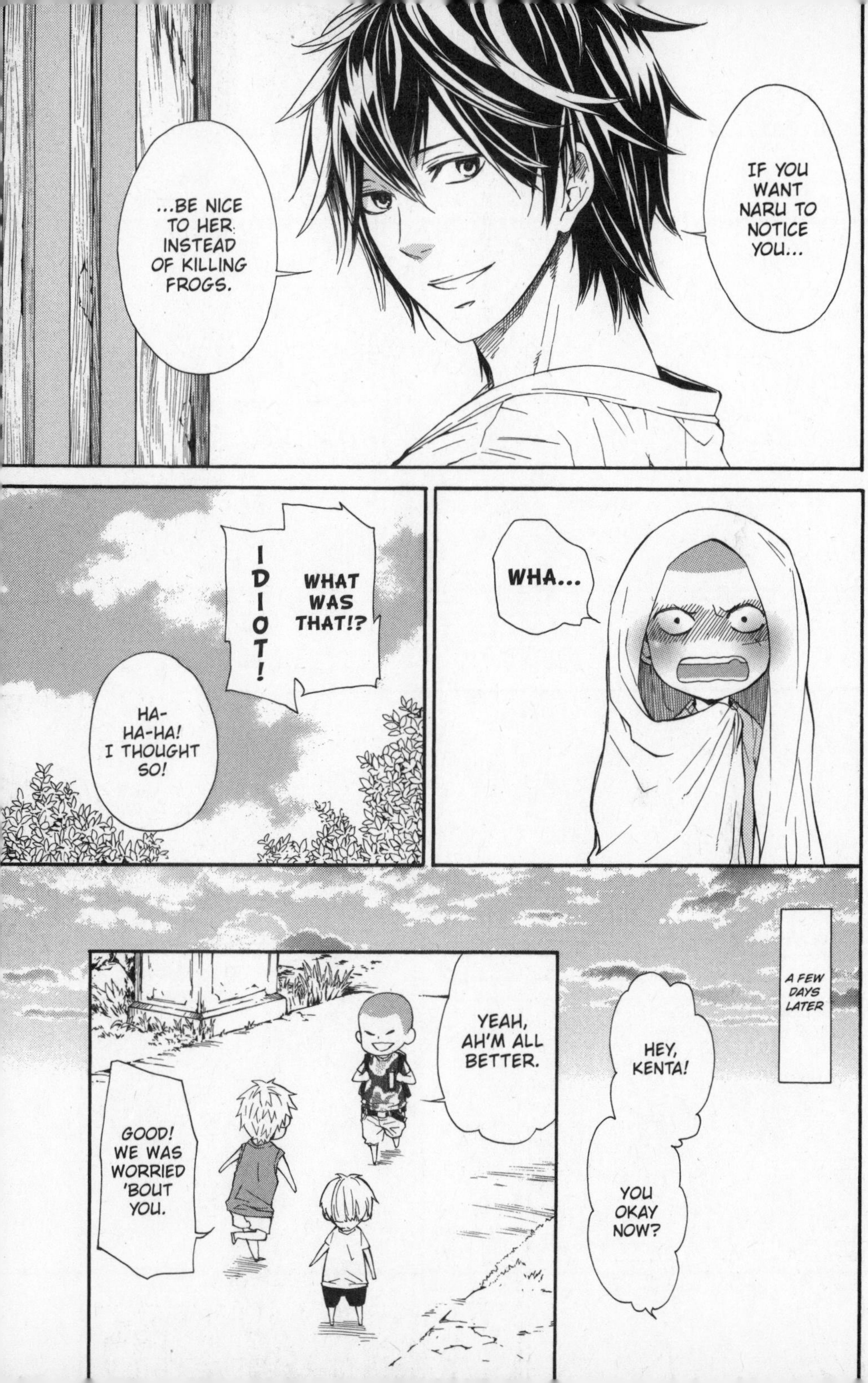
IF YOU WANT NARU TO NOTICE YOU...
...BE NICE TO HER INSTEAD OF KILLING FROGS.
WHA...
WHAT WAS THAT!?
IDIOT!
HA-HA-HA! I THOUGHT SO!
A FEW DAYS LATER
HEY, KENTA!
YOU OKAY NOW?
YEAH, AH'M ALL BETTER.
GOOD! WE WAS WORRIED 'BOUT YOU.

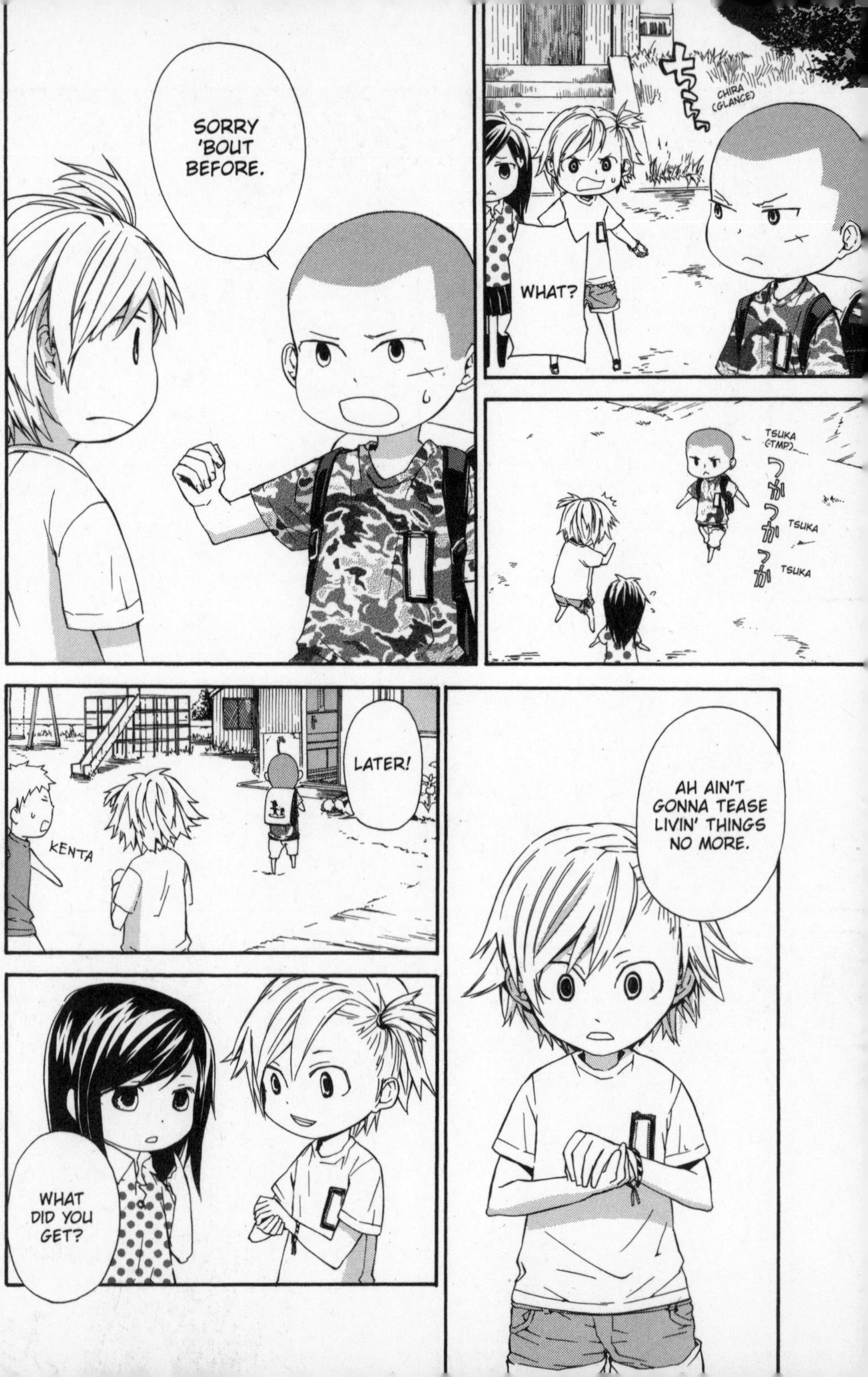

CHIRA (GLANCE)
WHAT?
TSUKA (TMP)
つかつかつか
TSUKA
TSUKA
SORRY 'BOUT BEFORE.
AH AIN'T GONNA TEASE LIVIN' THINGS NO MORE.
LATER!
KENTA
WHAT DID YOU GET?

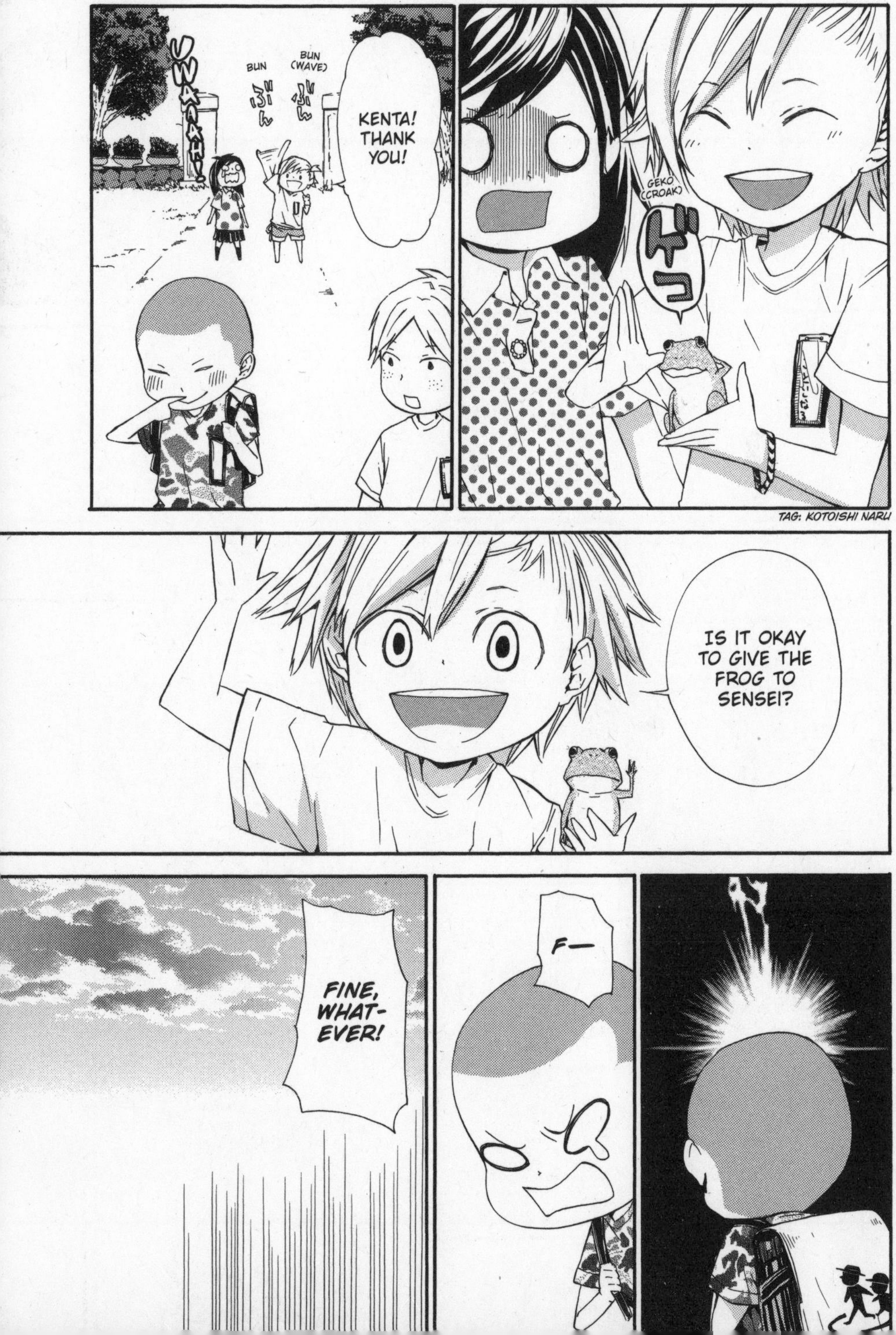
GEKO (CROAK)
ゲコッ
KENTA! THANK YOU!
BUN (WAVE)
ぶん
BUN
ぶん
UWAAAH!
TAG: KOTOISHI NARU
IS IT OKAY TO GIVE THE FROG TO SENSEI?
F—
FINE, WHATEVER!

ACT.3.5
HITOKKURUMA
(Translation: Unicycle)

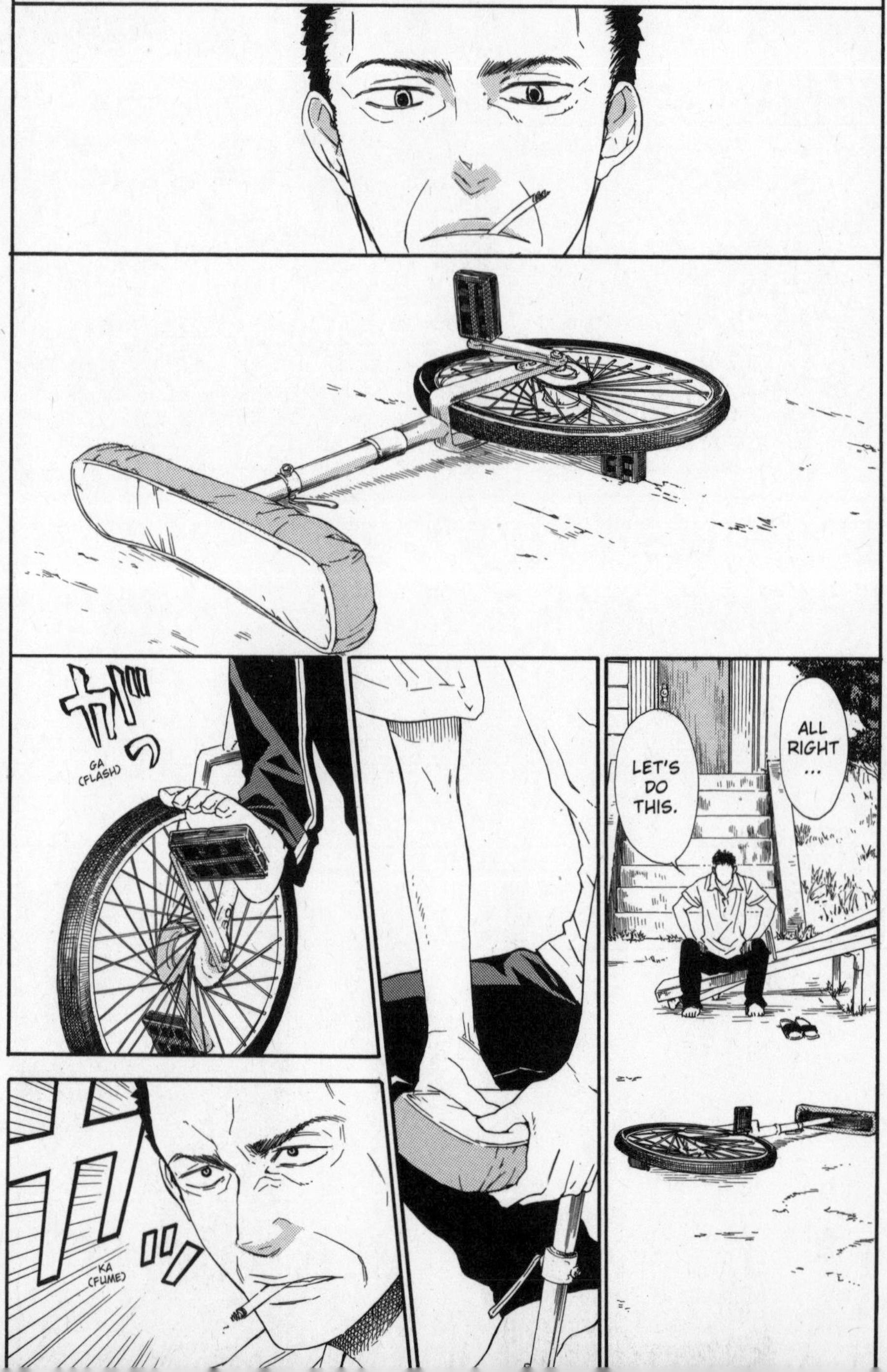
ALL RIGHT ...
LET'S DO THIS.
GA (FLASH)
KA (FUME)

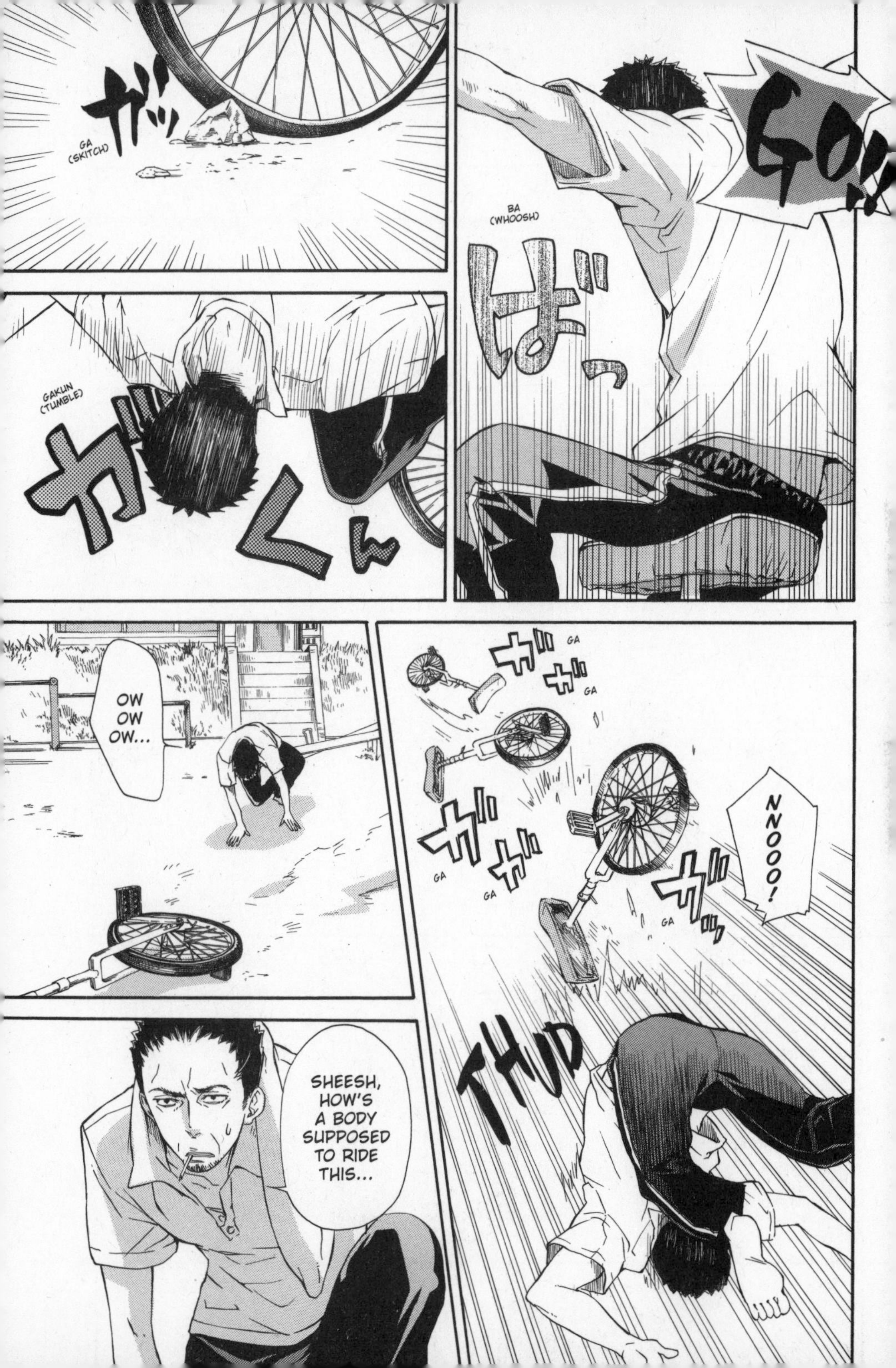
GO!!
BA (WHOOSH)
GA (SKITCH)
GAKUN (TUMBLE)
GA
GA
NNOOOO!
GA
GA
GA
THUD
OW OW OW...
SHEESH, HOW'S A BODY SUPPOSED TO RIDE THIS...

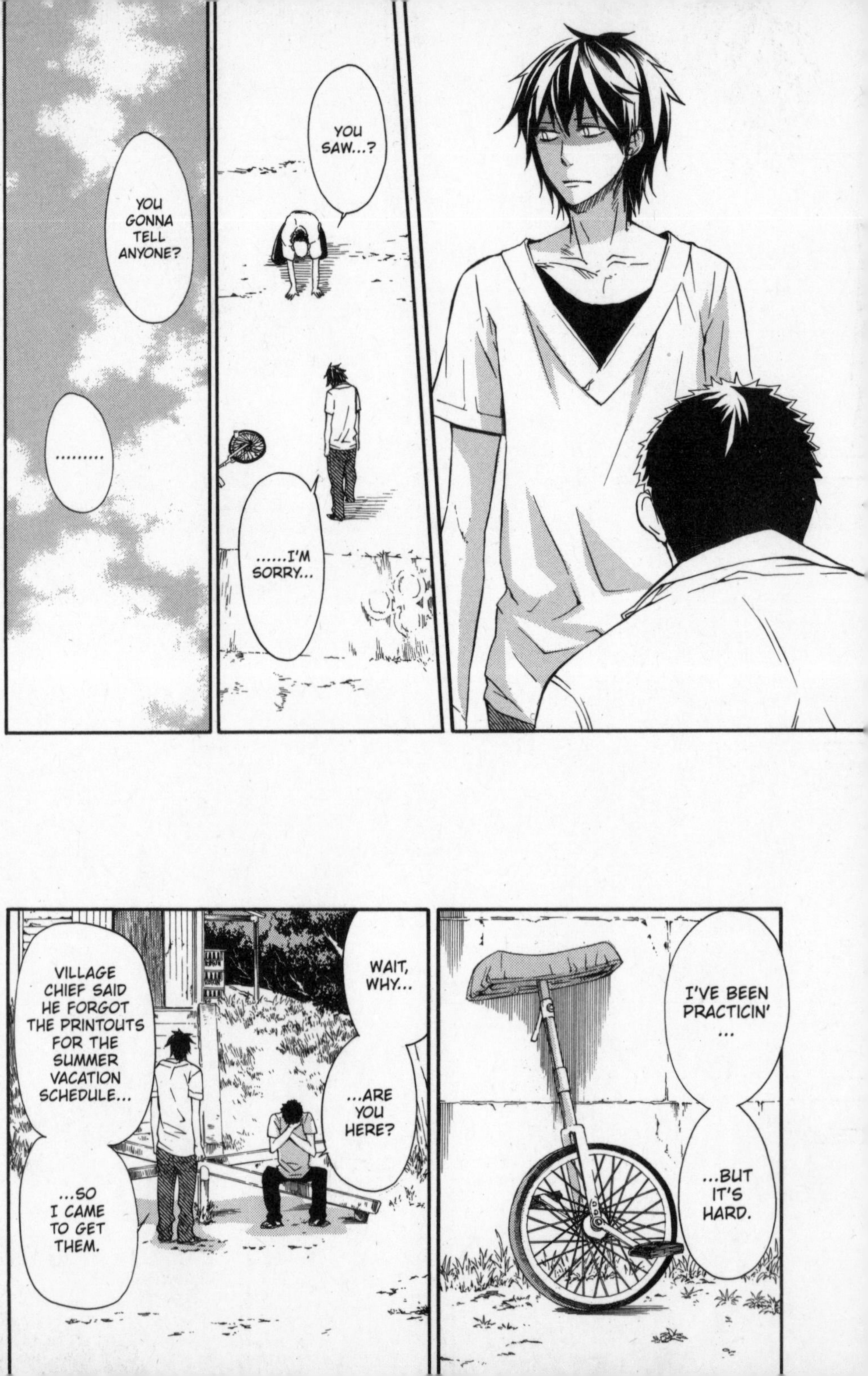
YOU SAW...?
......I'M SORRY...
YOU GONNA TELL ANYONE?
....
I'VE BEEN PRACTICIN' ...
...BUT IT'S HARD.
WAIT, WHY...
...ARE YOU HERE?
VILLAGE CHIEF SAID HE FORGOT THE PRINTOUTS FOR THE SUMMER VACATION SCHEDULE...
...SO I CAME TO GET THEM.

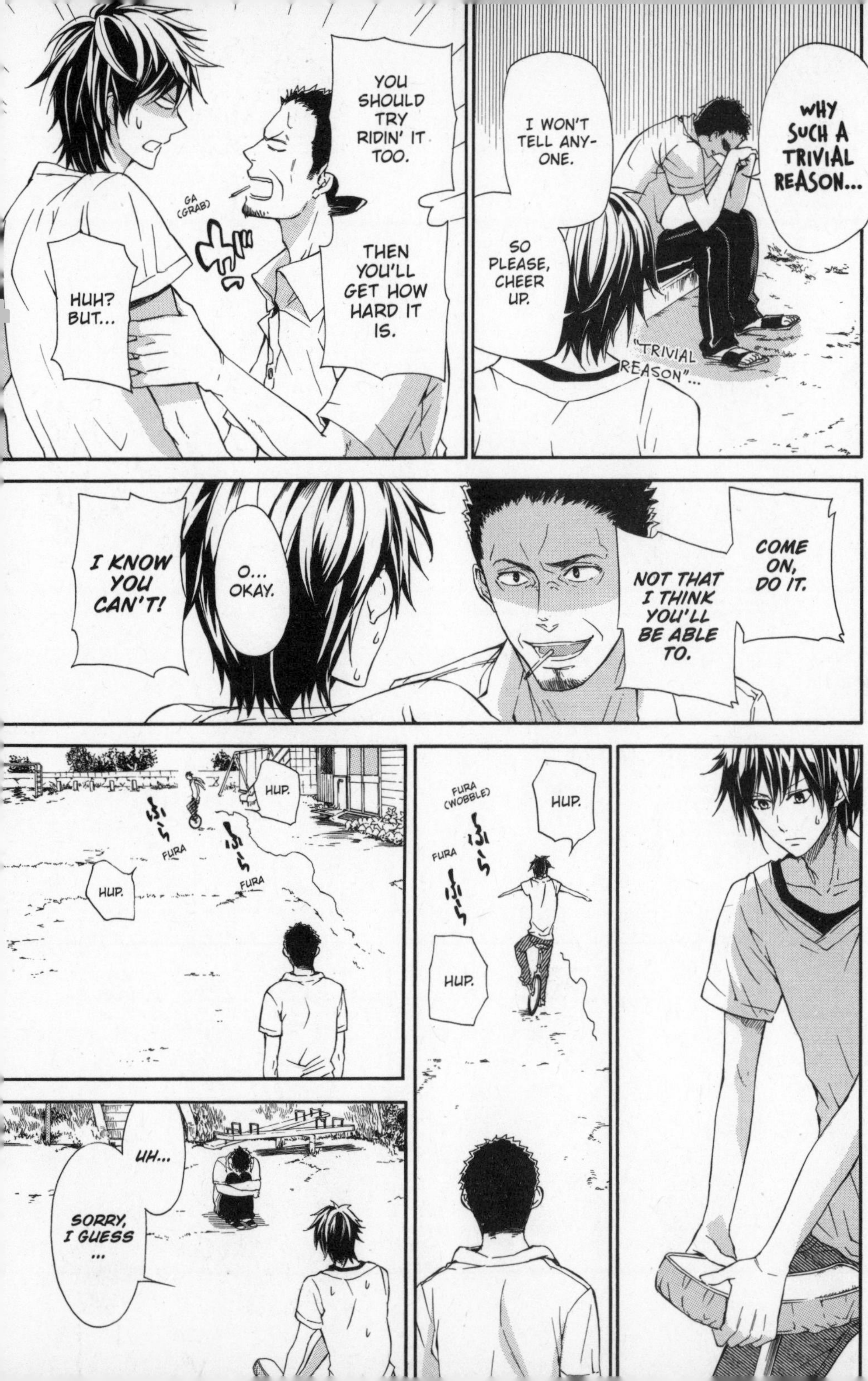
WHY SUCH A TRIVIAL REASON...
I WON'T TELL ANY-ONE.
SO PLEASE, CHEER UP.
"TRIVIAL REASON"...
YOU SHOULD TRY RIDIN' IT TOO.
THEN YOU'LL GET HOW HARD IT IS.
GA (GRAB)
HUH? BUT...
COME ON, DO IT.
NOT THAT I THINK YOU'LL BE ABLE TO.
O... OKAY.
I KNOW YOU CAN'T!
HUP.
FURA (WOBBLE)
FURA
HUP.
HUP.
FURA
FURA
HUP.
UH...
SORRY, I GUESS ...

ACT.4
ONNANKODON
(Translation: Girls)

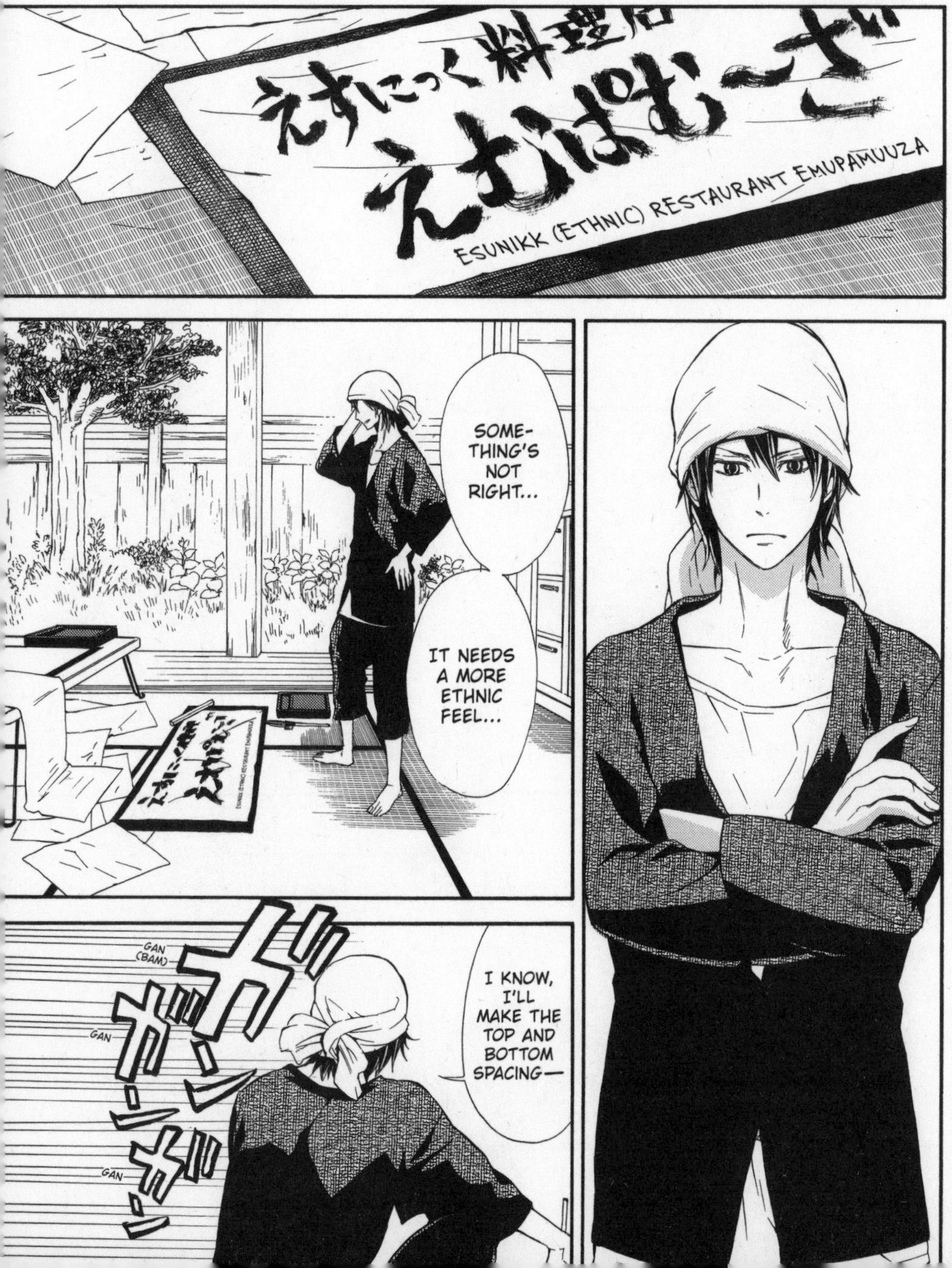
えすにっく料理店
えむぱむ～ざ
ESUNIKK (ETHNIC) RESTAURANT EMUPAMUUZA
SOME-THING'S NOT RIGHT...
IT NEEDS A MORE ETHNIC FEEL...
I KNOW, I'LL MAKE THE TOP AND BOTTOM SPACING—
GAN (BAM)
GAN
GAN

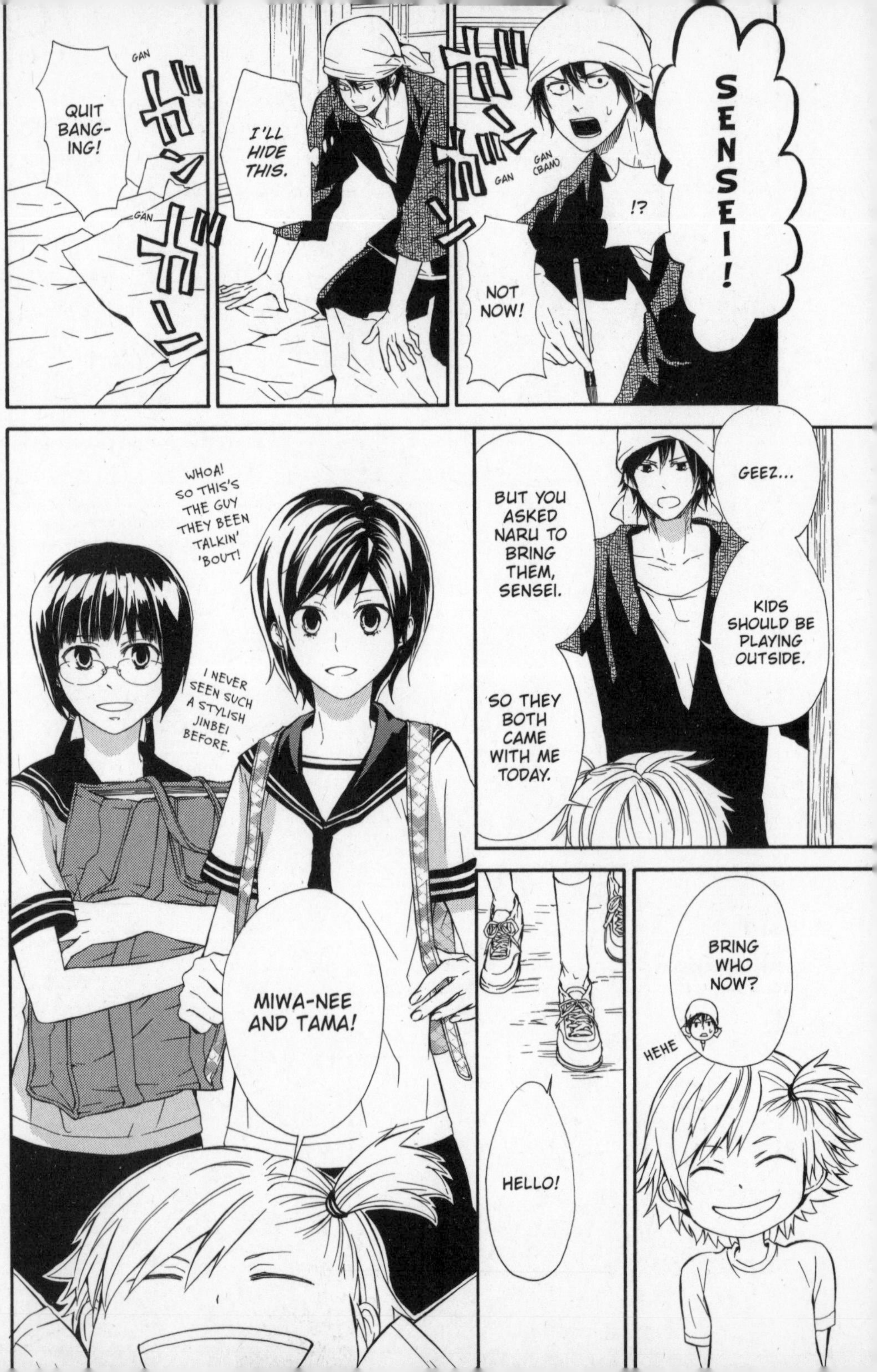
SENSEI!
!?
GAN
GAN (BAM)
NOT NOW!
I'LL HIDE THIS.
GAN
QUIT BANGING!
GAN
GEEZ...
KIDS SHOULD BE PLAYING OUTSIDE.
BUT YOU ASKED NARU TO BRING THEM, SENSEI.
SO THEY BOTH CAME WITH ME TODAY.
BRING WHO NOW?
HEHE
HELLO!
WHOA! SO THIS'S THE GUY THEY BEEN TALKIN' 'BOUT!
I NEVER SEEN SUCH A STYLISH JINBEI BEFORE.
MIWA-NEE AND TAMA!

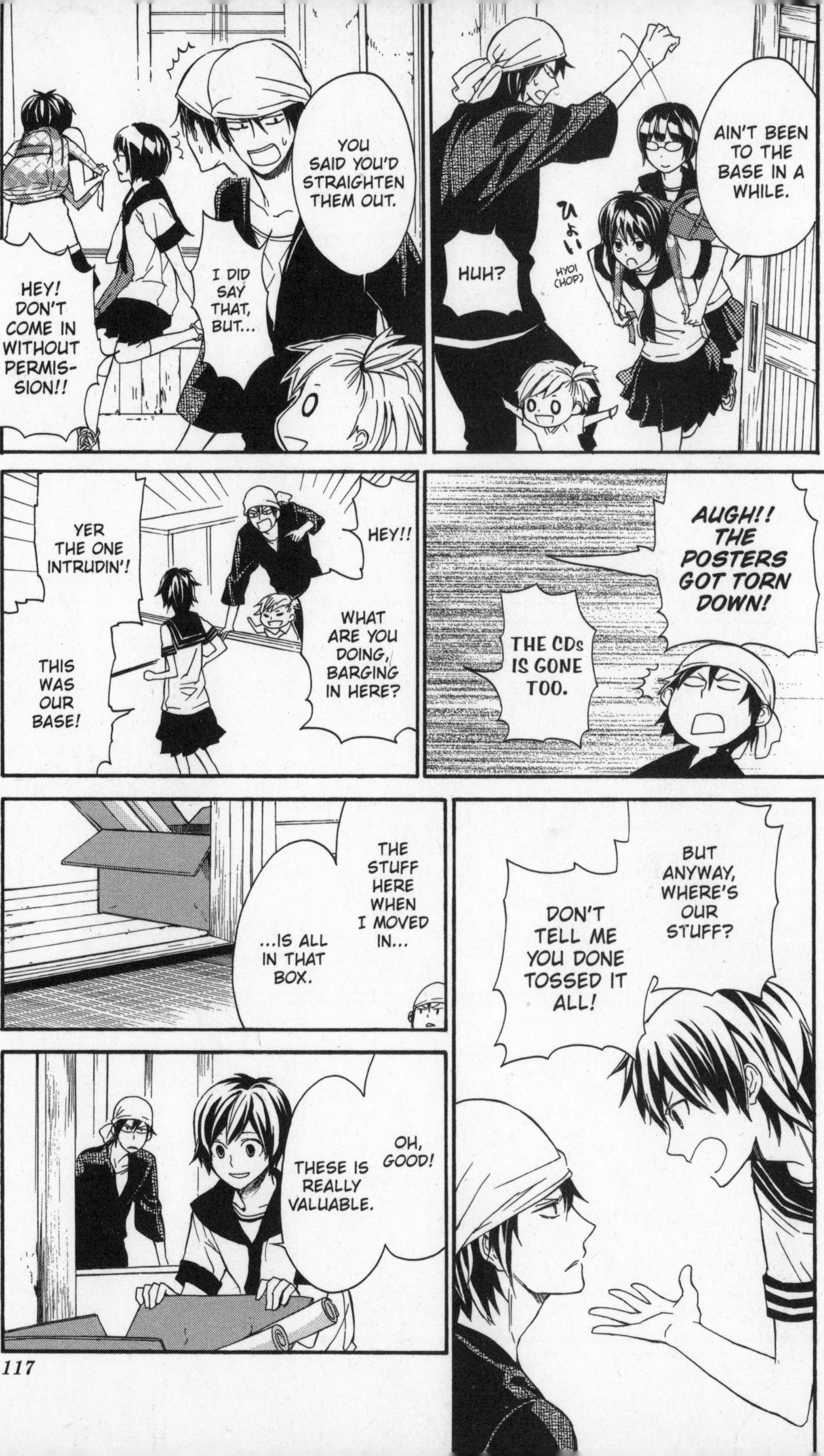
AIN'T BEEN TO THE BASE IN A WHILE.
ひょい
HYOI (HOP)
HUH?
YOU SAID YOU'D STRAIGHTEN THEM OUT.
I DID SAY THAT, BUT...
HEY! DON'T COME IN WITHOUT PERMIS-SION!!
AUGH!! THE POSTERS GOT TORN DOWN!
THE CDs IS GONE TOO.
HEY!!
WHAT ARE YOU DOING, BARGING IN HERE?
YER THE ONE INTRUDIN'!
THIS WAS OUR BASE!
BUT ANYWAY, WHERE'S OUR STUFF?
DON'T TELL ME YOU DONE TOSSED IT ALL!
THE STUFF HERE WHEN I MOVED IN...
...IS ALL IN THAT BOX.
OH, GOOD!
THESE IS REALLY VALUABLE.

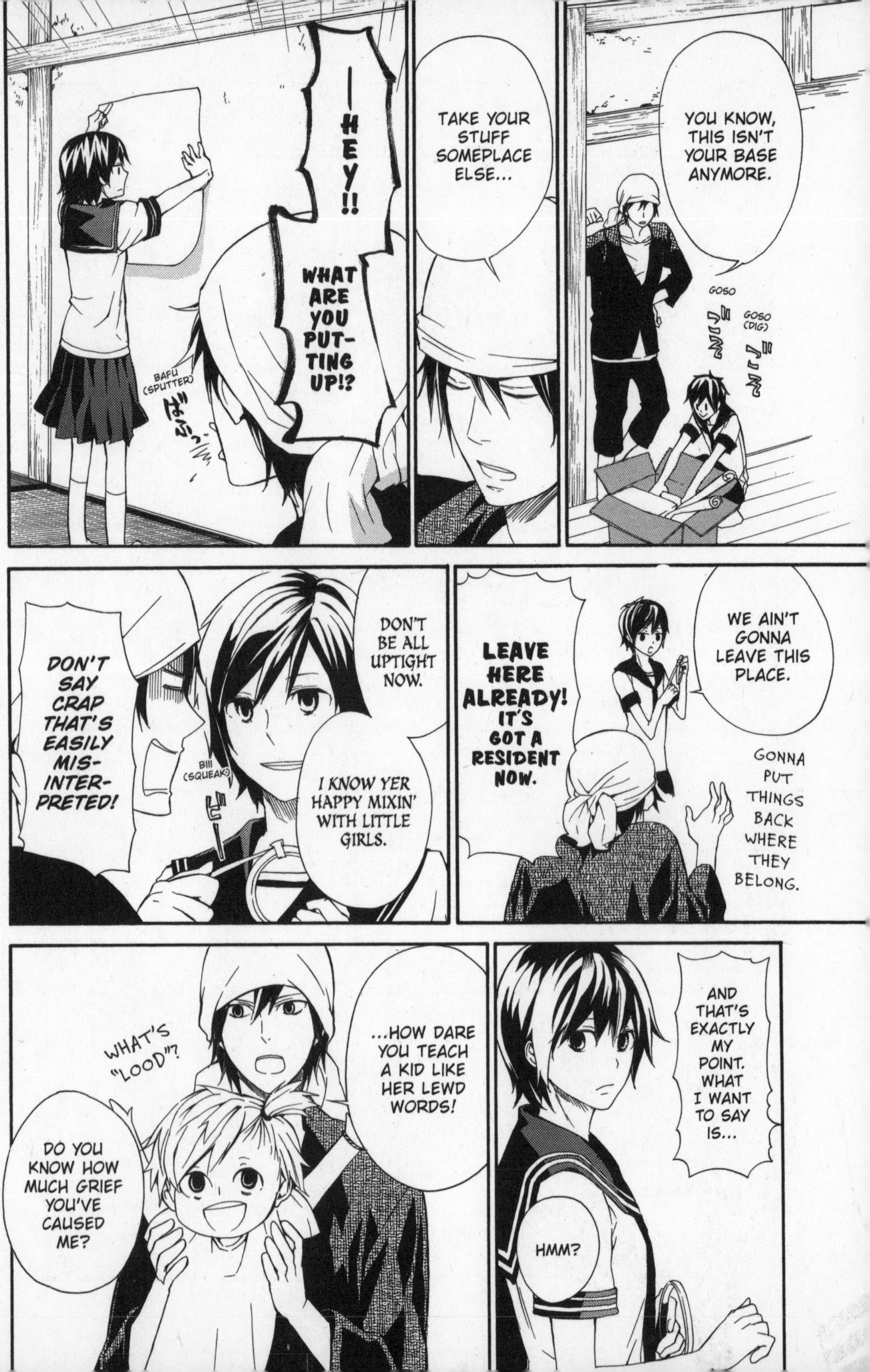

YOU KNOW, THIS ISN'T YOUR BASE ANYMORE.
GOSO
GOSO (DIG)
TAKE YOUR STUFF SOMEPLACE ELSE...
—HEY!!
WHAT ARE YOU PUT-TING UP!?
BAFU (SPUTTER)
ばふっ
WE AIN'T GONNA LEAVE THIS PLACE.
LEAVE HERE ALREADY! IT'S GOT A RESIDENT NOW.
GONNA PUT THINGS BACK WHERE THEY BELONG.
DON'T BE ALL UPTIGHT NOW.
I KNOW YER HAPPY MIXIN' WITH LITTLE GIRLS.
BIII (SQUEAK)
DON'T SAY CRAP THAT'S EASILY MIS-INTER-PRETED!
AND THAT'S EXACTLY MY POINT. WHAT I WANT TO SAY IS...
HMM?
...HOW DARE YOU TEACH A KID LIKE HER LEWD WORDS!
WHAT'S "LOOD"?
DO YOU KNOW HOW MUCH GRIEF YOU'VE CAUSED ME?

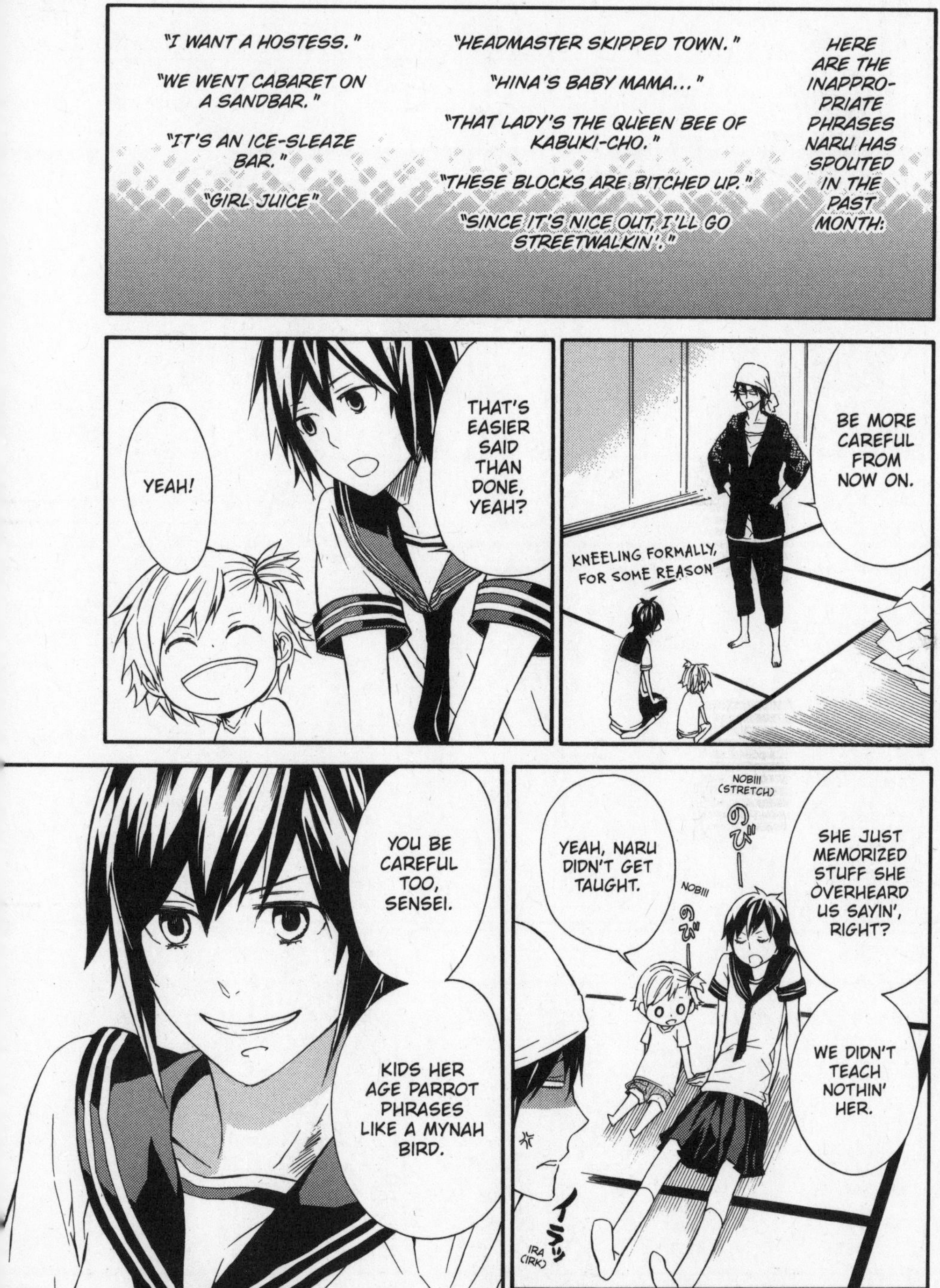
HERE ARE THE INAPPROPRIATE PHRASES NARU HAS SPOUTED IN THE PAST MONTH:
"HEADMASTER SKIPPED TOWN."
"HINA'S BABY MAMA..."
"THAT LADY'S THE QUEEN BEE OF KABUKI-CHO."
"THESE BLOCKS ARE BITCHED UP."
"SINCE IT'S NICE OUT, I'LL GO STREETWALKIN'."
"I WANT A HOSTESS."
"WE WENT CABARET ON A SANDBAR."
"IT'S AN ICE-SLEAZE BAR."
"GIRL JUICE"
BE MORE CAREFUL FROM NOW ON.
KNEELING FORMALLY, FOR SOME REASON
THAT'S EASIER SAID THAN DONE, YEAH?
YEAH!
NOBIII (STRETCH)
SHE JUST MEMORIZED STUFF SHE OVERHEARD US SAYIN', RIGHT?
YEAH, NARU DIDN'T GET TAUGHT.
NOBIII
WE DIDN'T TEACH NOTHIN' HER.
IRA (IRK)
YOU BE CAREFUL TOO, SENSEI.
KIDS HER AGE PARROT PHRASES LIKE A MYNAH BIRD.

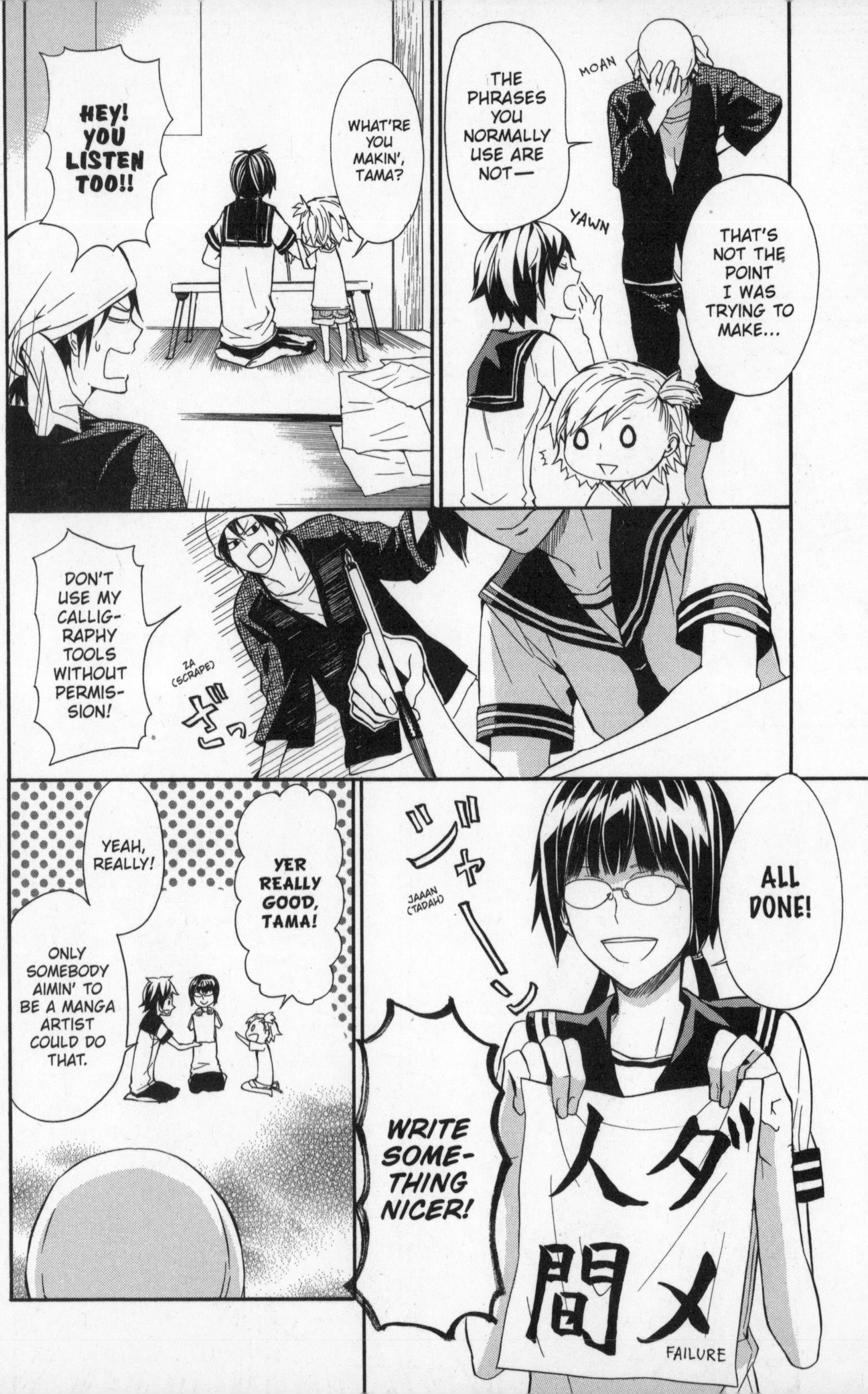
MOAN
THE PHRASES YOU NORMALLY USE ARE NOT—
THAT'S NOT THE POINT I WAS TRYING TO MAKE...
YAWN
WHAT'RE YOU MAKIN', TAMA?
HEY! YOU LISTEN TOO!!
DON'T USE MY CALLIG-RAPHY TOOLS WITHOUT PERMIS-SION!
ざっ
ZA (SCRAPE)
ALL DONE!
ジャーン
JAAAN (TADAH)
ダメ人間
FAILURE
WRITE SOME-THING NICER!
YER REALLY GOOD, TAMA!
YEAH, REALLY!
ONLY SOMEBODY AIMIN' TO BE A MANGA ARTIST COULD DO THAT.

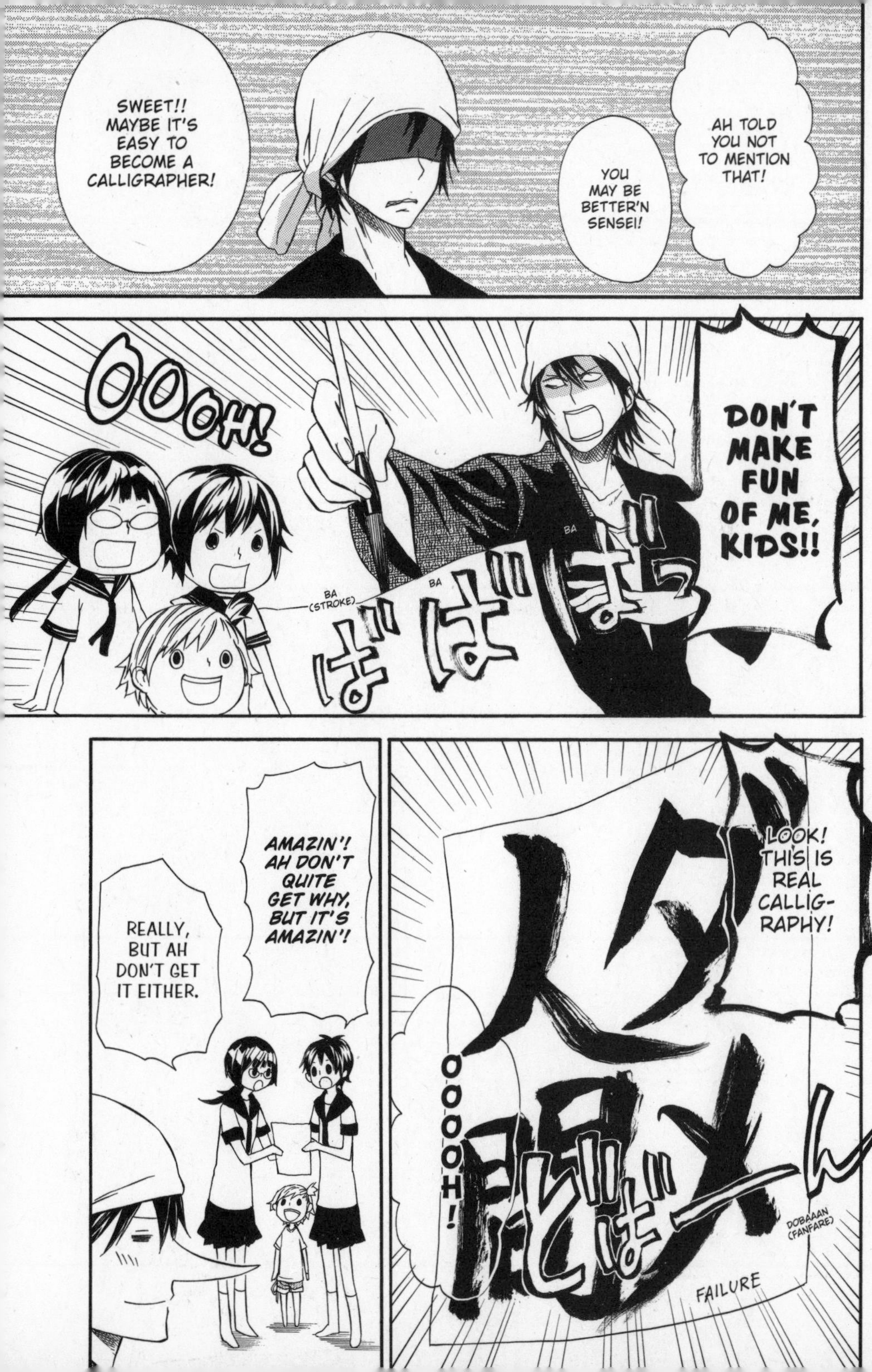
AH TOLD YOU NOT TO MENTION THAT!
YOU MAY BE BETTER'N SENSEI!
SWEET!! MAYBE IT'S EASY TO BECOME A CALLIGRAPHER!
DON'T MAKE FUN OF ME, KIDS!!
BA
BA
BA (STROKE)
OOOOH!
LOOK! THIS IS REAL CALLIG-RAPHY!
OOOOOH!
DOBAAAN (FANFARE)
FAILURE
AMAZIN'! AH DON'T QUITE GET WHY, BUT IT'S AMAZIN'!
REALLY, BUT AH DON'T GET IT EITHER.

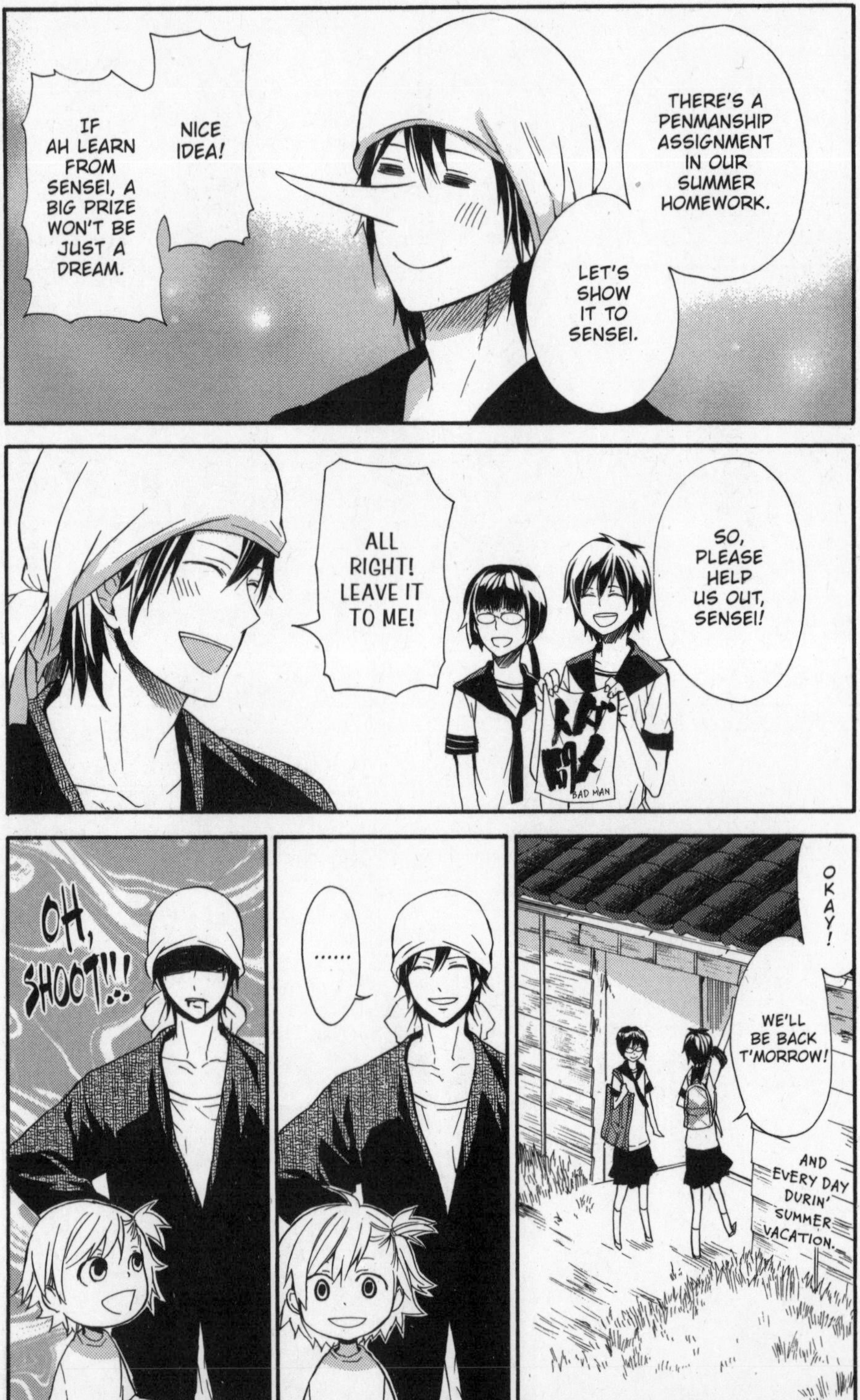
THERE'S A PENMANSHIP ASSIGNMENT IN OUR SUMMER HOMEWORK.
LET'S SHOW IT TO SENSEI.
NICE IDEA!
IF AH LEARN FROM SENSEI, A BIG PRIZE WON'T BE JUST A DREAM.
SO, PLEASE HELP US OUT, SENSEI!
BAD MAN
ALL RIGHT! LEAVE IT TO ME!
OKAY!
WE'LL BE BACK T'MORROW!
AND EVERY DAY DURIN' SUMMER VACATION.
......
OH, SHOOT!!!

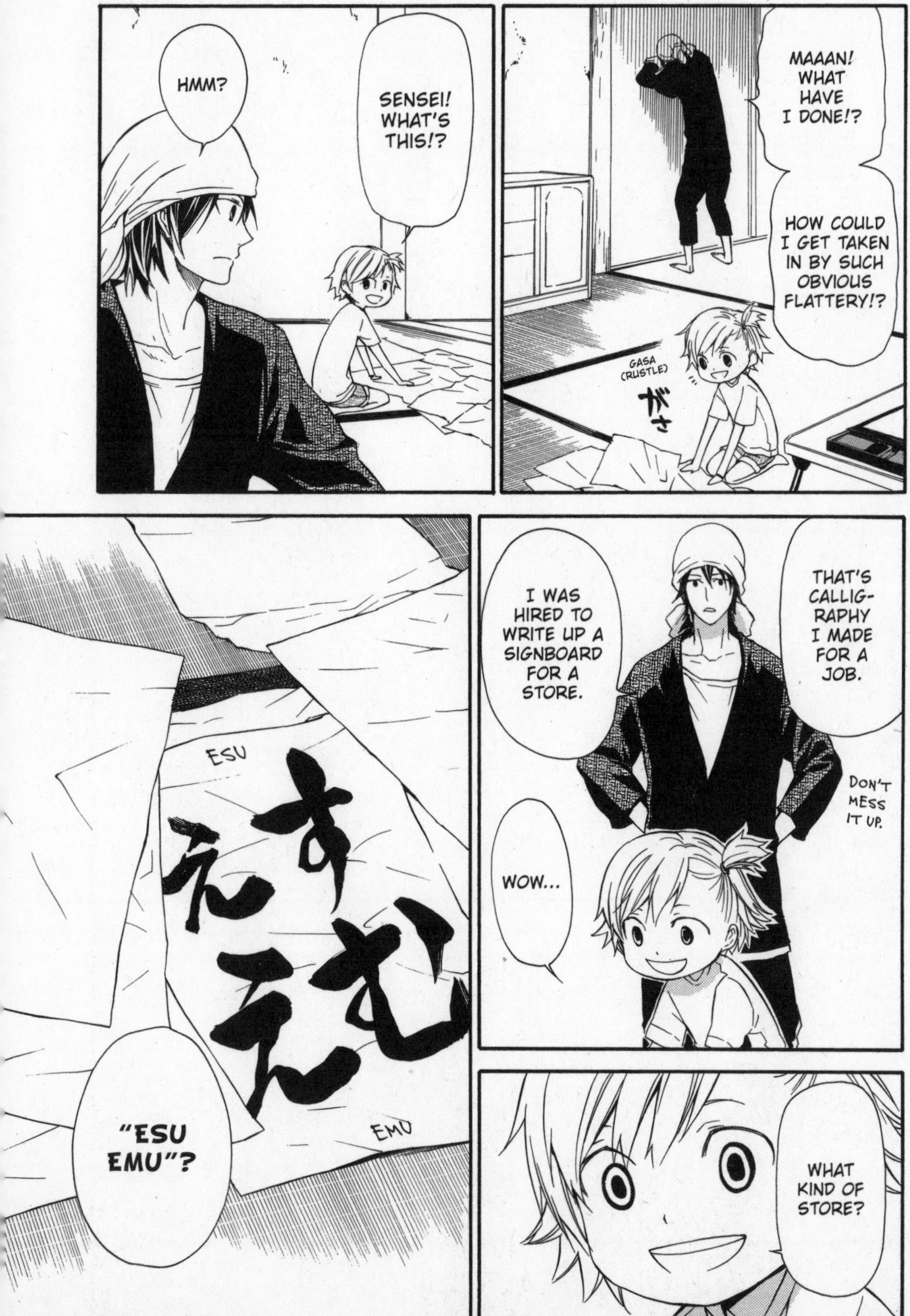
MAAAN! WHAT HAVE I DONE!?
HOW COULD I GET TAKEN IN BY SUCH OBVIOUS FLATTERY!?
GASA (RUSTLE)
がさ
SENSEI! WHAT'S THIS!?
HMM?
THAT'S CALLIG-RAPHY I MADE FOR A JOB.
I WAS HIRED TO WRITE UP A SIGNBOARD FOR A STORE.
DON'T MESS IT UP.
WOW...
WHAT KIND OF STORE?
ESU
EMU
"ESU EMU"?

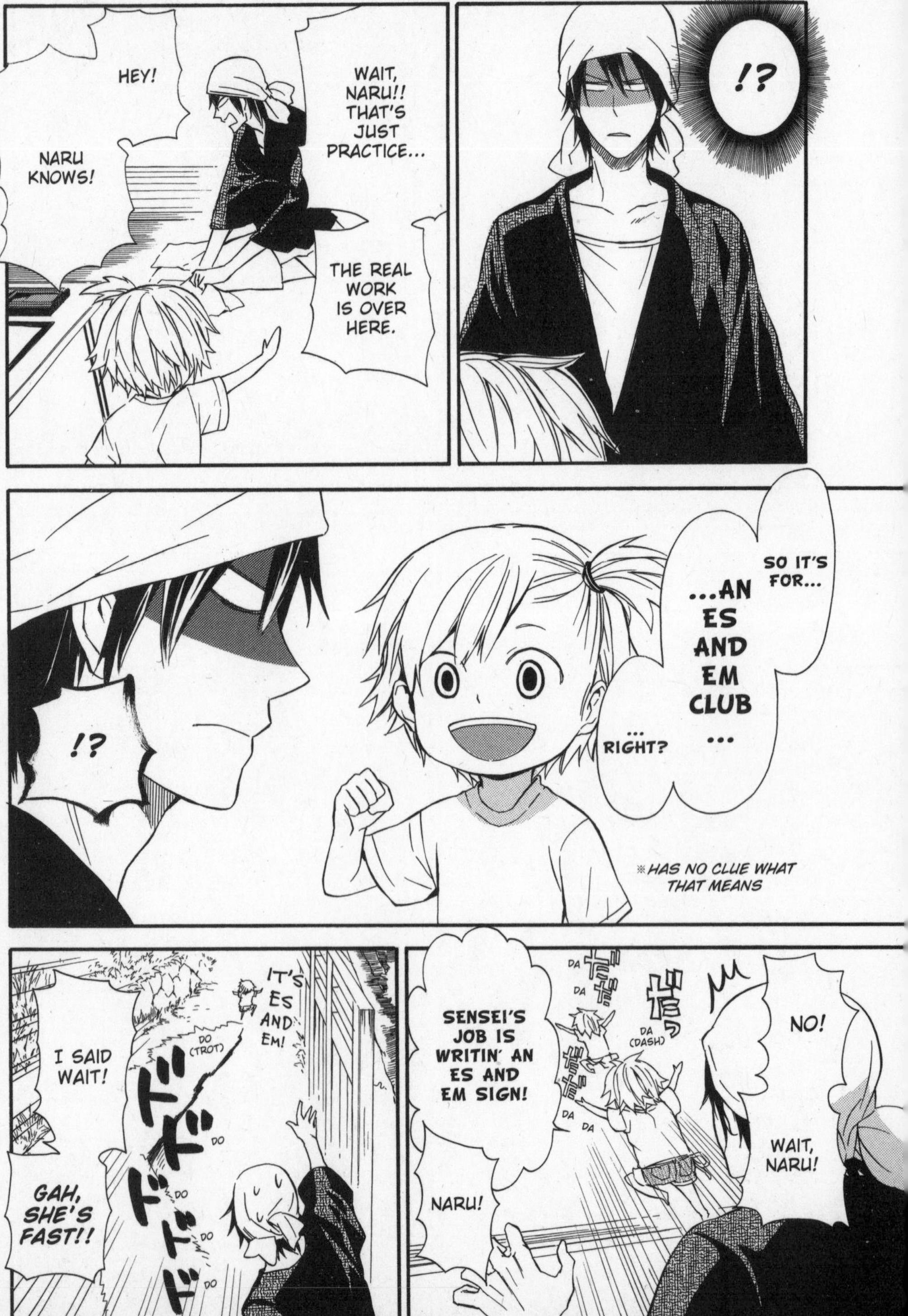
!?
WAIT, NARU!! THAT'S JUST PRACTICE...
THE REAL WORK IS OVER HERE.
HEY!
NARU KNOWS!
SO IT'S FOR...
...AN ES AND EM CLUB...
...RIGHT?
!?
※HAS NO CLUE WHAT THAT MEANS
NO!
WAIT, NARU!
DA DA
DA (DASH)
DA DA
SENSEI'S JOB IS WRITIN' AN ES AND EM SIGN!
NARU!
IT'S ES AND EM!
DO (TROT)
I SAID WAIT!
DO DO DO DO
GAH, SHE'S FAST!!

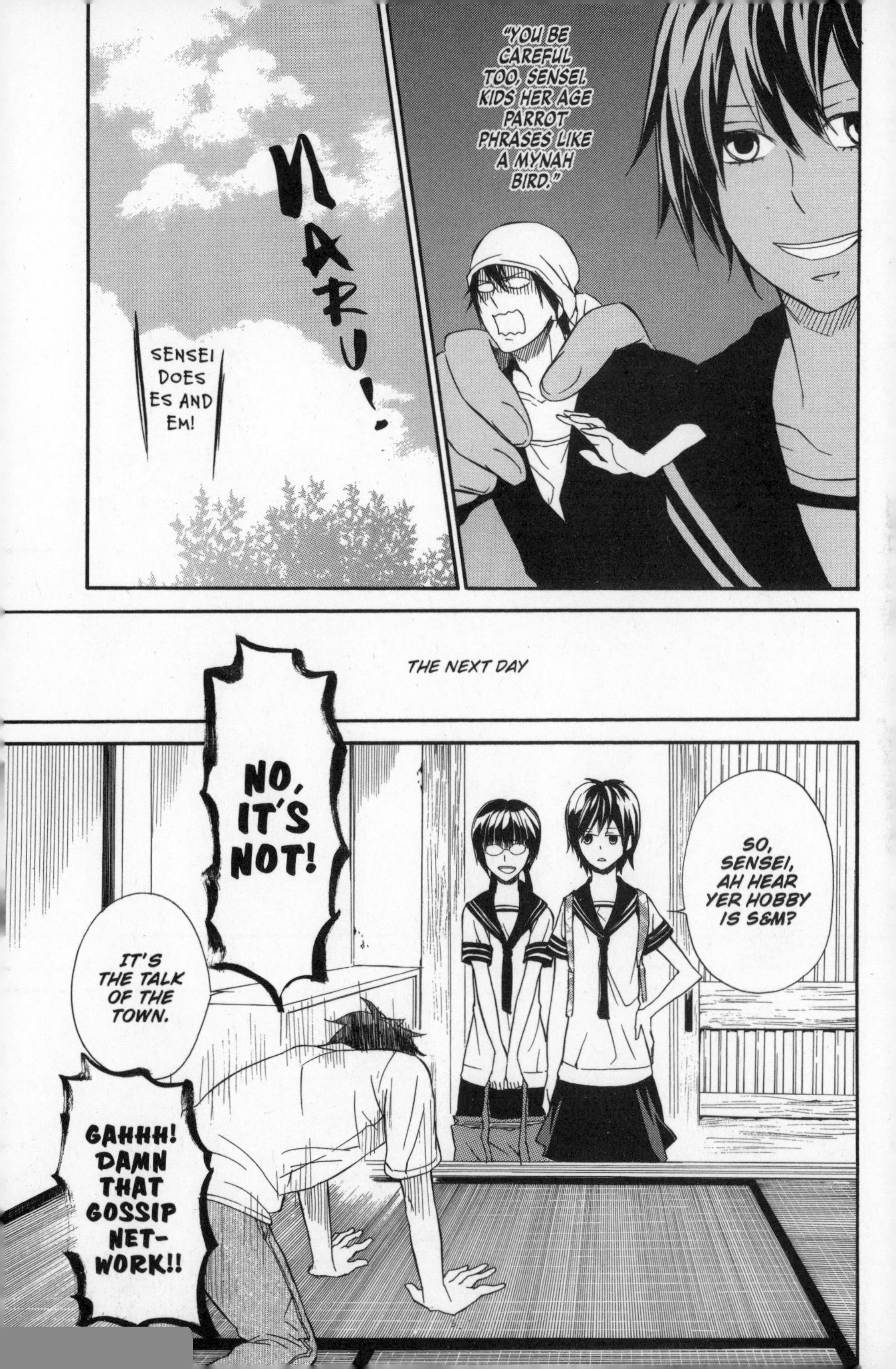
"YOU BE CAREFUL TOO, SENSEI. KIDS HER AGE PARROT PHRASES LIKE A MYNAH BIRD."
NARU!
SENSEI DOES ES AND EM!
THE NEXT DAY
SO, SENSEI, AH HEAR YER HOBBY IS S&M?
NO, IT'S NOT!
IT'S THE TALK OF THE TOWN.
GAHHH! DAMN THAT GOSSIP NET-WORK!!

ACT.5
SHA
(Translation: Side Dishes)

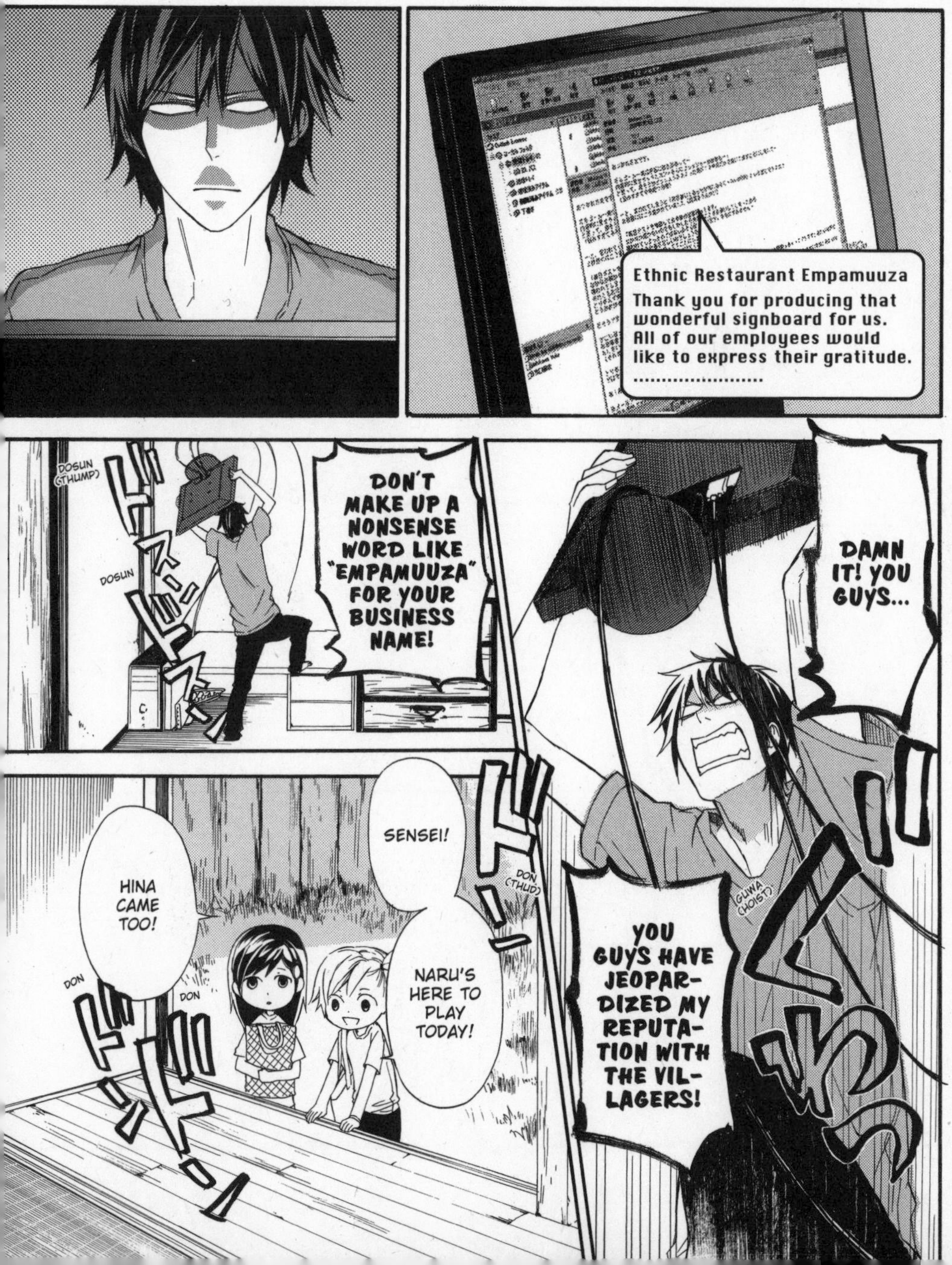
Ethnic Restaurant Empamuuza
Thank you for producing that wonderful signboard for us. All of our employees would like to express their gratitude. ....
DAMN IT! YOU GUYS...
GUWA (HOIST)
YOU GUYS HAVE JEOPARDIZED MY REPUTATION WITH THE VILLAGERS!
DOSUN (THUMP)
DOSUN
DON'T MAKE UP A NONSENSE WORD LIKE "EMPAMUUZA" FOR YOUR BUSINESS NAME!
DON (THUD)
SENSEI!
NARU'S HERE TO PLAY TODAY!
HINA CAME TOO!
DON
DON

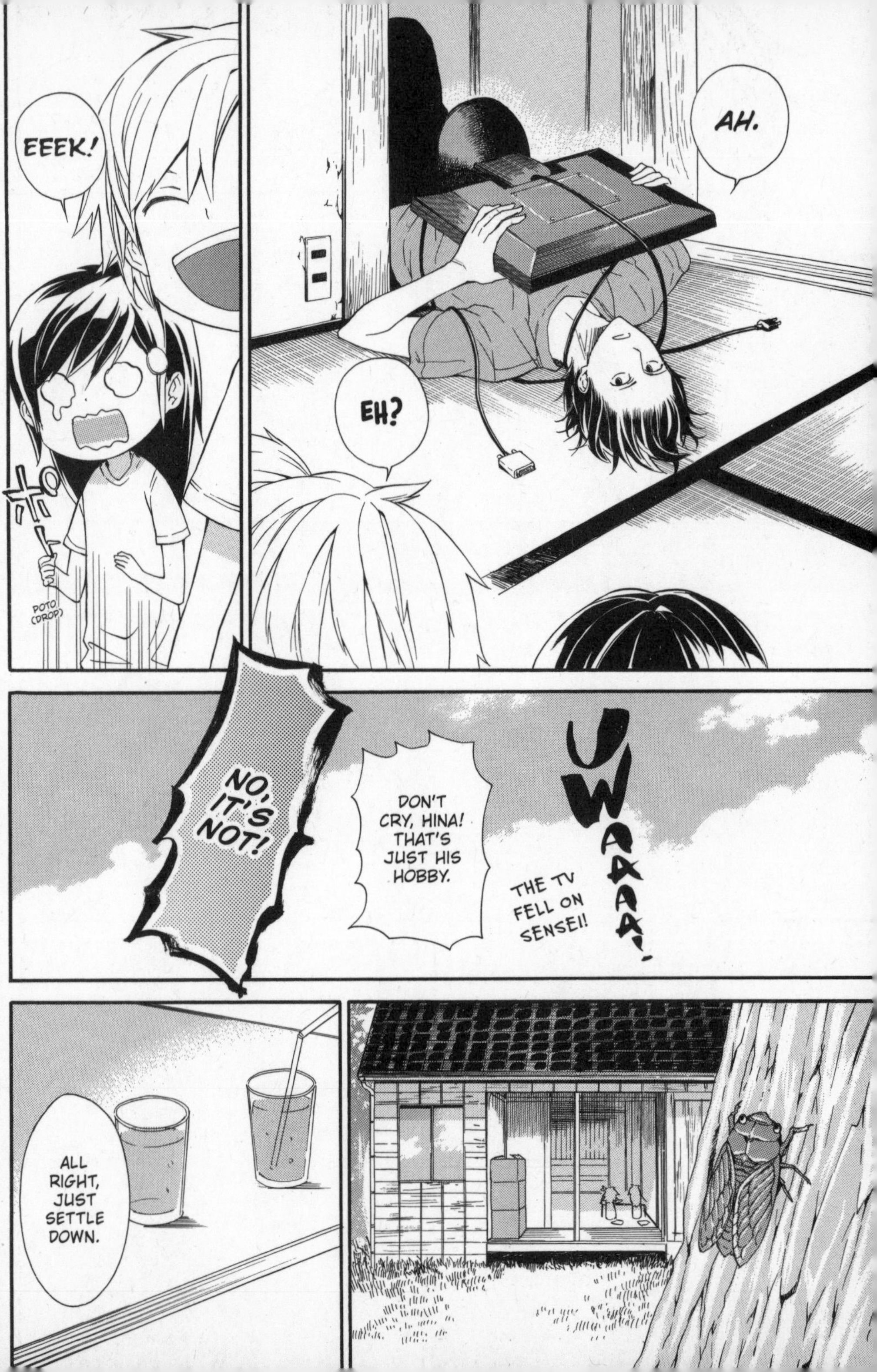
AH.
EH?
EEEK!
POTO (DROP)
UWAAAA!
THE TV FELL ON SENSEI!
DON'T CRY, HINA! THAT'S JUST HIS HOBBY.
NO, IT'S NOT!
ALL RIGHT, JUST SETTLE DOWN.

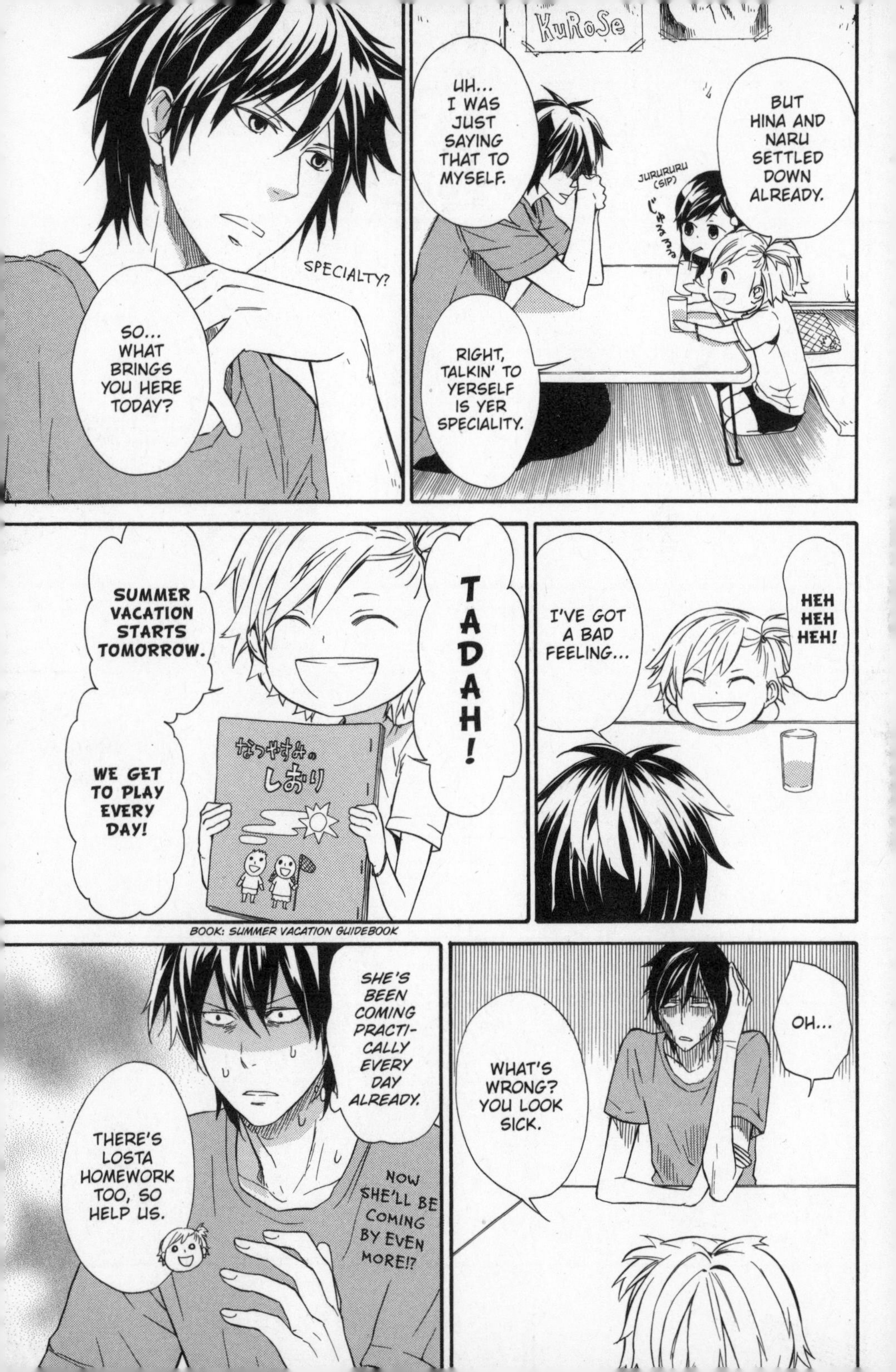
KuRoSe
BUT HINA AND NARU SETTLED DOWN ALREADY.
JURURURU (SIP)
UH... I WAS JUST SAYING THAT TO MYSELF.
RIGHT, TALKIN' TO YERSELF IS YER SPECIALITY.
SPECIALTY?
SO... WHAT BRINGS YOU HERE TODAY?
HEH HEH HEH!
I'VE GOT A BAD FEELING...
TADAH!
SUMMER VACATION STARTS TOMORROW.
WE GET TO PLAY EVERY DAY!
なつやすみの
しおり
BOOK: SUMMER VACATION GUIDEBOOK
OH...
WHAT'S WRONG? YOU LOOK SICK.
SHE'S BEEN COMING PRACTI-CALLY EVERY DAY ALREADY.
THERE'S LOSTA HOMEWORK TOO, SO HELP US.
NOW SHE'LL BE COMING BY EVEN MORE!?

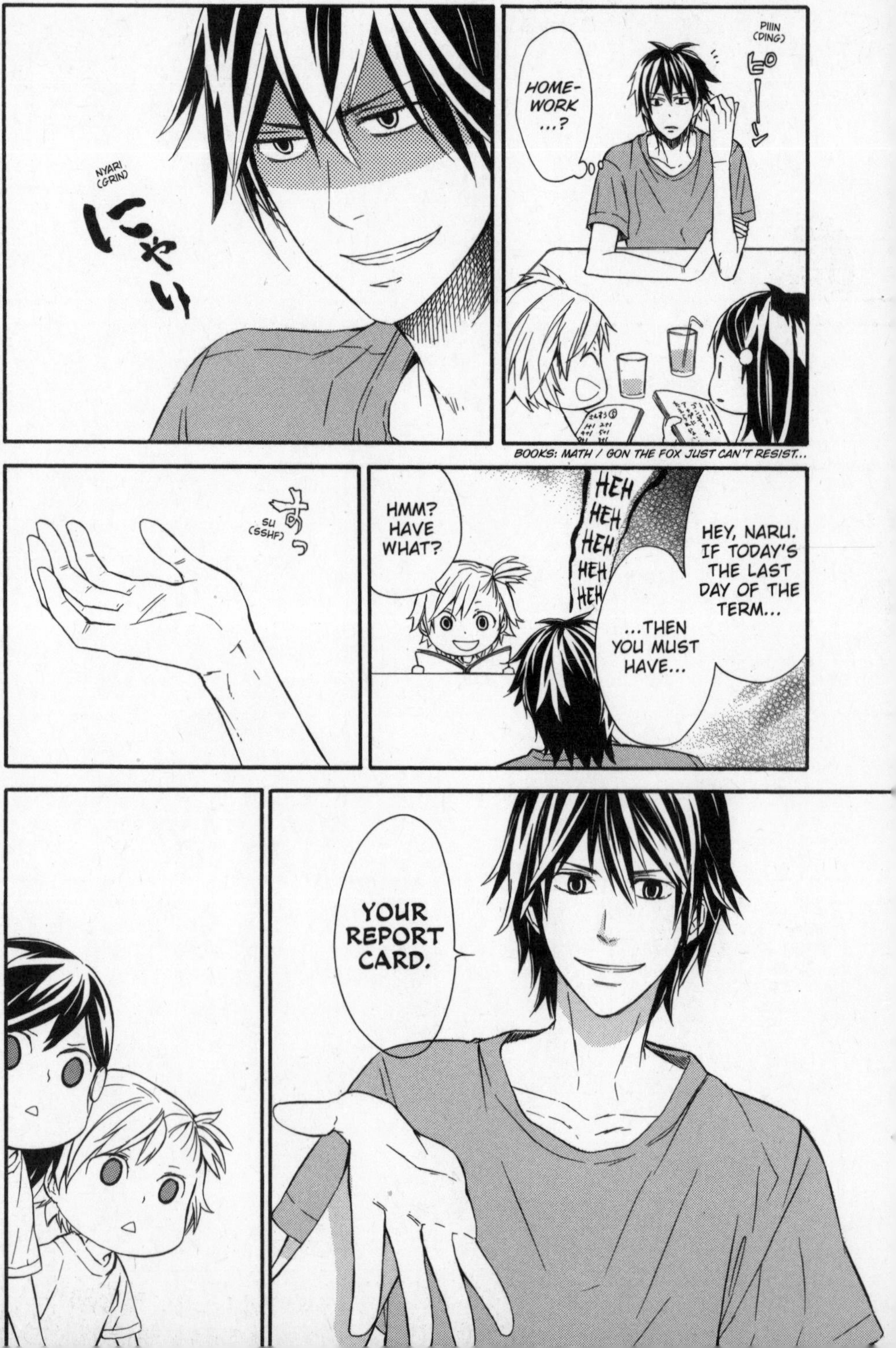
PIIIN (DING)
ピーン
HOME-WORK...?
BOOKS: MATH / GON THE FOX JUST CAN'T RESIST...
NYARI (GRIN)
にやり
HEH HEH HEH HEH HEH
HEY, NARU. IF TODAY'S THE LAST DAY OF THE TERM...
...THEN YOU MUST HAVE...
HMM? HAVE WHAT?
SU (SSHF)
すっ
YOUR REPORT CARD.

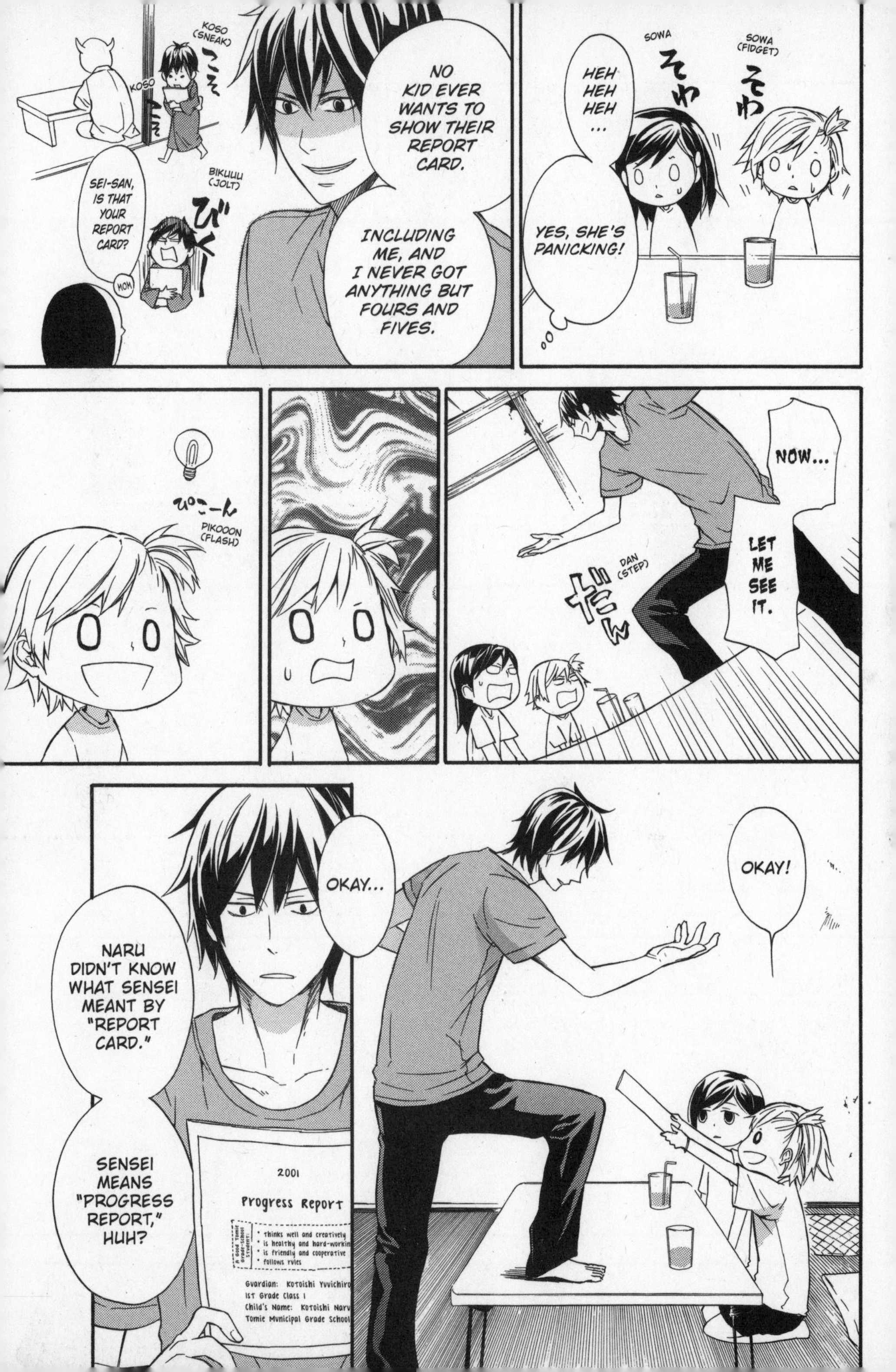

SOWA
SOWA (FIDGET)
HEH HEH HEH ...
YES, SHE'S PANICKING!
NO KID EVER WANTS TO SHOW THEIR REPORT CARD.
KOSO (SNEAK)
KOSO
SEI-SAN, IS THAT YOUR REPORT CARD?
BIKUUU (JOLT)
MOM
INCLUDING ME, AND I NEVER GOT ANYTHING BUT FOURS AND FIVES.
NOW...
LET ME SEE IT.
DAN (STEP)
PIKOOON (FLASH)
OKAY!
OKAY...
NARU DIDN'T KNOW WHAT SENSEI MEANT BY "REPORT CARD."
SENSEI MEANS "PROGRESS REPORT," HUH?
2001
Progress Report
A Good Tomie Grade-School Student:
* thinks well and creatively
* is healthy and hard-working
* is friendly and cooperative
* follows rules
Guardian: Kotoishi Yuuichiro
1st Grade Class 1
Child's Name: Kotoishi Naru
Tomie Municipal Grade School

SHE'S SO OPEN-MINDED!!

...BUT THERE'S MORE TO LIFE THAN JUST STUDYIN', RIGHT?

IT'S NOT SO GREAT...

HERE'S MINE TOO...

ARE YOU SURE YOU WANT ME TO SEE IT?

UH-HUH.

not MATURE

WELL, FINE.

...FOR HER BAD GRADES.

I'LL GIVE HER A MILD LECTURE...

Japanese — Interest, motivation, attitude towards Japanese language / Expression — Speaking, Writing, Listening, Reading; Comprehension ability — Basic Facts, Penmanship

Social Studies — Interest, motivation and attitude towards social issues; Social consideration / judgment; Skill and comprehension in observation and data use; Knowledge, comprehension of social issues

Math — Interest, motivation and attitude towards arithmetic; Mathematical thinking; ...tion and processing ...es and figures

HAVE YOU CALMED DOWN, SENSEI?

PANT PANT

AND MOST OF THEM ARE "VERY SATISFAC-TORY"!

WHY HASN'T THAT HEADMASTER BEEN CENSURED FOR LAZY GRADING!?

CHILDREN GROW WITH PRAISE.

THEY'RE ALL "SATIS-FACTORY"! I CAN'T DO ANY SCOLDING FOR THIS!

CURSE YOU, RELAXED EDUCA-TION SYSTEM!

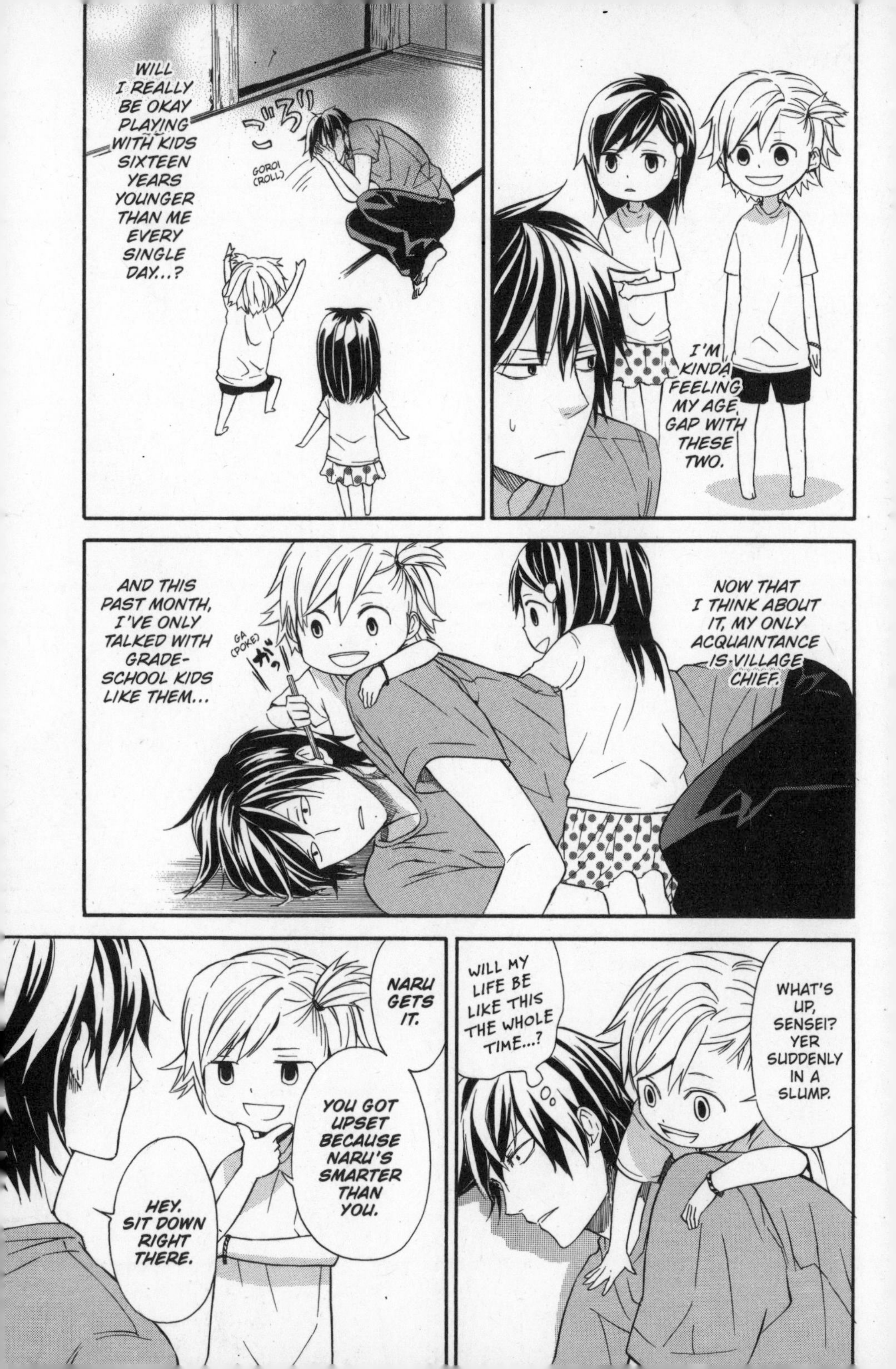
I'M KINDA FEELING MY AGE GAP WITH THESE TWO.
WILL I REALLY BE OKAY PLAYING WITH KIDS SIXTEEN YEARS YOUNGER THAN ME EVERY SINGLE DAY...?
GOROI (ROLL)
NOW THAT I THINK ABOUT IT, MY ONLY ACQUAINTANCE IS VILLAGE CHIEF.
AND THIS PAST MONTH, I'VE ONLY TALKED WITH GRADE-SCHOOL KIDS LIKE THEM...
GA (POKE)
WHAT'S UP, SENSEI? YER SUDDENLY IN A SLUMP.
WILL MY LIFE BE LIKE THIS THE WHOLE TIME...?
NARU GETS IT.
YOU GOT UPSET BECAUSE NARU'S SMARTER THAN YOU.
HEY. SIT DOWN RIGHT THERE.

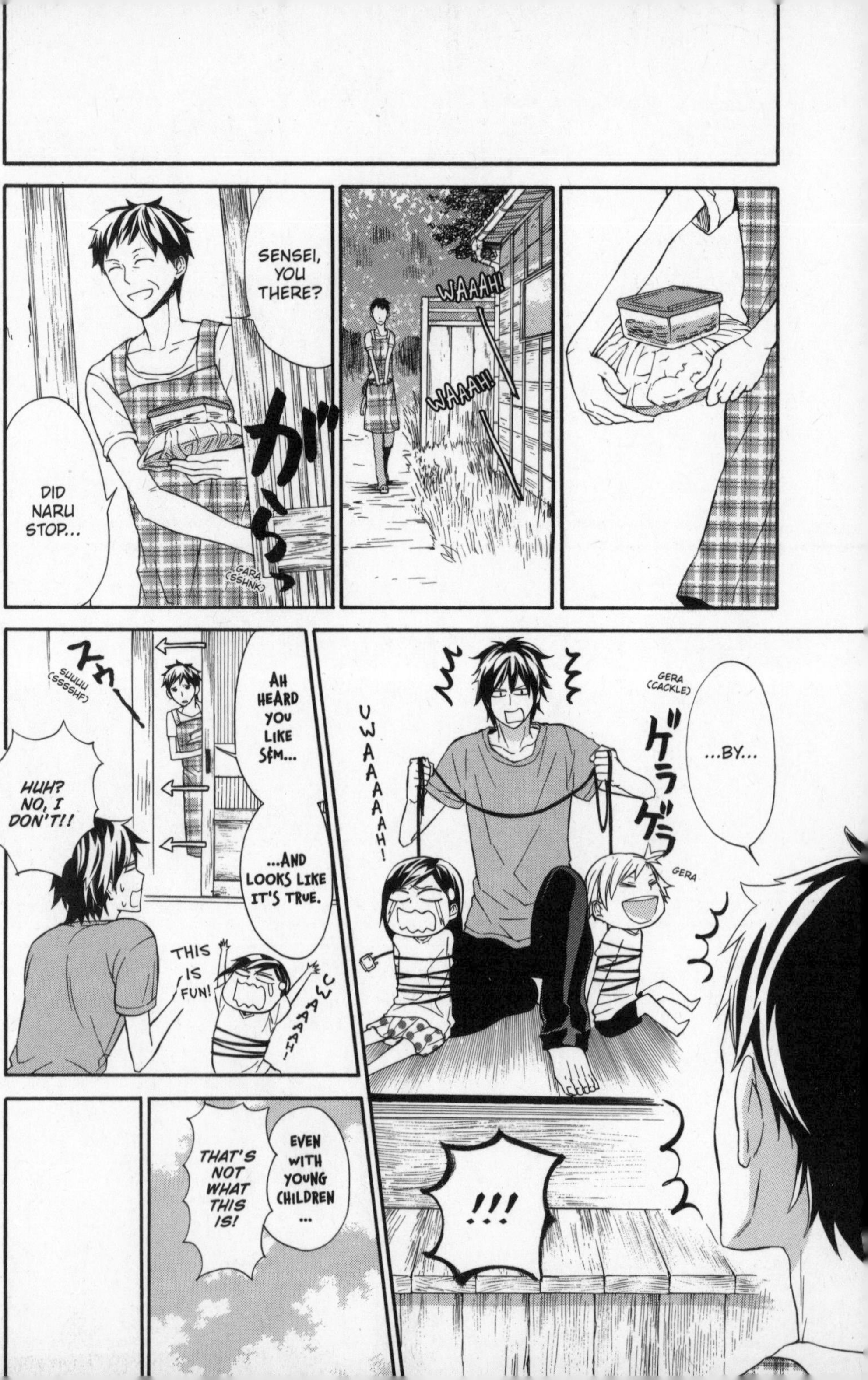
WAAAH!
WAAAH!
SENSEI, YOU THERE?
DID NARU STOP...
GARA (SSHNK)
GERA (CACKLE)
...BY...
GERA
UWAAAAAAAH!
SUUUU (SSSSHF)
AH HEARD YOU LIKE S&M...
HUH? NO, I DON'T!!
...AND LOOKS LIKE IT'S TRUE.
THIS IS FUN!
UWAAAAH!
!!!
EVEN WITH YOUNG CHILDREN...
THAT'S NOT WHAT THIS IS!

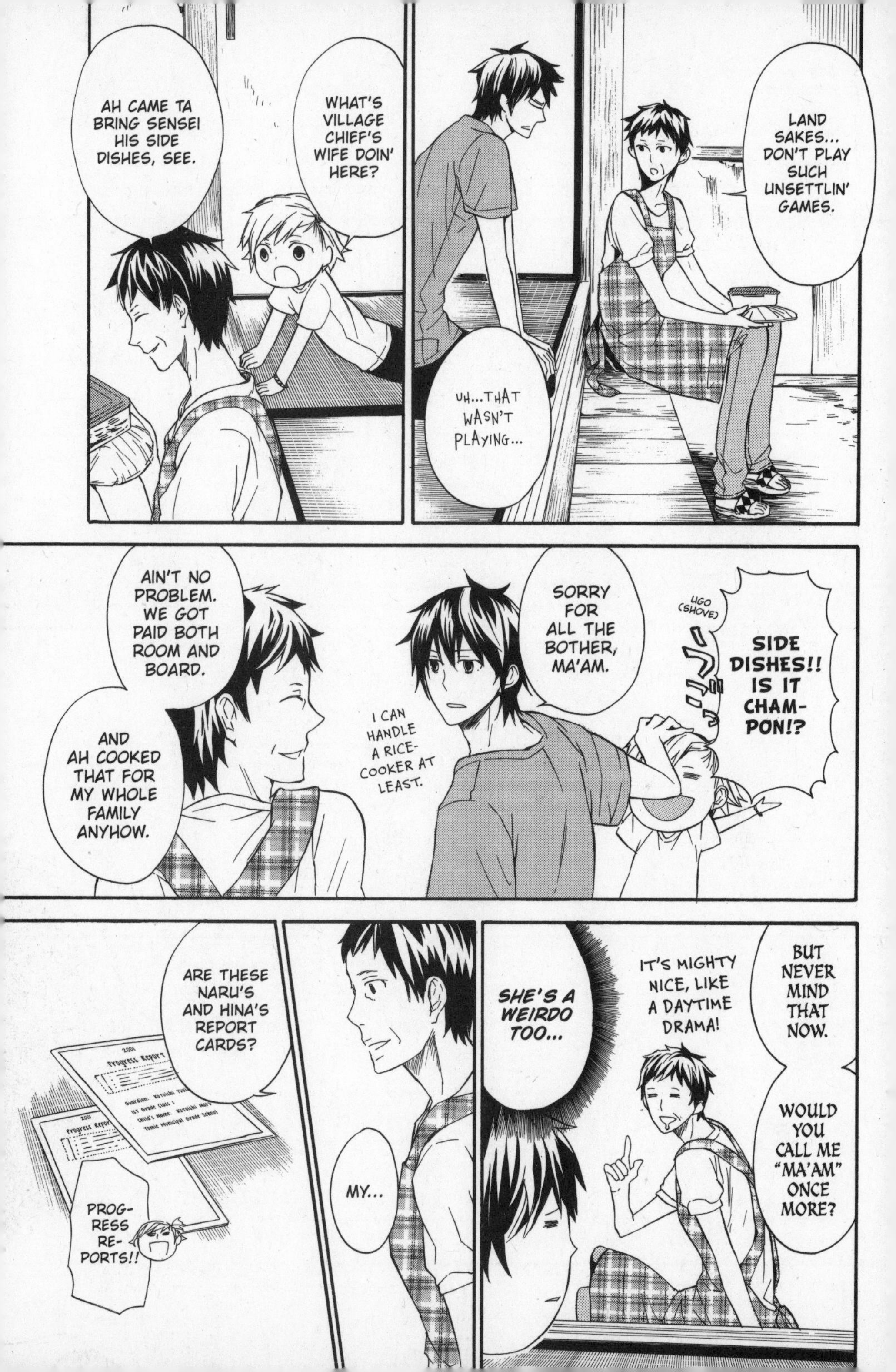

LAND SAKES... DON'T PLAY SUCH UNSETTLIN' GAMES.
UH...THAT WASN'T PLAYING...
WHAT'S VILLAGE CHIEF'S WIFE DOIN' HERE?
AH CAME TA BRING SENSEI HIS SIDE DISHES, SEE.
UGO (SHOVE)
SIDE DISHES!! IS IT CHAMPON!?
SORRY FOR ALL THE BOTHER, MA'AM.
I CAN HANDLE A RICE-COOKER AT LEAST.
AIN'T NO PROBLEM. WE GOT PAID BOTH ROOM AND BOARD.
AND AH COOKED THAT FOR MY WHOLE FAMILY ANYHOW.
BUT NEVER MIND THAT NOW.
IT'S MIGHTY NICE, LIKE A DAYTIME DRAMA!
WOULD YOU CALL ME "MA'AM" ONCE MORE?
SHE'S A WEIRDO TOO...
MY...
ARE THESE NARU'S AND HINA'S REPORT CARDS?
Progress Report
Progress Report
PROG-RESS RE-PORTS!!

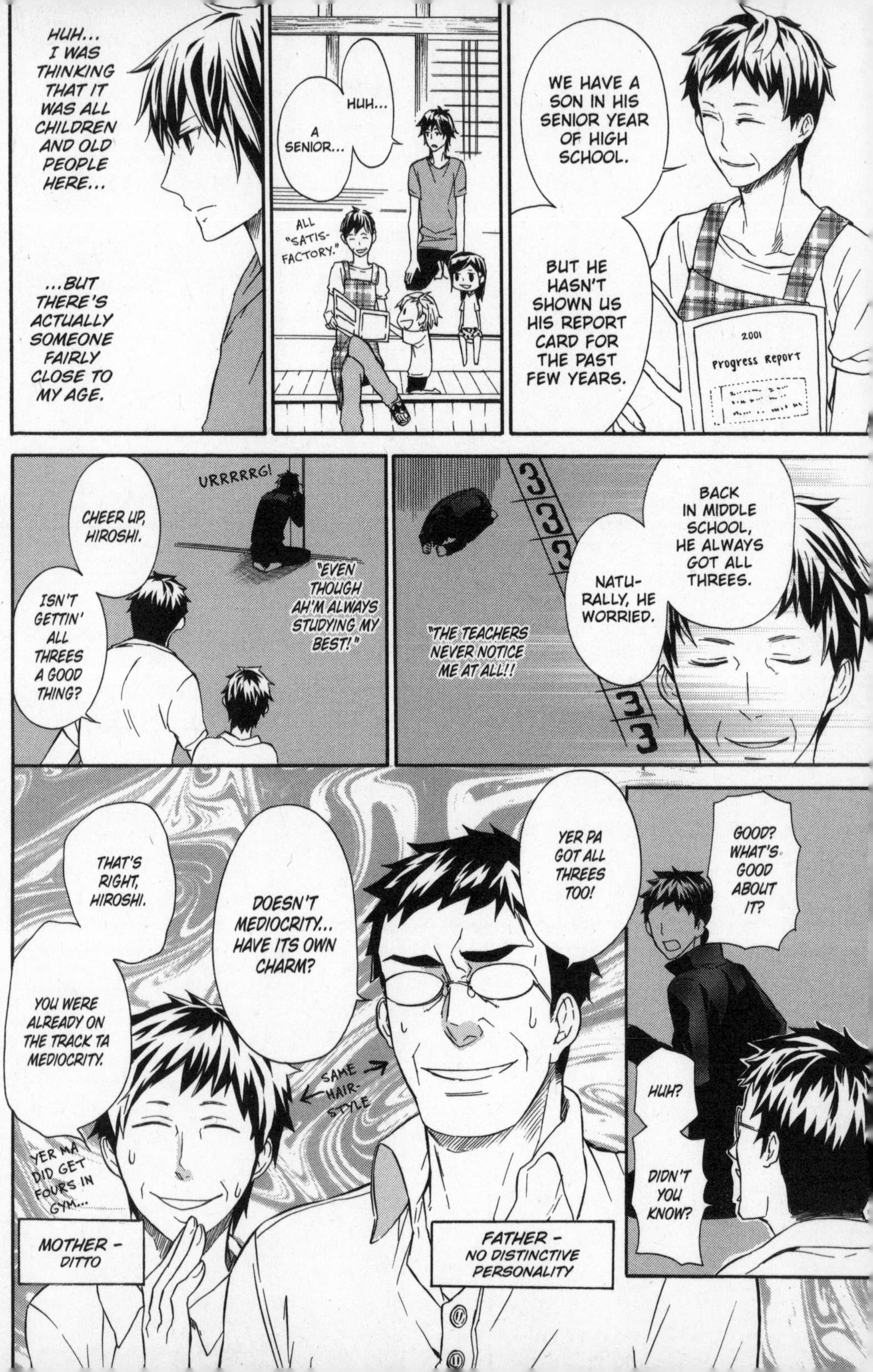
WE HAVE A SON IN HIS SENIOR YEAR OF HIGH SCHOOL.
BUT HE HASN'T SHOWN US HIS REPORT CARD FOR THE PAST FEW YEARS.
2001
Progress Report
HUH... A SENIOR...
ALL "SATIS-FACTORY."
HUH... I WAS THINKING THAT IT WAS ALL CHILDREN AND OLD PEOPLE HERE...
...BUT THERE'S ACTUALLY SOMEONE FAIRLY CLOSE TO MY AGE.
BACK IN MIDDLE SCHOOL, HE ALWAYS GOT ALL THREES.
NATU-RALLY, HE WORRIED.
"THE TEACHERS NEVER NOTICE ME AT ALL!!
URRRRRG!
CHEER UP, HIROSHI.
"EVEN THOUGH AH'M ALWAYS STUDYING MY BEST!"
ISN'T GETTIN' ALL THREES A GOOD THING?
GOOD? WHAT'S GOOD ABOUT IT?
HUH?
DIDN'T YOU KNOW?
YER PA GOT ALL THREES TOO!
DOESN'T MEDIOCRITY... HAVE ITS OWN CHARM?
THAT'S RIGHT, HIROSHI.
YOU WERE ALREADY ON THE TRACK TA MEDIOCRITY.
SAME HAIR-STYLE
FATHER - NO DISTINCTIVE PERSONALITY
YER MA DID GET FOURS IN GYM...
MOTHER - DITTO

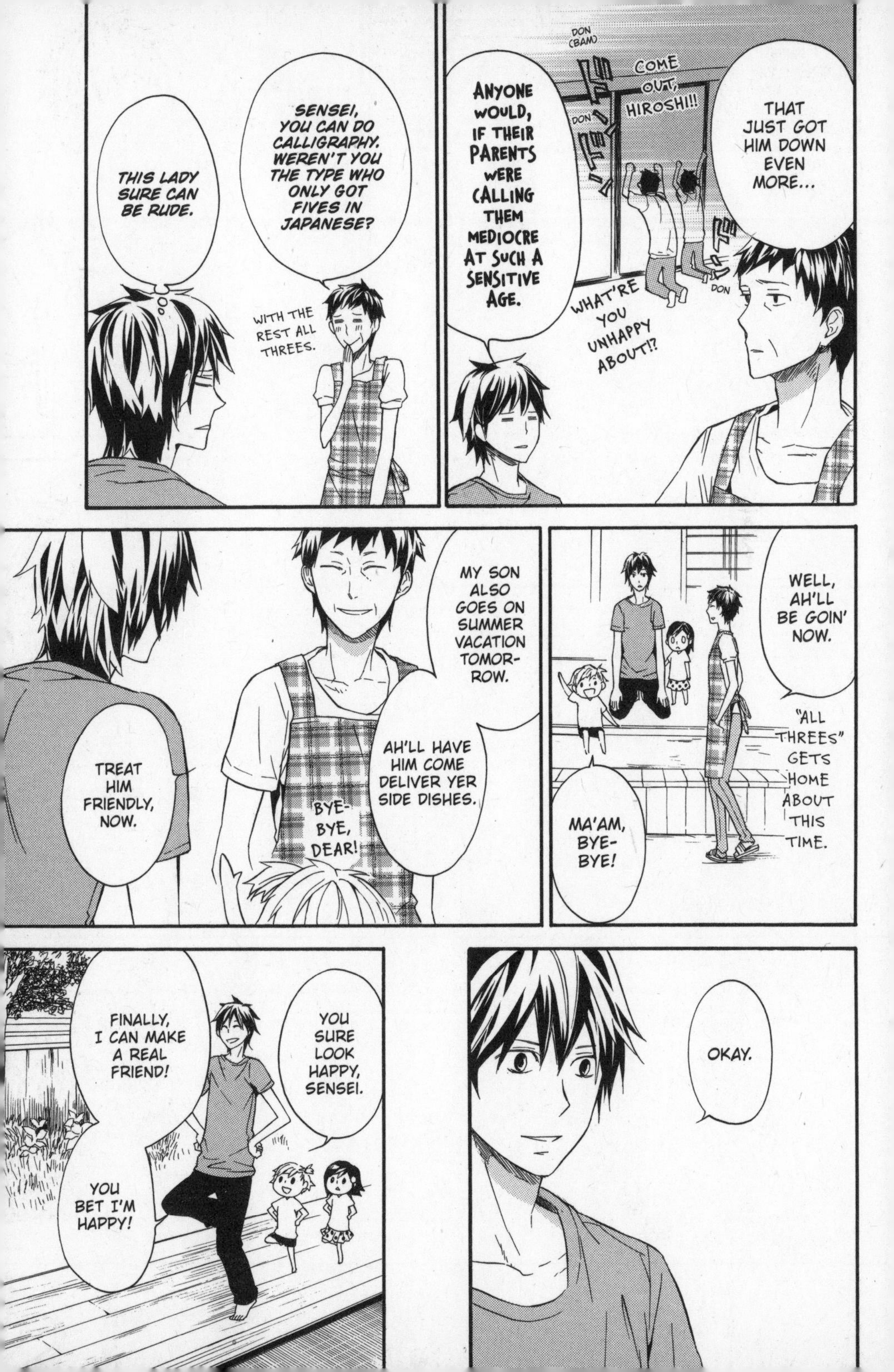
THAT JUST GOT HIM DOWN EVEN MORE...
DON (BAM)
COME OUT, HIROSHI!!
DON
DON
WHAT'RE YOU UNHAPPY ABOUT!?
ANYONE WOULD, IF THEIR PARENTS WERE CALLING THEM MEDIOCRE AT SUCH A SENSITIVE AGE.
SENSEI, YOU CAN DO CALLIGRAPHY. WEREN'T YOU THE TYPE WHO ONLY GOT FIVES IN JAPANESE?
WITH THE REST ALL THREES.
THIS LADY SURE CAN BE RUDE.
WELL, AH'LL BE GOIN' NOW.
"ALL THREES" GETS HOME ABOUT THIS TIME.
MA'AM, BYE-BYE!
MY SON ALSO GOES ON SUMMER VACATION TOMOR-ROW.
AH'LL HAVE HIM COME DELIVER YER SIDE DISHES.
BYE-BYE, DEAR!
TREAT HIM FRIENDLY, NOW.
OKAY.
YOU SURE LOOK HAPPY, SENSEI.
FINALLY, I CAN MAKE A REAL FRIEND!
YOU BET I'M HAPPY!

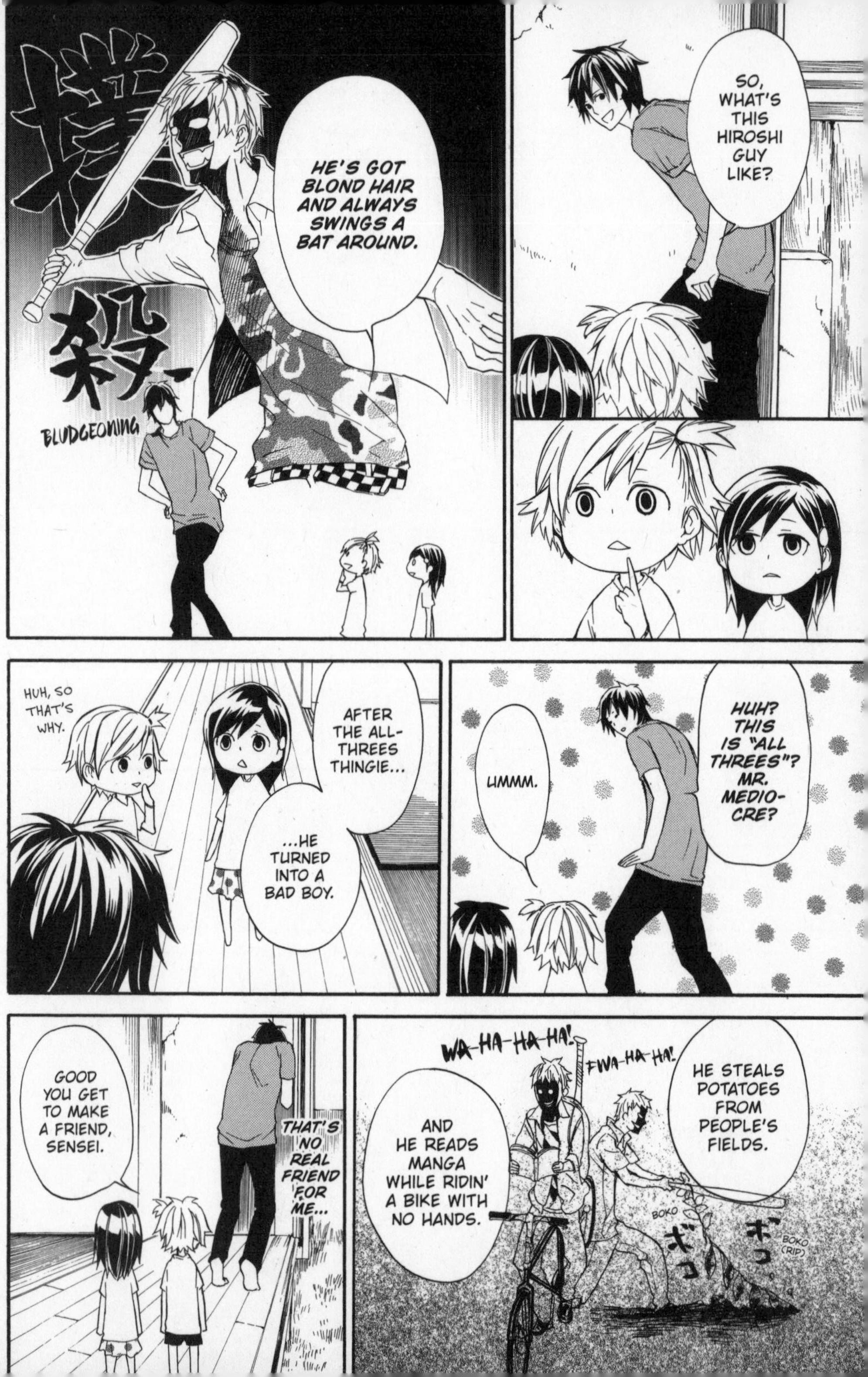
SO, WHAT'S THIS HIROSHI GUY LIKE?
撲
殺
BLUDGEONING
HE'S GOT BLOND HAIR AND ALWAYS SWINGS A BAT AROUND.
HUH? THIS IS "ALL THREES"? MR. MEDIOCRE?
UMMM.
AFTER THE ALL-THREES THINGIE...
...HE TURNED INTO A BAD BOY.
HUH, SO THAT'S WHY.
HE STEALS POTATOES FROM PEOPLE'S FIELDS.
FWA-HA-HA!
WA-HA-HA-HA!
AND HE READS MANGA WHILE RIDIN' A BIKE WITH NO HANDS.
BOKO
ボコ
ボコッ
BOKO (RIP)
GOOD YOU GET TO MAKE A FRIEND, SENSEI.
THAT'S NO REAL FRIEND FOR ME...

an interest in the subject and tackles it with motiv...	3	3
express own thoughts precisely		
ability to comprehend		
use language correctly		
high interest in social issues, tackles subject with motivation	3	3
...e to consider social issues correctly		
...e to choose effective materials and apply them well		
...us knowledge and comprehension of social issues		
Has an interest in the subject and tackles it with motivation	3	3
Able to see and think mathematically		
Can express equations and figures, and perform related calculations		
Has knowledge and comprehension of quantities and figures		
Has interest in the state of nature and can progress and research it	3	3
Able to see and think in scientific terms		
Can learn research and observation skills, and express results		
Has knowledge and comprehension of natural events		
Tackles music activities with a motivated attitude	3	3
Can feel the beauty of music, and express it creatively		
Has skill in expression (instrumental, singing, creation)		
Can appreciate musical works		
...nterest in the subject and tackles it with motivation	3	3

IT'S THE SUMMER OF MY THIRD YEAR OF HIGH SCHOOL...

AH'VE BEEN ANGUISHIN' OVER THE UPCOMIN' ENTRANCE EXAMS.

MY MUSIC TEACHER SAYS...

YOU NEED TO SING A LITTLE LOUDER.

YOU NEED TO RUN A LITTLE LONGER.

MY GYM TEACHER SAYS...

MY HOME-ROOM TEACHER SAYS...

YOU NEED TO TRY A LITTLE HARDER.

THAT'S WHAT AH'M DOIN'!

BUT AH'VE BEEN WORKIN'... SO HARD...

NOBODY UNDER-STANDS ME.

ACT.6 YOSONMON

(Translation: City Person)

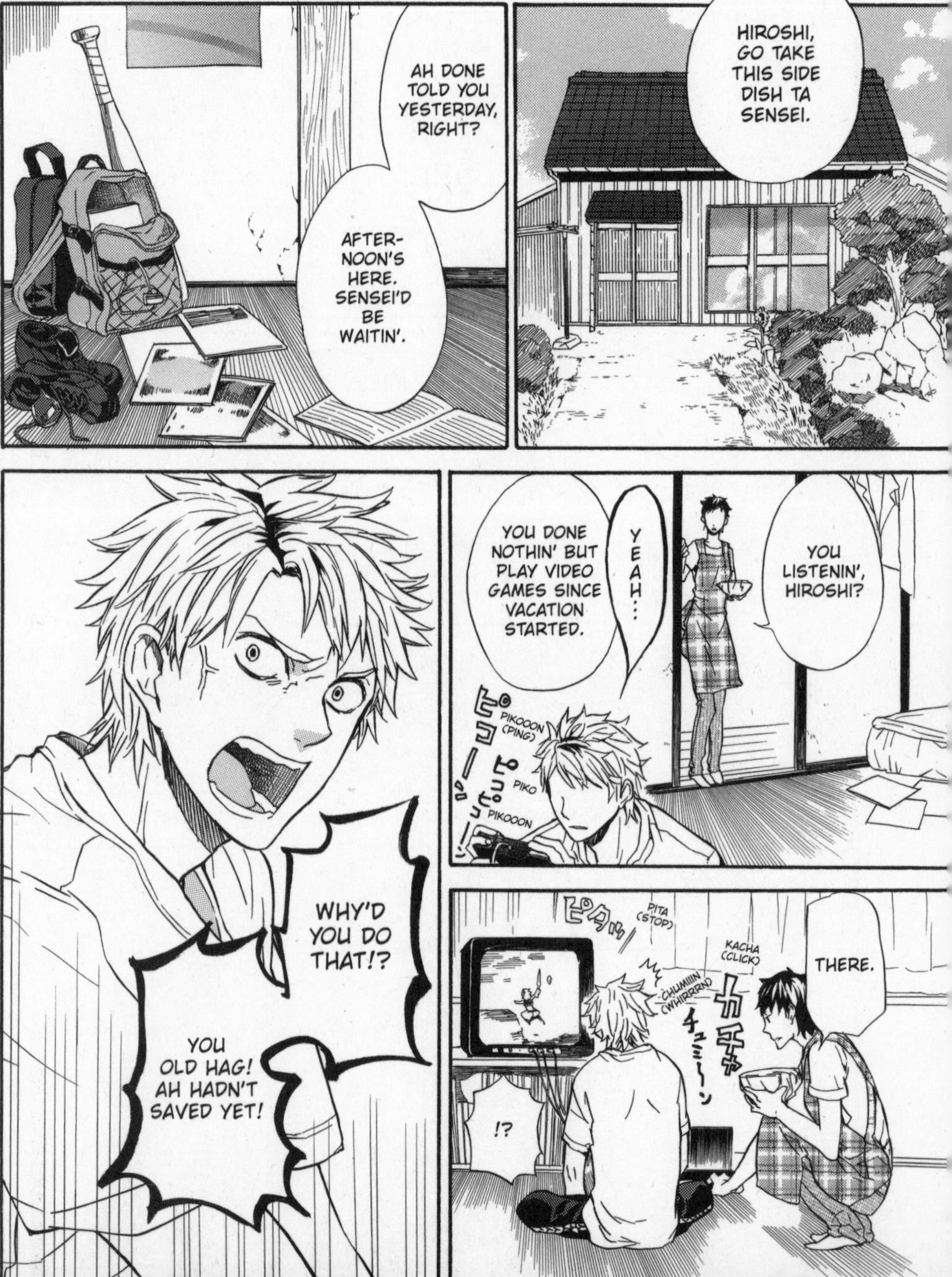
HIROSHI, GO TAKE THIS SIDE DISH TA SENSEI.
AH DONE TOLD YOU YESTERDAY, RIGHT?
AFTER-NOON'S HERE. SENSEI'D BE WAITIN'.
YOU LISTENIN', HIROSHI?
YEAH...
YOU DONE NOTHIN' BUT PLAY VIDEO GAMES SINCE VACATION STARTED.
PIKOOON (PING)
PIKO
PIKOOON
THERE.
KACHA (CLICK)
PITA (STOP)
CHUMIIIN (WHIRRRN)
!?
WHY'D YOU DO THAT!?
YOU OLD HAG! AH HADN'T SAVED YET!

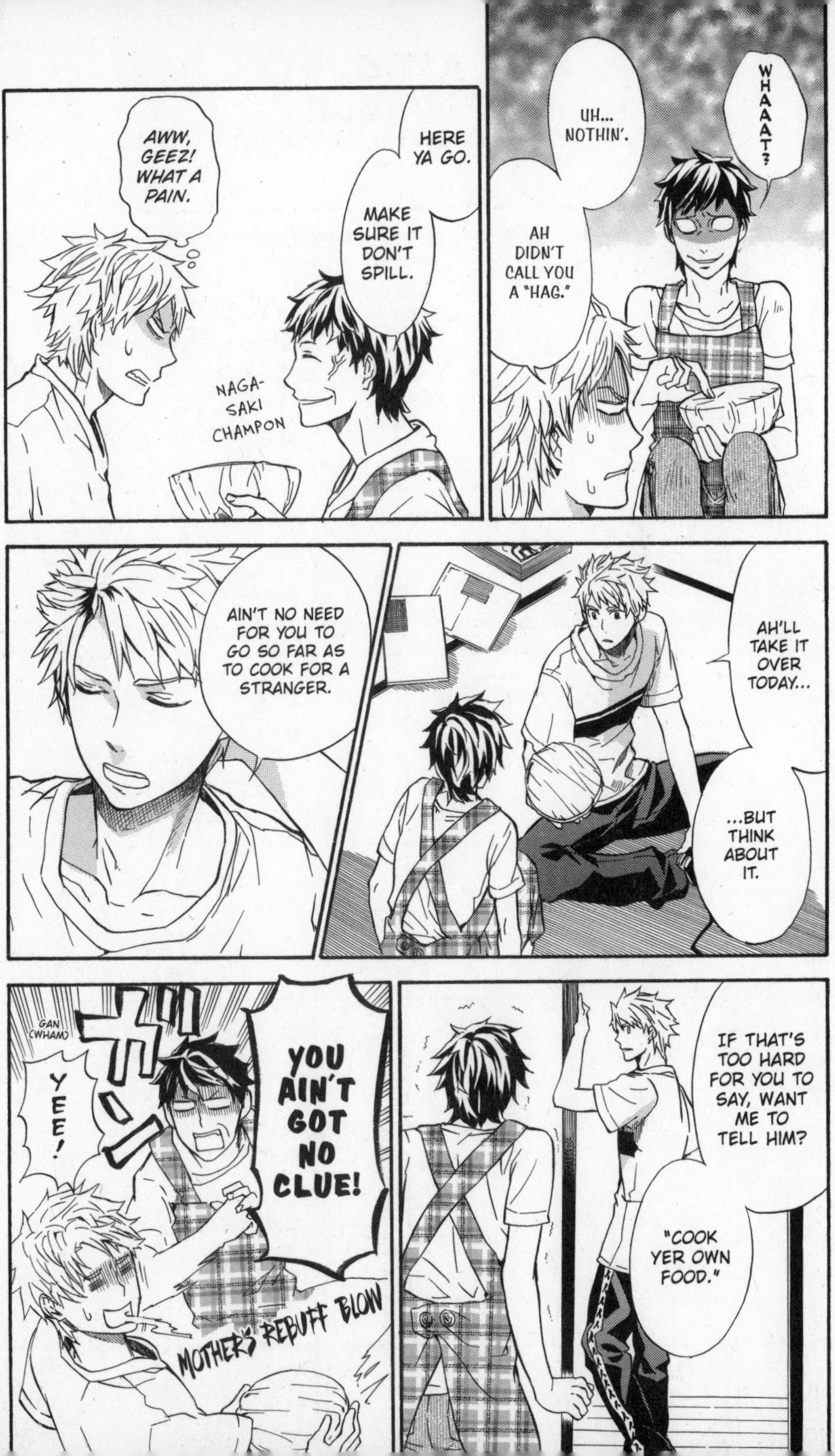
WHAAAT?
UH... NOTHIN'.
AH DIDN'T CALL YOU A "HAG."
HERE YA GO.
MAKE SURE IT DON'T SPILL.
NAGA-SAKI CHAMPON
AWW, GEEZ! WHAT A PAIN.
AH'LL TAKE IT OVER TODAY...
...BUT THINK ABOUT IT.
AIN'T NO NEED FOR YOU TO GO SO FAR AS TO COOK FOR A STRANGER.
IF THAT'S TOO HARD FOR YOU TO SAY, WANT ME TO TELL HIM?
"COOK YER OWN FOOD."
YOU AIN'T GOT NO CLUE!
GAN (WHAM)
YEE!
MOTHER'S REBUFF BLOW

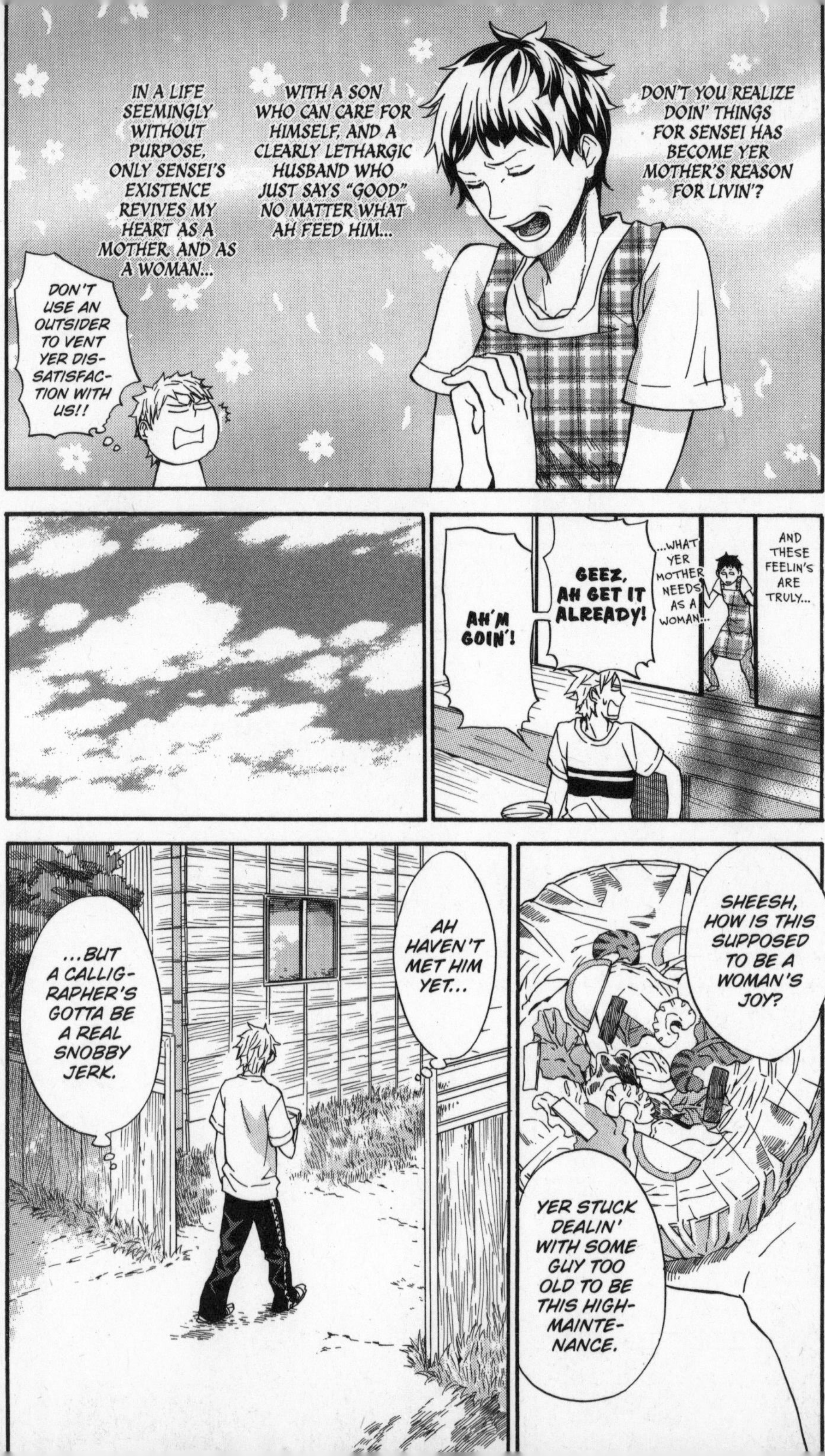
DON'T YOU REALIZE DOIN' THINGS FOR SENSEI HAS BECOME YER MOTHER'S REASON FOR LIVIN'?
WITH A SON WHO CAN CARE FOR HIMSELF, AND A CLEARLY LETHARGIC HUSBAND WHO JUST SAYS "GOOD" NO MATTER WHAT AH FEED HIM...
IN A LIFE SEEMINGLY WITHOUT PURPOSE, ONLY SENSEI'S EXISTENCE REVIVES MY HEART AS A MOTHER AND AS A WOMAN...
DON'T USE AN OUTSIDER TO VENT YER DIS-SATISFAC-TION WITH US!!
AND THESE FEELIN'S ARE TRULY...
...WHAT YER MOTHER NEEDS AS A WOMAN...
GEEZ, AH GET IT ALREADY!
AH'M GOIN'!
SHEESH, HOW IS THIS SUPPOSED TO BE A WOMAN'S JOY?
YER STUCK DEALIN' WITH SOME GUY TOO OLD TO BE THIS HIGH-MAINTE-NANCE.
AH HAVEN'T MET HIM YET...
...BUT A CALLIG-RAPHER'S GOTTA BE A REAL SNOBBY JERK.

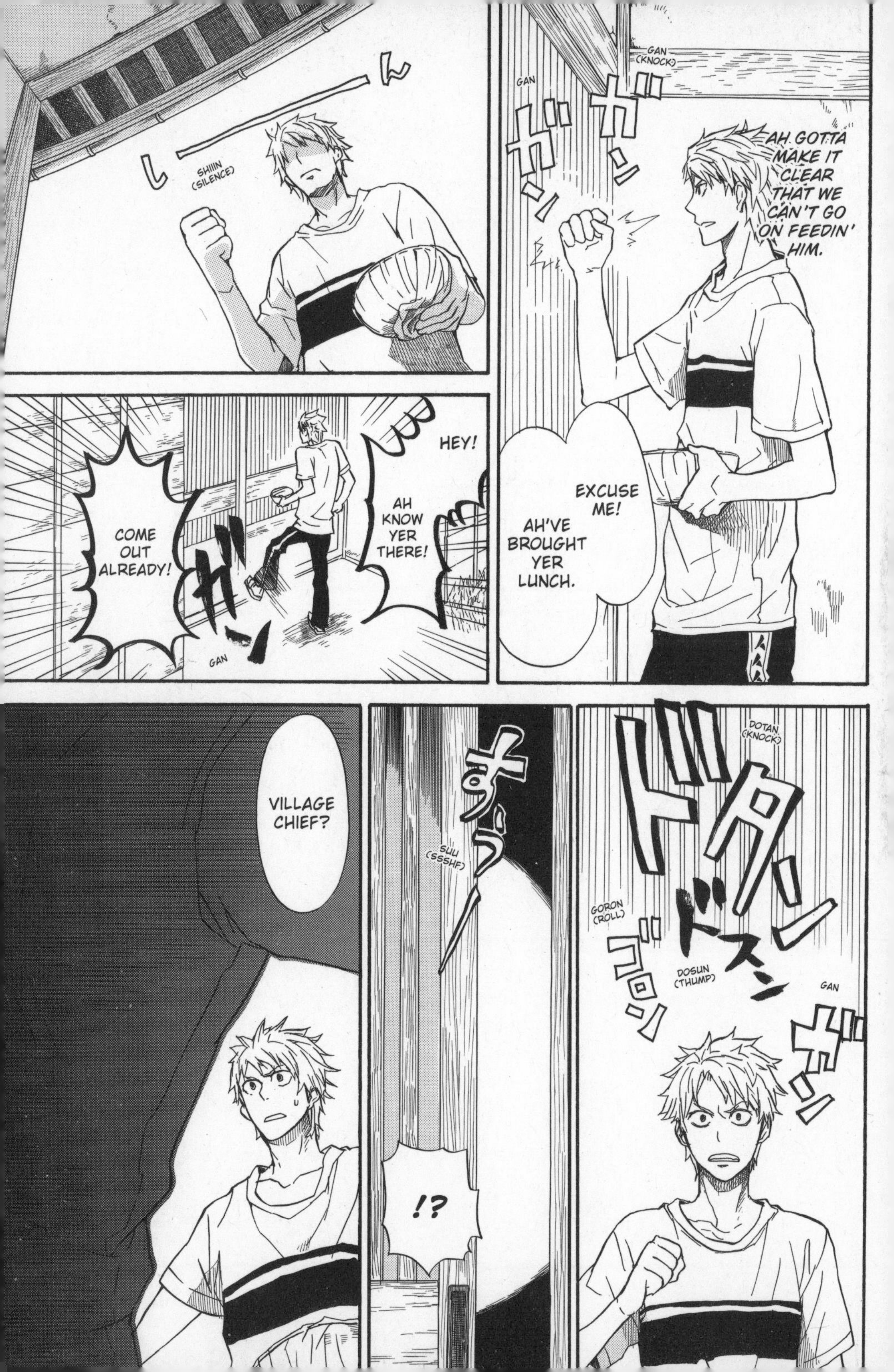
GAN
(KNOCK)
GAN
AH GOTTA MAKE IT CLEAR THAT WE CAN'T GO ON FEEDIN' HIM.
EXCUSE ME! AH'VE BROUGHT YER LUNCH.
SHIIN
(SILENCE)
HEY!
AH KNOW YER THERE!
COME OUT ALREADY!
GAN
DOTAN
(KNOCK)
GORON
(ROLL)
DOSUN
(THUMP)
GAN
SUU
(SSSHF)
!?
VILLAGE CHIEF?

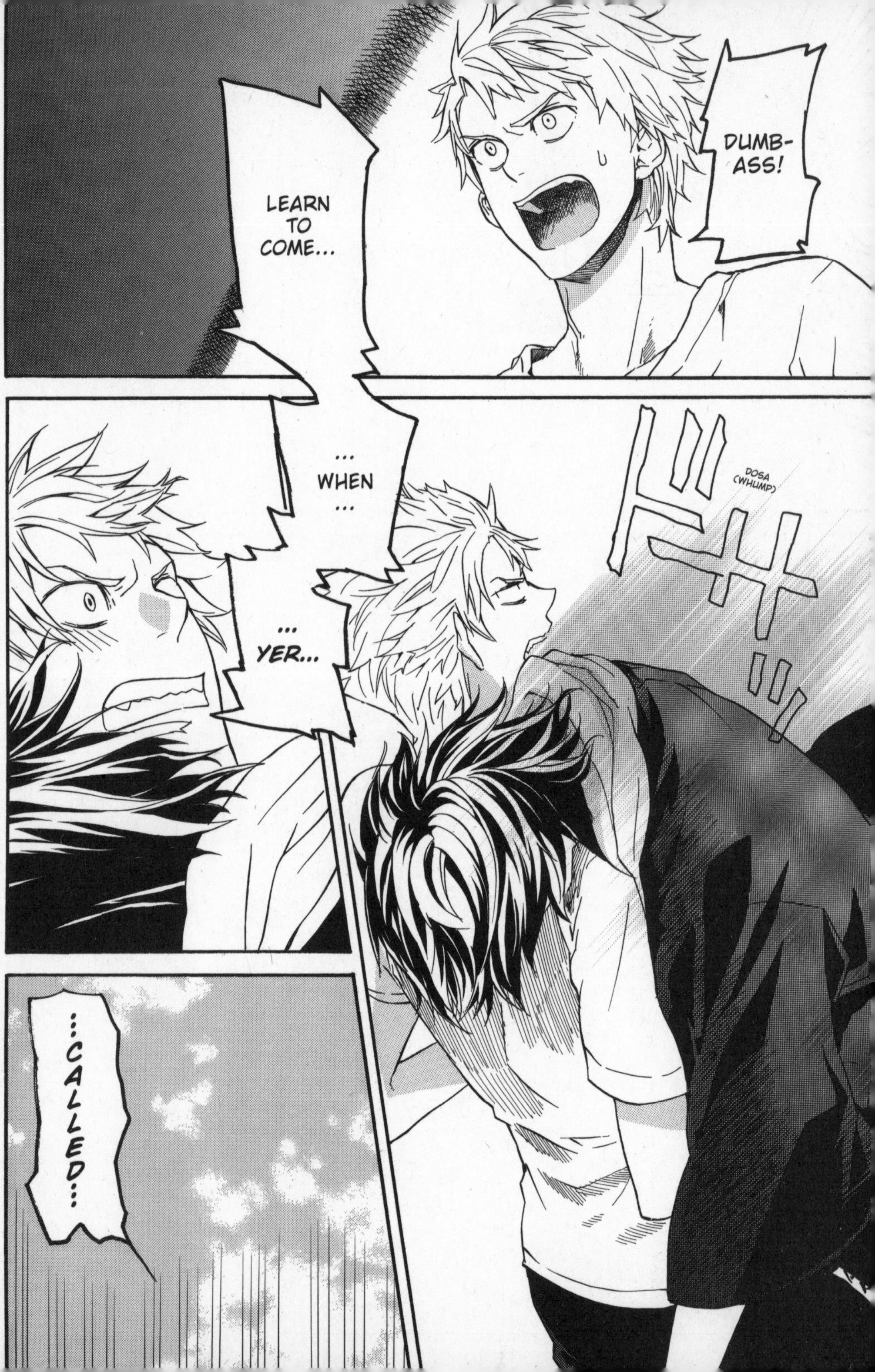
DUMB-ASS!
LEARN TO COME...
DOSA (WHUMP)
... WHEN ...
... YER...
...CALLED...

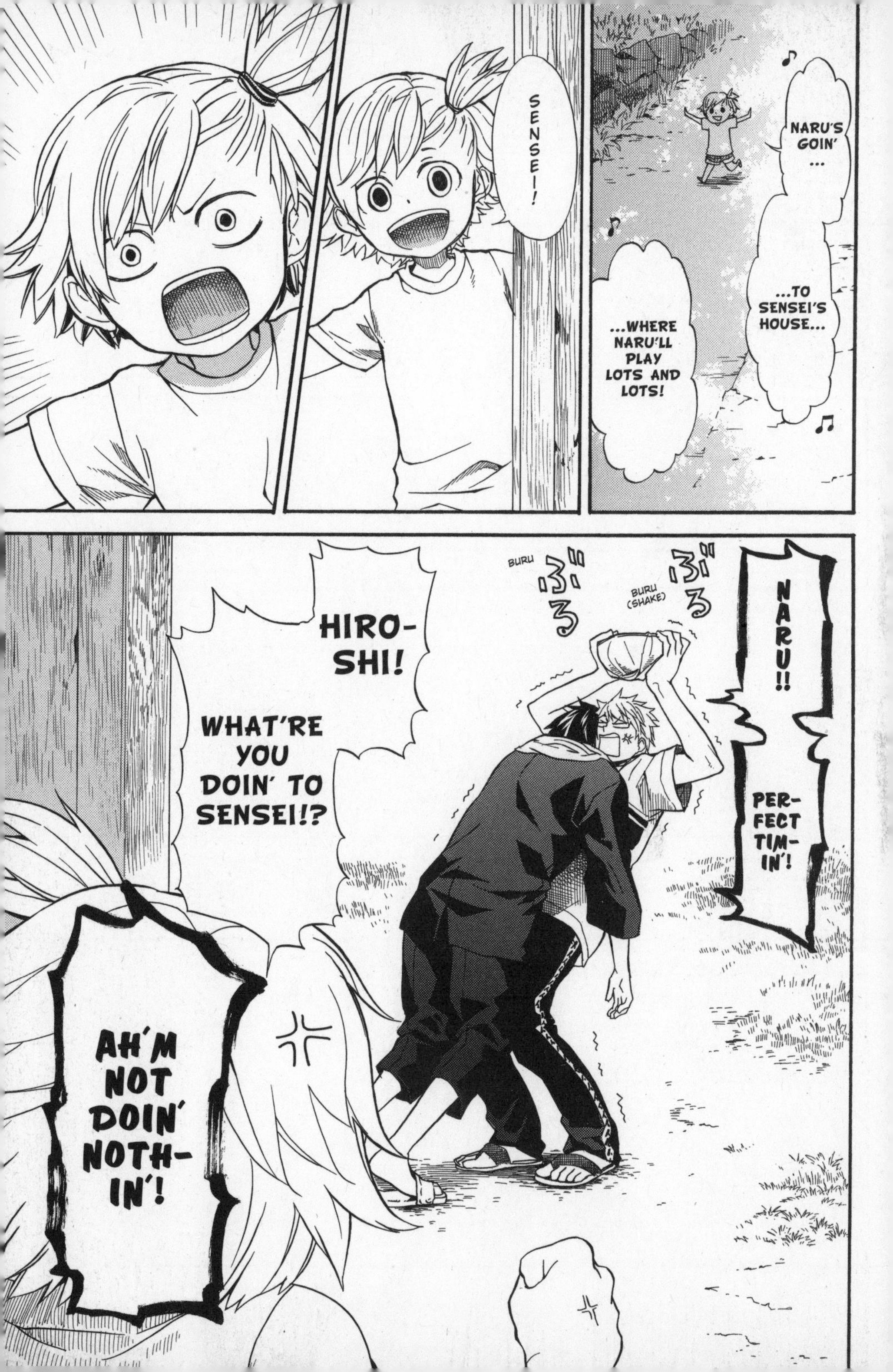
NARU'S GOIN'...
...TO SENSEI'S HOUSE...
...WHERE NARU'LL PLAY LOTS AND LOTS!
SENSEI!
NARU!!
PER-FECT TIM-IN'!
ぶる
BURU (SHAKE)
ぶる
BURU
HIRO-SHI!
WHAT'RE YOU DOIN' TO SENSEI!?
AH'M NOT DOIN' NOTH-IN'!

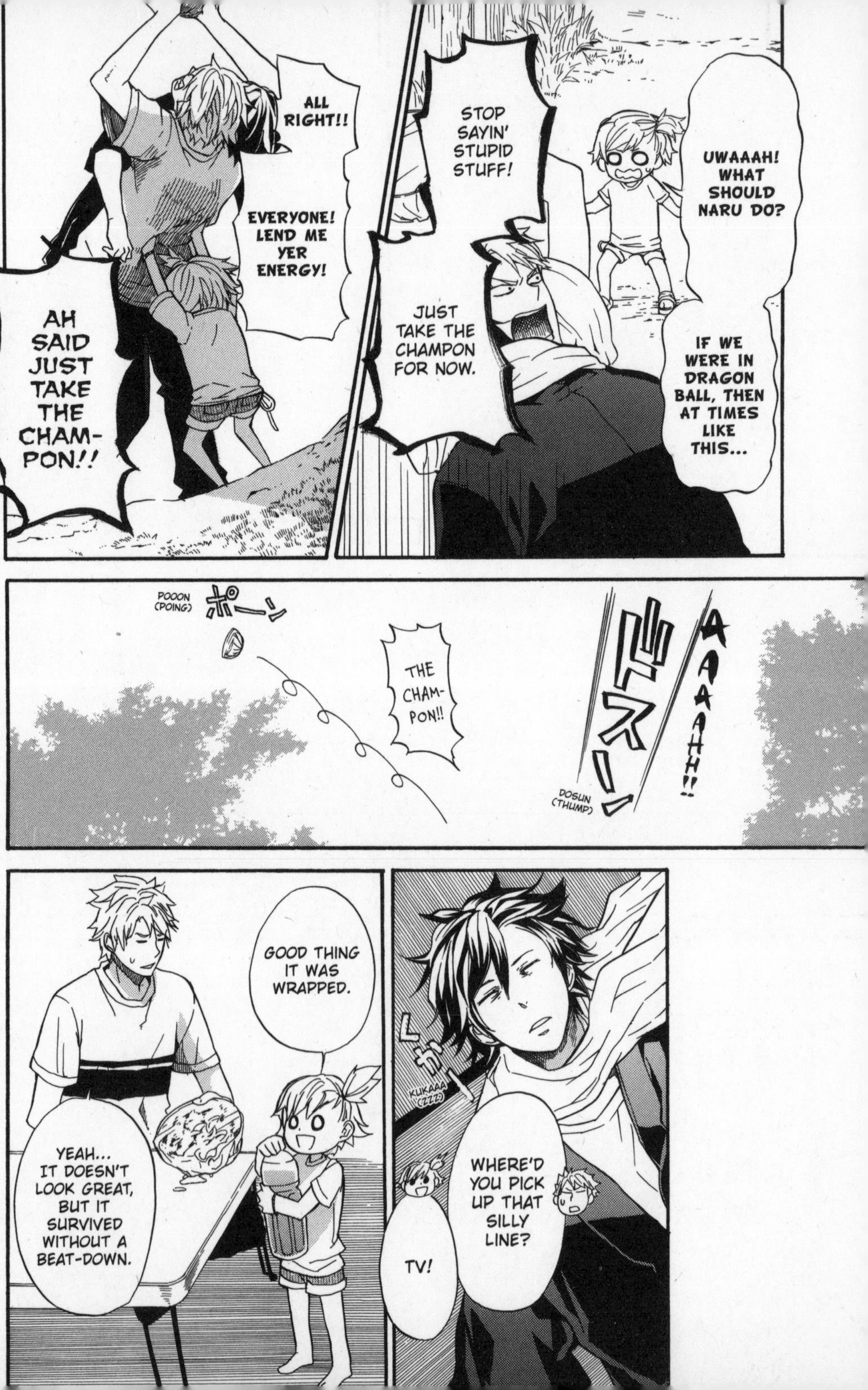
UWAAAH! WHAT SHOULD NARU DO?
IF WE WERE IN DRAGON BALL, THEN AT TIMES LIKE THIS...
STOP SAYIN' STUPID STUFF!
JUST TAKE THE CHAMPON FOR NOW.
ALL RIGHT!!
EVERYONE! LEND ME YER ENERGY!
AH SAID JUST TAKE THE CHAM-PON!!
AAAAHH!!
ドスーン
DOSUN (THUMP)
THE CHAM-PON!!
ポーン
POOON (POING)
KUKAAA (ZZZ)
WHERE'D YOU PICK UP THAT SILLY LINE?
TV!
GOOD THING IT WAS WRAPPED.
YEAH... IT DOESN'T LOOK GREAT, BUT IT SURVIVED WITHOUT A BEAT-DOWN.

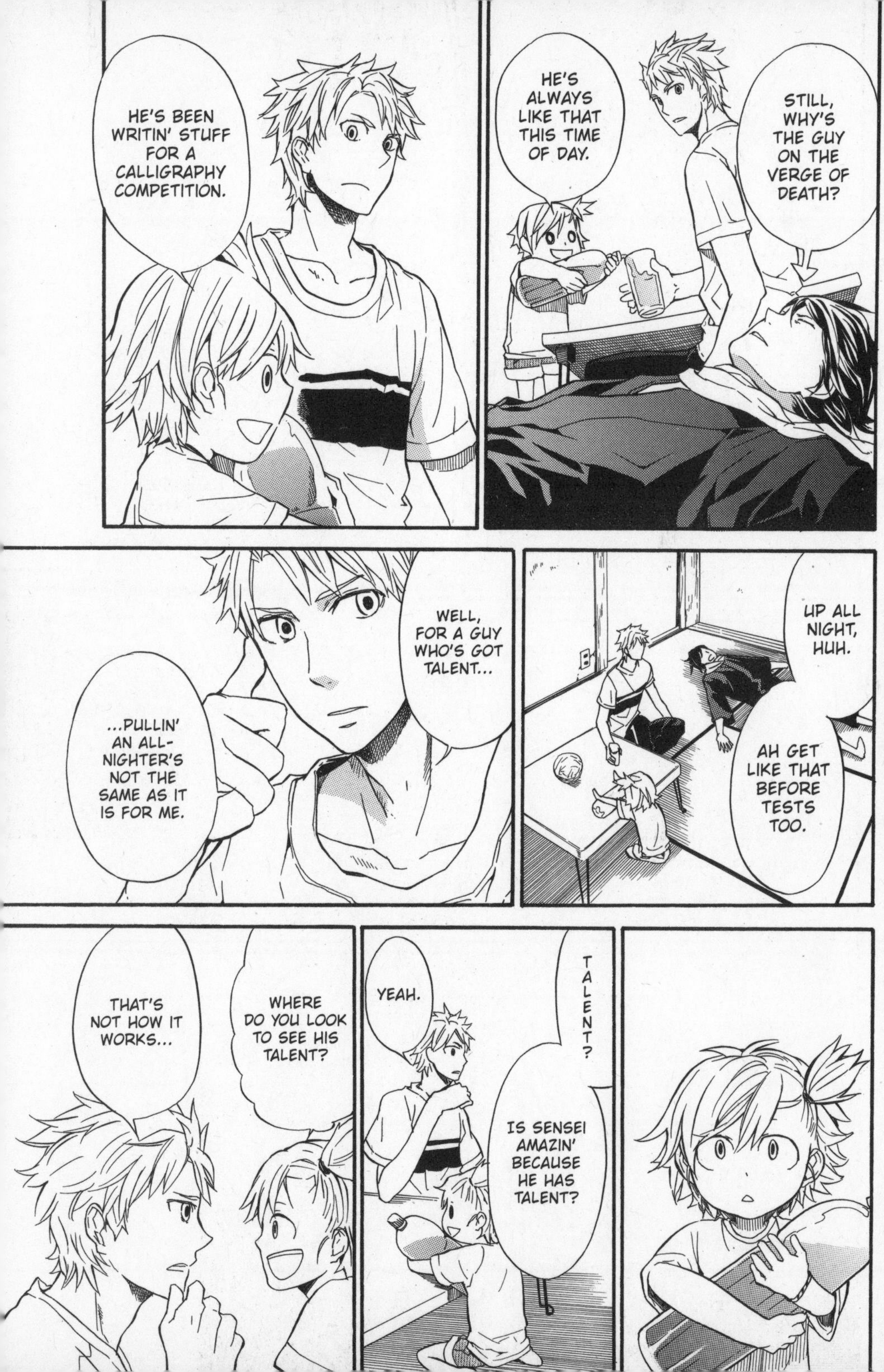
STILL, WHY'S THE GUY ON THE VERGE OF DEATH?
HE'S ALWAYS LIKE THAT THIS TIME OF DAY.
HE'S BEEN WRITIN' STUFF FOR A CALLIGRAPHY COMPETITION.
UP ALL NIGHT, HUH.
AH GET LIKE THAT BEFORE TESTS TOO.
WELL, FOR A GUY WHO'S GOT TALENT...
...PULLIN' AN ALL-NIGHTER'S NOT THE SAME AS IT IS FOR ME.
TALENT?
YEAH.
IS SENSEI AMAZIN' BECAUSE HE HAS TALENT?
WHERE DO YOU LOOK TO SEE HIS TALENT?
THAT'S NOT HOW IT WORKS...

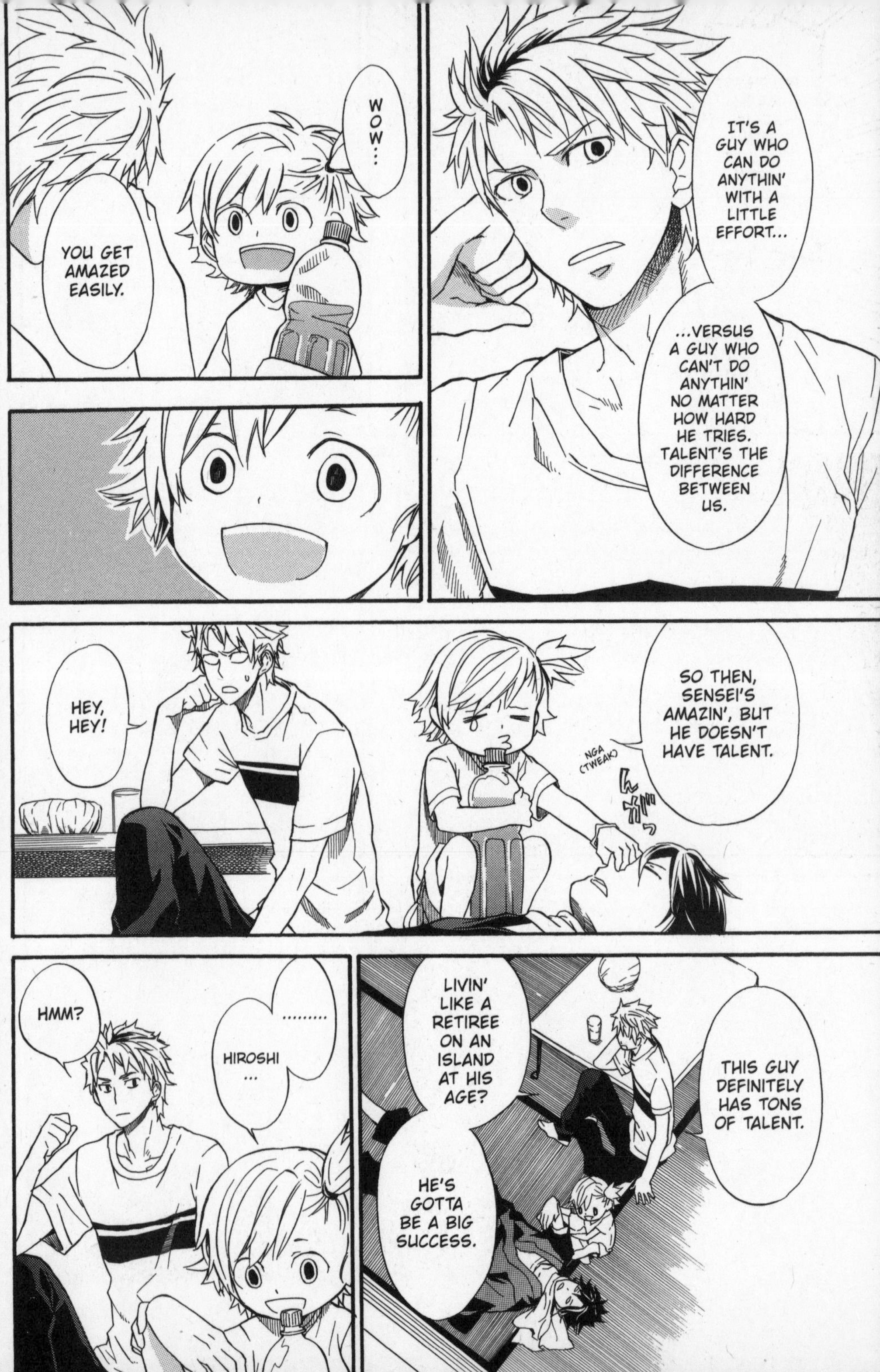
IT'S A GUY WHO CAN DO ANYTHIN' WITH A LITTLE EFFORT...
...VERSUS A GUY WHO CAN'T DO ANYTHIN' NO MATTER HOW HARD HE TRIES. TALENT'S THE DIFFERENCE BETWEEN US.
WOW...
YOU GET AMAZED EASILY.
SO THEN, SENSEI'S AMAZIN', BUT HE DOESN'T HAVE TALENT.
NGA (TWEAK)
HEY, HEY!
THIS GUY DEFINITELY HAS TONS OF TALENT.
LIVIN' LIKE A RETIREE ON AN ISLAND AT HIS AGE?
HE'S GOTTA BE A BIG SUCCESS.
....
HIROSHI ...
HMM?

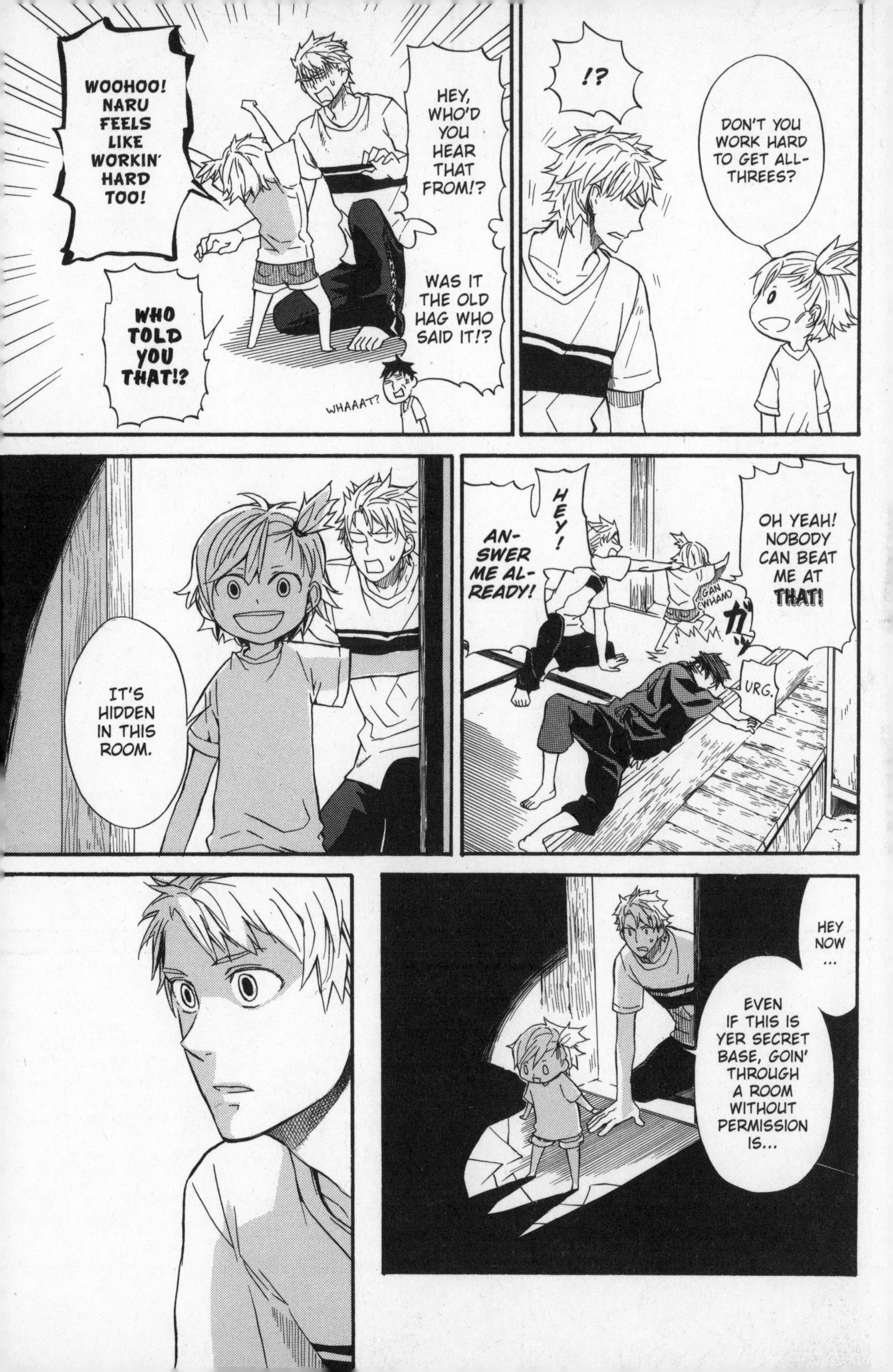
!?
DON'T YOU WORK HARD TO GET ALL-THREES?
HEY, WHO'D YOU HEAR THAT FROM!?
WAS IT THE OLD HAG WHO SAID IT!?
WOOHOO! NARU FEELS LIKE WORKIN' HARD TOO!
WHO TOLD YOU THAT!?
WHAAAT?
OH YEAH! NOBODY CAN BEAT ME AT THAT!
HEY!
ANSWER ME ALREADY!
GAN (WHAM)
ガッ
URG.
IT'S HIDDEN IN THIS ROOM.
HEY NOW...
EVEN IF THIS IS YER SECRET BASE, GOIN' THROUGH A ROOM WITHOUT PERMISSION IS...

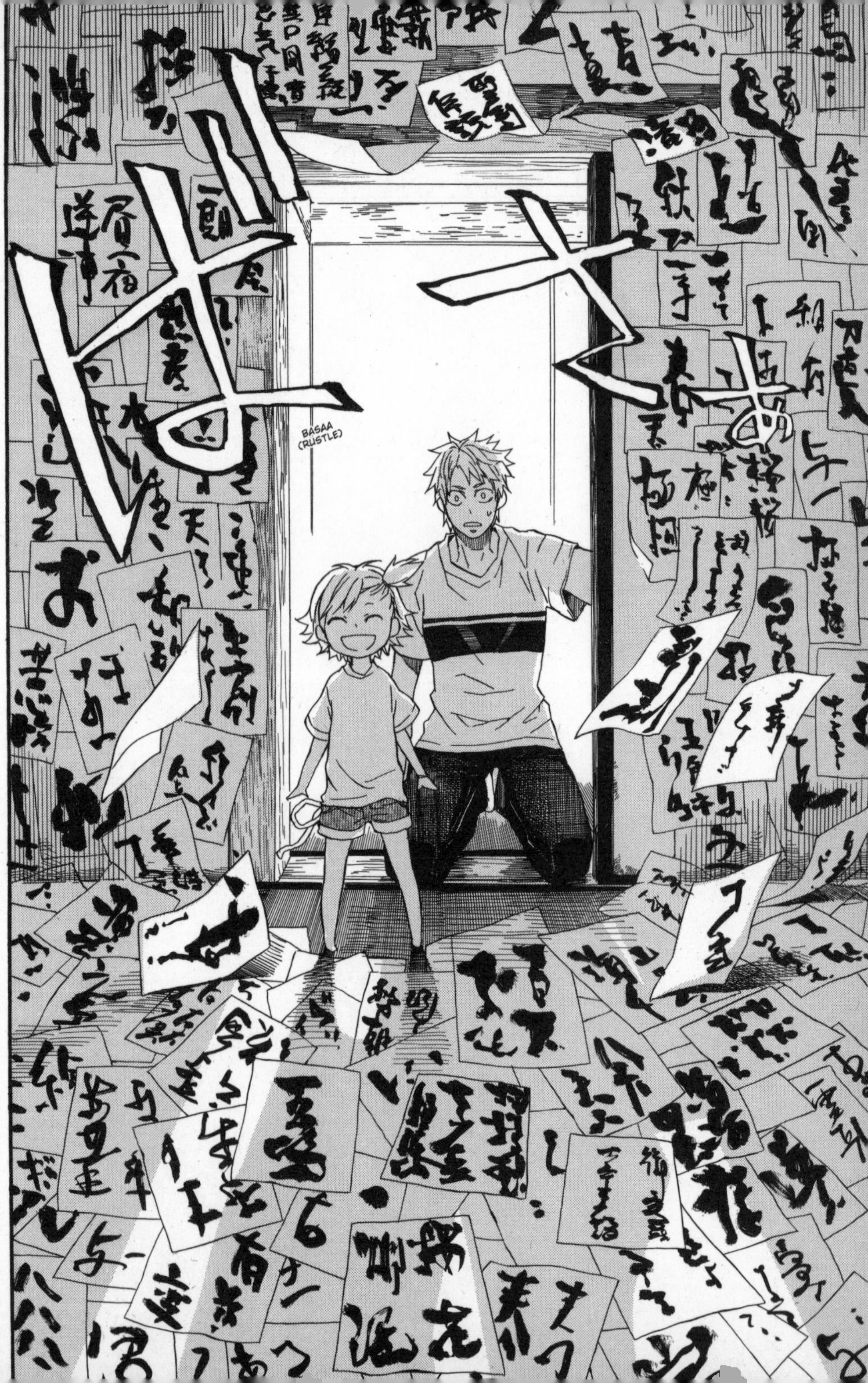
BASAA (RUSTLE)

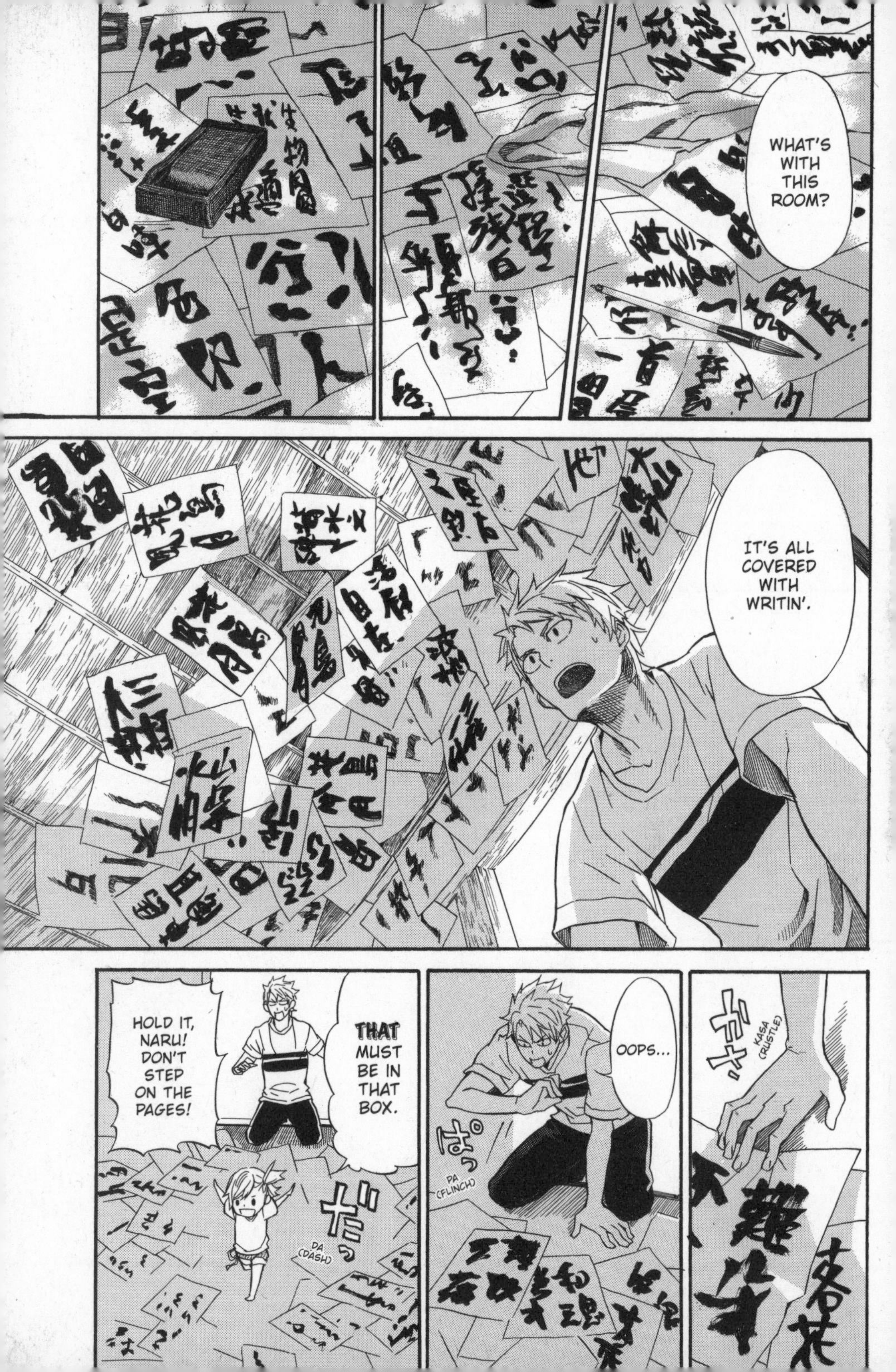
WHAT'S WITH THIS ROOM?
IT'S ALL COVERED WITH WRITIN'.
かさ
KASA (RUSTLE)
OOPS...
ぱっ
PA (FLINCH)
THAT MUST BE IN THAT BOX.
HOLD IT, NARU! DON'T STEP ON THE PAGES!
だっ
DA (DASH)

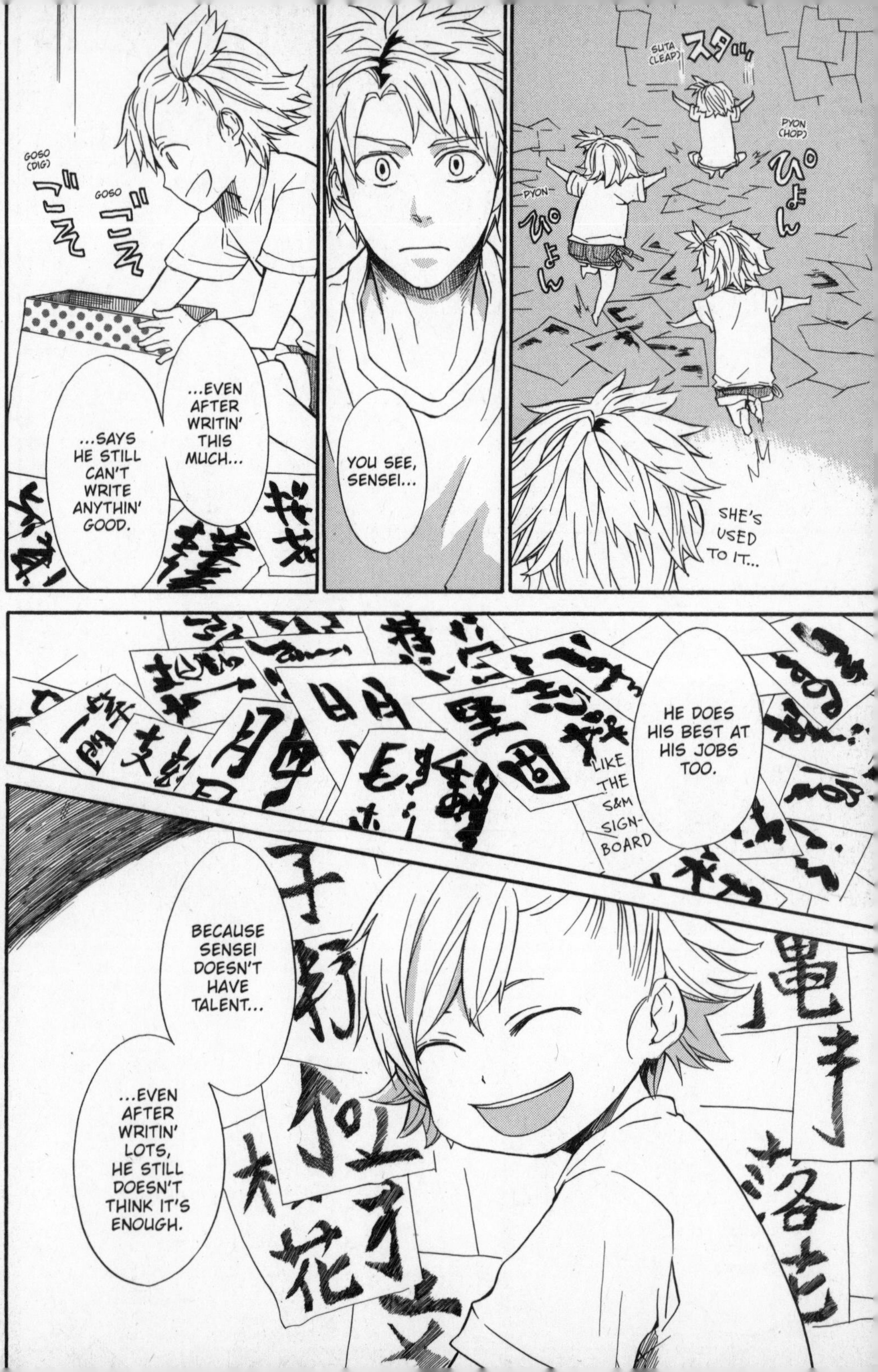
SUTA (LEAP)
PYON (HOP)
PYON
SHE'S USED TO IT...
YOU SEE, SENSEI...
GOSO (DIG)
GOSO
...EVEN AFTER WRITIN' THIS MUCH...
...SAYS HE STILL CAN'T WRITE ANYTHIN' GOOD.
HE DOES HIS BEST AT HIS JOBS TOO.
LIKE THE S&M SIGN-BOARD
BECAUSE SENSEI DOESN'T HAVE TALENT...
...EVEN AFTER WRITIN' LOTS, HE STILL DOESN'T THINK IT'S ENOUGH.

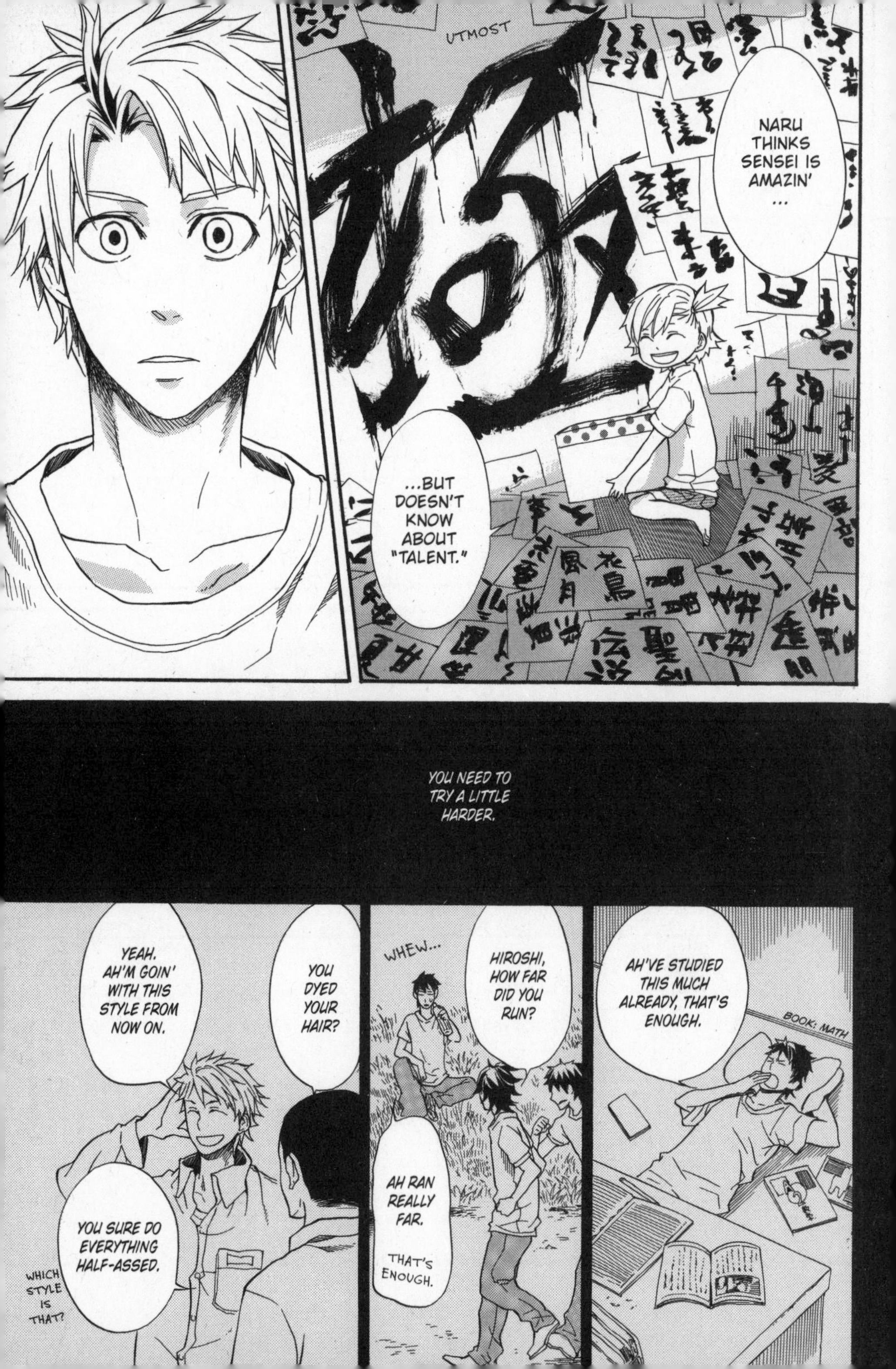
UTMOST
NARU THINKS SENSEI IS AMAZIN' ...
...BUT DOESN'T KNOW ABOUT "TALENT."
YOU NEED TO TRY A LITTLE HARDER.
AH'VE STUDIED THIS MUCH ALREADY, THAT'S ENOUGH.
BOOK: MATH
WHEW...
HIROSHI, HOW FAR DID YOU RUN?
AH RAN REALLY FAR.
THAT'S ENOUGH.
YOU DYED YOUR HAIR?
YEAH. AH'M GOIN' WITH THIS STYLE FROM NOW ON.
YOU SURE DO EVERYTHING HALF-ASSED.
WHICH STYLE IS THAT?

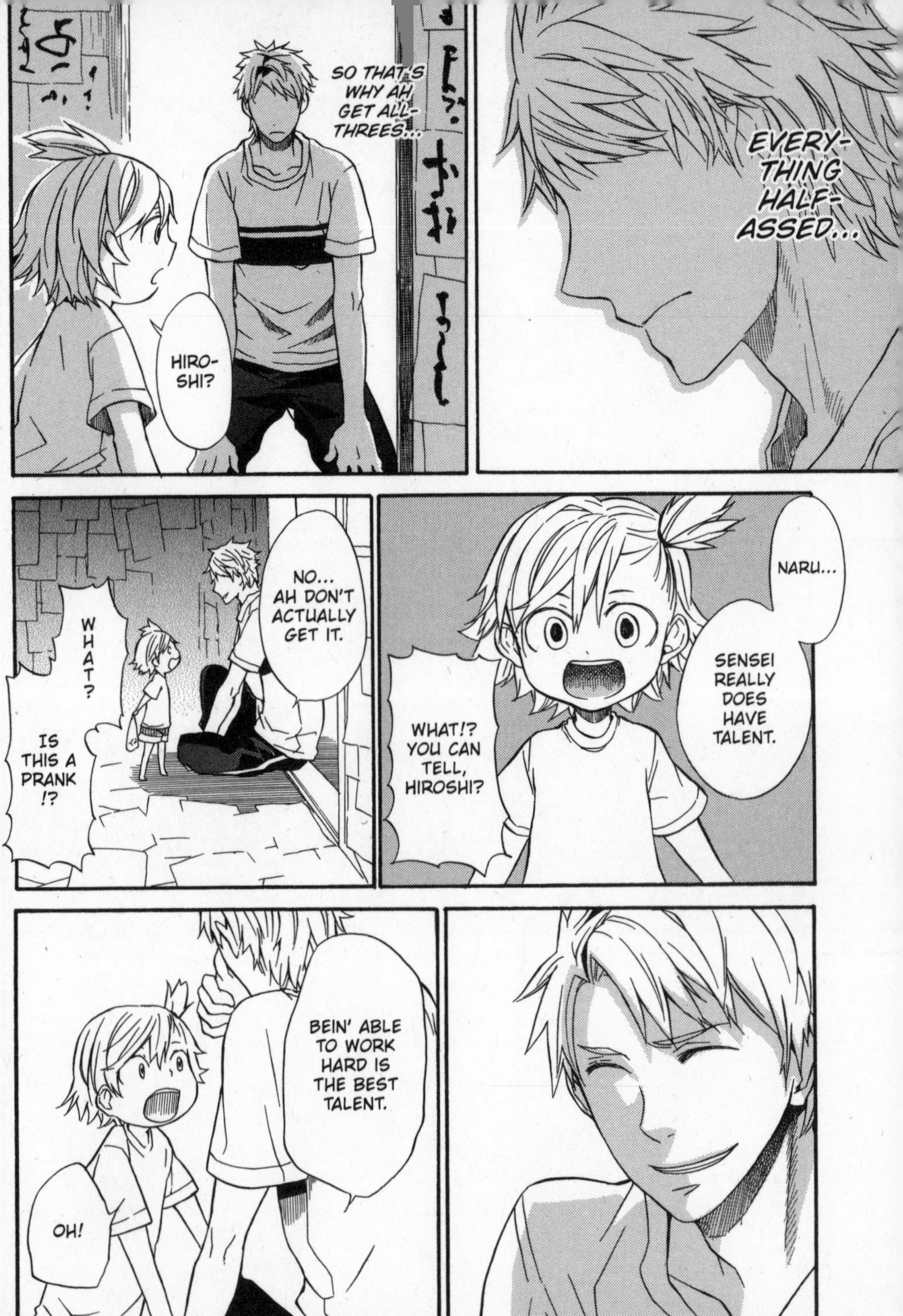
EVERY-THING HALF-ASSED...
SO THAT'S WHY AH GET ALL-THREES...
HIRO-SHI?
NARU...
SENSEI REALLY DOES HAVE TALENT.
WHAT!? YOU CAN TELL, HIROSHI?
NO... AH DON'T ACTUALLY GET IT.
WHAT?
IS THIS A PRANK !?
BEIN' ABLE TO WORK HARD IS THE BEST TALENT.
OH!

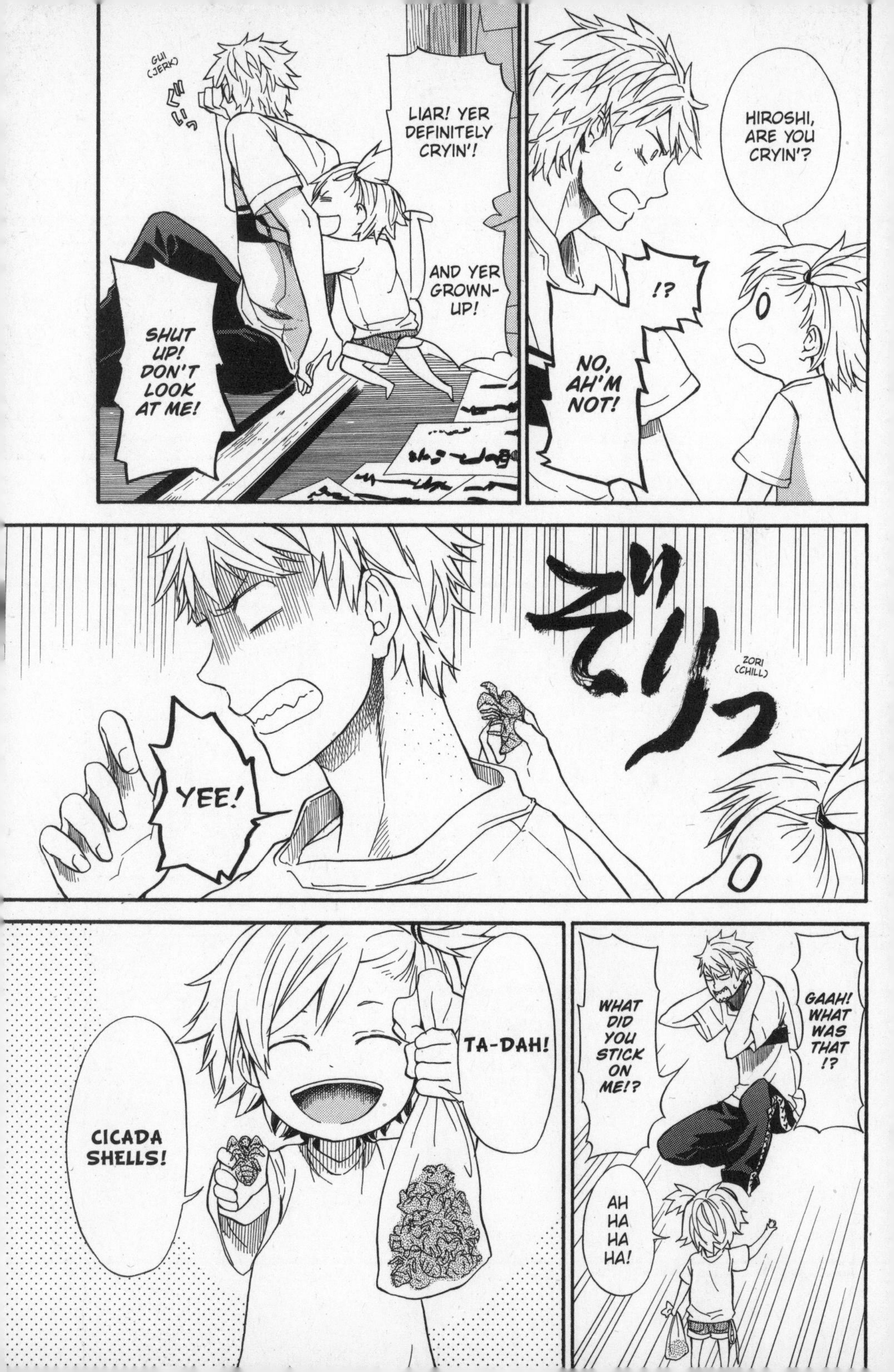
HIROSHI, ARE YOU CRYIN'?
!?
NO, AH'M NOT!
LIAR! YER DEFINITELY CRYIN'!
AND YER GROWN-UP!
GUI (JERK)
SHUT UP! DON'T LOOK AT ME!
ZORI (CHILL)
YEE!
GAAH! WHAT WAS THAT!?
WHAT DID YOU STICK ON ME!?
AH HA HA HA!
TA-DAH!
CICADA SHELLS!

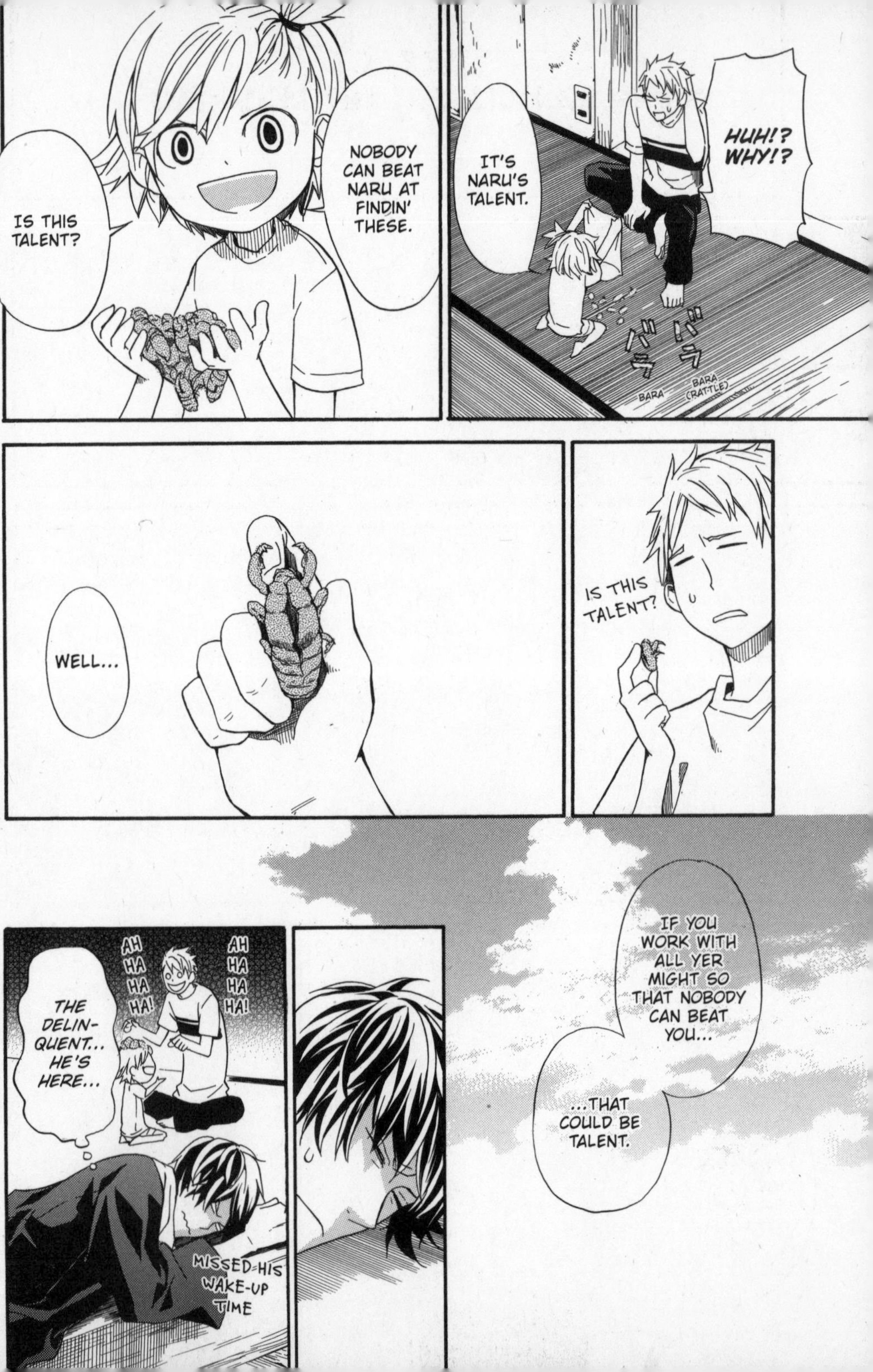
IT'S NARU'S TALENT.
HUH!? WHY!?
BARA BARA (RATTLE)
NOBODY CAN BEAT NARU AT FINDIN' THESE.
IS THIS TALENT?
IS THIS TALENT?
WELL...
IF YOU WORK WITH ALL YER MIGHT SO THAT NOBODY CAN BEAT YOU...
...THAT COULD BE TALENT.
AH HA HA HA HA!
AH HA HA HA HA!
THE DELIN-QUENT... HE'S HERE...
MISSED HIS WAKE-UP TIME

ACT.6.5
GOUCHOU-GAI NO MUSHIKO
(Translation: Village Chief's Son)

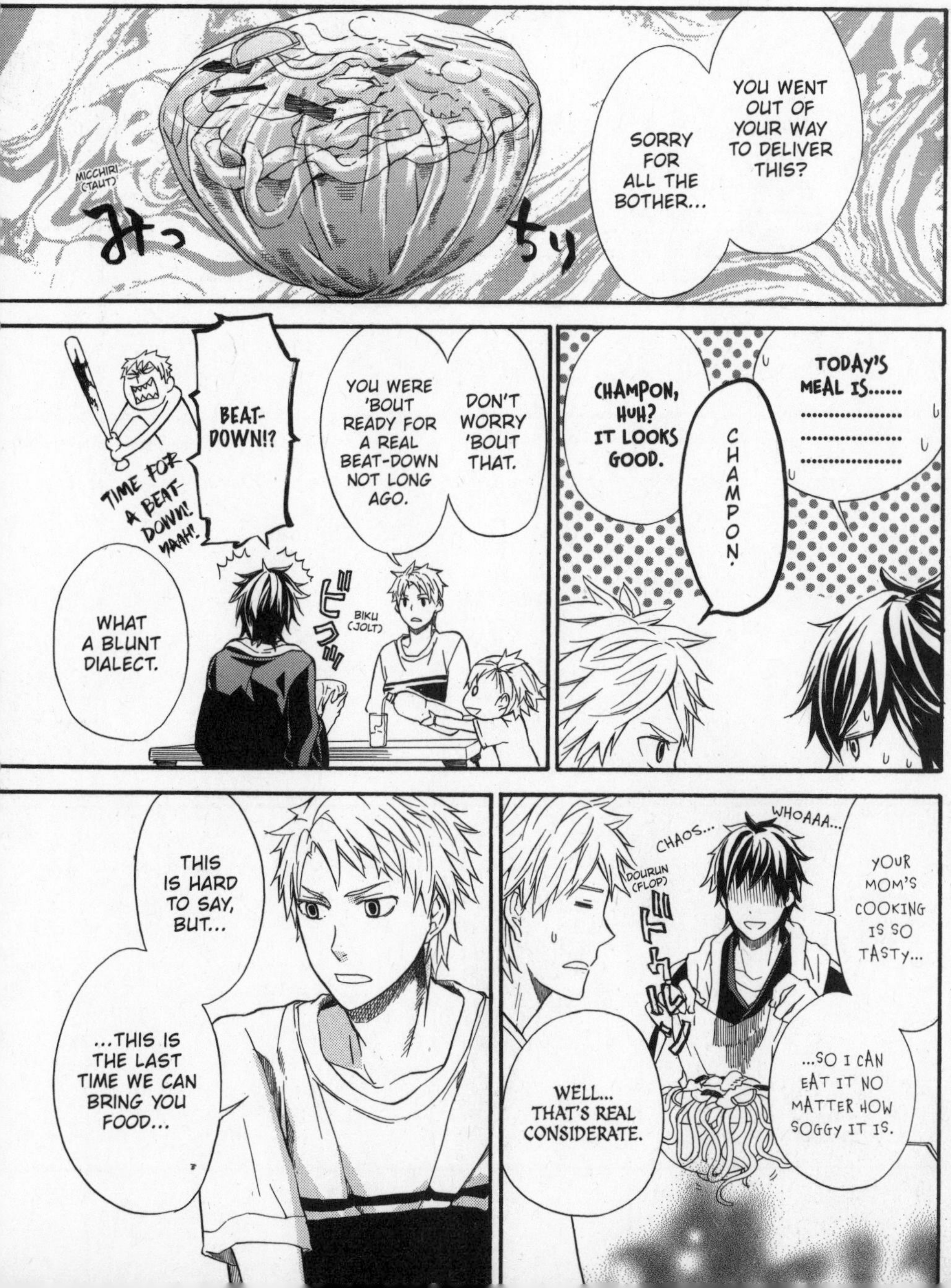
YOU WENT OUT OF YOUR WAY TO DELIVER THIS?
SORRY FOR ALL THE BOTHER...
MICCHIRI (TAUT)
TODAY'S MEAL IS...... ....
CHAMPON.
CHAMPON, HUH? IT LOOKS GOOD.
DON'T WORRY 'BOUT THAT.
YOU WERE 'BOUT READY FOR A REAL BEAT-DOWN NOT LONG AGO.
BEAT-DOWN!?
TIME FOR A BEAT-DOWN!! MAAH!
BIKU (JOLT)
WHAT A BLUNT DIALECT.
WHOAAA...
CHAOS...
YOUR MOM'S COOKING IS SO TASTY...
...SO I CAN EAT IT NO MATTER HOW SOGGY IT IS.
DOURUN (FLOP)
WELL... THAT'S REAL CONSIDERATE.
THIS IS HARD TO SAY, BUT...
...THIS IS THE LAST TIME WE CAN BRING YOU FOOD...

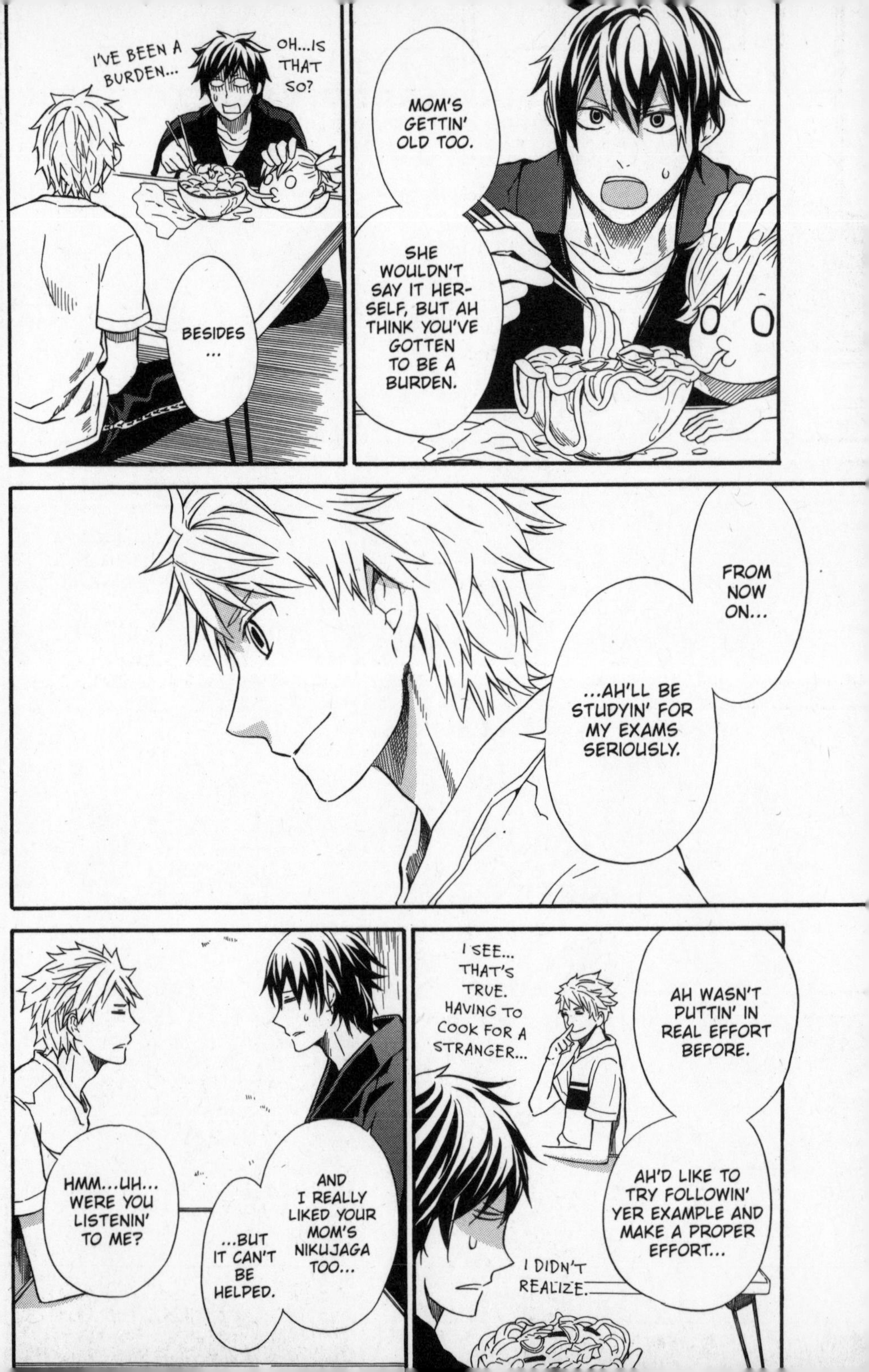
MOM'S GETTIN' OLD TOO.
SHE WOULDN'T SAY IT HER-SELF, BUT AH THINK YOU'VE GOTTEN TO BE A BURDEN.
OH...IS THAT SO?
I'VE BEEN A BURDEN...
BESIDES...
FROM NOW ON...
...AH'LL BE STUDYIN' FOR MY EXAMS SERIOUSLY.
AH WASN'T PUTTIN' IN REAL EFFORT BEFORE.
I SEE... THAT'S TRUE. HAVING TO COOK FOR A STRANGER...
AH'D LIKE TO TRY FOLLOWIN' YER EXAMPLE AND MAKE A PROPER EFFORT...
I DIDN'T REALIZE.
AND I REALLY LIKED YOUR MOM'S NIKUJAGA TOO...
...BUT IT CAN'T BE HELPED.
HMM...UH... WERE YOU LISTENIN' TO ME?

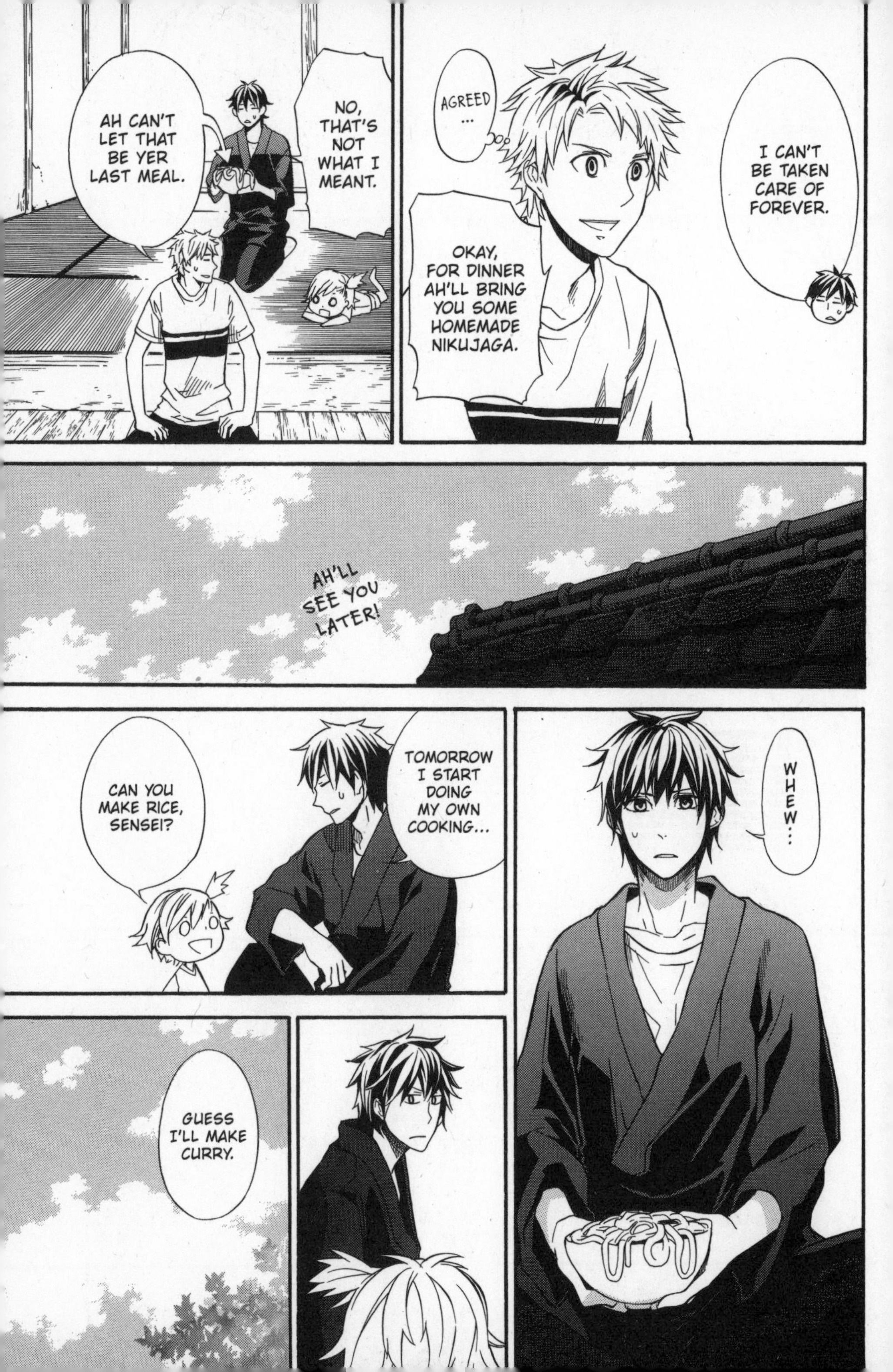
I CAN'T BE TAKEN CARE OF FOREVER.
AGREED ...
OKAY, FOR DINNER AH'LL BRING YOU SOME HOMEMADE NIKUJAGA.
NO, THAT'S NOT WHAT I MEANT.
AH CAN'T LET THAT BE YER LAST MEAL.
AH'LL SEE YOU LATER!
WHEW...
TOMORROW I START DOING MY OWN COOKING...
CAN YOU MAKE RICE, SENSEI?
GUESS I'LL MAKE CURRY.

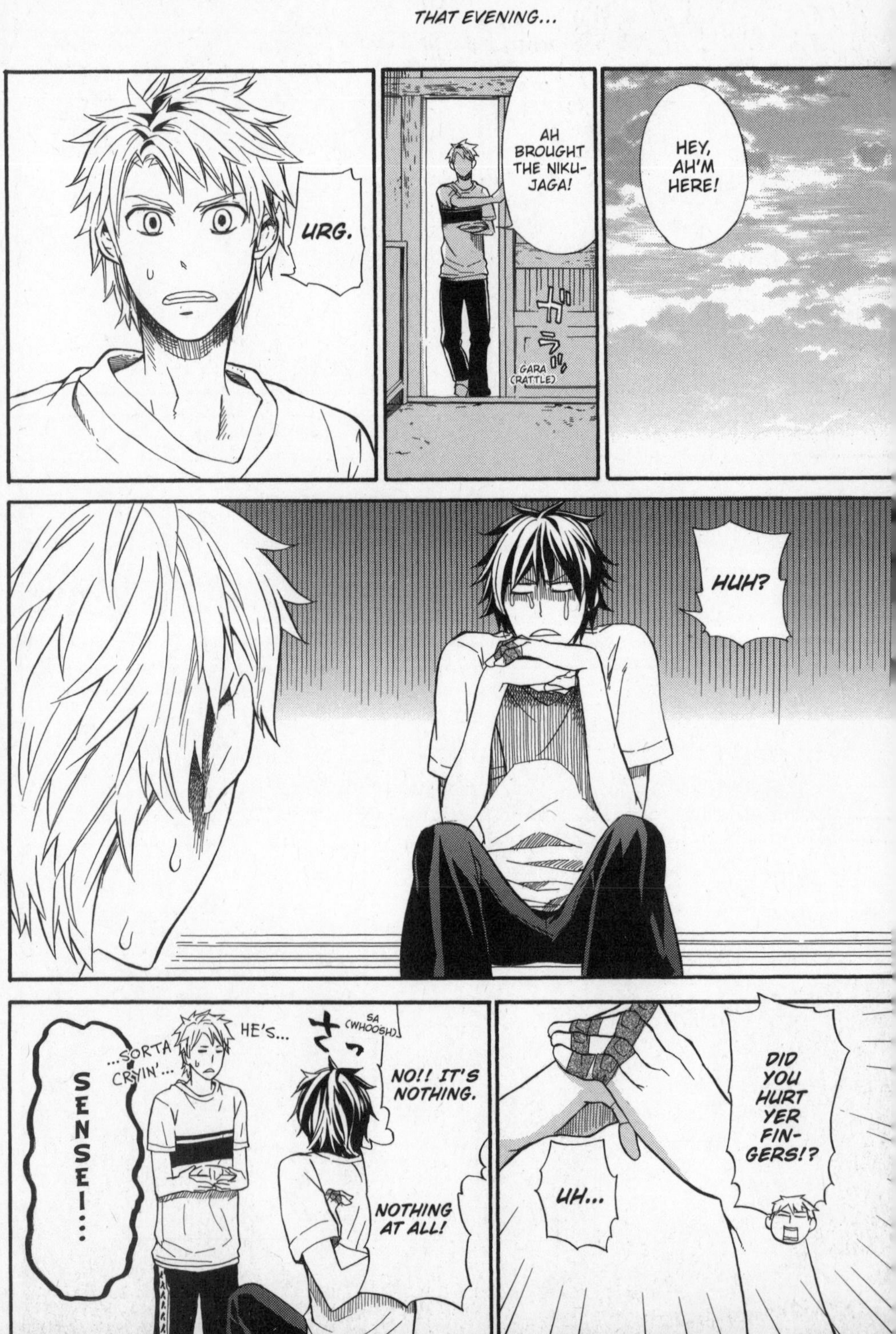
THAT EVENING...
HEY, AH'M HERE!
AH BROUGHT THE NIKU-JAGA!
ガラ
GARA (RATTLE)
URG.
HUH?
DID YOU HURT YER FINGERS!?
UH...
さっ
SA (WHOOSH)
NO!! IT'S NOTHING.
NOTHING AT ALL!
HE'S...
...SORTA CRYIN'...
SENSEI!...

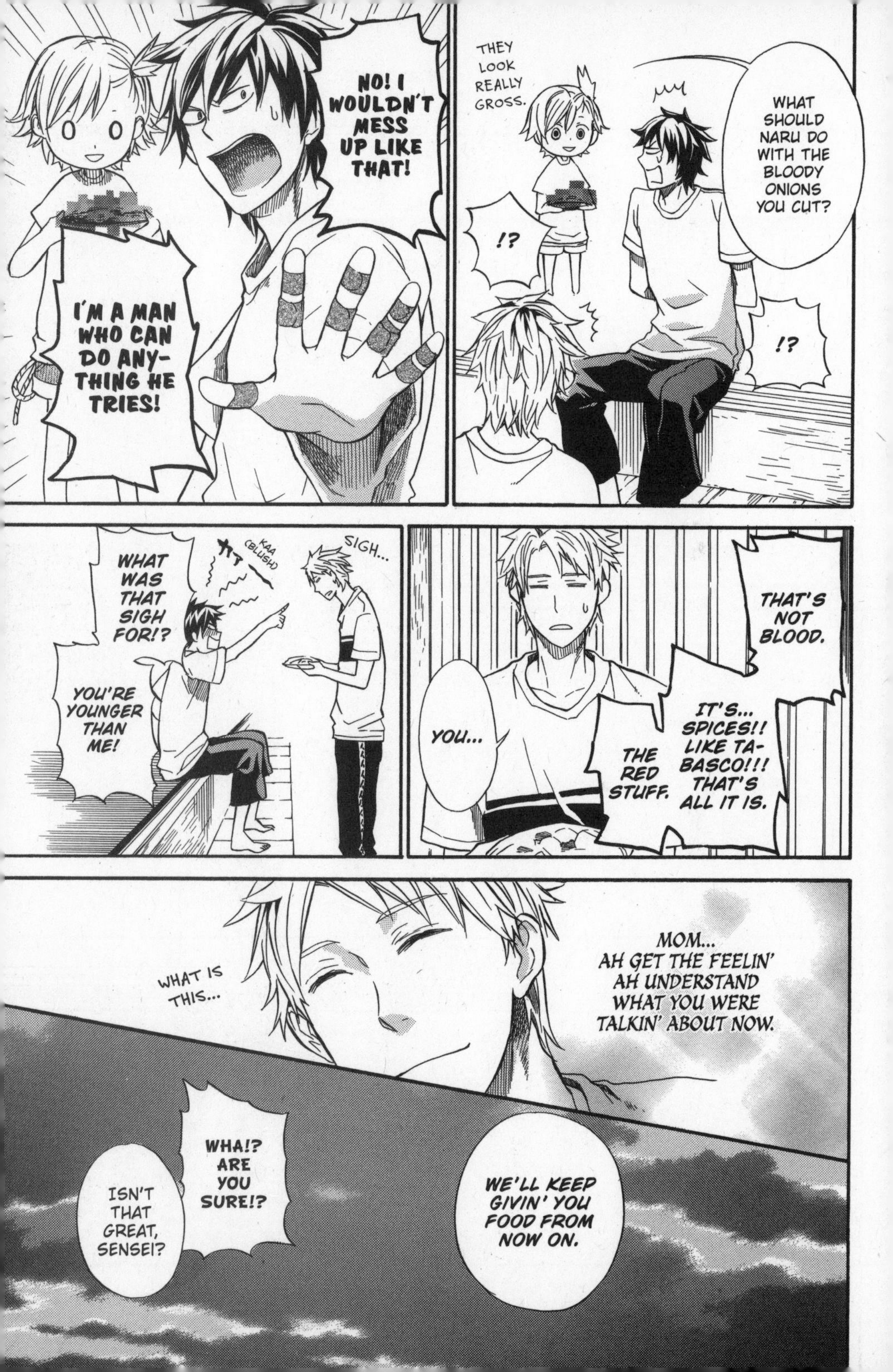

WHAT SHOULD NARU DO WITH THE BLOODY ONIONS YOU CUT?
THEY LOOK REALLY GROSS.
!?
!?
NO! I WOULDN'T MESS UP LIKE THAT!
I'M A MAN WHO CAN DO ANY-THING HE TRIES!
THAT'S NOT BLOOD.
IT'S... SPICES!! LIKE TA-BASCO!!! THAT'S ALL IT IS.
THE RED STUFF.
YOU...
SIGH...
KAA (BLUSH)
WHAT WAS THAT SIGH FOR!?
YOU'RE YOUNGER THAN ME!
MOM... AH GET THE FEELIN' AH UNDERSTAND WHAT YOU WERE TALKIN' ABOUT NOW.
WHAT IS THIS...
WE'LL KEEP GIVIN' YOU FOOD FROM NOW ON.
WHA!? ARE YOU SURE!?
ISN'T THAT GREAT, SENSEI?

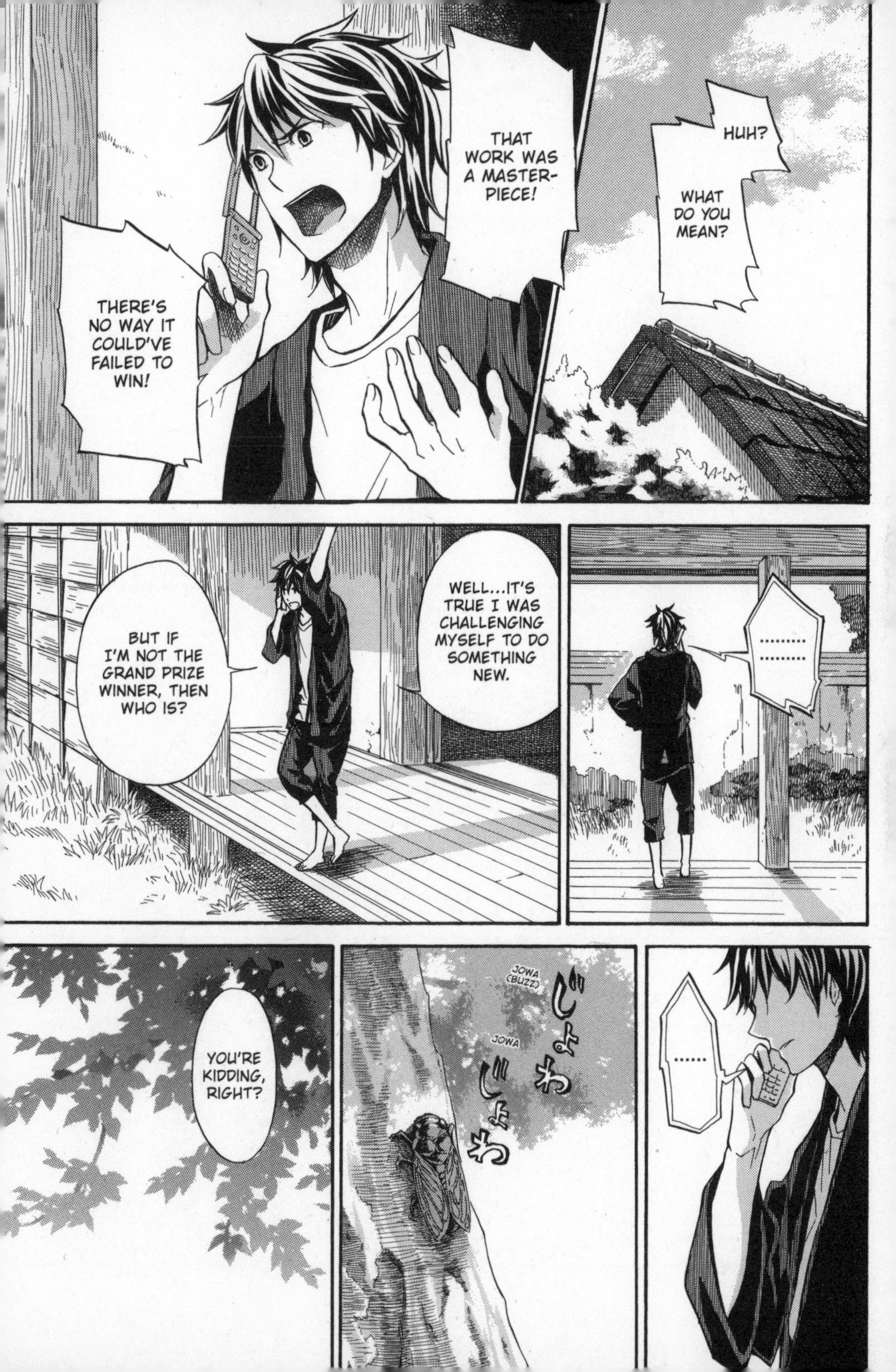
HUH?
WHAT DO YOU MEAN?
THAT WORK WAS A MASTER-PIECE!
THERE'S NO WAY IT COULD'VE FAILED TO WIN!
....
....
WELL...IT'S TRUE I WAS CHALLENGING MYSELF TO DO SOMETHING NEW.
BUT IF I'M NOT THE GRAND PRIZE WINNER, THEN WHO IS?
......
じょわ
JOWA (BUZZ)
じょわ
JOWA
YOU'RE KIDDING, RIGHT?

ACT.7
HITONMOCHI
(Translation: Mochi Thrown in Celebration)

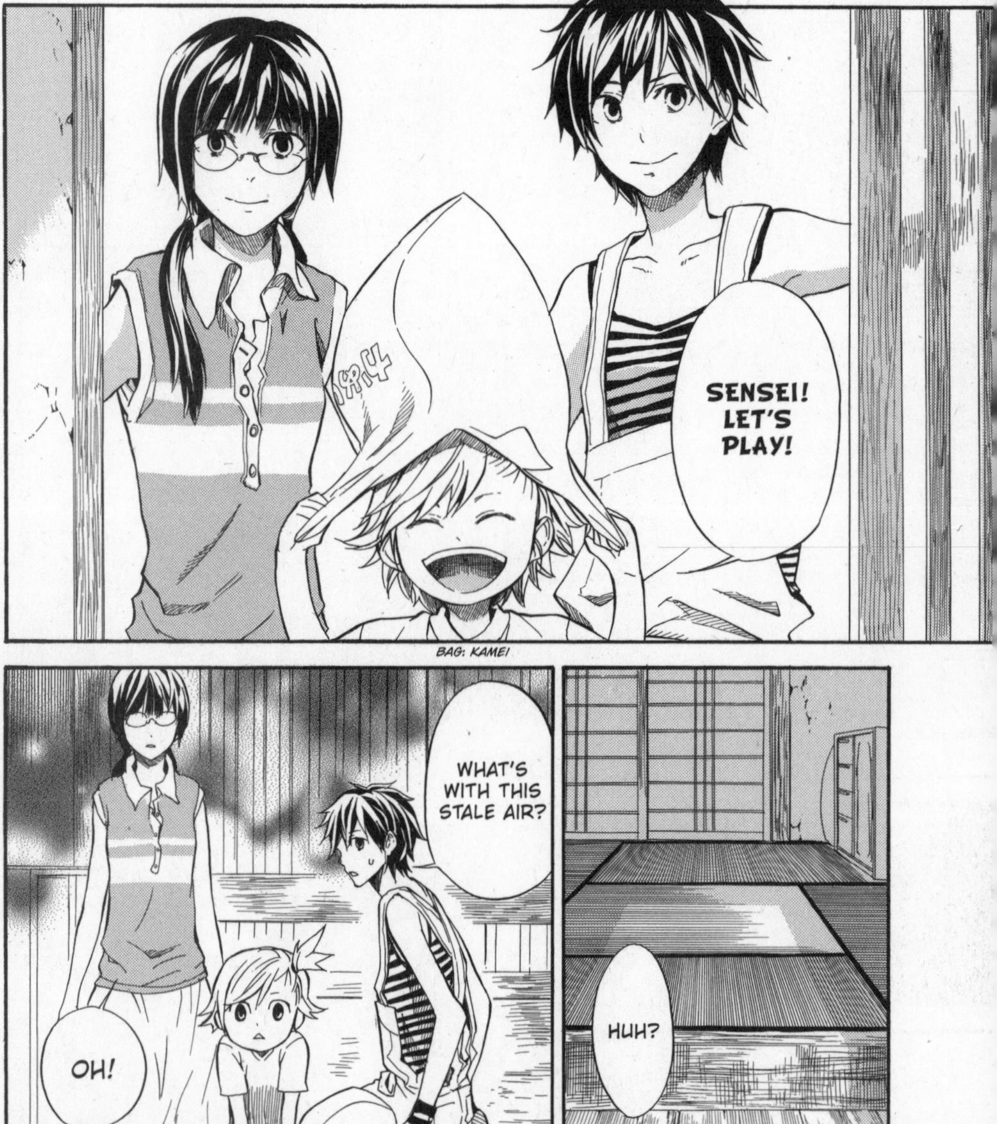
SENSEI! LET'S PLAY!
BAG: KAMEI
HUH?
WHAT'S WITH THIS STALE AIR?
OH!

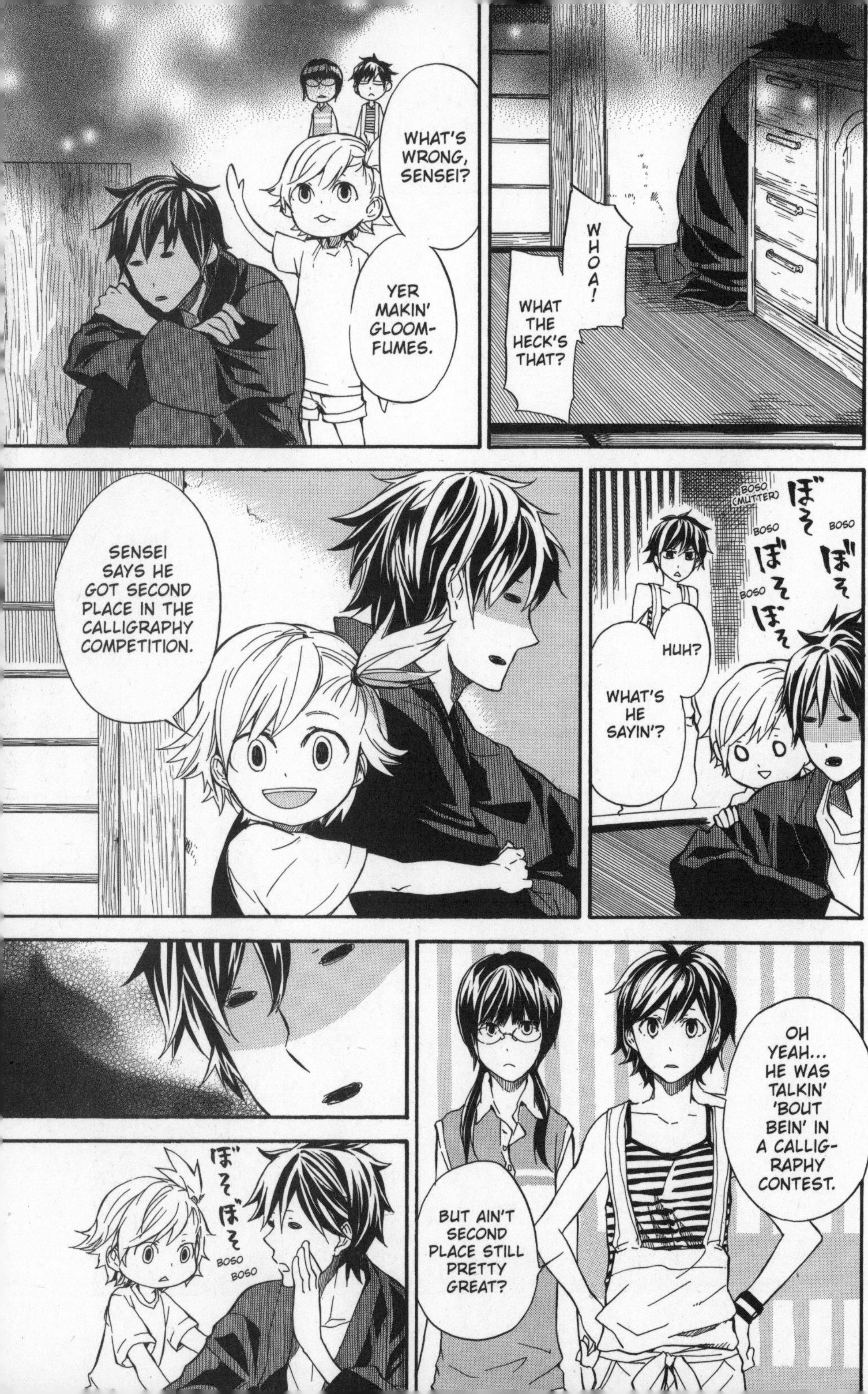
WHOA!
WHAT THE HECK'S THAT?
WHAT'S WRONG, SENSEI?
YER MAKIN' GLOOM-FUMES.
ぼそ BOSO (MUTTER)
ぼそ BOSO
ぼそ BOSO
ぼそ BOSO
HUH?
WHAT'S HE SAYIN'?
SENSEI SAYS HE GOT SECOND PLACE IN THE CALLIGRAPHY COMPETITION.
OH YEAH... HE WAS TALKIN' 'BOUT BEIN' IN A CALLIG-RAPHY CONTEST.
BUT AIN'T SECOND PLACE STILL PRETTY GREAT?
ぼそぼそ
BOSO BOSO

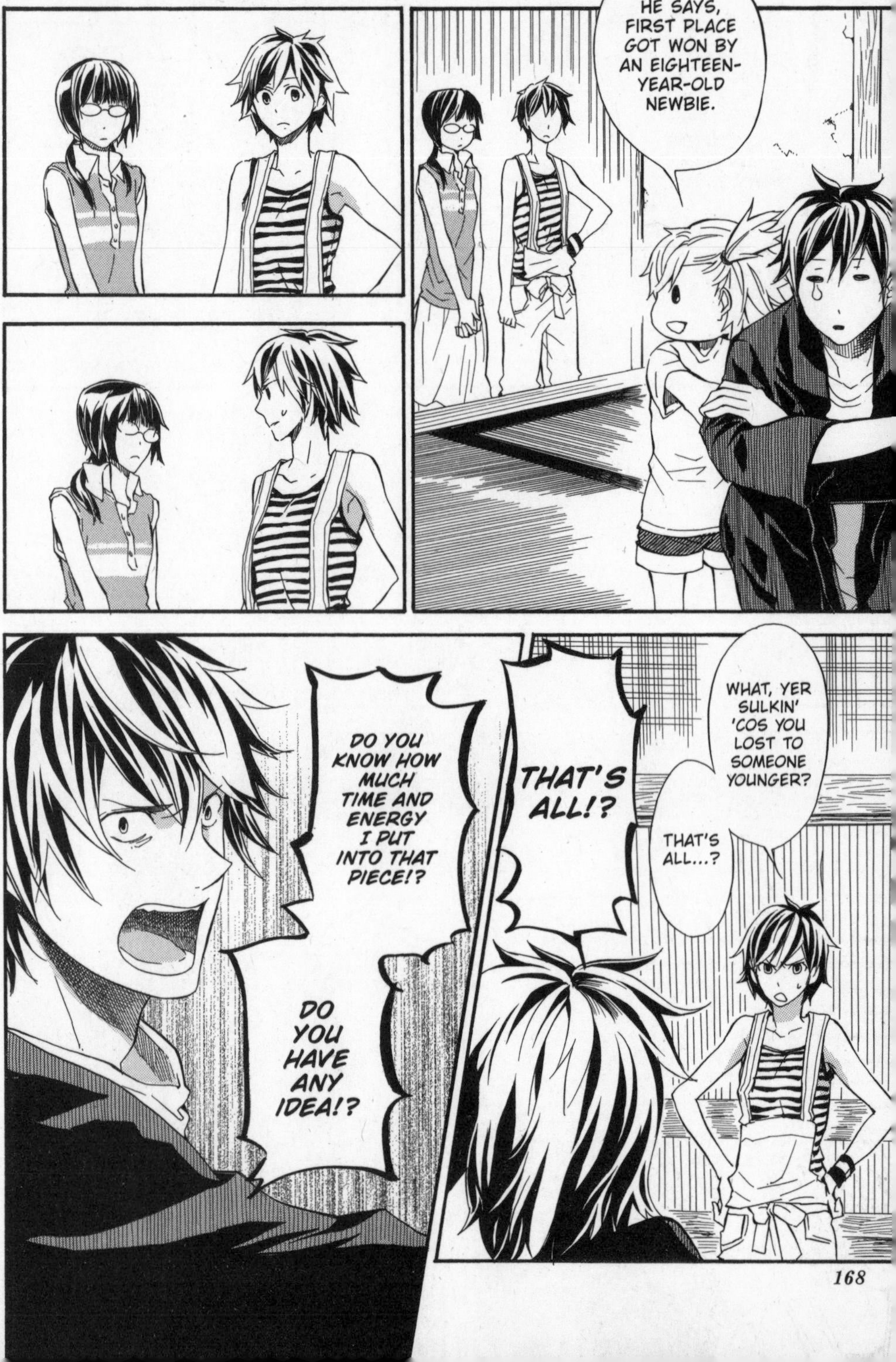
HE SAYS, FIRST PLACE GOT WON BY AN EIGHTEEN-YEAR-OLD NEWBIE.
WHAT, YER SULKIN' 'COS YOU LOST TO SOMEONE YOUNGER?
THAT'S ALL...?
THAT'S ALL!?
DO YOU KNOW HOW MUCH TIME AND ENERGY I PUT INTO THAT PIECE!?
DO YOU HAVE ANY IDEA!?

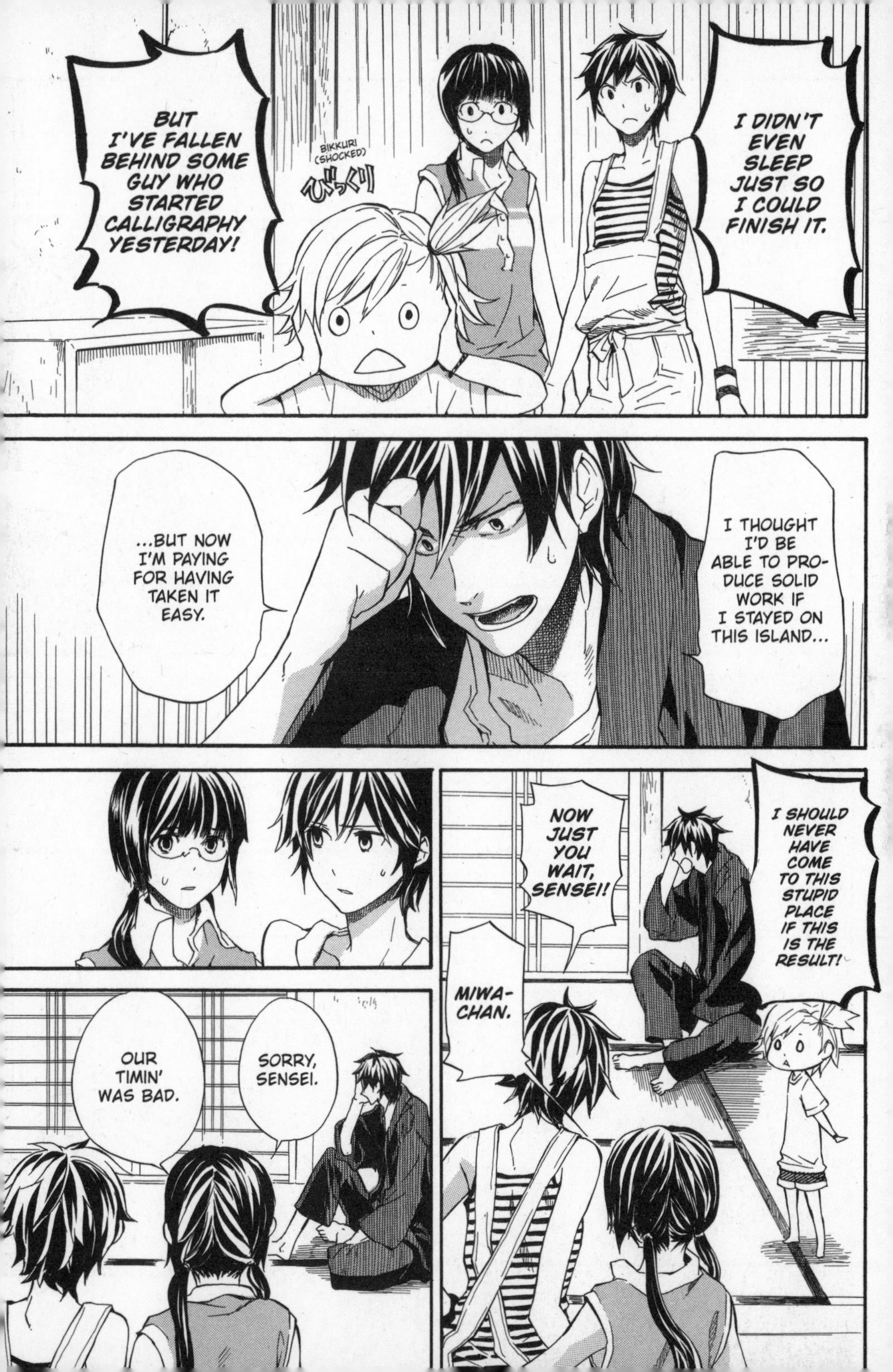

I DIDN'T EVEN SLEEP JUST SO I COULD FINISH IT.
BUT I'VE FALLEN BEHIND SOME GUY WHO STARTED CALLIGRAPHY YESTERDAY!
BIKKURI (SHOCKED)
びっくり
I THOUGHT I'D BE ABLE TO PRO-DUCE SOLID WORK IF I STAYED ON THIS ISLAND...
...BUT NOW I'M PAYING FOR HAVING TAKEN IT EASY.
I SHOULD NEVER HAVE COME TO THIS STUPID PLACE IF THIS IS THE RESULT!
NOW JUST YOU WAIT, SENSEI!!
MIWA-CHAN.
SORRY, SENSEI.
OUR TIMIN' WAS BAD.

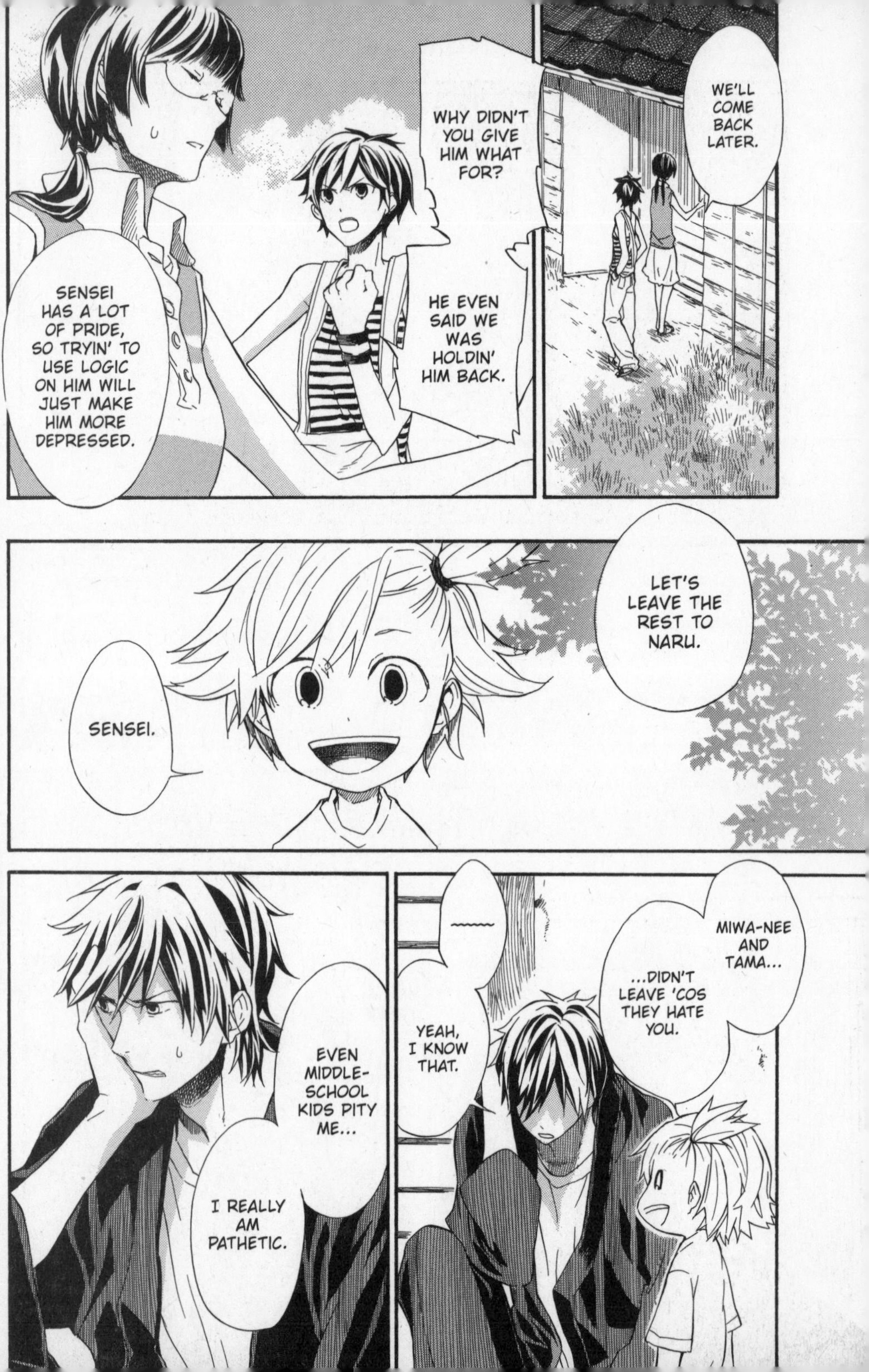
WE'LL COME BACK LATER.
WHY DIDN'T YOU GIVE HIM WHAT FOR?
HE EVEN SAID WE WAS HOLDIN' HIM BACK.
SENSEI HAS A LOT OF PRIDE, SO TRYIN' TO USE LOGIC ON HIM WILL JUST MAKE HIM MORE DEPRESSED.
LET'S LEAVE THE REST TO NARU.
SENSEI.
MIWA-NEE AND TAMA...
...DIDN'T LEAVE 'COS THEY HATE YOU.
~~~~~
YEAH, I KNOW THAT.
EVEN MIDDLE-SCHOOL KIDS PITY ME...
I REALLY AM PATHETIC.
~~~~~

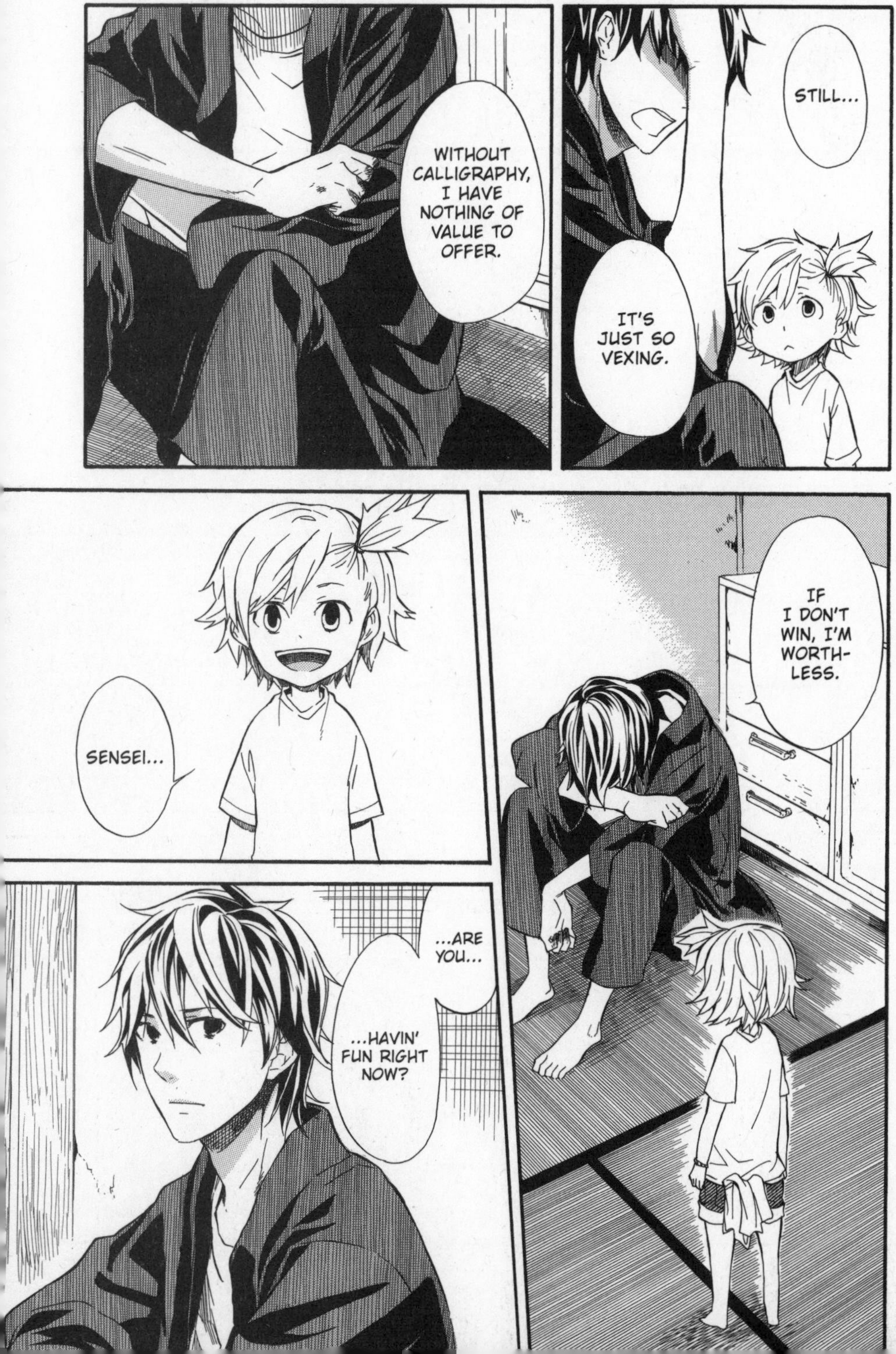

STILL...
IT'S JUST SO VEXING.
WITHOUT CALLIGRAPHY, I HAVE NOTHING OF VALUE TO OFFER.
IF I DON'T WIN, I'M WORTHLESS.
SENSEI...
...ARE YOU...
...HAVIN' FUN RIGHT NOW?

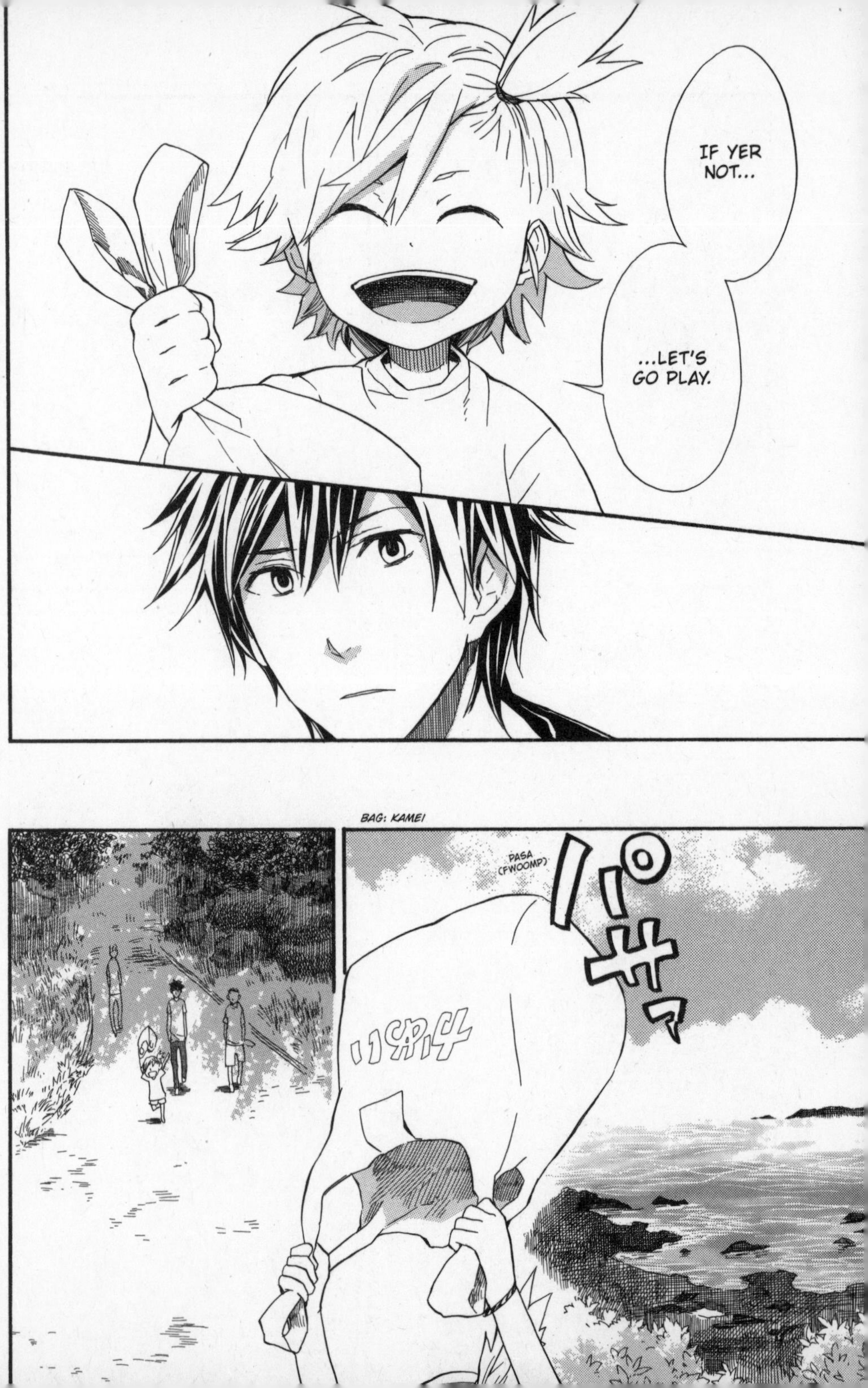
IF YER NOT...
...LET'S GO PLAY.
BAG: KAMEI
PASA (FWOOMP)

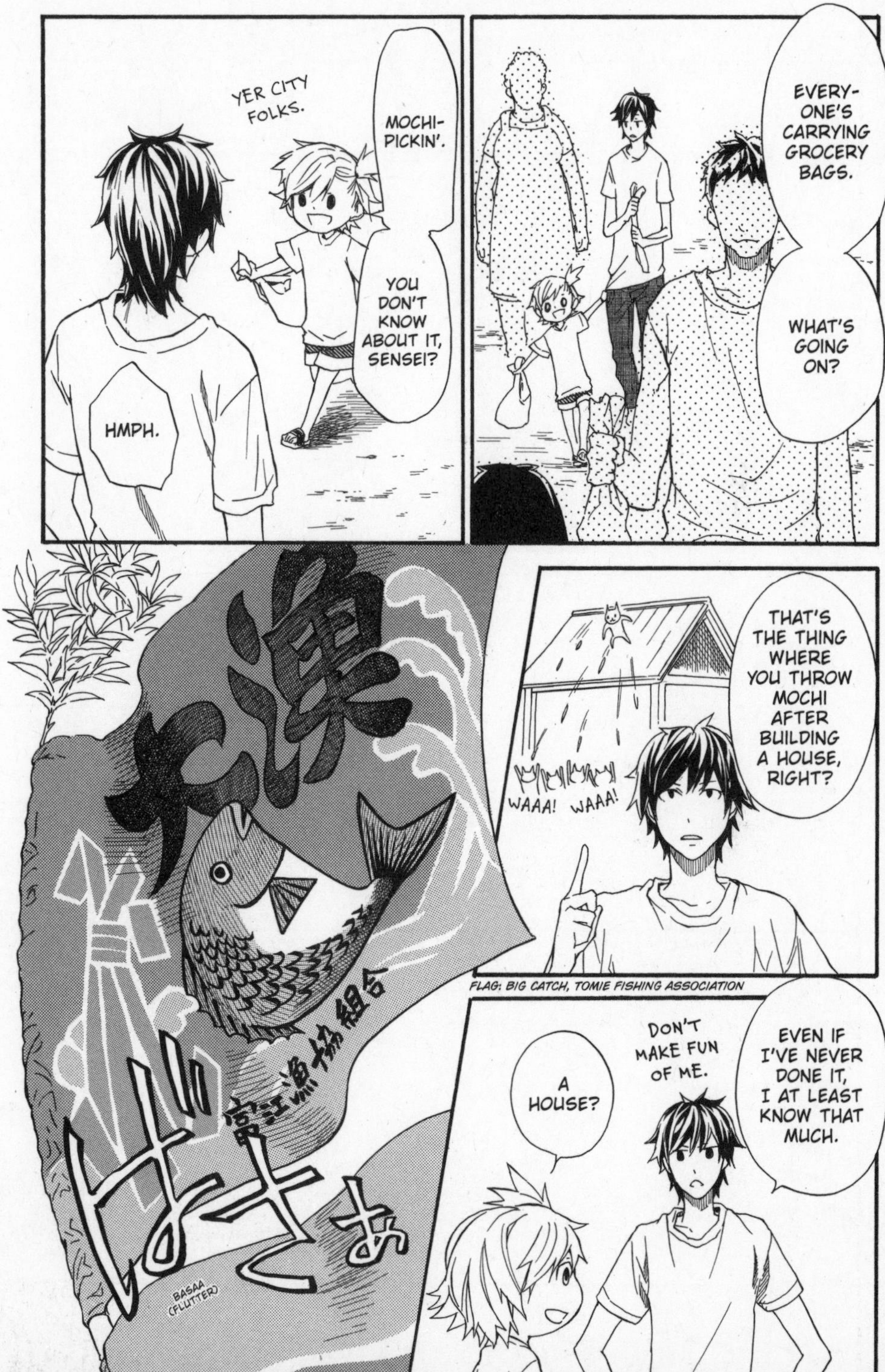
EVERY-ONE'S CARRYING GROCERY BAGS.
WHAT'S GOING ON?
MOCHI-PICKIN'.
YOU DON'T KNOW ABOUT IT, SENSEI?
YER CITY FOLKS.
HMPH.
THAT'S THE THING WHERE YOU THROW MOCHI AFTER BUILDING A HOUSE, RIGHT?
WAAA! WAAA!
FLAG: BIG CATCH, TOMIE FISHING ASSOCIATION
EVEN IF I'VE NEVER DONE IT, I AT LEAST KNOW THAT MUCH.
DON'T MAKE FUN OF ME.
A HOUSE?
大漁
富江漁協組合
BASAA (FLUTTER)

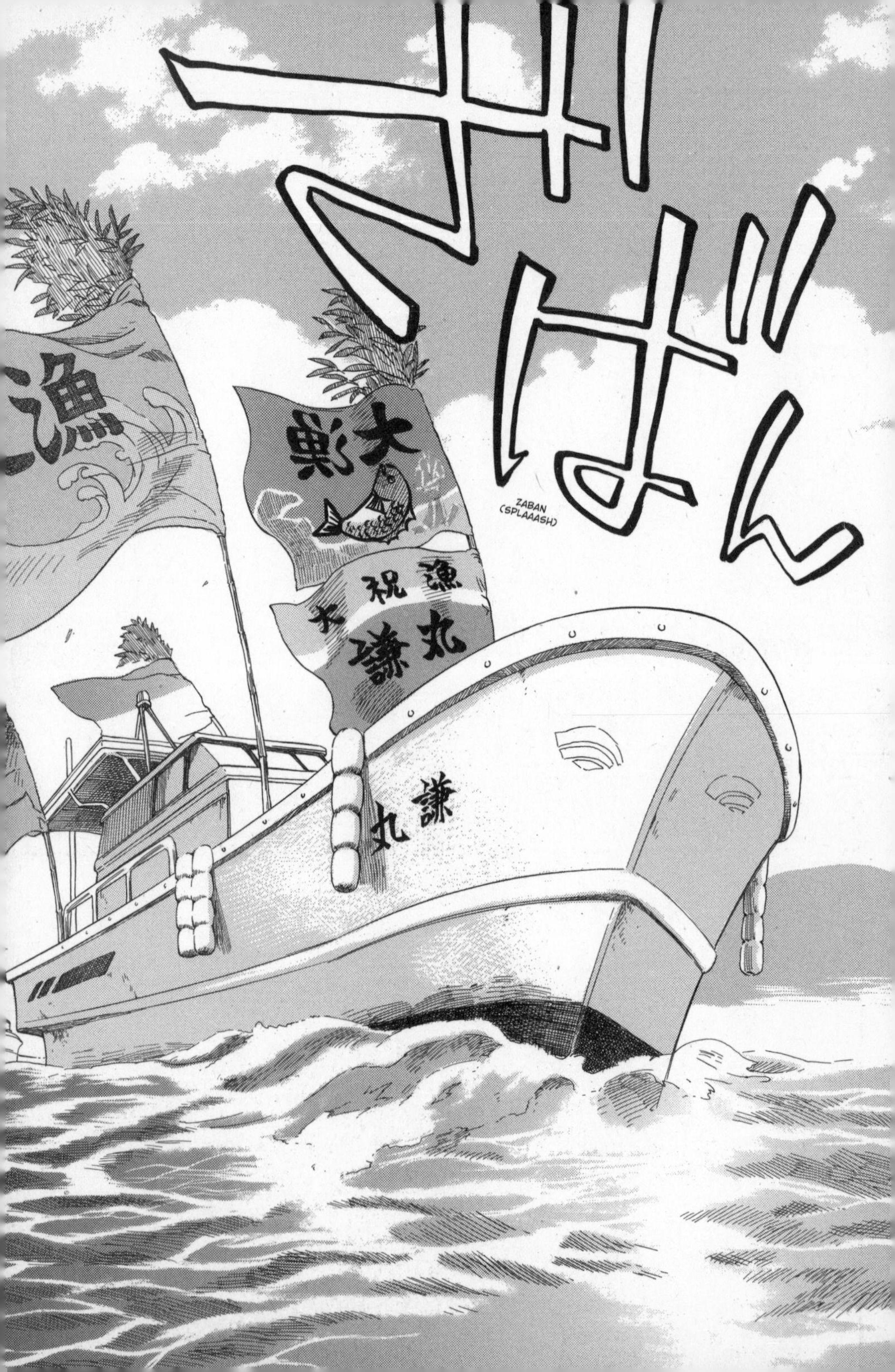
ざばん
ZABAN
(SPLAAASH)
謙丸

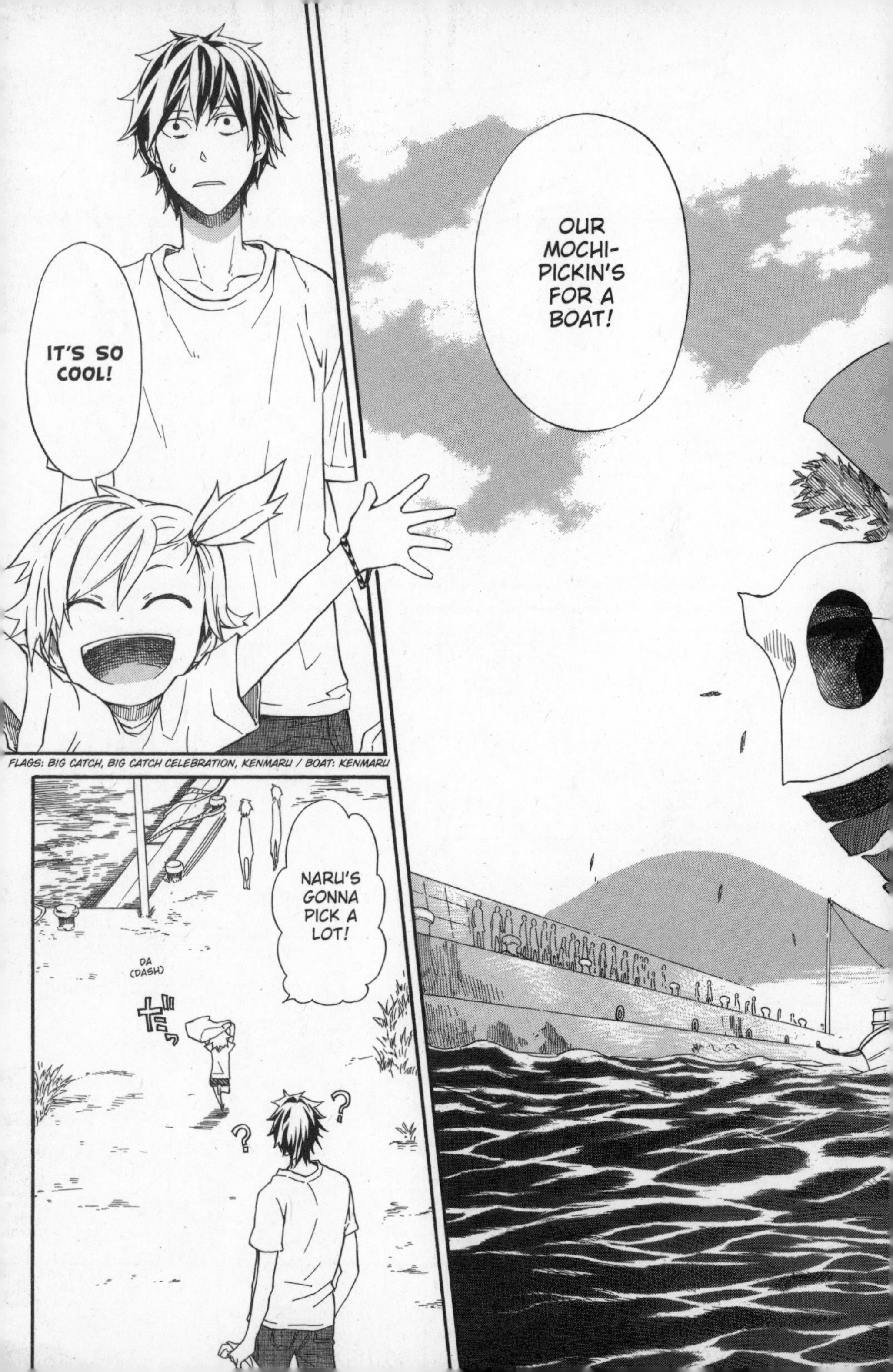
OUR MOCHI-PICKIN'S FOR A BOAT!
IT'S SO COOL!
FLAGS: BIG CATCH, BIG CATCH CELEBRATION, KENMARU / BOAT: KENMARU
NARU'S GONNA PICK A LOT!
DA (DASH)

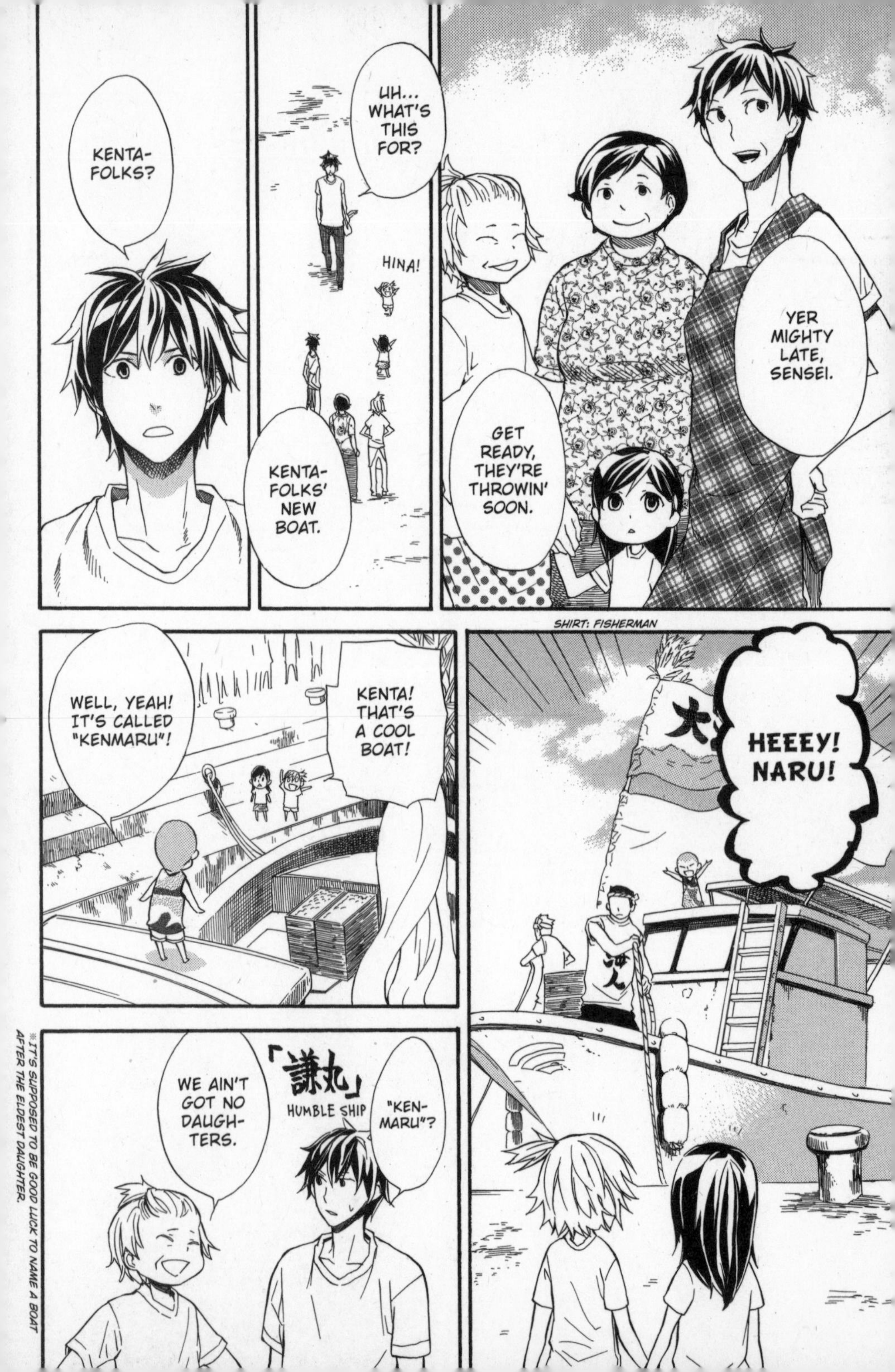
YER MIGHTY LATE, SENSEI.
GET READY, THEY'RE THROWIN' SOON.
SHIRT: FISHERMAN
UH... WHAT'S THIS FOR?
HINA!
KENTA-FOLKS' NEW BOAT.
KENTA-FOLKS?
HEEEY! NARU!
KENTA! THAT'S A COOL BOAT!
WELL, YEAH! IT'S CALLED "KENMARU"!
「謙丸」
HUMBLE SHIP
"KEN-MARU"?
WE AIN'T GOT NO DAUGHTERS.
※IT'S SUPPOSED TO BE GOOD LUCK TO NAME A BOAT AFTER THE ELDEST DAUGHTER.

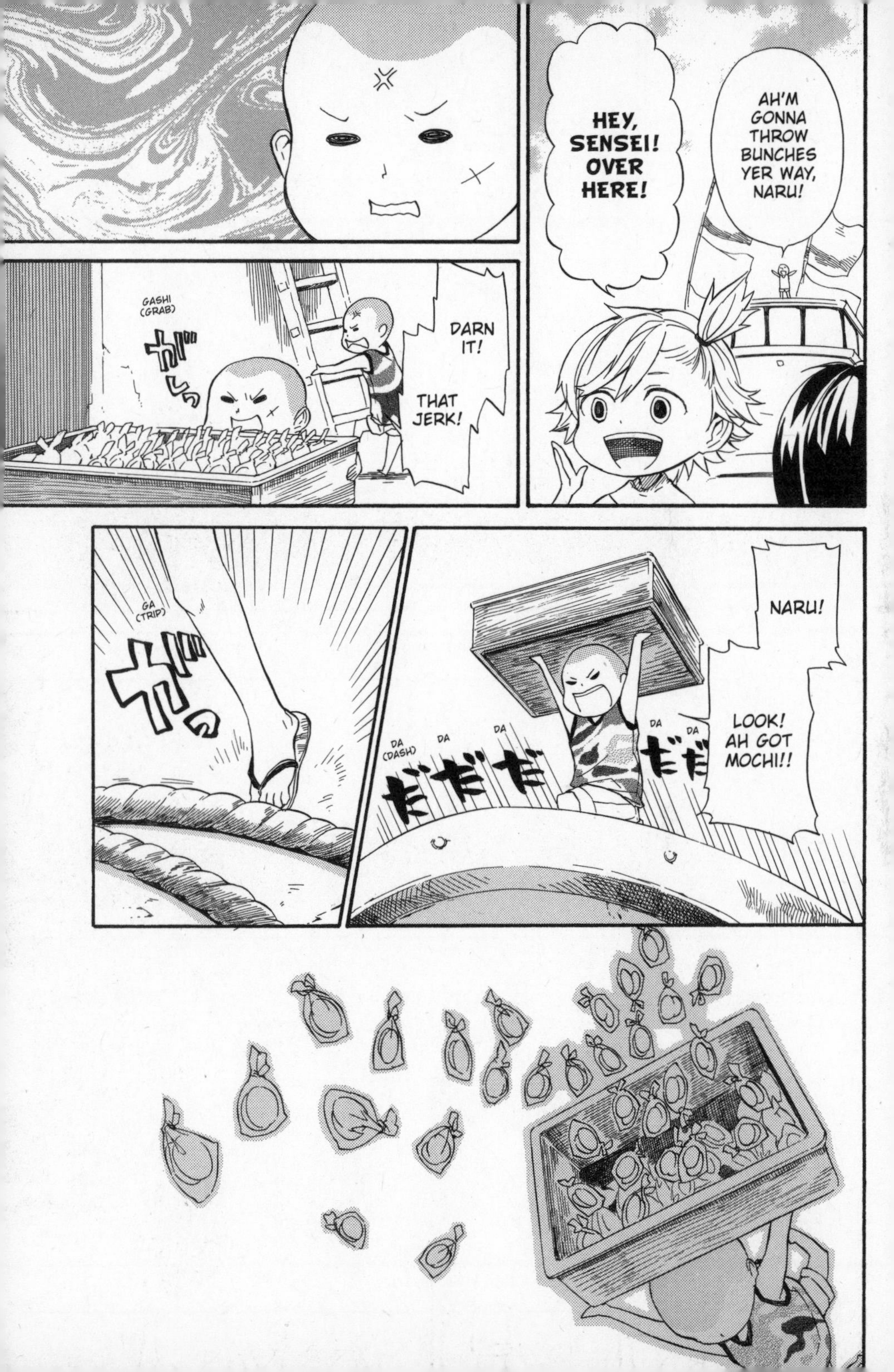

AH'M GONNA THROW BUNCHES YER WAY, NARU!
HEY, SENSEI! OVER HERE!
DARN IT!
THAT JERK!
GASHI (GRAB)
がしっ
NARU!
LOOK! AH GOT MOCHI!!
DA DA
だだ
DA DA DA (DASH)
だだだ
GA (TRIP)
ガッ

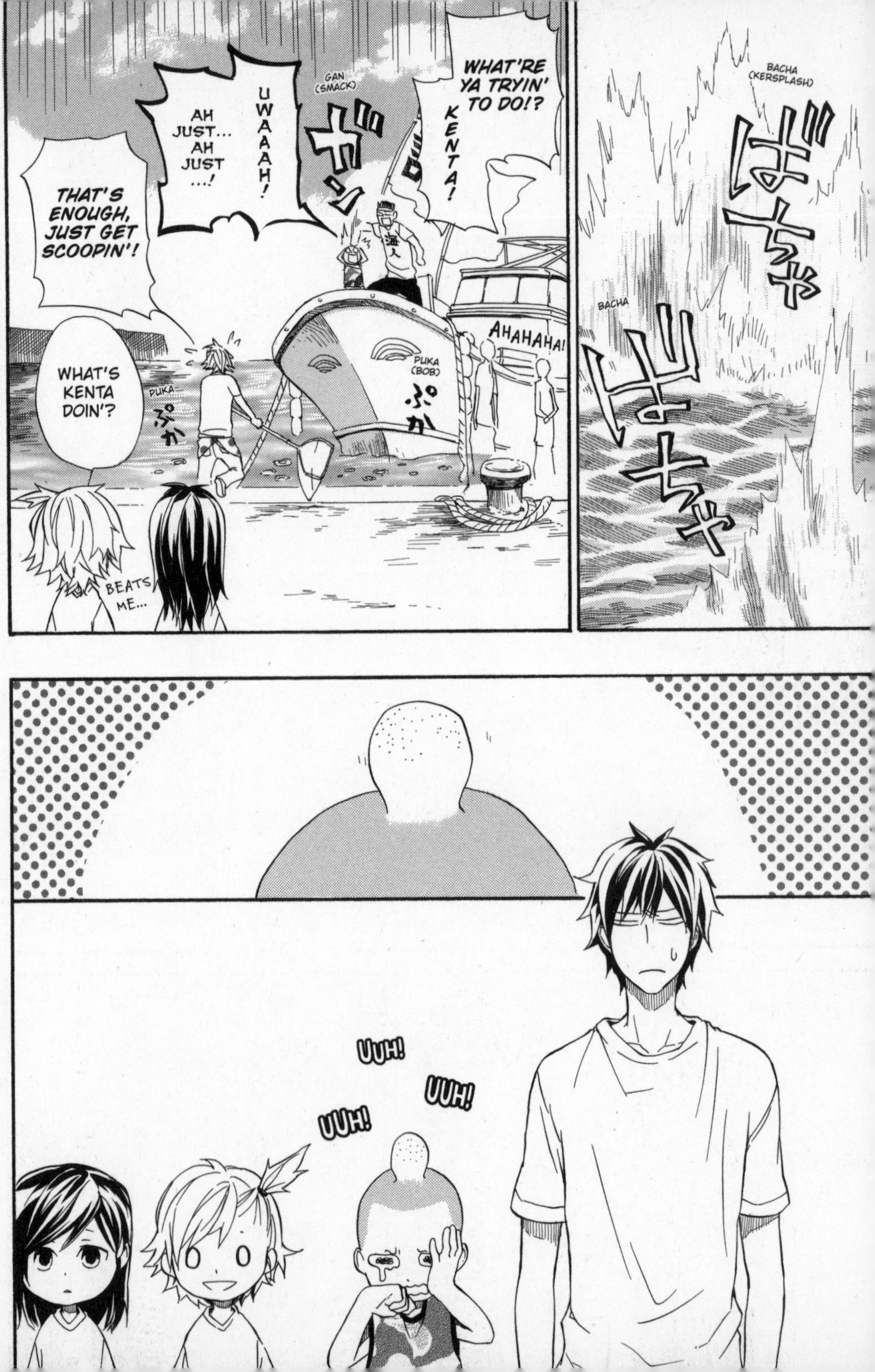
BACHA (KERSPLASH)
ばちゃ
BACHA
ばちゃ
WHAT'RE YA TRYIN' TO DO!?
KENTA!
GAN (SMACK)
ガン
UWAAAAH!
AH JUST... AH JUST ...!
THAT'S ENOUGH, JUST GET SCOOPIN'!
AHAHAHA!
PUKA (BOB)
ぷか
PUKA
ぷか
WHAT'S KENTA DOIN'?
BEATS ME...
UUH!
UUH!
UUH!

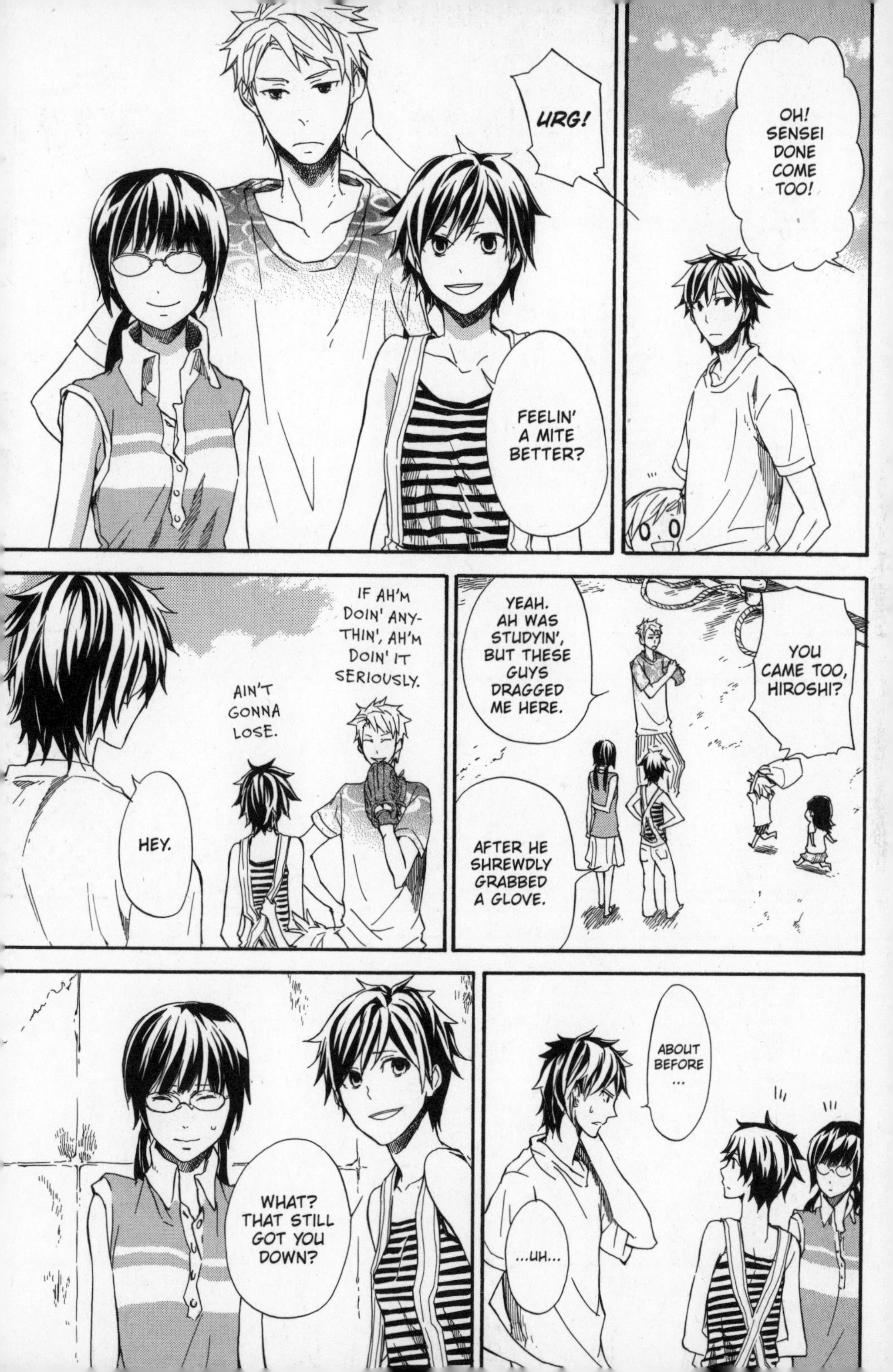
OH! SENSEI DONE COME TOO!
URG!
FEELIN' A MITE BETTER?
YOU CAME TOO, HIROSHI?
YEAH. AH WAS STUDYIN', BUT THESE GUYS DRAGGED ME HERE.
AFTER HE SHREWDLY GRABBED A GLOVE.
IF AH'M DOIN' ANY-THIN', AH'M DOIN' IT SERIOUSLY.
AIN'T GONNA LOSE.
HEY.
ABOUT BEFORE ...
...UH...
WHAT? THAT STILL GOT YOU DOWN?

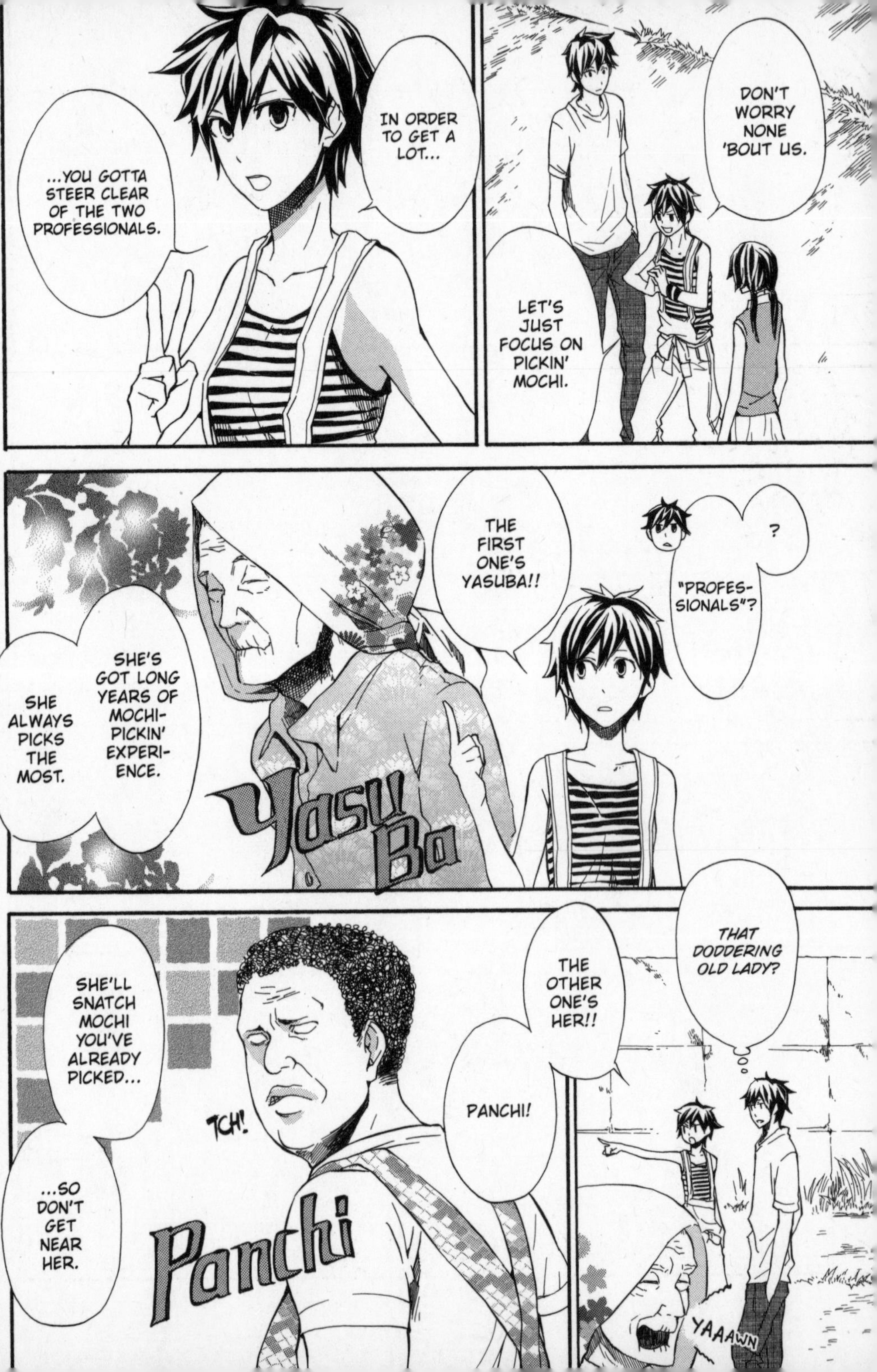
DON'T WORRY NONE 'BOUT US.
LET'S JUST FOCUS ON PICKIN' MOCHI.
IN ORDER TO GET A LOT...
...YOU GOTTA STEER CLEAR OF THE TWO PROFESSIONALS.
?
"PROFES-SIONALS"?
THE FIRST ONE'S YASUBA!!
SHE'S GOT LONG YEARS OF MOCHI-PICKIN' EXPERI-ENCE.
SHE ALWAYS PICKS THE MOST.
Yasu Ba
THAT DODDERING OLD LADY?
YAAAWN
THE OTHER ONE'S HER!!
PANCHI!
SHE'LL SNATCH MOCHI YOU'VE ALREADY PICKED...
TCH!
...SO DON'T GET NEAR HER.
Panchi

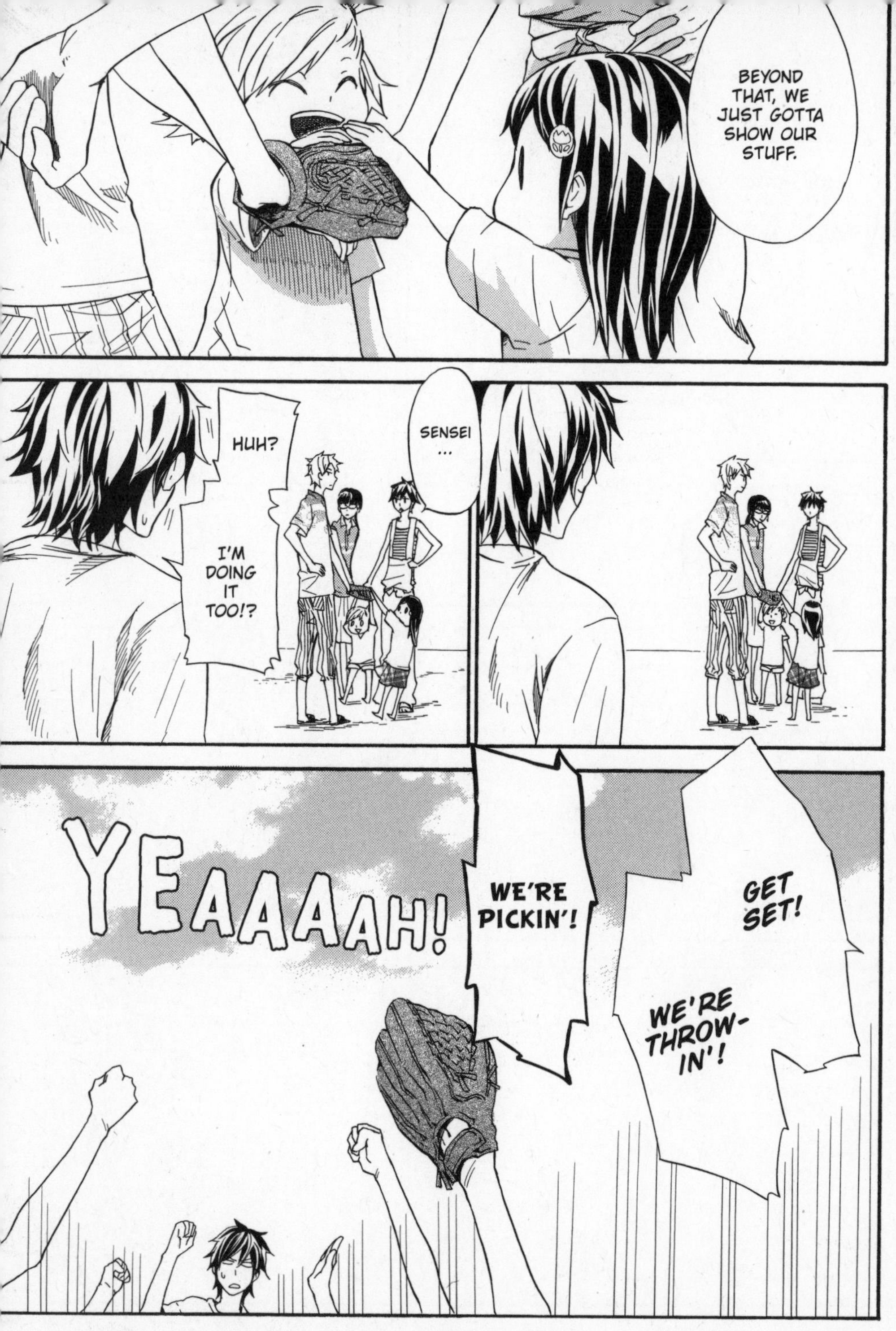
BEYOND THAT, WE JUST GOTTA SHOW OUR STUFF.
SENSEI ...
HUH?
I'M DOING IT TOO!?
GET SET!
WE'RE THROW-IN'!
WE'RE PICKIN'!
YEAAAAAH!

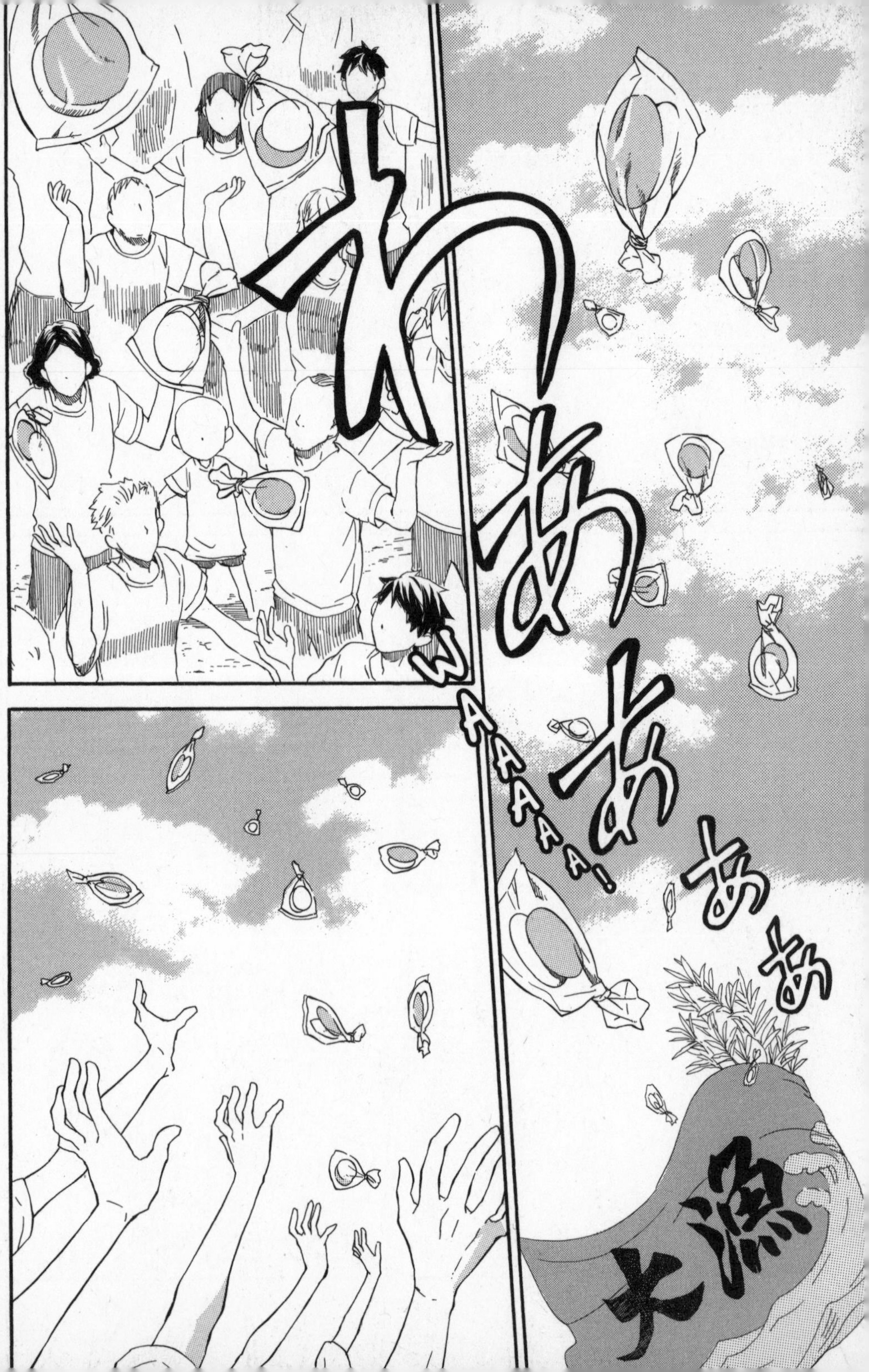
わああああ
WAAAAA!
大漁

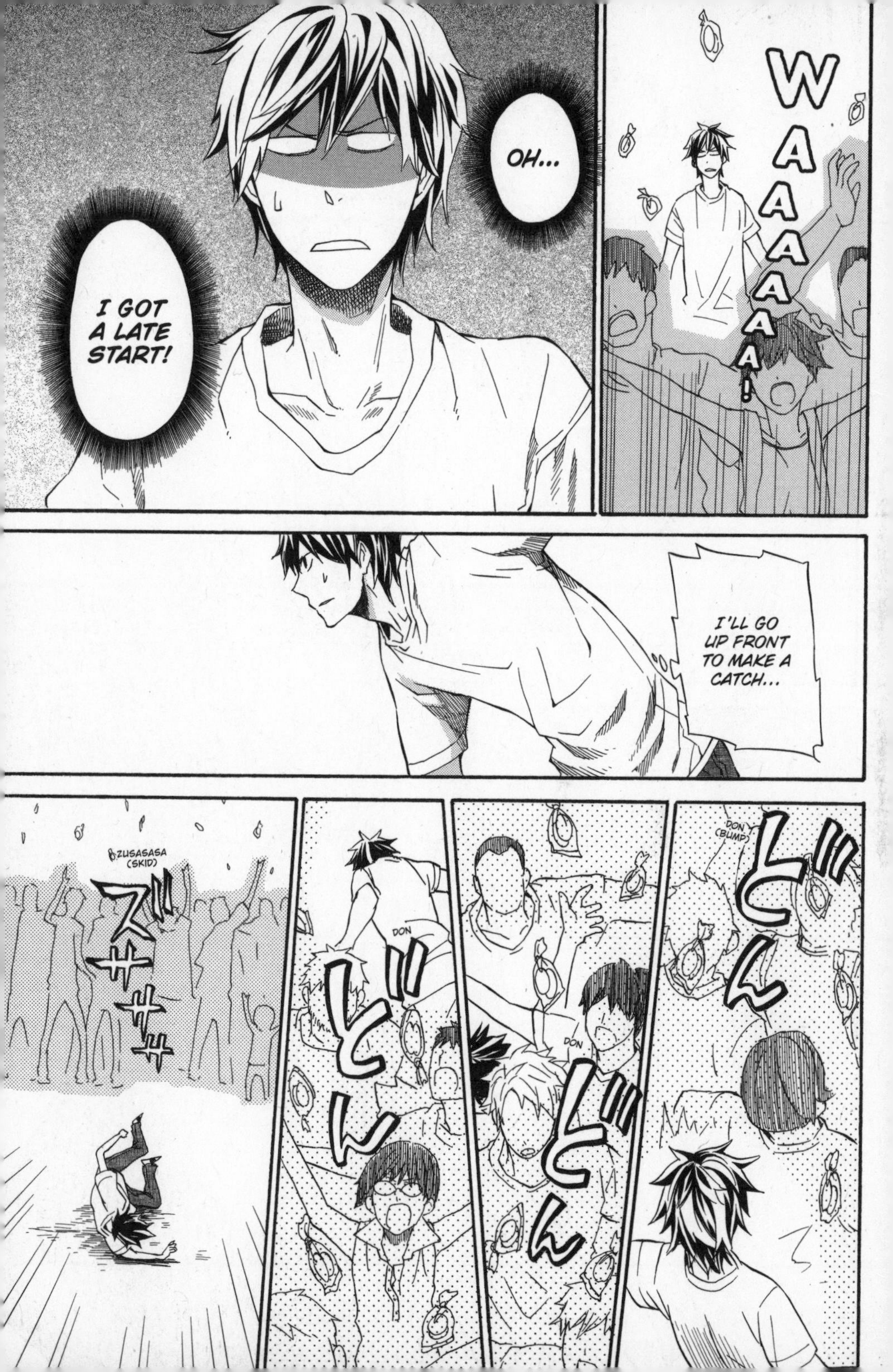
WAAAAAAA!
OH...
I GOT A LATE START!
I'LL GO UP FRONT TO MAKE A CATCH...
DON (BUMP)
どん
DON
どん
DON
どん
ZUSASASA (SKID)
ズサササ

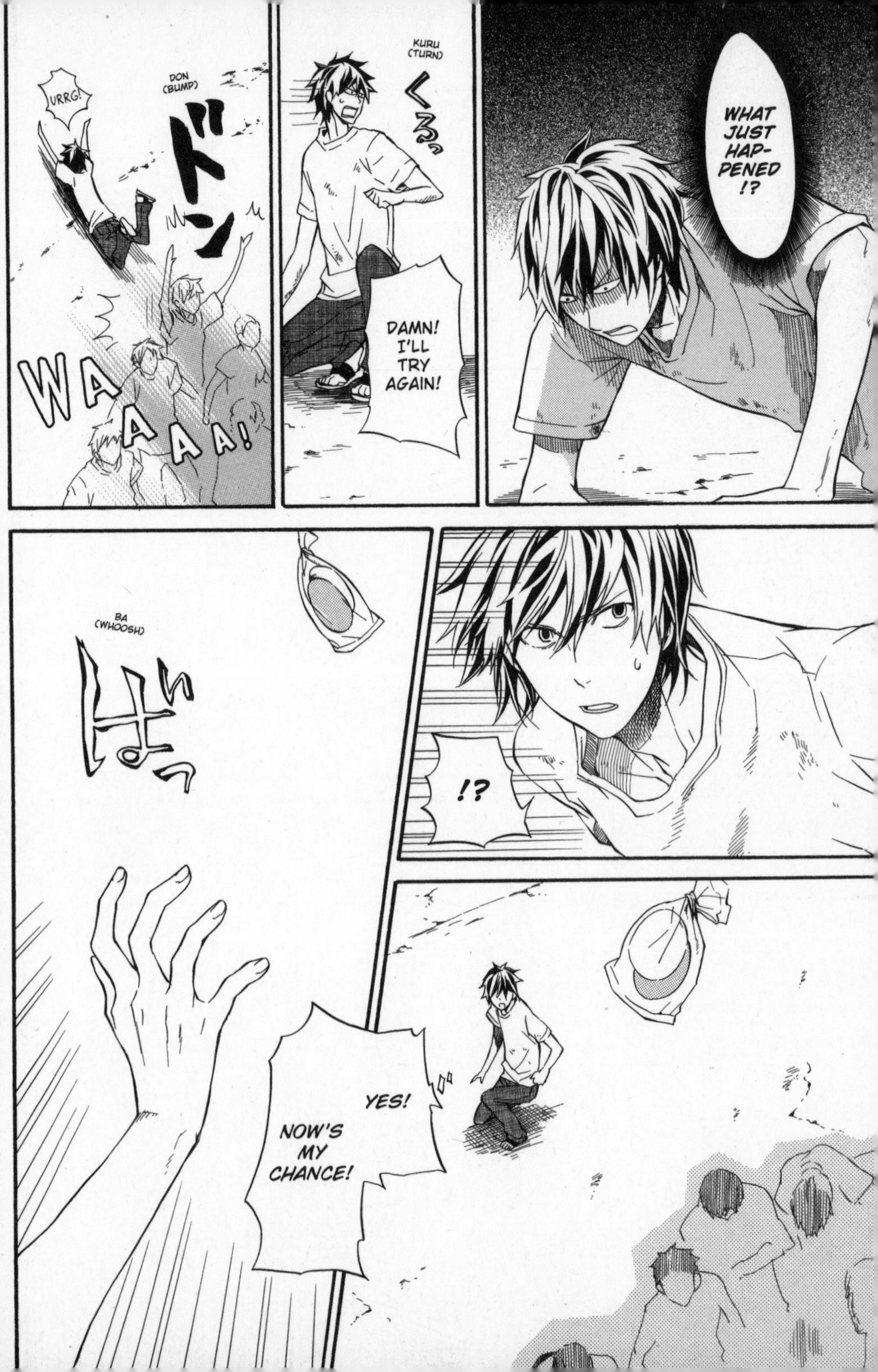
WHAT JUST HAP-PENED !?
KURU (TURN)
くるっ
DAMN! I'LL TRY AGAIN!
DON (BUMP)
ドン
URRG!
WAAAA!
!?
BA (WHOOSH)
ばっ
YES!
NOW'S MY CHANCE!

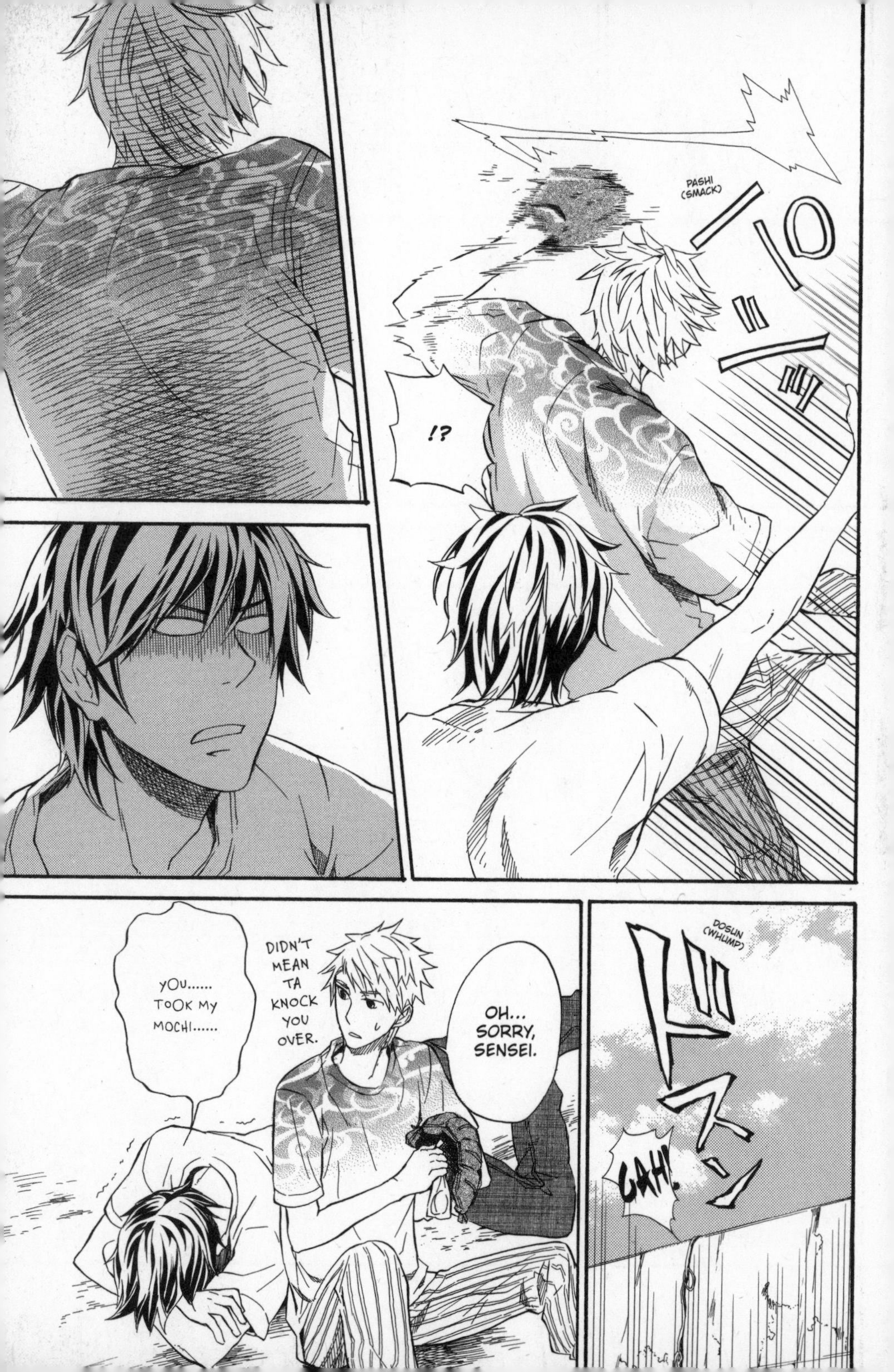

PASHI (SMACK)
!?
DOSUN (WHUMP)
GAH!
OH... SORRY, SENSEI.
DIDN'T MEAN TA KNOCK YOU OVER.
YOU...... TOOK MY MOCHI......

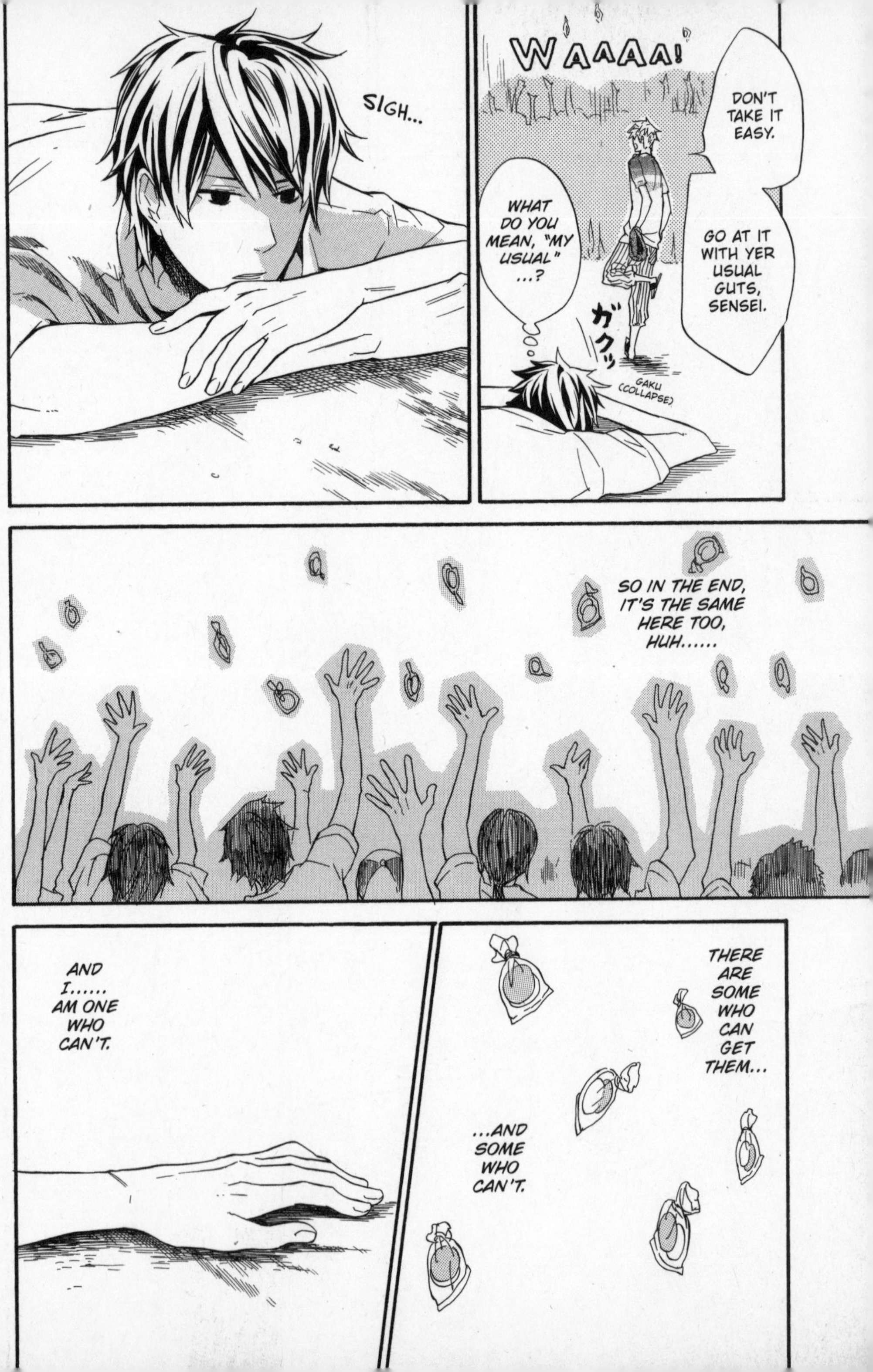
WAAAA!
DON'T TAKE IT EASY.
GO AT IT WITH YER USUAL GUTS, SENSEI.
WHAT DO YOU MEAN, "MY USUAL"...?
ガクッ
GAKU (COLLAPSE)
SIGH...
SO IN THE END, IT'S THE SAME HERE TOO, HUH......
THERE ARE SOME WHO CAN GET THEM...
...AND SOME WHO CAN'T.
AND I...... AM ONE WHO CAN'T.

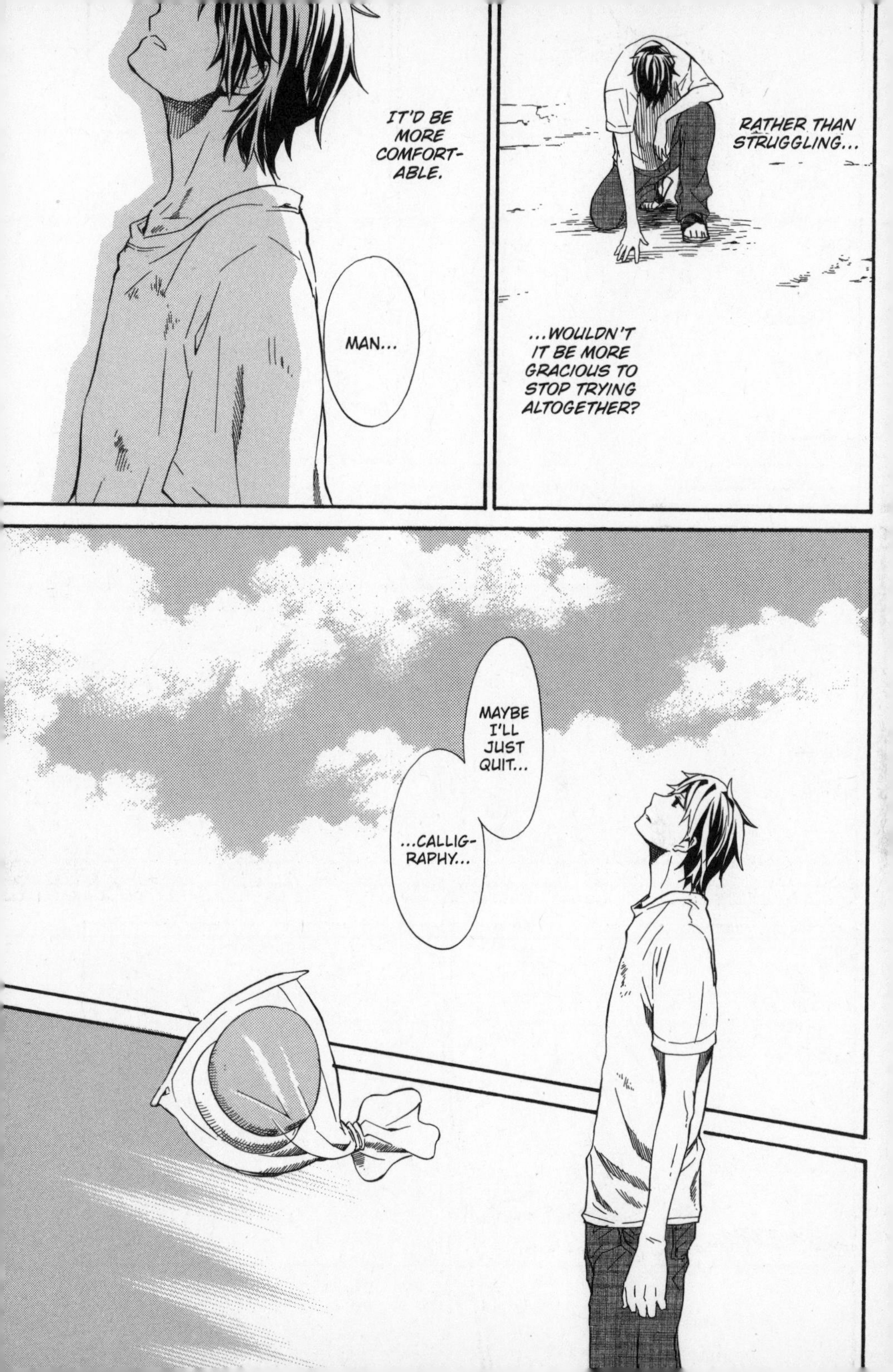
RATHER THAN STRUGGLING...
...WOULDN'T IT BE MORE GRACIOUS TO STOP TRYING ALTOGETHER?
IT'D BE MORE COMFORT-ABLE.
MAN...
MAYBE I'LL JUST QUIT...
...CALLIG-RAPHY...

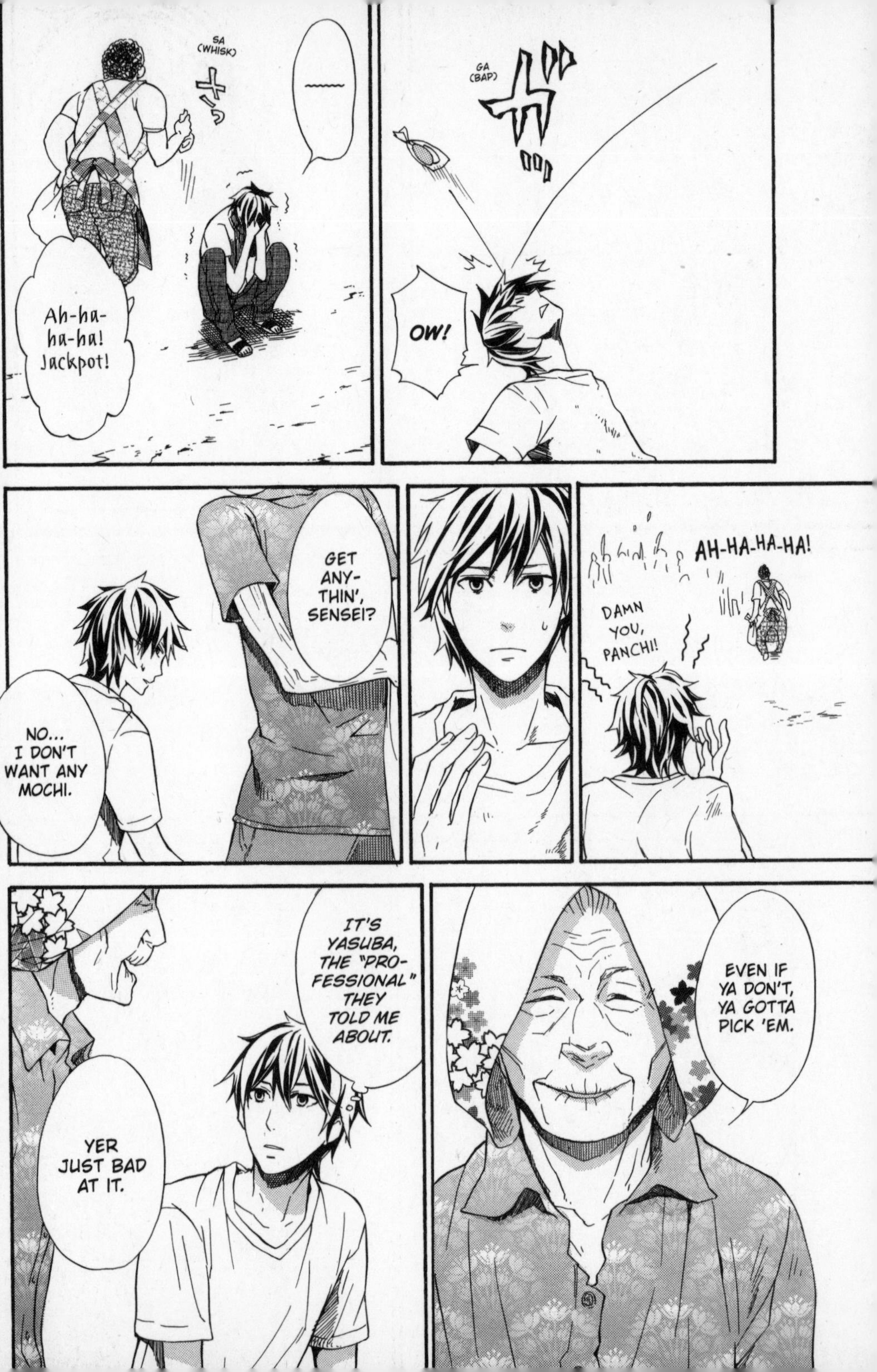
GA (BAP)
OW!
——
SA (WHISK)
Ah-ha-ha-ha! Jackpot!
AH-HA-HA-HA!
DAMN YOU, PANCHI!
GET ANYTHIN', SENSEI?
NO... I DON'T WANT ANY MOCHI.
EVEN IF YA DON'T, YA GOTTA PICK 'EM.
IT'S YASUBA, THE "PROFESSIONAL" THEY TOLD ME ABOUT.
YER JUST BAD AT IT.

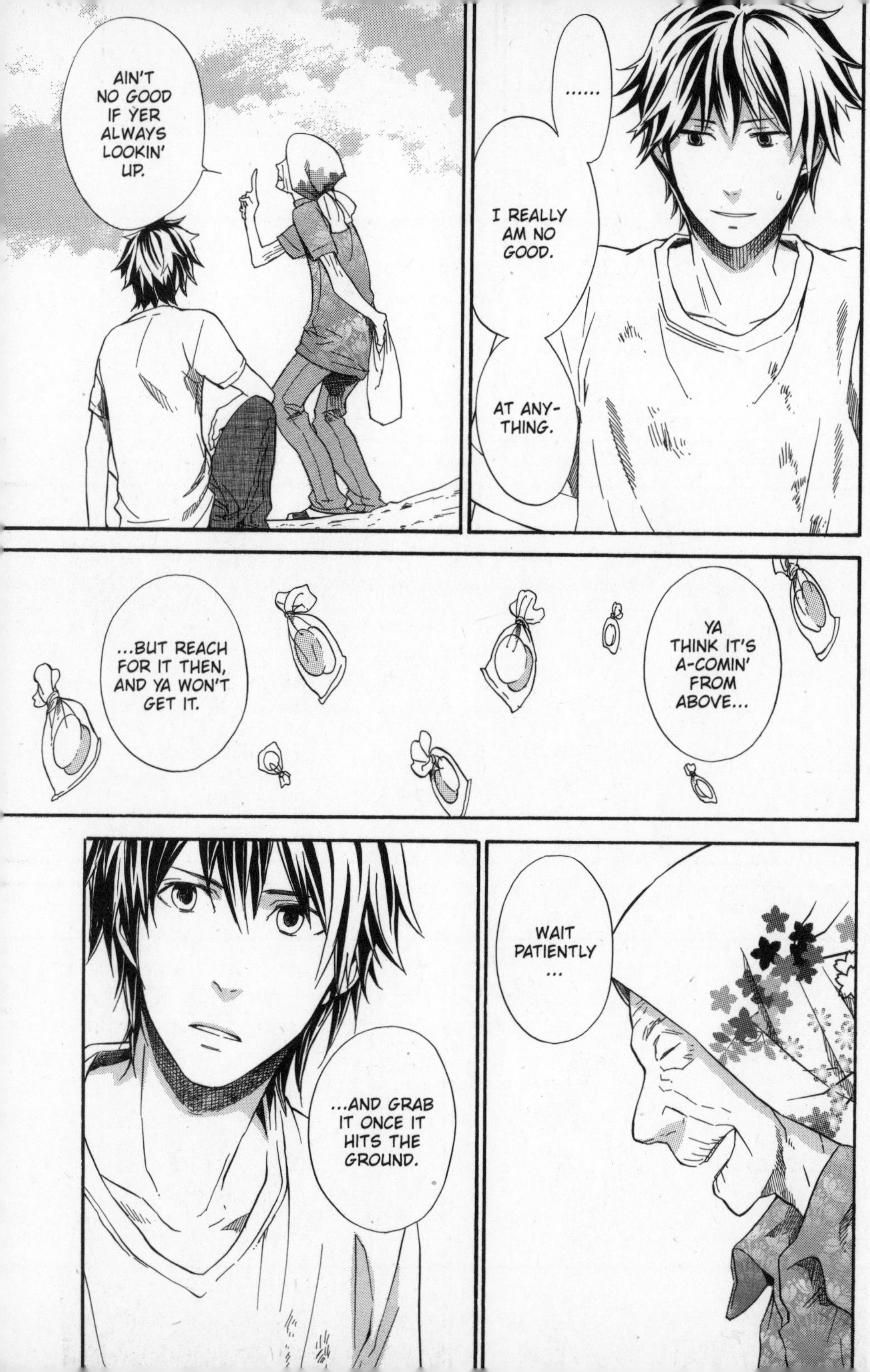
......
I REALLY AM NO GOOD.
AT ANY-THING.
AIN'T NO GOOD IF YER ALWAYS LOOKIN' UP.
YA THINK IT'S A-COMIN' FROM ABOVE...
...BUT REACH FOR IT THEN, AND YA WON'T GET IT.
WAIT PATIENTLY ...
...AND GRAB IT ONCE IT HITS THE GROUND.

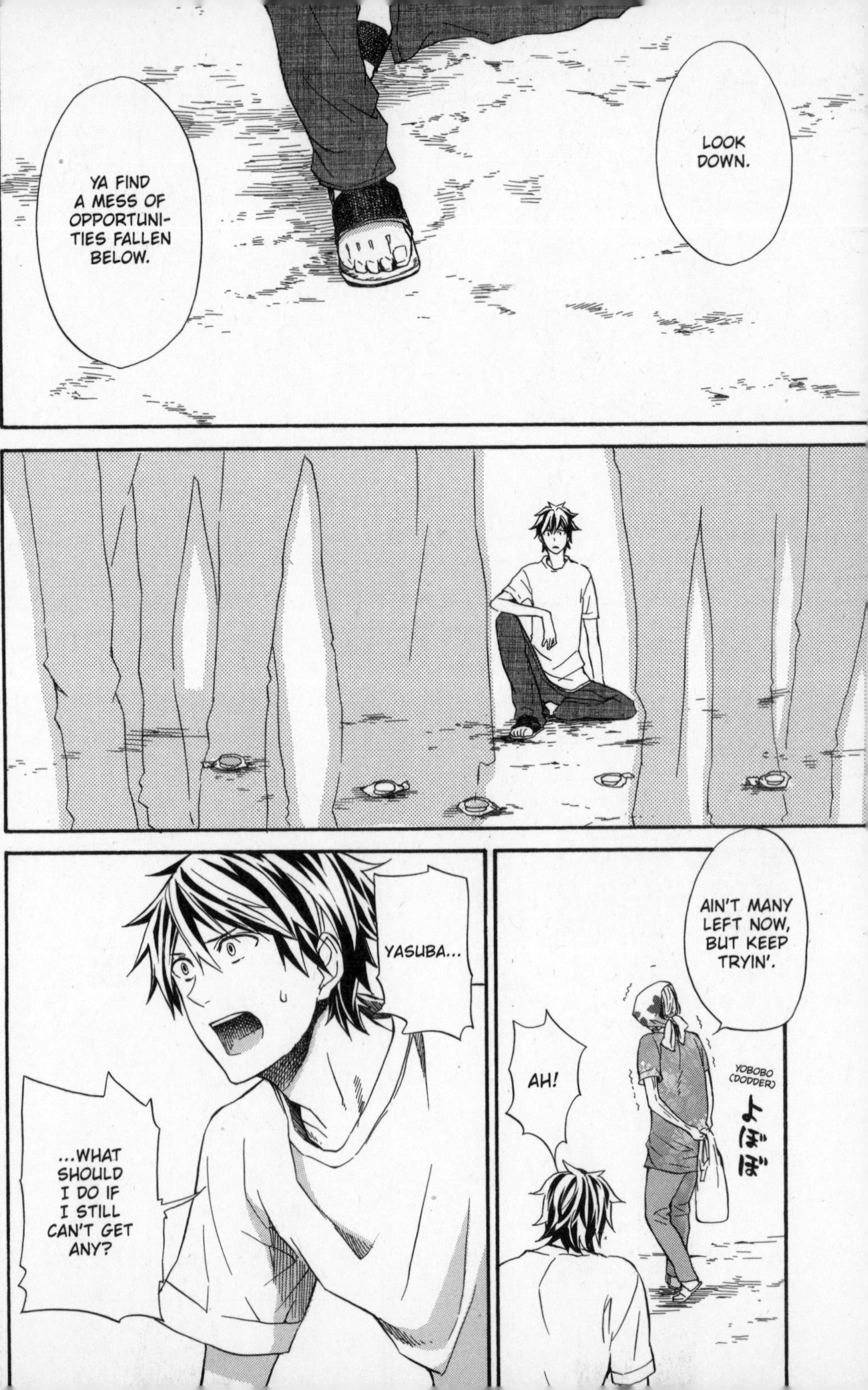
LOOK DOWN.
YA FIND A MESS OF OPPORTUNITIES FALLEN BELOW.
AIN'T MANY LEFT NOW, BUT KEEP TRYIN'.
YOBOBO (DODDER)
よぼぼ
AH!
YASUBA...
...WHAT SHOULD I DO IF I STILL CAN'T GET ANY?

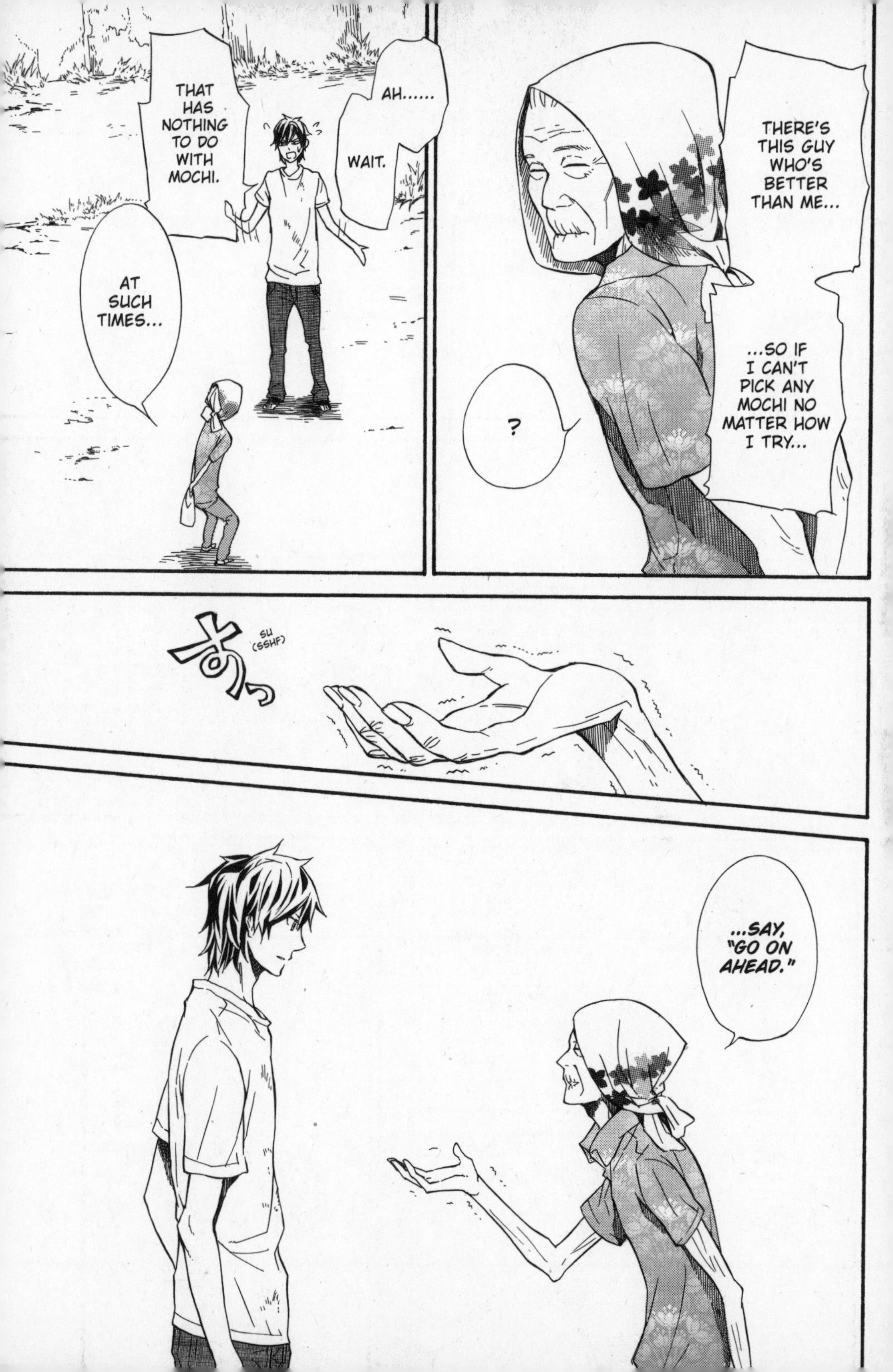
THERE'S THIS GUY WHO'S BETTER THAN ME...
...SO IF I CAN'T PICK ANY MOCHI NO MATTER HOW I TRY...
?
AH......
WAIT.
THAT HAS NOTHING TO DO WITH MOCHI.
AT SUCH TIMES...
SU (SSHF)
...SAY, "GO ON AHEAD."

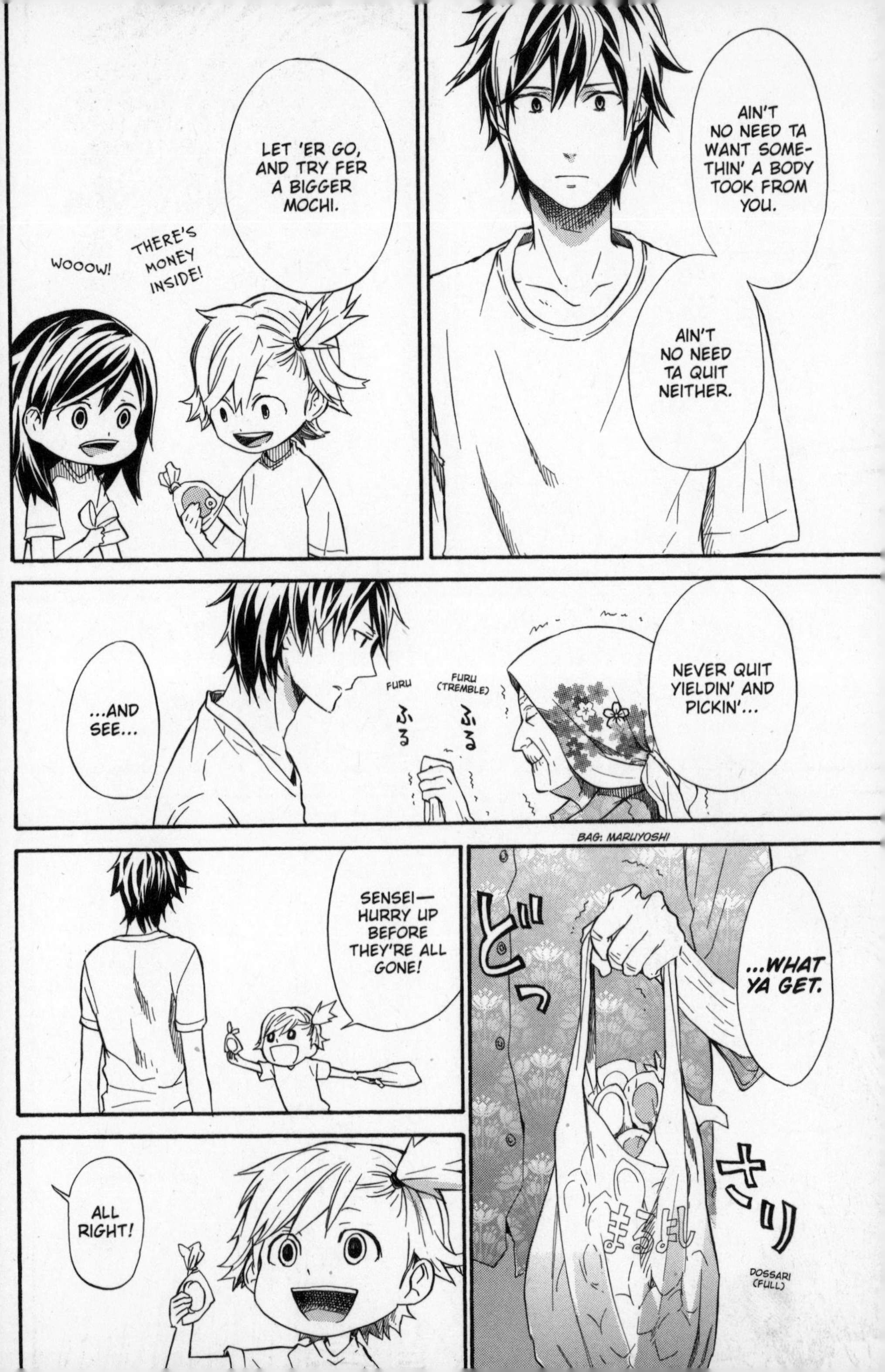
AIN'T NO NEED TA WANT SOMETHIN' A BODY TOOK FROM YOU.
AIN'T NO NEED TA QUIT NEITHER.
LET 'ER GO, AND TRY FER A BIGGER MOCHI.
THERE'S MONEY INSIDE!
WOOOW!
NEVER QUIT YIELDIN' AND PICKIN'...
FURU (TREMBLE)
ふる
FURU
ふる
...AND SEE...
BAG: MARUYOSHI
...WHAT YA GET.
どっさり
まるよし
DOSSARI (FULL)
SENSEI— HURRY UP BEFORE THEY'RE ALL GONE!
ALL RIGHT!

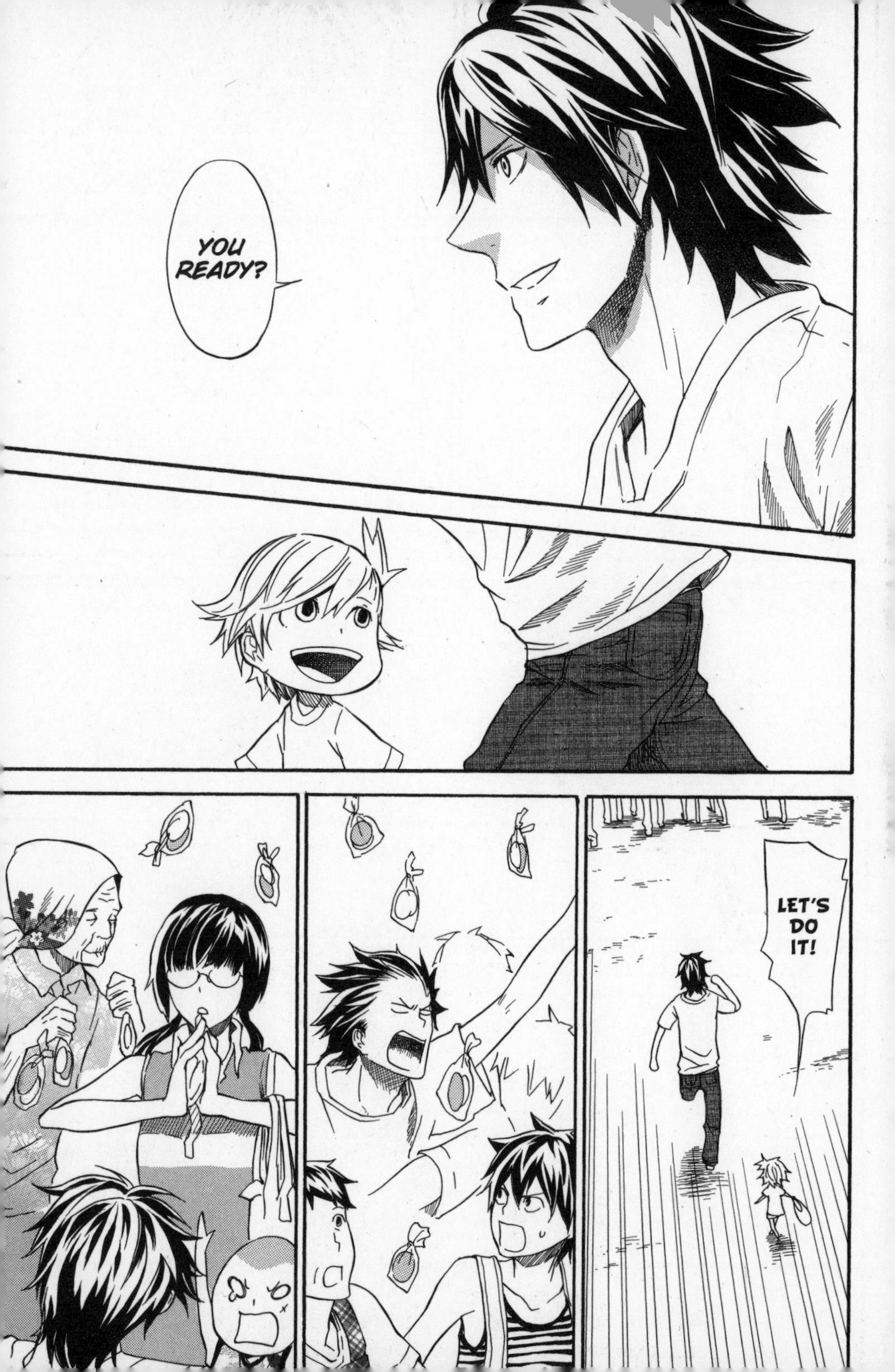
YOU READY?
LET'S DO IT!

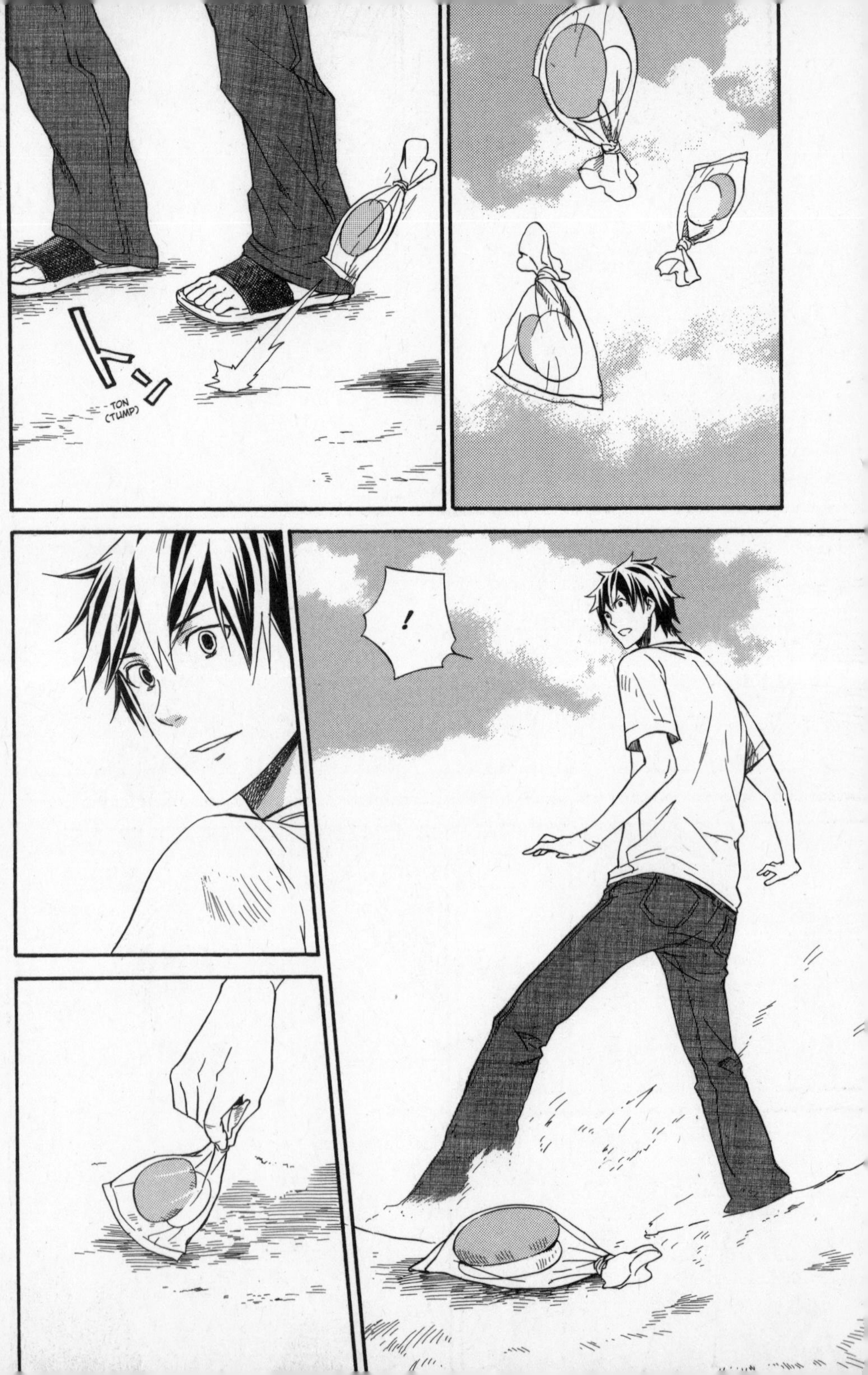
トーン
TON
(TUMP)
!

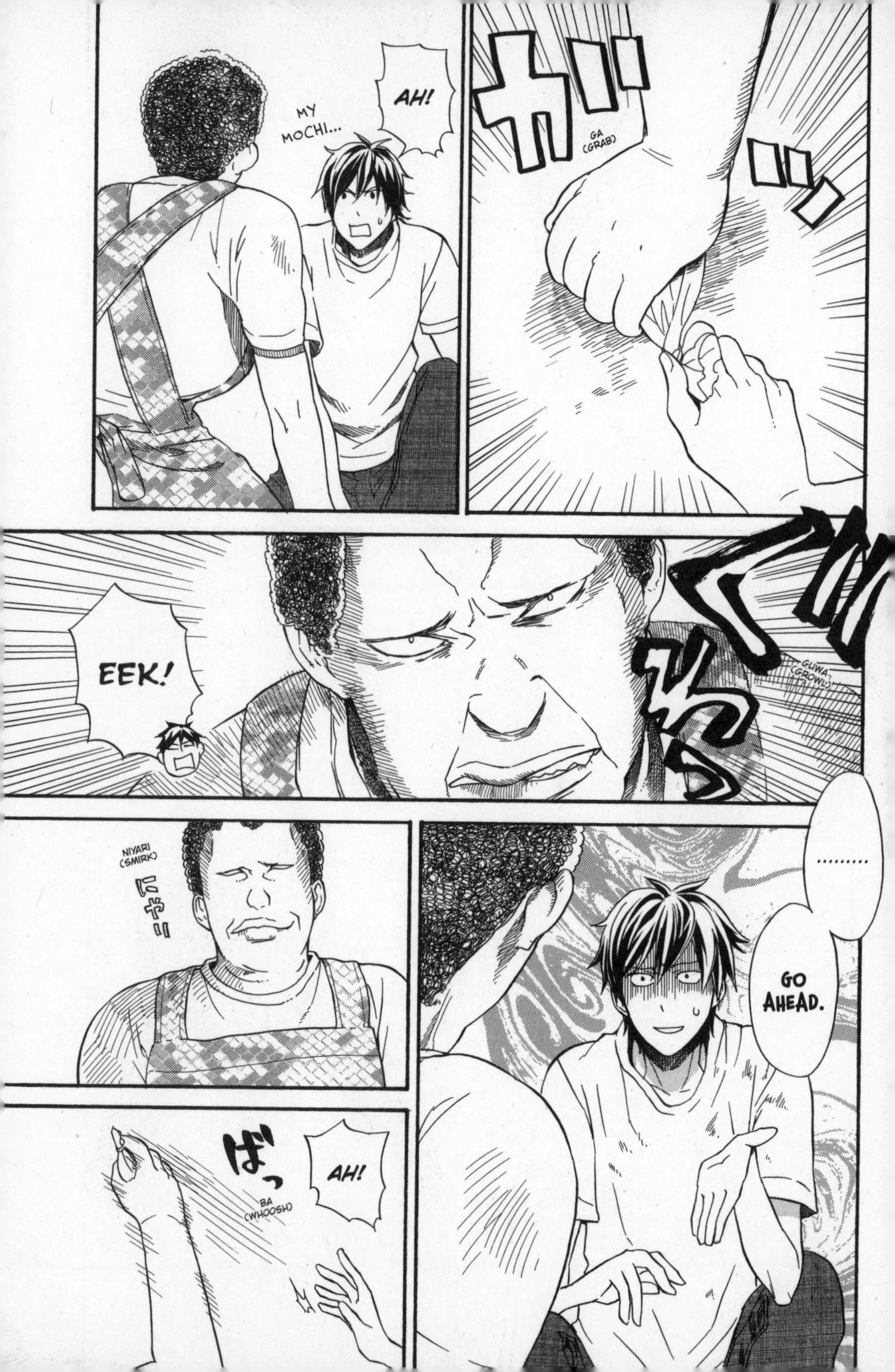
GA (GRAB)
AH!
MY MOCHI...
GUWA (GROWL)
EEK!
....
GO AHEAD.
NIYARI (SMIRK)
にやり
AH!
ばっ
BA (WHOOSH)

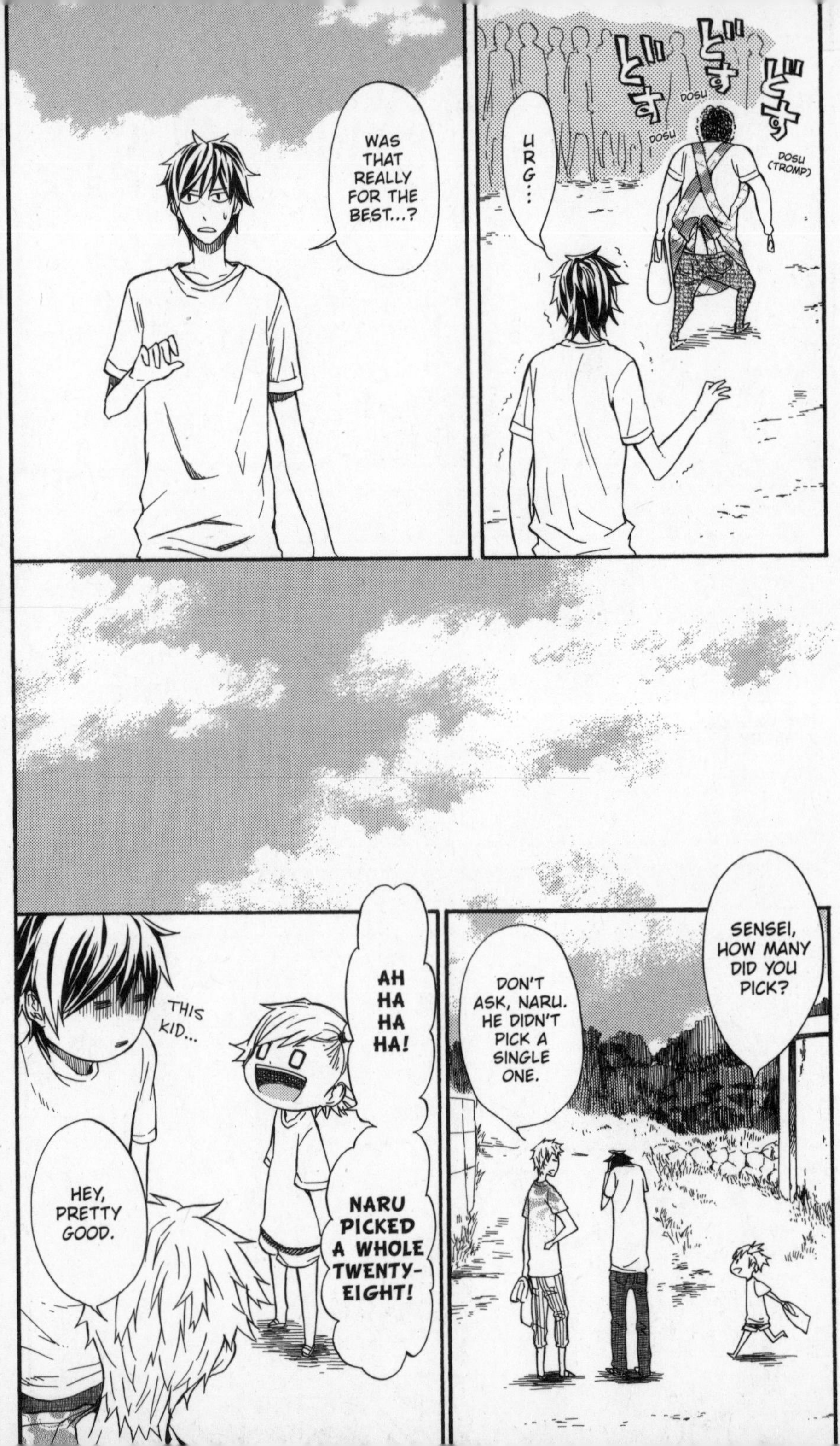
どす
DOSU (TROMP)
どす
DOSU
どす
DOSU
URG...
WAS THAT REALLY FOR THE BEST...?
SENSEI, HOW MANY DID YOU PICK?
DON'T ASK, NARU. HE DIDN'T PICK A SINGLE ONE.
AH HA HA HA!
NARU PICKED A WHOLE TWENTY-EIGHT!
THIS KID...
HEY, PRETTY GOOD.

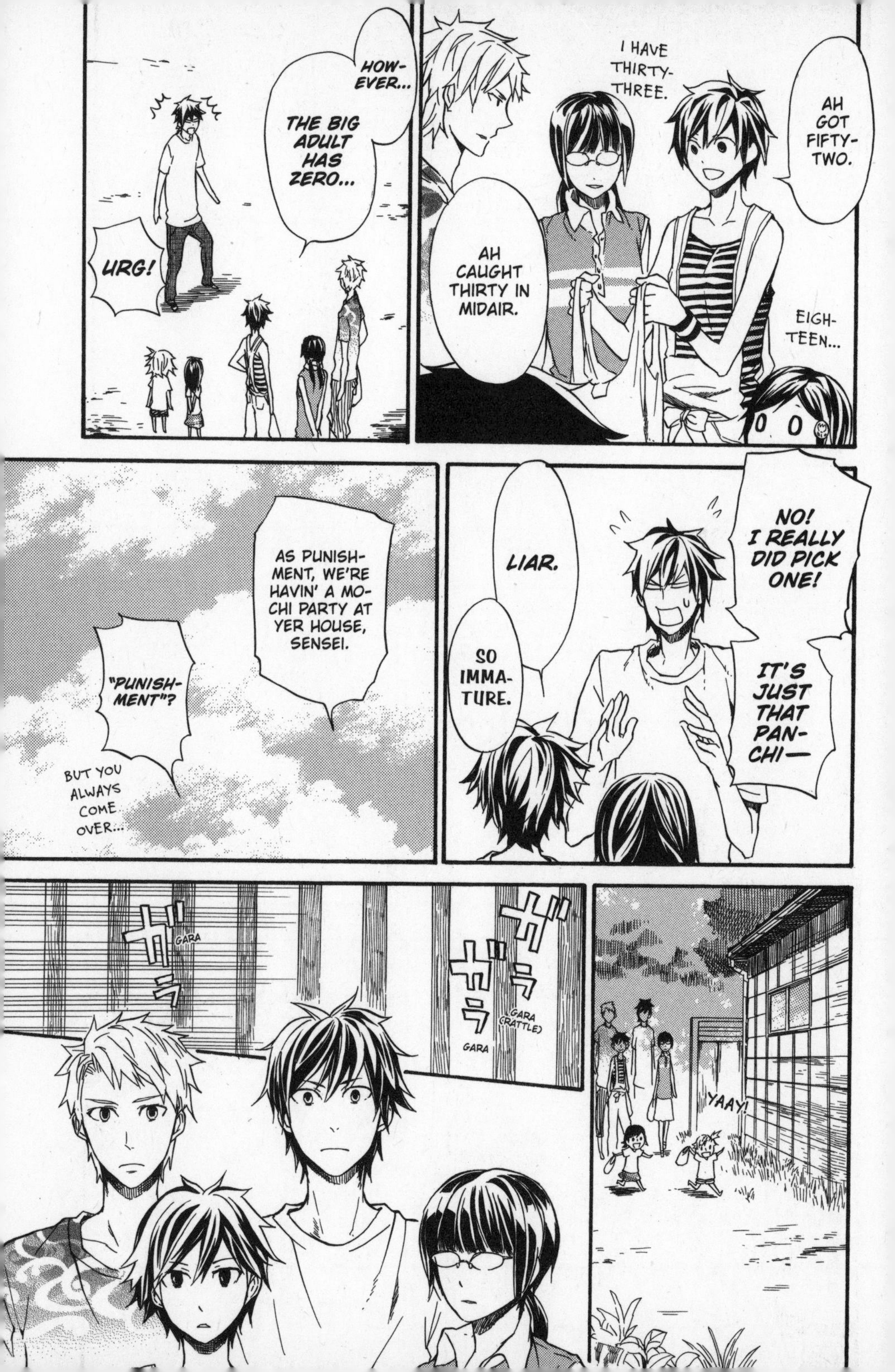
AH GOT FIFTY-TWO.
I HAVE THIRTY-THREE.
AH CAUGHT THIRTY IN MIDAIR.
EIGHTEEN...
HOWEVER...
THE BIG ADULT HAS ZERO...
URG!
NO! I REALLY DID PICK ONE!
IT'S JUST THAT PANCHI—
LIAR.
SO IMMATURE.
AS PUNISHMENT, WE'RE HAVIN' A MOCHI PARTY AT YER HOUSE, SENSEI.
"PUNISHMENT"?
BUT YOU ALWAYS COME OVER...
YAAY!
ガラ
GARA
ガラ
GARA (RATTLE)
ガラ
GARA

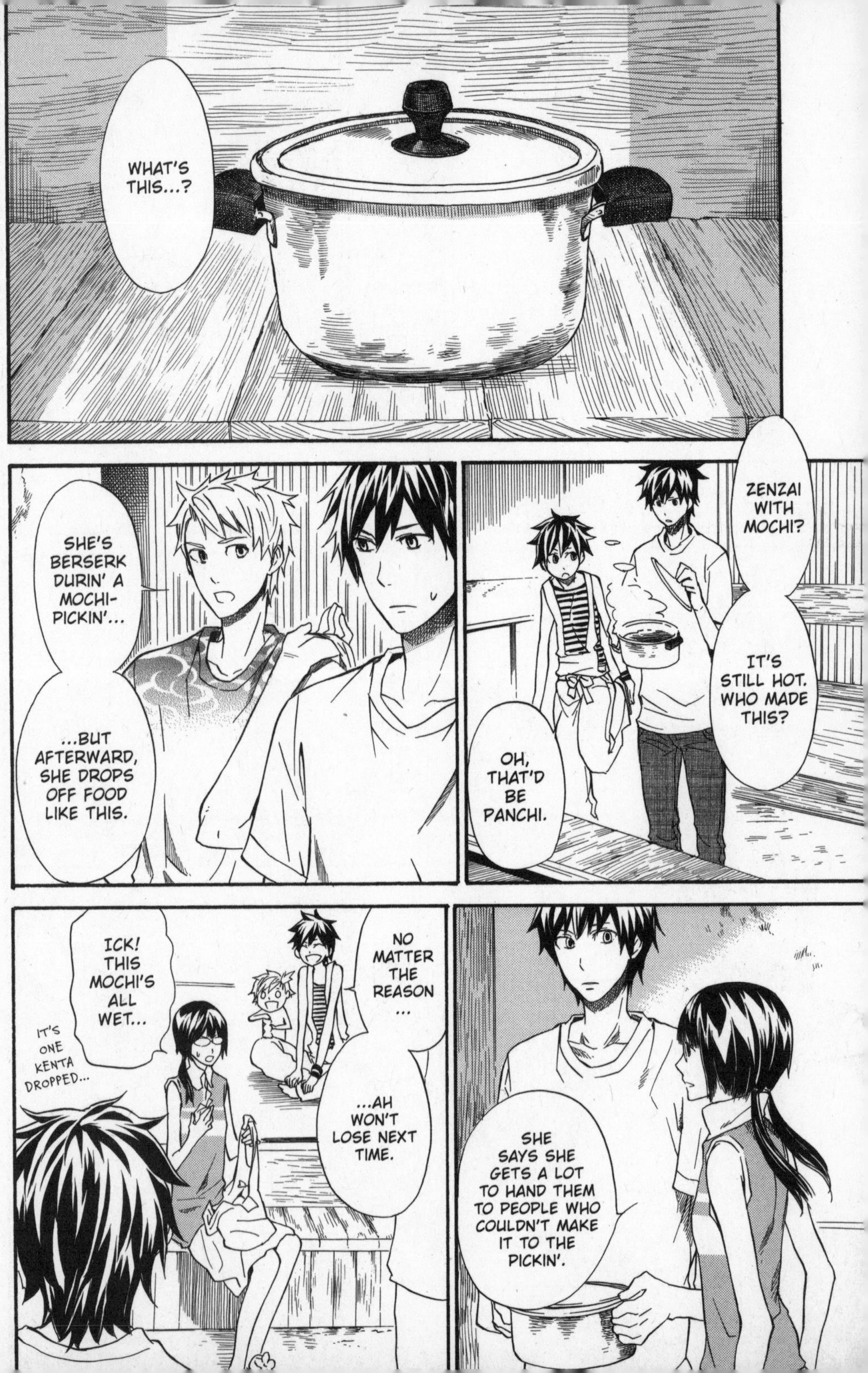
WHAT'S THIS...?
ZENZAI WITH MOCHI?
IT'S STILL HOT. WHO MADE THIS?
OH, THAT'D BE PANCHI.
SHE'S BERSERK DURIN' A MOCHI-PICKIN'...
...BUT AFTERWARD, SHE DROPS OFF FOOD LIKE THIS.
SHE SAYS SHE GETS A LOT TO HAND THEM TO PEOPLE WHO COULDN'T MAKE IT TO THE PICKIN'.
NO MATTER THE REASON ...
ICK! THIS MOCHI'S ALL WET...
IT'S ONE KENTA DROPPED...
...AH WON'T LOSE NEXT TIME.

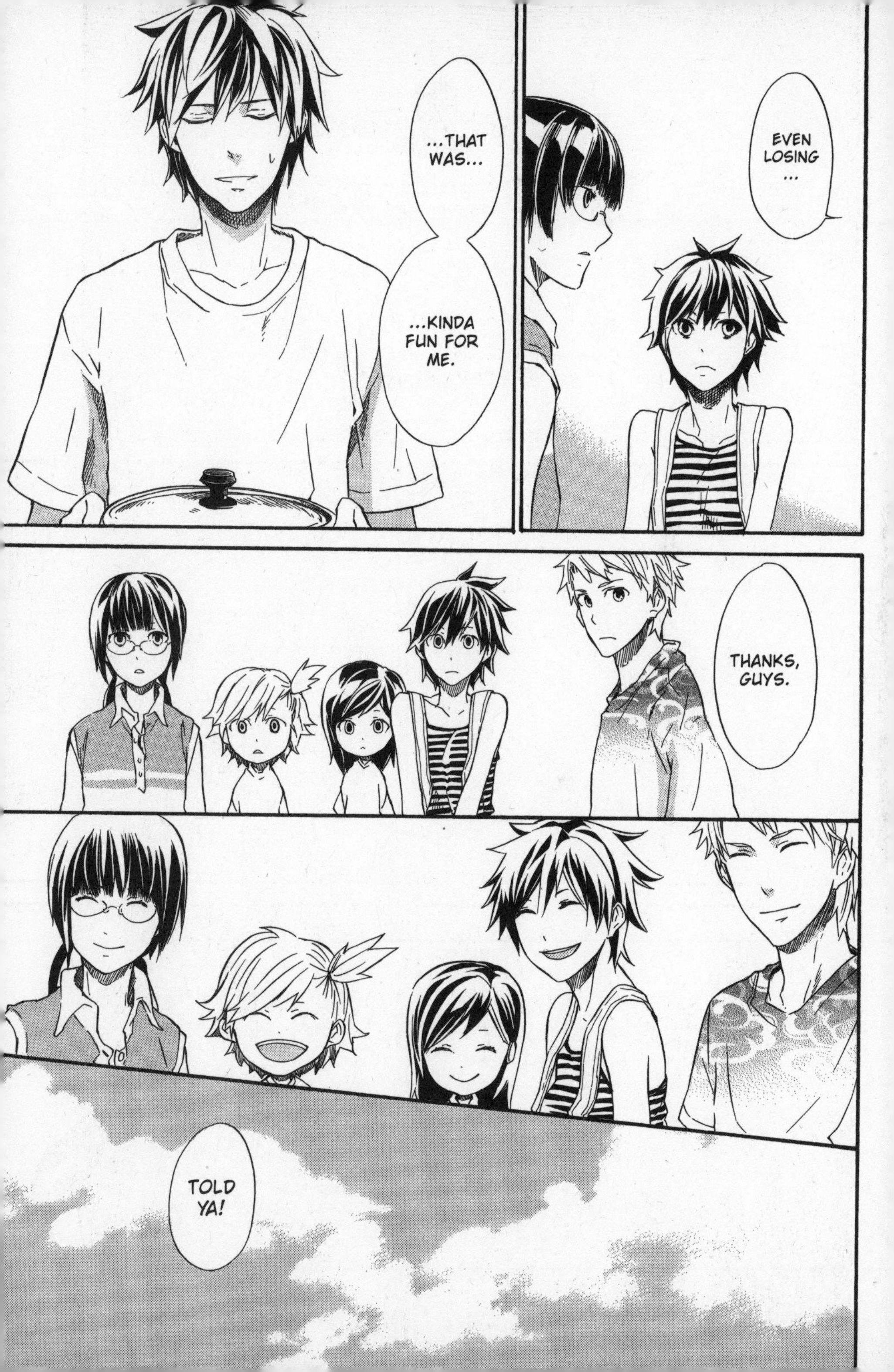
EVEN LOSING...
...THAT WAS...
...KINDA FUN FOR ME.
THANKS, GUYS.
TOLD YA!

BONUS: DANPO

(Translation: Pond)

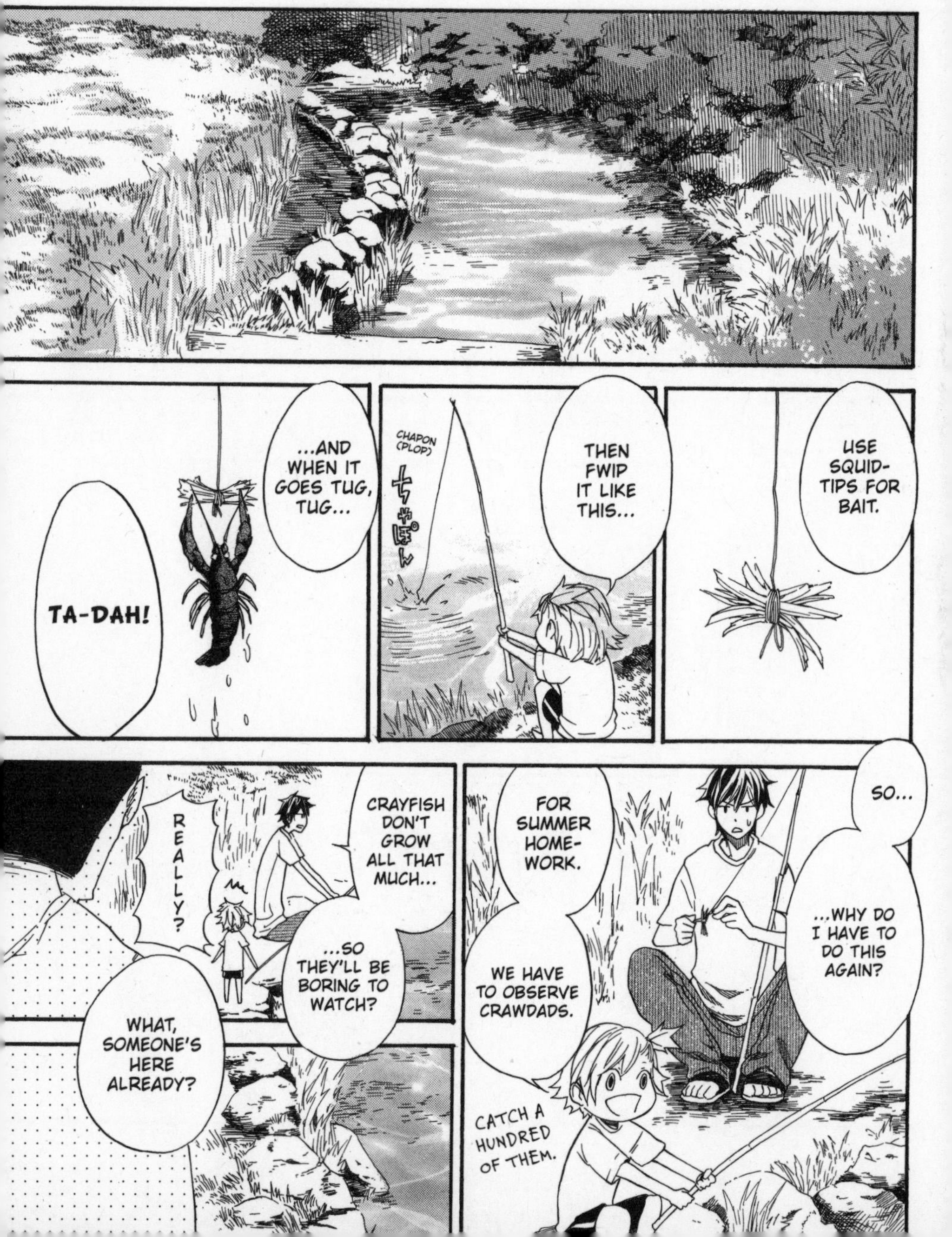
USE SQUID-TIPS FOR BAIT.
THEN FWIP IT LIKE THIS...
CHAPON (PLOP)
ちゃぽん
...AND WHEN IT GOES TUG, TUG...
TA-DAH!
SO...
...WHY DO I HAVE TO DO THIS AGAIN?
FOR SUMMER HOMEWORK.
WE HAVE TO OBSERVE CRAWDADS.
CATCH A HUNDRED OF THEM.
CRAYFISH DON'T GROW ALL THAT MUCH...
REALLY?
...SO THEY'LL BE BORING TO WATCH?
WHAT, SOMEONE'S HERE ALREADY?

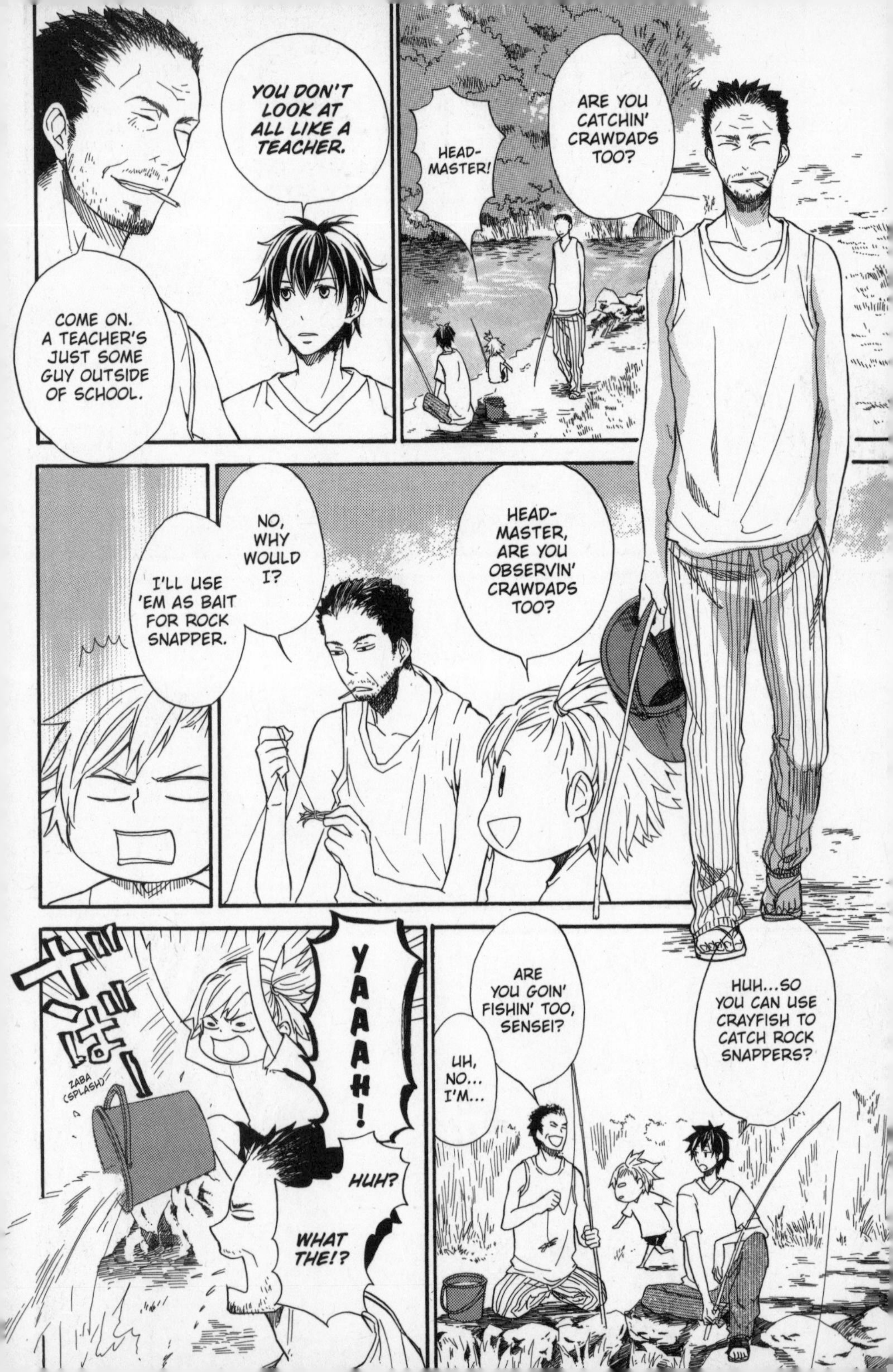
ARE YOU CATCHIN' CRAWDADS TOO?
HEAD-MASTER!
YOU DON'T LOOK AT ALL LIKE A TEACHER.
COME ON. A TEACHER'S JUST SOME GUY OUTSIDE OF SCHOOL.
HEAD-MASTER, ARE YOU OBSERVIN' CRAWDADS TOO?
NO, WHY WOULD I?
I'LL USE 'EM AS BAIT FOR ROCK SNAPPER.
HUH...SO YOU CAN USE CRAYFISH TO CATCH ROCK SNAPPERS?
ARE YOU GOIN' FISHIN' TOO, SENSEI?
UH, NO... I'M...
YAAAH!
ZABA (SPLASH)
HUH?
WHAT THE!?

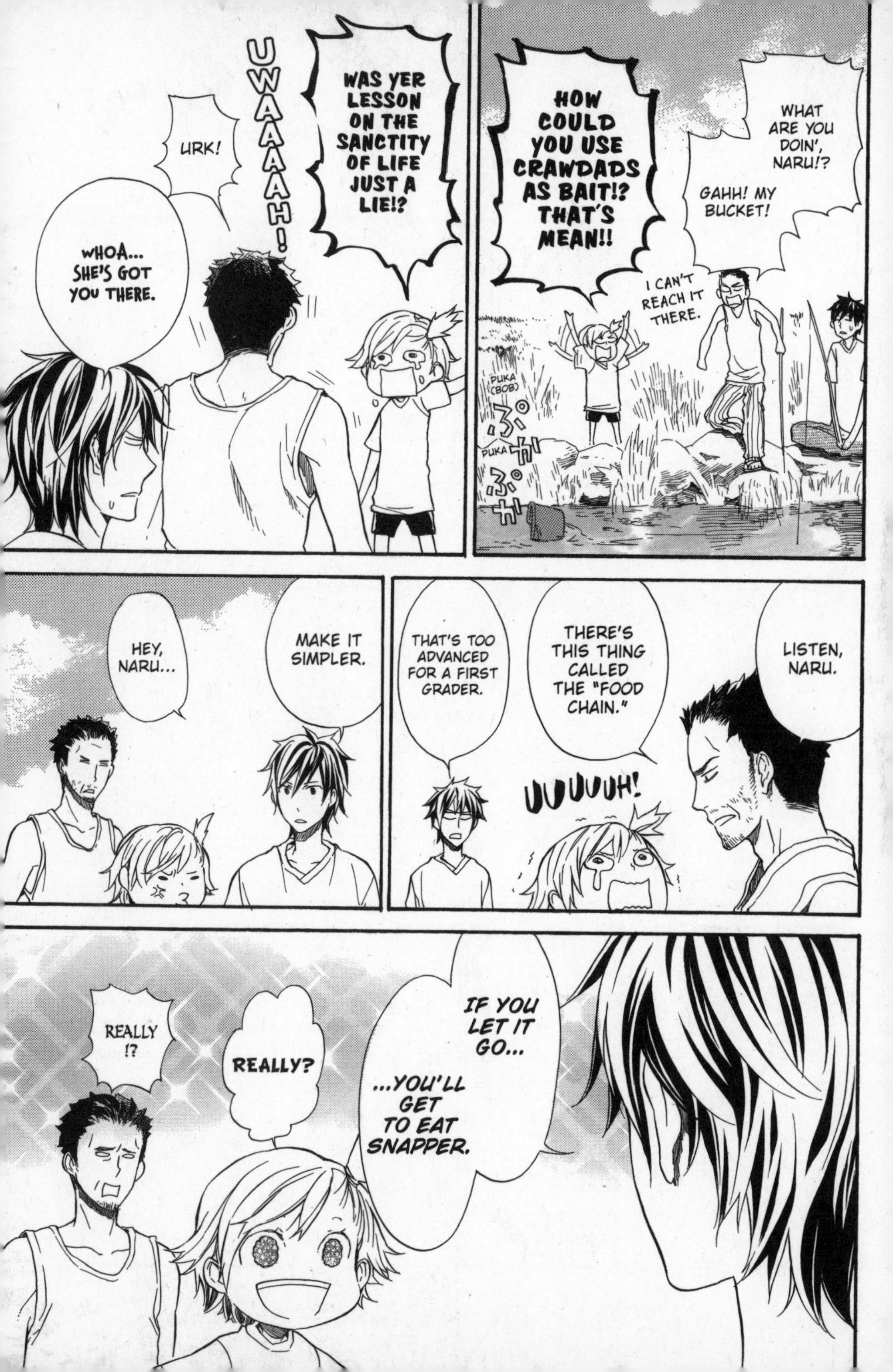
WHAT ARE YOU DOIN', NARU!?
GAHH! MY BUCKET!
HOW COULD YOU USE CRAWDADS AS BAIT!? THAT'S MEAN!!
I CAN'T REACH IT THERE.
PUKA (BOB)
ぷか
PUKA
ぷか
WAS YER LESSON ON THE SANCTITY OF LIFE JUST A LIE!?
UWAAAAAH!
URK!
WHOA... SHE'S GOT YOU THERE.
LISTEN, NARU.
THERE'S THIS THING CALLED THE "FOOD CHAIN."
UUUUUH!
THAT'S TOO ADVANCED FOR A FIRST GRADER.
MAKE IT SIMPLER.
HEY, NARU...
IF YOU LET IT GO...
...YOU'LL GET TO EAT SNAPPER.
REALLY?
REALLY !?

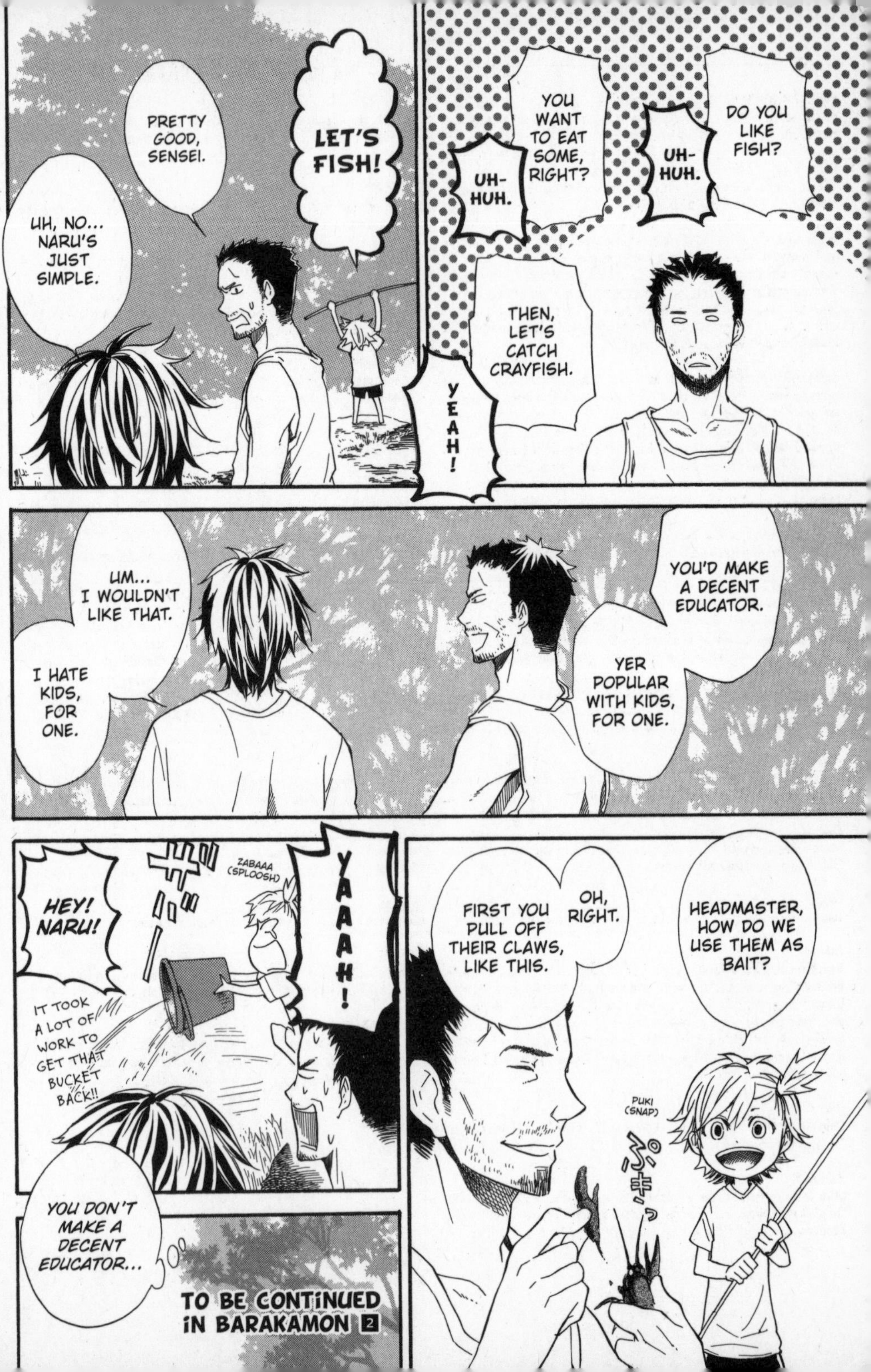
DO YOU LIKE FISH?
UH-HUH.
YOU WANT TO EAT SOME, RIGHT?
UH-HUH.
THEN, LET'S CATCH CRAYFISH.
YEAH!
LET'S FISH!
PRETTY GOOD, SENSEI.
UH, NO... NARU'S JUST SIMPLE.
YOU'D MAKE A DECENT EDUCATOR.
YER POPULAR WITH KIDS, FOR ONE.
UM... I WOULDN'T LIKE THAT.
I HATE KIDS, FOR ONE.
HEADMASTER, HOW DO WE USE THEM AS BAIT?
OH, RIGHT.
FIRST YOU PULL OFF THEIR CLAWS, LIKE THIS.
PUKI (SNAP)
YAAAAH!
ZABAAA (SPLOOSH)
HEY! NARU!
IT TOOK A LOT OF WORK TO GET THAT BUCKET BACK!!
YOU DON'T MAKE A DECENT EDUCATOR...
TO BE CONTINUED IN BARAKAMON 2

TRANSLATION NOTES

COMMON HONORIFICS

no honorific: Indicates familiarity or closeness; if used without permission or reason, addressing someone in this manner would constitute an insult.

-san: The Japanese equivalent of Mr./Mrs./Miss. If a situation calls for politeness, this is the fail-safe honorific.

-sama: Conveys great respect; may also indicate that the social status of the speaker is lower than that of the addressee.

-kun: Used most often when referring to boys, this indicates affection or familiarity. Occasionally used by older men among their peers, but it may also be used by anyone referring to a person of lower standing.

-chan: An affectionate honorific indicating familiarity used mostly in reference to girls; also used in reference to cute persons or animals of either gender.

-sensei: A Japanese term of respect commonly used for teachers, but can also refer to doctors, writers, and artists. Hence, Village Chief is not implying that Handa is a teacher when he calls him "sensei."

Calligraphy: Japanese calligraphy has a long history and tradition, with roots stemming from ancient China. One of the traditions carried over was the Chinese expression of the "Four Treasures," which refers to the brush, ink, paper, and ink stone used in calligraphy. Traditionally, an inkstick—solidified ink—is ground against an inkstone filled with water in order to produce ink with which to write. This time-consuming process helped to teach patience, which is important in the art of calligraphy. However, modern advances have developed a bottled liquid ink, commonly used by beginners and within the Japanese school system.

Gotou Dialect: Many of the villagers, especially the elderly ones, are actually speaking the local Gotou dialect in the original Japanese. This dialect is reflected in the English translation with some of the grammar elements of older Southern American English to give it a more rustic, rural coastal feel without making it too hard to read (it's not meant to replicate any particular American accent exactly). This approach is similar to how dialect is made accessible in Japanese media, including *Barakamon*, because a complete dialect with all of its different vocabulary would be practically incomprehensible to most Tokyo residents.

Chapter Titles: The chapter titles on the Table of Contents, as well as the interior of the book, were left untranslated to show real examples of Gotou dialect vocabulary. The translation notes next to them were originally standard Japanese.

PAGE 23
Junon Boy: *Junon* is a monthly fashion magazine in Japan geared toward teenaged girls and young women, which has a famous beauty contest for boys.

PAGE 26
Sacred Sword Legend: "*Seiken Densetsu*" is the original Japanese name of the "Mana" JRPG series published by Square ENIX.

PAGE 27
Tomgari Corn: The actual name of the cone-shaped corn snacks is Tongari Corn.

PAGE 65
Urashima: This chapter has a long reference to the story of Urashima Taro, a poor fisherman who, after rescuing a sea turtle, is rewarded with a visit to the undersea Dragon Palace. When he leaves to return home after three days, the Princess gives him a box that she says he must not open. Upon returning home, he finds his village unrecognizable and learns that 300 years have passed since he left. In despair he opens the treasure box, which contains his missing years, and is turned into an extremely old man.

PAGE 72
Fishcess: in the original, Naru mispronounced "*Hime-sama* (Princess)" as "*shimesaba* (vinegared mackerel)"

PAGE 80
pitch in: in the original, the old woman Yasuba says *kase*, a dialect word for "help" that's very different from the standard Japanese *tetsudai*, which is why Handa doesn't recognize it at all.

PAGE 91-92
butt-jab: the infamous *kancho*, which literally means "enema," is a Japanese schoolboy practice of bullying someone by jabbing their fingers at/up the person's butt.

PAGE 116
jinbei: The clothes Handa's wearing are traditional Japanese casual summer clothes normally worn only at home and consist of matching short jacket and trousers.

PAGE 119:
bad language: This sampling of things Naru said is mostly her substituting regular words with ones related to nightlife or the sex trade. For example, Kabuki-cho is a neighborhood in Tokyo famous for its entertainment/red-light district. The meanings are consistent for most of the terms, with two exceptions: "Baby mama" was originally *chiimama*, which refers to a female heir to the proprietress of a bar, and "streetwalking" was originally *makura-eigyou* (pillow business), where a salesperson etc., has sexual relations with a client as a bargaining point.

PAGE 128
Ah Eh Eee: The original was an alphabet joke naming off the first 3 of the Japanese vowels "Ah Ee Oo Eh Oh"; here it's been changed to use the European vowel sequence sounds "Ah Eh Ee Oh Oo" in a way that also makes sense as reaction sounds.

PAGE 131-132
Report Cards vs. Progress Reports, "relaxed education system": In recent decades, there has been increasing concern in Japan about children being burdened by academic pressure at young ages, leading to a gradual reduction in requirements for primary education as part of the "*Yutori Kyoiku* (relaxed education)" system. In public grade schools, report cards with number grades ranging from 1 (poor) to 5 (excellent) have mostly been replaced with progress reports (*ayumi*) that only use "Very Satisfactory," "Satisfactory," and "Needs Improvement" as evaluations. Circles, the Japanese equivalent of a plus or check mark, are used to mark satisfactory points, while Xs would be used to mark points that need work (if Naru had any). Most of Naru's grades are "Very Satisfactory," with one amusing exception being Penmanship.

PAGE 143
Nagasaki champon: A dish of ramen noodles and various ingredients such as seafood and vegetables, cooked together in broth (Ma'am is right to be concerned about it getting spilled).

PAGE 148
"Lend me yer energy!": A reference to Goku's Spirit Bomb from *Dragon Ball Z*.

PAGE 160
nikujaga: A beef and potato stew made using Japanese seasonings.

PAGE 198
zenzai: A sweet red-bean soup with pieces of mochi; often served cold in summer, but requires heat to make the red-bean part in the first place.

PAGE 202
rock snapper: The original term, *ishidai*, generally means "striped beakfish." Here the more literal term of "rock snapper" is used to better match when Handa tells Naru she can eat "snapper" (*tai*) on the next page.

BARAKAMON NEWS

Vol.510

A column that answers the question, "What's Barakamon?"

This column will answer your burning questions about the series. First, the setting for Barakamon is the Gotou Archipelago in Nagasaki Prefecture, where creator Yoshino-sensei was born and raised. These islands, located at the west end of Japan, are a paradise of beautiful sunsets.

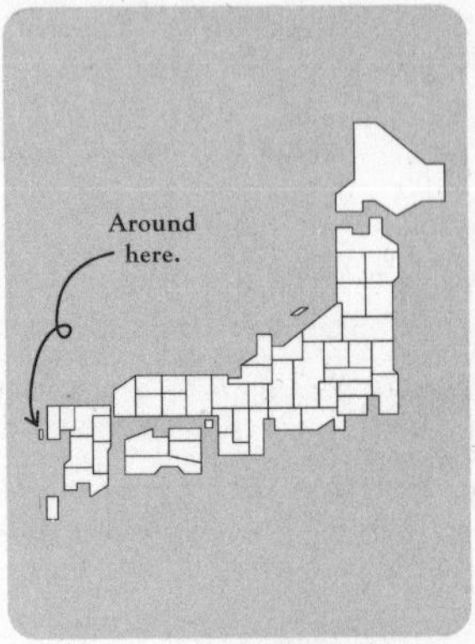
Around here.

Next is the meaning of the word "Barakamon," which has hardly shown up in this volume despite being the title of the series. "Baramon" means "energetic person" in the Gotou dialect, and in the area where the protagonist and villagers are living, they specifically use the word "Barakamon." By the way, Gotou has kites called Baramontako, the making of which have been passed down since ancient times. They appear as shown.

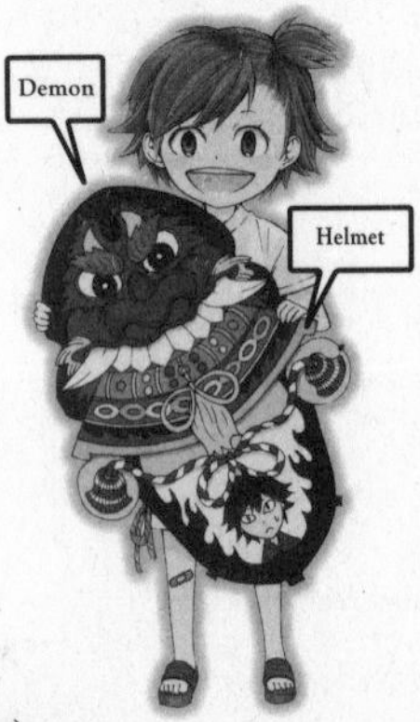
Demon
Helmet

These kites use a ferocious design of a demon biting a helmet. Because the demon face is biting down, you may think that the "baramon (energetic person)" is the demon, but it's actually the one wearing the helmet, looking forward and making progress in spite of the demon. This means that the helmet is the subject of the kite.

LOVELY GOTOU GALLERY

Introducing lovely scenes of Gotou photographed by creator Yoshino-sensei and the editor in charge!

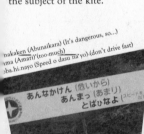

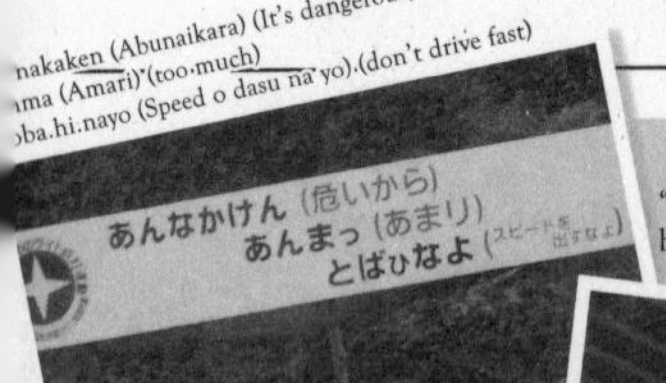
nakaken (Abunaikara) (It's dangerous, so...)
ma (Amari) (too much)
oba.hi.nayo (Speed o dasu na yo).(don't drive fast)
あんなかけん（危いから）
あんまっ（あまり）
とばひなよ

⬅Did Japanese always have a small "ひ(hi)" symbol!? The editor can't hide the culture shock...

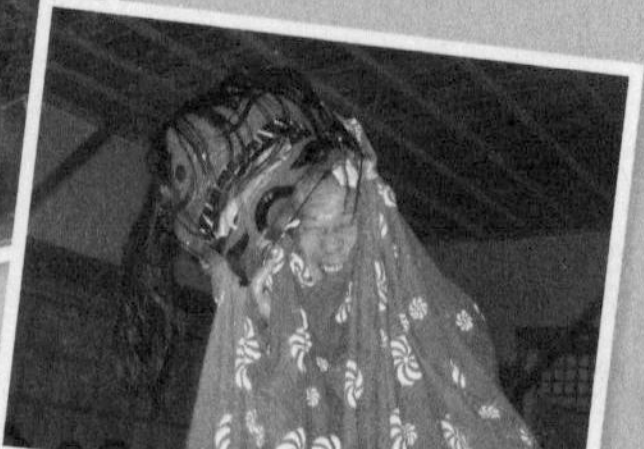

⬆A festival scene photographed by Yoshino-sensei! As Yoshino-sensei cheers, "Lion come out!" the person inside merrily shows himself like so!

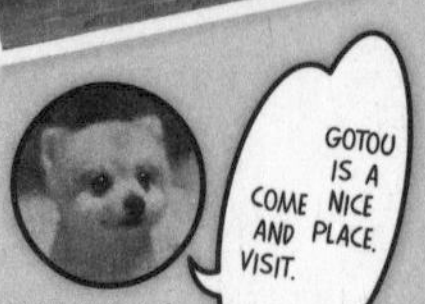
GOTOU IS A NICE PLACE. COME AND VISIT.

Yoshino family dog, **Yoichi.**

These ➡ are from when the editor first visited Gotou for a business meeting, and actually got picked up by a tractor....

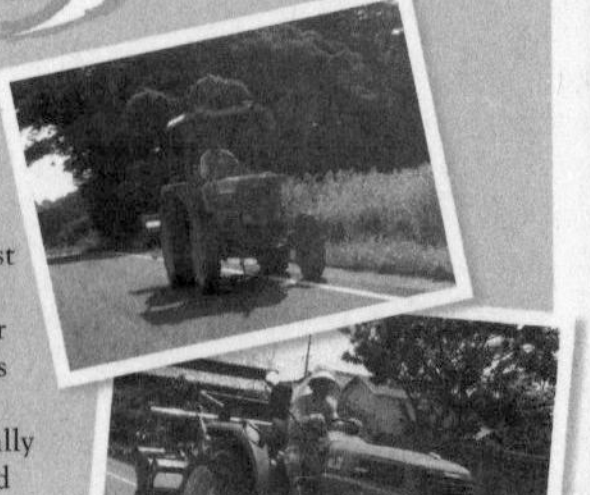

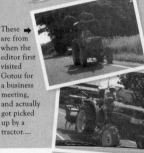

BARAKAMON 1

SATSUKI YOSHINO

Translation/Adaptation: Krista Shipley, Karie Shipley
Lettering: Lys Blakeslee

This book is a work of fiction. Names, characters, places, and incidents are the product of the author's imagination or are used fictitiously. Any resemblance to actual events, locales, or persons, living or dead, is coincidental.

Barakamon vol. 1 © 2009 Satsuki Yoshino SQUARE ENIX CO., LTD. First published in Japan in 2009 by SQUARE ENIX CO., LTD. English translation rights arranged with SQUARE ENIX CO., LTD. and Yen Press, LLC through Tuttle-Mori Agency, Inc.

English translation © 2014 by SQUARE ENIX CO., LTD.

Yen Press
1290 Avenue of the Americas
New York, NY 10104

Visit us at yenpress.com
facebook.com/yenpress
twitter.com/yenpress
yenpress.tumblr.com
instagram.com/yenpress

First Yen Press Edition: October 2014

Yen Press is an imprint of Yen Press, LLC.
The Yen Press name and logo are trademarks of Yen Press, LLC.

The publisher is not responsible for websites (or their content) that are not owned by the publisher.

ISBN: 978-0-316-33608-6

10

WOR

Printed in the United States of America